Tongues of Fire

Tongues of Fire

How Charismatic Prayer Changes Evangelical Brains and Inspires Spirit-Filled Activism

Josh Brahinsky

BLOOMSBURY ACADEMIC
NEW YORK • LONDON • OXFORD • NEW DELHI • SYDNEY

BLOOMSBURY ACADEMIC
Bloomsbury Publishing Inc, 1359 Broadway, New York, NY 10018, USA
Bloomsbury Publishing Plc, 50 Bedford Square, London, WC1B 3DP, UK
Bloomsbury Publishing Ireland, 29 Earlsfort Terrace, Dublin 2, D02 AY28, Ireland

BLOOMSBURY, BLOOMSBURY ACADEMIC and the Diana logo are
trademarks of Bloomsbury Publishing Plc

First published in the United States of America 2026

Cover design: Diana Nuhn
Cover image of bird © DrPAS / iStock.com
Neuron image © by Vitalii Dumma/ iStock.com

Some of the data and stories in this book were published previously in Brahinsky, Josh.
2012. "Pentecostal Body Logics: Cultivating a Modern Sensorium." Cultural Anthropology
27 (2): 215–38., Brahinsky, Josh. 2013. "Cultivating Discontinuity: Pentecostal Pedagogies
of Yielding and Control." Anthropology & Education Quarterly 44 (4): 399–422, Brahinsky,
Josh. 2018. "The Effects of Scale: What Pentecostalism and Neuroscience Teach Us About
Habit, Affect and Agency." Anthropological Theory 18 (4): 478–501., Brahinsky, Josh. 2020.
"Crossing the Buffer: Ontological Anxiety among US Evangelicals and an Anthropological
Theory of Mind." Journal of the Royal Anthropological Institute 26 (S1): 45–60, and
Brahinsky, Josh, Jonas Mago, Mark Miller, Shaila Catherine, and Michael Lifshitz. 2024.
"The Spiral of Attention, Arousal, and Release: A Comparative Phenomenology of Jhāna
Meditation and Speaking in Tongues." American Journal of Human Biology 36 (12): e24189.
https://doi.org/10.1002/ajhb.24189.

Bloomsbury Publishing Inc does not have any control over, or responsibility for, any
third-party websites referred to or in this book. All internet addresses given in this
book were correct at the time of going to press. The author and publisher regret
any inconvenience caused if addresses have changed or sites have ceased
to exist, but can accept no responsibility for any such changes.

Library of Congress Cataloging-in-Publication Data Available

ISBN: HB: 979-8-8818-0498-5
       ePDF: 979-8-7651-6320-7
       eBook: 979-8-8818-0499-2

Typeset by Integra Software Services Pvt. Ltd.
Printed and bound in the United States of America

To find out more about our authors and books visit www.bloomsbury.com
and sign up for our newsletters.

Contents

Figures

Acknowledgments

This book took lots of people: my mother Naomi, father David, and sister Rachel for inspiration to always do things that I enjoy; Benjamin for amazing hugs and brilliant smiles that made writing possible; and Jen for comic genius, love, and kindness, as well as fantastic editing.

Thank you to Tanya Luhrmann for an unbelievable decade of mentorship; Michael Lifshitz for making space for my wild flights of research fantasy; Jonas Mago for being my most esteemed teacher and friend; thanks also to Felicity Aulino, Emily Ng, John Dulin, Rachel Smith, Kara Weisman, Vivian Dzokoto, and Mar Estarellas, who are kind and brilliant colleagues; Jon Bialecki, who outlined the book on a napkin; Joel Robbins, who made me think I was an anthropologist; Dacher Keltner and Alison Gopnik, who invited me to play psychologist; Cliff Saron, who kindly told me I couldn't or maybe shouldn't but somehow enticed me in the process; Ivan R. Gillis and Madeline Lane-Mckinley, who helped the words come out with their editing; and Barbara Epstein, Nancy van Deusen, Jim Clifford, Susan Harding, and Lenny Helfgott as embracing advisors.

Shavon, Tim, Hope, Sherol, Ginny, and Susan helped organize the research. Without them, there is nothing to talk about. Dan Albrecht and Everett Wilson at Bethany really started the whole conversation for me and Charlie Self hooked me up with amazing folks to talk with. My editor Richard Brown and agent Rita Rosenkranz helped me turn it into a book. And I want to thank Oliver Sacks, who I never met but who is simply an abiding inspiration to write and ponder. This was lots of fun to think about with all of you. I so appreciate the opportunity.

Human Subjects Research: This book includes data from multiple studies, approved by the UCSC, UC Berkeley, Stanford University, and McGill University IRBs; all participants provided informed consent for any interviews, brain scans, cognitive tasks and psychological scales, and conversations that were not public facing, i.e., in class or in church. All classroom access was approved by the president of Bethany University and the participating faculty. All church notes were taken with permission from lead pastors. All quotes are from field notes or recordings; they are as close to verbatim as I could get and still have them make sense. Names for all students and interviewees are anonymized except with permission from Shavon, Bethany faculty, and Darrin Rodgers who spoke more as experts than informants.

Prologue

Letting Go

Believer's Night at Glad Tidings Church feels more like a vibrant rock concert than a traditional gospel choir. The hall is enveloped in a mysteriously dim lighting, a space where miracles and rebirths are said to unfold. Built in the 1930s, this venue long served as the epicenter for regional charismatic gatherings within the Northern California Assemblies of God (AG). Now, as the crowd of three hundred people swells with anticipation, the band bursts forth, breathing life into the air. The rhythmic pulsations stir the gathering, prompting fervent jumps and spirited singing. Amidst this swirling sea of energy, Pastor Beiser, a diminutive figure on the stage, seizes the moment. With masterful timing, he disrupts the musical cadence, bringing the harmony to an abrupt halt. It is time for a sermon, to teach us something of shyness and personal growth. For me, the lesson becomes far more visceral.

"Go beyond your comfort zone, fully yield to God," he whispers gently. The room quiets further. His arms shake and his body contracts; his Parkinson's is quite visible. Yet, after a few moments of hushed whisper, a surge of spirit begins to fill him. He steadies himself and rises to his full height. The drummer begins to press the beat.

"Now!" Pastor speaks with strength, "stretch yourself," he says, "Sing louder!" He stands even taller. The music crests.

"Try it now! Let go!" he commands.

I find myself captivated by the interplay of passion and the language of release. At the peak of intensity, he shifts again, calling for a sweet, rolling ballad. Again, a quiet rains down upon us, and we sing softly, our voices intertwined in a gentle chorus: "Holy Spirit Fall. Holy Spirit Fall. Holy Spirit Fall." As the echoes of our collective song subside, a peculiar sensation stirs within me. I become aware of a tingling in my skull. Little pricks of sharp awareness caress my temples. It is as though a gentle crown of thorns encircles me, its subtle pressure tracing a path across the front and back of my forehead. The top of my head, oddly enough, remains untouched. In that moment, a fleeting opportunity presents itself. I imagine I could allow the pressure squeezing my temples to sink into me and enter deep into my brain. Perhaps I can open and surrender control of my head or of my body more fully. I observe this possibility for a quick moment, paused on what feels like a precipice. But instead of release, I shake myself to disperse the sensations. I regain clarity. The ethereal crown drifts away, retreating into the realm of possibility. Meanwhile, all around me, others succumb to the floor, their bodies gracefully surrendering to being "slain in the spirit." The pastor asks the crowd to remain there on the ground, encouraging them to "soak, soak in the spirit," as he says it. For the next half hour, the savoring of release envelops the space as many lie fully immobile, flopped in between the seats. Silence, and then a bit of rustling. I tiptoe out to the lobby, quietly, so as not to disturb.

***

I had found myself at a crossroads, unable to fully embrace the act of "letting go." It beckoned to me, whispering promises of relaxation, acceptance, openness, and the sheer pleasure of surrender. Yet, I felt hesitant—a trepidation intertwined with the echoes of my own epileptic history. But it was more than fear alone that held me back. There was also the matter of understanding. Charismatic preachers implore their followers to "let go," assuming it to be a concept easily grasped. Yet, what does it truly mean to let go? And especially in this Christian context? To release desires, thoughts, control, the very essence of my self? These are intangible, not objects clenched within a fist. And once untethered, where could they drift? Will they plummet into the earth's embrace or aimlessly drift, perhaps toward distant stars? Maybe God scoops them up? Letting go has become a metaphor ingrained within the charismatic community, an integral facet of their collective wisdom. Yet, their comfort with the term obscures what is, by many measures, an exceptionally enigmatic idea.

As I ventured further into the muddle of this phenomenon, I couldn't help but notice its reverberations extending far beyond the bounds of the charismatic world. Even within my own Jewish/secular sphere, we are well acquainted with the idea of letting go, yet our familiarity also obscures its inherent vagueness. As I continued on my journey into the charismatic subculture, it became evident that these particular words can shape the very wellspring of our embodied experience. The messy entanglement of word and body, the elusive dance between letting go and holding on—this was the realm I found myself exploring.

The words themselves carried weight, I mused. And they might exert a mysterious influence on our bodily selves. I entertained the idea that these words were more than metaphors—that the mere act of speaking or even contemplating the phrases "let go" or "release" invoked the power of speech acts, to weave intimate connections between words and bodies. And perhaps, just perhaps, the simple process of giving voice could prod us toward the act of release, even if only in the subtlest of ways.

Anselm in the Magnetic Resonance Imaging Scanner (MRI)

On the day of the MRI, Anselm was hurting. The air hung heavy with intensity, foreboding, and an underlying struggle. He exuded a fierce energy, from his baldhead and stark visage to his wide smile, brash holler, and thickly muscled hug.

The drama became especially visible when Anselm realized that we would ask him to seek God while lying on his injured back for the next three hours. It was a departure from his usual prayer postures—typically curled up in humble submission on the floor, sometimes pacing with fervor or whirling through the church while gesticulating brightly. But within the confining tube of the MRI, he couldn't use his arms to emphasize his arguments or his agreement with God. Just days before, I had witnessed Anselm and other leaders of Glad

Tidings Church cleansing the prayer hall through vigorous, rapid-fire worship in preparation for Wednesday night services. He hadn't stood still for one moment the entire evening.

As he reclined on the MRI table, the repetitive grind of the magnet was punctuated by the machine's loud ringing. Anselm's back tensed, a pinched nerve unhappy in such cramped quarters. Soon, he was caught in a full-blown spasm. He later confided that he rarely lay on his back, not even at night. Lingering injuries from his time in foster care and a stint as a bank robber (yes, really!) roused him from slumber after just a few hours. During his time with us, he relied on ibuprofen, but after an hour of struggling to concentrate amid the cacophony and pain, he asked to be released.

We had just listened to him recite the Lord's Prayer, which we were comparing with everyday "praise prayer," an improvisational blend of affectionate devotion to the divine—and also with speaking in tongues, which we will discuss a lot here. Anselm was not feeling any of them. "I feel God with my senses, and I can't feel him in here," he explained, pointing to the MRI machine as the hindrance. "The machinery disrupts it. It's so loud that I can't focus on God."

Anselm explained that he accessed God through both his mind and his body, and if he could control the environment, he might forge a stronger connection. Also, that morning's journey to the MRI had likely thrown him off balance. We had endured an hour-long drive beset with car troubles. My engine nearly froze en route, and we barely limped into the Stanford Medical Center parking lot—I spent the evening navigating tow trucks. Then an additional hour was taken up with pretest questionnaires. By the time Anselm changed into a hospital gown, removing every trace of metal that could heat up in the scanner, and then lay on his back uncomfortably, his mind was growing increasingly agitated. All this had consumed three hours of the day. And now he was hurting.

Concerned about the cumulative stress, I thought he might need a break. I asked if he preferred a ride home or if he wanted to give it one last attempt. To even begin a second reading would mean approximately thirty minutes of sitting and lying in wait while we set up the MRI. Anselm emerged from the testing room, walked around for a bit, and then, to my surprise, drank some water, shook his legs, and climbed back onto the table. We began anew. Only then did he experience the shift.

Within a few minutes of the restart, he shouted out that his pain was subsiding. He had "let it go." Five minutes later, he was soaring. When the time came to pause, a smile illuminated his face, and he insisted on another sequence of prayer. Anselm had achieved communion with God in the MRI.

The Significance of Charismatic Evangelicalism

For charismatics, it's all about the release.

Most of us are at least vaguely familiar with the evangelical experience of being "born again." Full submission to God can sever previously messy life threads, providing renewed energy and the vulnerability of a newborn baby. Baptism, the baptism of the spirit, revival, and faith healing are all related moments of worship where individuals relinquish control and even their sense of self. Afterward, things come back together as new. Repeated letting go and renewal builds a sense of possibility. In this manner, for charismatics, personal rebirth becomes an engine for all sorts of personal and even social change.

Recall the events of January 2021 when protesters engaged in the Senate Hall takeover raised their hands in the classic charismatic style of prayer. Or think of the legislators flopped across the floor, praying in tongues in the Arizona Statehouse before the vote to revitalize an ancient abortion restriction. These visible incidents exposed only the surface of a vast social and political network developed over the past two centuries. Originating from an encounter between the Great Awakenings of the late 1700s and 1800s and emerging forms of slave Christianity, evangelicals emerged as central figures in major social movements of their time: abolition, anti-vice campaigns, temperance, and numerous other moral reforms. Around the year 1900, a group, mostly made up of the underprivileged, discovered their own stirring way forward. These were Pentecostal Christians who embraced the foundational tenets of evangelicalism, emphasizing the literal or near-literal truth of the Bible, fostering a personal relationship with Jesus, inviting participants to evangelize, and experiencing spiritual rebirth, the experience of being born again.[1] But

Figure 0.1 *Glad Tidings Church, San Francisco. Glad Tidings Archive.*

Pentecostals also valued what they call the "gifts of the spirit"—prophecy, faith healing, being slain in the spirit—where they find themselves wilted on the floor in a deeply altered state of mind—and "speaking in tongues," a practice of rapidly generating word-like sounds that are felt to communicate directly to God.[2] The unconventional energy of Pentecostal practices meant their churches lived on the margins but also gained immense appeal.

Fast-forward one hundred years, and these churches have seen impressive growth, with their practices permeating mainstream, Catholic, fundamentalist, and particularly "nondenominational" churches. Their global membership now stands at nearly half a billion. The mere 11 million in the United States may seem comparatively middling—unless we stack it against almost any other social movement. Throughout the first half of the twentieth century, this fringe group of spiritual radicals—known for advocating feminism, pacifism, and anti-racism, and inspiring movements among the impoverished—penetrated the leadership of the broader evangelical movement.

In the process of gaining influence, the white leaders among them very clearly reversed political course. Charismatics have become a crucial source of energy and activism for the Christian Right. The AG, boasting 69 million members and the largest Pentecostal group in the world, served as the focal point of my fieldwork.[2] While the majority of my informants were people of color, many African American, this is not a study of a Black Church which is, at least a somewhat, if not very, different formation.

Along the way, there were ongoing debates over terminology. As new waves of churches with similar practices spread globally, some began using the term *charismatic* to describe emerging elements within the movement. Others adopted the broader label *Pentecostal/Charismatic* (P/C) to encompass the full range of expression.[3] The churches I worked with were mostly affiliated with the AG, a historically Pentecostal denomination. However, these particular congregations aligned more closely with the broader charismatic movement in practice. As such, I use the terms *charismatic* and *evangelical* somewhat loosely—but deliberately and with respect. A quick aside: at this point, you might have noticed the footnotes, but if you want to delve even deeper, every chapter is partnered with a bibliographic discussion at the back of the book.

The Science of Contemplation

Charismatic practices have been largely left out of the recent explosion of research revealing the effects of contemplation on our bodies. With roughly 1,000 studies done annually on mindfulness, many showing increased brain plasticity and health benefits related to stress reduction, only a handful focus on prayer, and charismatic worship is almost entirely unexplored.

Perhaps this is because Buddhist practices taught in the United States emphasize the mind rather than the spirit. Such an orientation may be more comfortable for secular audiences than the charismatic focus on God. But also, charismatic worship is intensely physical, emotional, and rife with an altered sense of reality. Psychologists have frequently drawn comparisons between speaking in tongues and extreme or abnormal behaviors, such as schizophrenia, hysteria, and neuroses.[4] Consequently, charismatic worship did not readily present itself as an obvious mechanism for beneficial health effects, or really for any research at all.

It doesn't help that white charismatics translate their spiritual experience into political will, often voting in unison against health care, welfare, and social support. This alignment might seem at odds with the needs of a predominantly working-class movement, leading observers to view charismatics either as easily manipulated individuals or as pawns of influential church leaders who exploit their voting power and financial contributions. In turn, charismatics grew increasingly wary of researchers, fearing that studies would mock their practices or seek to undermine the importance of their prayers.

Things, however, are changing. Some evangelicals now imagine God working through science, not in opposition to it. They find they can engage in the study of natural laws and processes, embracing scientific inquiry with the eager intensity of any young atheist scientist, so long as they keep in mind who ultimately runs the show. Moreover, the field of contemplative science is broadening, as researchers delve into forms of Buddhism that go beyond the usual "be here now." These explorations now embrace practices that weave in both imagination and intense emotions, asking us to imagine sitting on the top of a mountain, having sex with a goddess, facing mortality, or simply contemplating the future.[5] In this evolving context, charismatic worship seems an increasingly reasonable candidate for scientific investigation.

In fact, the very qualities that earned charismatics scorn—strong emotions, altered minds, and spontaneity—are now recognized by cognitive scientists as vital elements for both happiness and good decision-making. Neuroscientist Antonio Damasio and his colleagues have argued that emotions are at the core of effective rational thought,[6] while numerous scholars have demonstrated that creative thinking flourishes when cognitive control is relaxed.[7] Others suggest that experiencing awe and embracing spontaneity are essential for overall happiness.[8] More recently, a surge of research suggests that mystical experiences enable us to break free from entrenched thought patterns that hold us captive.[9] Naturally, this research elevates certain forms of emotionalism and relinquishing of control, favoring the likes of Thoreau and the Romantics over Hitler and the Nazis.

At one point in the midst of my research, I found myself sitting in the office among a pile of training manuals and lists of coaches claiming they could teach the uninitiated the art of speaking in tongues. To my surprise, it seemed that speaking in tongues could be viewed as simply another form of prayer or meditation—carefully taught and extensively studied, yet often experienced as a spontaneous and liberating release. I had recently learned that experienced charismatics can speak in tongues at will. I also discovered that many, if not most, people fake it at first.[10] The funny thing is, this simple fact, that people pretend to speak in tongues in the process of learning to let go, strikes most outsiders I've talked to about this phenomenon as mind-boggling. Most observers buy into the Protestant idea that to be authentic requires surrender and a lack of effort. Genuine tongues prayer is something that happens, not something a person does, and it is certainly not learned by pretending, they suppose. And yet, the reality is quite different.

As charismatics saturate their thoughts with passion for God, their mouths produce a rush of nonsense words, sweeping aside all other considerations, they say. While the experience may appear noisy and active, within the very heart of this whirlwind, practitioners find moments of utter tranquility. This stillness enables them to listen intently, hoping to capture a whisper of response—a fleeting audible voice or an encounter with the physical touch of the divine. In this manner, charismatics oscillate between states close to the quiet of mindfulness and others more like the raucous play of psychedelic experiences, both key comparators in this story as we try and understand what it is to speak in tongues.

This charismatic approach to mindful attention is fierce, fueled in part by their overwhelming sense that spiritual practice is a matter of life and death. Unlike mindfulness practitioners who seek to empty themselves of thoughts, charismatics fill themselves so intensely with love for God that, like other forms of passion, their prayer focuses the mind. They frequently describe a purifying "fire"—a stark contrast to the detached coolness often linked to popular mindfulness practices. This heightened intensity of charismatic practice traces its roots back to slave religion and the experiences of impoverished farmers and laborers in the late 1800s, both white and Black communities.[11] The vividly emotional prayer practices common to the Black prophetic tradition may have held clues to an alternate way of inhabiting the body, one that liberated individuals from the shackles of daily violence and toil. Despite their current impulse toward consumerism and capitalist competition, the ferocity of charismatic release continues, in many ways, to signal rebellion against the modern world surrounding them.

My Research Project

Before I go much further in this story of charismatic release, I should note that my father, a therapist of the sixties generation, performs the kind of therapy in which letting go is a, if not the, central goal of the practice. So, "letting go" is a term I have heard my whole life—a background concept whose meaning seemed self-evident as I grew up (although not so much after this research). My father believes that social transformation requires an expansion of the mind, a relaxation of the body, and a release from everyday conventions. Think of The Doors singing "Break on Through" or, for that matter, the hippie Christians of the 1960s. Around the dinner table, I would often challenge his therapist's mantra that the inner life is reflected in the outer, and that a healthy society requires work on our inner selves. My focus was always first and foremost on the social. This is why I chose to study charismatic evangelicals. I was intrigued by how they built their movement, how they worked together to make social change, and why they seemed so remarkably good at all of this. I wanted to study their organizing power. I was not especially curious about their inner worlds. That was twenty years ago.

There was much to explore—even when simply seeing them as movement builders. I followed the Promise Keepers, a charismatic evangelical men's group. They filled football stadiums with men who came to pray, to shout, and somehow, to sit with me for hours of interviews. Later, I moved to Santa Cruz, California. I began visiting Bethany University, a small liberal arts college and missionary training center, linked to the AG. With a six-month-old baby, the idea of a traditional anthropological field journey to a distant part of the world seemed a bit far-fetched. Fortunately, Bethany's president, Everett Wilson, welcomed me warmly. He granted me full access to the campus.

Over the next three years, I immersed myself: I sat in on classes, especially those focused on missionary training, and conducted interviews—dozens of them—with faculty, students, and administrators involved in foreign missions.

I also spoke with scores of AG missionaries in the field, working in places like El Salvador and Turkey, among others. After six years in Lebanon, one missionary's main takeaway was a growing fondness for soccer.[12] In 2014, I finished my dissertation. It looked at how the AG trained missionaries—how they were organized and what ideas shaped their work.[13]

In 2016, psychological anthropologist Tanya Luhrmann at Stanford invited me onto a remarkable team of anthropologists and psychologists. They became some of my closest friends. Tanya had Templeton Foundation funding to compare the spiritual experiences of charismatics in China, Ghana, Vanuatu, Thailand, and the United States. For my part, I conducted over sixty extended interviews, primarily at two churches: one in Madera, California, that had split from the AG, and an AG church in San Francisco. That's where I met Anselm. It's also where I started working with neuroscientist Michael Lifshitz. His infectious curiosity and enthusiasm helped me imagine that maybe we could actually study charismatic experiences with the tools of neuroscience. Michael's lab at McGill University in Montreal later became my intellectual home and training ground.

Over time, it became increasingly clear that much of the dynamic energy in charismatic organizing stemmed from the inner sensations that surged forth during worship. People told me again and again that regular prayer transformed their minds and bodies—this wasn't just a metaphor. Tanya had previously observed how the inner attention of charismatics made God feel near, often accompanied by vivid sensory experiences.[14] Together, we began to wonder whether the act of "letting go" during worship—surrender, release—could produce measurable effects on the brain.

Release and attention are now major subjects in research on mindfulness and psychedelics. But earlier, a similar notion had emerged in the few brain scan studies of prayer—particularly tongues prayer. I looked at the work of Michael Persinger and Andrew Newberg, who tried to show that this form of prayer might generate a neural signature—something that could, perhaps, reflect a shift in willed control or volition.[15] Their combined sample was small—only six people—still the findings were inspiring. Could we show that the passionate, focused attention in charismatic worship reshaped the body and mind in distinctive ways? We wrote a grant proposal to the National Science Foundation and were given the go-ahead.

As we began to design this study, we hit immediate barriers. Big ones. Getting a reliable measure would turn out to be far more difficult than I had naively anticipated. MRIs are not churches. Scientists are not preachers. And prayer means lots of mouth movement—not good for brain scans that require stillness. Further, in even the most rigorous research contexts, psychologists today struggle to replicate foundational work. In our case, it seemed very possible—likely even—that a straight-up MRI study would yield no meaningful data at all.

We found ourselves considering an unusual approach. The regular tools of the laboratory—however precise—were not enough. They couldn't catch what we were seeing and hearing. Instead, we needed a mixed-methods design: to hold data from many domains, we could weave disciplines together rather than flatten them. Maybe we could hold on to the subtle details that often get lost when things are oversimplified—and take seriously the challenges of doing research that speaks to real-world settings, not just on paper.

We turned to a little-known branch of science known as *neurophenomenology*—a field that attempts to bring first-person experience into dialogue with the measurements of brain and body. We "front-loaded" our neuroscience, as we put it, with clinical-style extended interviews where we delved into the fine details of spiritual experience. Looking back, there was even more front-loading than that—a decade of ethnographic observation.

In some ways, the plan had unfolded naturally. At the time, I had formal training in history, anthropology, and philosophy. I knew very little of the brain. Yet, through my work with Michael, I found myself, almost unwittingly, becoming a neurophenomenologist of sorts. He meanwhile was traveling in the opposite direction, steadily weaving cultural frames into his neuroscience research. Now, after eight years of working with brain scans (MRI, Electroencephalograph (EEG)) and other psychological methods, things have grown a bit more intentional. But looking back, I like to describe our initial somewhat accidental design like this: begin not with hypotheses, but with immersion—years of watching, listening, questioning—before ever sliding someone into a scanner. Let science be led by lived experience.

This approach required us not only to use multiple methods but to look carefully at the relationships between them. We began paying close attention to what we, following philosopher of science Ian Hacking, call "looping."[16] This may sound a bit abstract, so let me break it down. Looping means that people's beliefs, expectations, and practices shape what they feel—and those feelings, in turn, shape what they believe and do.

For instance, charismatics live within a tradition that emphasizes submission to God—not only as a theological concept but as a daily, practiced reality. This orientation shapes everything: the structure of the church, the rhythms of family life, and the ordinary experience of a Tuesday afternoon. The act of yielding is not only spiritual—it is conceptual, behavioral, postural, and, as we now know, neurobiological. In worship, submission takes on obvious physical form: opened arms, trembling voices, and collapsed bodies. And what we see here is not random. It is the result of centuries of crowdsourcing the emotional and bodily techniques designed to express, even induce, a state of openness to God that permeates the charismatic culture. The loop generates a shared neurobiology. A bodily language of release.

Each layer of the loop supports the others. They resonate. The logic of one becomes more compelling, sometimes more pleasurable, in the face of the other. The structure of this book itself follows one of those loops: from the practice and training of release, into the deep recesses of the mind, and then outward again, into social and cultural life. You may find yourself reading in circles. Then you will know you are really in it.

For me, looping became a way to embrace dialogue—between disciplines, between methodologies, between different ways of knowing, and between myself and very different people. This method allowed Tanya, Michael, and me to imagine a fully biocultural research project. We call it ethnographic neurophenomenology. A mouthful, perhaps—but behind it, something we find generous, clear, and rigorous: a deeply interdisciplinary lens on charismatic worship.

I went to talk with Pastor Shavon at Glad Tidings Church to see if this could work. After graduating from UCLA, Shavon had moved to San Francisco, married a former baseball player turned youth pastor, and took a job as a tech worker as they raised three kids. The kids basically grew up in the church.

In our first interview, we had talked for more than five hours. I found her perspective inspiring and her enthusiasm catching.

To my surprise, Shavon loved the idea of studying her prayer with neuroscience. It was a good call—she also enjoyed when we did it. Eventually, others joined in. In the end, following seventy-five multi-hour interviews, ninety-three participants then generously let us scan their brains while they prayed (some with MRI, some with EEG).[17] We got some good brain data. Some of it matched what we saw in the field. That's why this book exists.

As we began to uncover how worship shaped both the mind and culture, I started to reconsider my father's perspective. He could be right: this practice of inner release may be key to why charismatics are so effective—why they build movements, why they influence politics. It's strange, but all this "letting go" might be exactly what fuels spirited and influential engagement with the world.

That is the central puzzle of this book: What do charismatics truly mean when they say they are "letting go"? What does this tell us about how they see the world? And how has this impulse—so personal, and so inward—helped shape their outsized impact on the world around them? The structure of this book follows a similar trajectory: it begins with interview data exploring experiences of charismatic release, then turns to the neurobiology underlying those experiences, and finally examines how personal experience and biology interact to shape the culture and politics of charismatic communities.

1

Letting Go

Pablo

Pablo's slicked-back hair and smooth stride marked him as a musician, but he was on pause. "Letting go" had meant bidding farewell to his thriving music career—a sacrifice of monumental proportions, considering his role producing music for iconic figures like Michael Jackson and Lionel Richie. The weight of this difficult release seemed to give him the ability to articulate with unparalleled clarity and depth the essence of letting go. Our initial conversation lasted an impressive five hours. When we met again, he greeted me with an infectious grin and a warm embrace. Pablo's vibrant energy was contagious. His story laid bare his innermost thoughts, recounting a profound liberation, both in body and in spirit. He had felt himself reborn—and in the process unearthed a raw, unadorned version of his inner self.

Pablo grew up in an African American neighborhood in San Francisco and spent his summers with his grandma in Merced, a small town in the Central Valley of California, worshipping in an apostolic church[1] five mornings a week. However, at eleven years old, tragedy struck when his cherished grandmother passed away. Consumed by fury and resentment toward an unyielding fate, he severed his connection with God. It was rebellion. He flung grocery carts off highway bridges and spent hours in street brawls, honing his fighting skills under the tutelage of his uncle, a champion within the California prison boxing league. Oddly enough, through the same period, straight-A academics earned him a spot at UC Berkeley.

It was not an easy transition. Pablo's first year of college was marred by a protracted court case. While back home, a Clinton-era drug sweep hit his neighborhood. He was literally caught up with his friends and their marijuana—and in a schoolyard, no less. Drugs on school grounds meant severe punishment. Pablo's situation seemed dire, especially when the authorities realized that, given his recent birthday, he was the sole eighteen-year-old who could be held accountable for any serious charge. The district attorney presented him with a harrowing choice: plead guilty and face a six-year prison sentence or proceed to trial and potentially endure twenty-eight years of incarceration. Things did not look good. But the morning of the trial, the judge called Pablo in. The judge had been brought into work early that day because the cops who busted Pablo had been caught dealing cocaine in the wee hours of the morning. The possession charges against Pablo were dropped, and the seeming miracle of his escape from the prison system brought Pablo back into the church.

The story, however, did not end there. The judge offered him a month of community service since arrest in a schoolyard was still grounds for trespassing. But Pablo refused to yield, turning down even a lesser punishment for a crime he refused to acknowledge. He spent the month in prison instead. "Stubborn," he explained. He then moved to Los Angeles, pouring his intense focus into a successful music career. There he met his wife, an exceptional gospel singer. Both of them were navigating what he later described as the superficial realm of worldly success, and it was slowly losing meaning. A musician, devoted father, and later a computer whiz, Pablo was in many ways a go-getter. Yet it was precisely this success that he hoped to relinquish.

Pablo recounted a pivotal day in worship, "I was being pressed down. I tried to get up and it was like, 'No.' Usually me, I like to be in control." Still, he managed to drop his internal push to be active, and he let himself collapse on the floor. This somehow generated heat. "My body was just hot. Have you ever seen how an iron rod, when it's put in the fire, it turns blue? It felt like that, my complete body, all over." The heat kicked off the release. "Shortly after that I started to speak in a different language." He was speaking in tongues.

Letting Go

"It is all about letting go," explained Stanford alumnus, long-term charismatic preacher, and Bethany University president Everett Wilson; he called it "The Flop." Charismatic practice clearly involves surrender, submitting oneself to a higher power. One must follow the rules of the church and obey the pastor. Wives and children submit to their husbands and fathers. All life decisions are guided by God. That part is relatively easy to understand. Yet, for charismatics, letting go is central to their practice precisely because it extends beyond a mere allegory for faith or a moral path. More than a metaphor, and more than a hierarchy, letting go is a tangible practice. Through regular spiritual exercises, charismatics surrender and release their thoughts, desires, the flesh, and even their sense of self—though not necessarily in that order. While religion can often reinforce social patterns, letting go introduces an element of unpredictability. When experienced viscerally, it infuses fluidity and creativity into our thoughts, sensations, and church practices, which might otherwise rely on relatively inflexible doctrines. Letting go can also, it seems, foster a sense of empowerment and a profound urge to act decisively.

To be born again, one must first surrender the old. This means shedding a prior sense of self and embracing a new one. This type of release can be felt to signal a complete break with the past, a full-on rejection of previous selves and old desires; some even enter into childlike vulnerability. Rebirth is the central premise of evangelical revivals. These breakthroughs, I suspect, are best understood as moments within a broader pattern of contraction and release. When evangelicals recount their life stories, they almost invariably describe a journey into the depths of depravity and despair before experiencing the transformative rebirth in God's intensity. Moreover, they speak of days, weeks, and even months of striving—and sometimes fully pretending—before realizing the release achievable through tongues prayer or other spiritual gifts. By considering these profound lows alongside the fiery highs and juxtaposing focused training with explosive release, we catch a glimpse of the oscillating rhythms of charismatic worship. Their training involves two distinct elements: learning to increase tension until it reaches a point of peak intensity and then knowing how to let it go.

Among charismatics, there's lively debate over the relative importance of that first big rebirth. Many prize the peak experience—the moment of fire and change. But speaking in tongues is often seen as another kind of renewal. Less dramatic, yes, but marked by a similar sense of breakthrough. Smaller waves, same current.

Critics easily identify instances where submission to authority among evangelicals has resulted in toxic obedience. The Shepherding Movement of the late 1970s, for instance, is quite aptly described as a time when a charismatic church undertook intense manipulation of its followers. Pastors created pyramid-like networks where "shepherds" controlled nearly all life decisions—about marriage, work, home, and medical concerns—among their "sheep."[2] The ideology of unquestioning obedience may flourish in hierarchical movements that demand this kind of compliance from their followers.[3] That kind of story makes it difficult to ignore the power dynamics in which affluent preachers convince their working-class followers that they have their best interests at heart.

Yet, one could also see letting go as a frugal, or even primal, rejection of the modern world—a romantic quest for an authentic, healthy self. This perspective is not far removed from the narrative within the church itself. Charismatics often cast themselves as rebels fighting the sickness of modern life.

Each of these perspectives has its moral direction. Undeniably, preachers exert control. But in the decentralized structure of charismatic churches, resistance to modern life is important. Letting go plays a role in both scenarios. This chapter traces out how charismatics let go—how it is enacted, how it moves through the body, and how it is felt from within. It is, in a sense, an attempt to build a taxonomy of a specific grammar of surrender as it is lived, spoken, shaken, and breathed by those who give themselves over to something beyond themselves.

Growing up, I thought that Buddhists had the lock on detachment. That seemed in sharp contrast to the Christian world I had encountered in central

New Jersey. Here faith seemed to mean more—more belief, more ritual, and maybe most prominently, more things. I was later surprised when I heard charismatics describe letting go as a central hope. They sounded Buddhist to my naive ears. I did later come to recognize that the charismatic idea of letting go linked to submission, which differed from the Buddhists who speak more to impermanence, watching things pass.[4] But still, both pointed to something shared: a loosening of grip, a shift in vision, a yielding to something beyond the self. That echo between them stayed with me.[5]

Pablo: Letting Go and Constructing a Self

At the core of Pablo's faith lay the felt need to relinquish control. A relentless inquiry reverberated through the depths of his being, "God, what do you want? Let me remove myself, because for years and years I did it my way. I poured education into myself and studied all these different things; music, computers, you name it, to build up myself and pat myself on the back." But, "That was just pride." Perhaps, he thought, he could step aside to allow God to do the work? "I banned myself, I removed my hand."

"You banned your 'self,'" I asked.

"Does it uproar sometimes?" he replied, "It does. Then I remember I'm a child of God, I'm being transformed. [God tells me to] Sit down!" Pablo then offered God control over his mind and body.

Bound together by their shared dedication to God above all else, Pablo and his wife decided to forsake their careers in the music industry and returned to the familiar embrace of San Francisco. Pablo now wakes at five every morning; he prays for several hours before he heads off to work. He listens to music, but no producing, no performing. Work is simply there to enable prayer, he says. This shift in priorities stemmed from a profound sensory experience.

Pablo frequently talks about the "self." An enigmatic but everyday concept I always find confusing. Scholars continue to debate whether the self exists, and if so, what is it. Is it an amalgamation of our memories, actions, relationships, or sensations? Different cultures harbor varying notions of the self, ranging from the most expansive visions that encompass multiple individuals' bodies (what we might call a family or community), while others view the self as encompassing the body, and still others quite narrowly imagine it simply as a facet of the mind.[6]

For our purposes, what matters is that charismatics experience their individualistic self as displaced and occasionally even dissolved as a result of their intense focus on God. Attention in one direction shifts the quality of attention elsewhere. "As soon as I started to dethrone myself more and more and enthrone who I called my God," explained Pablo, "my life started to change in a lot of other areas; how I dealt with people, how people dealt with me, my relationships. I was butting heads before, so many different areas; my parenting; my patience."

Every January, Glad Tidings Church embarks on a forty-day fast accompanied by morning prayer sessions from 5:00 a.m. to 8:00 a.m. Pablo described how the bodily experience of fasting facilitates his process of self-reformation. The three hours of structured morning prayer can infuse intensity into one's day, although oddly enough,[7] something about it felt spontaneous to Pablo. "Everything is amplified because I'm digging in. I'm surrounding my day with nothing but Him. I'm heightened and I'm making myself available in worship, then it's like, ping and it comes from nowhere." "It" was the shift of his mental state. This shift brought uncertainty. "Now I'm no longer at a stable place. I'm on ground that I'm not used to walking on. I'm used to wanting to be on a foundation I can control, where I can feel my feet. Now I'm in a place where it is unfamiliar territory." The transformative fire leaves its mark, forging and solidifying a new self, albeit temporarily. "It takes time for the burning and molding and cooling but I don't think you become solid for a permanent position. I think you become solid for that season before the new season." In prayer and through a relationship with God, the old self is unsettled, and a new self emerges, perhaps with a different set of sensibilities.

Music helps in the undoing. "I get lost in the music," said Pablo, "it tears me apart. It does its own thing. Music puts me in a place of availability, then God moves." Expectation also assists, so Pablo very explicitly works to set active expectations. "I try and make myself available to see what he had for me. I don't mean forcing myself to babble, I mean trying to see what he has for me." Paradoxically, personal will hinders progress. "By self-will, you're negating the process." This, of course, is oddly dissonant with the contemporary Western idea that the self relies on the will. Among evangelicals, by contrast, the self seems to emerge by releasing the will.

Pablo imagined letting go of layers of modern pretense. "I want to get past the entry point. Just like when you're in a relationship and you meet a young lady for the first time, at the entry point, you want to put on your best. I want to live beyond that surface level. That's the artificial level. It's real, but it's on the surface, it's cosmetic." Pointedly, he posed the question, "What's deep?" For Pablo, prayer served as a conduit toward authenticity, enabling him to be fully present in the immediate moment. "Prayer is a pre-requisite for being in the present." The raw child then became an ideal. "Recently, my son, he said, 'Mum, this is an amazing day. But it didn't start off amazing.' He said, 'Up until now, when you gave me this candy, I was not happy.'"

Pablo started laughing.

"He's six years old, what is he really saying? He's saying exactly what he means. Wow! He's raw, he's organic, he just says it. 'Give me that candy.'" Pablo aspired to this kind of enthusiasm. "I want that. I want to be raw at all times. I'm a student of life. Life is the alivest party I could attend. What that means for me is that I want to know it. I want to know it from its truest form." And the raw life comes, he says, from release.

While the idea of submission might evoke humility, it does not always imply sharing authority. Pablo, for instance, initially expressed a somewhat egalitarian perspective on marriage. "How does marriage work? We both have to submit ourselves." But, listening further, a hierarchy soon appeared. "As I submit myself to Christ, my wife submits herself to me." Humility, it seems, may be directional. I do give him credit for imagining a shared agency: "Really she's saying, 'I trust you because you're trusting Him [God] and so I'm going to hand you that gun.'" It turns out they both have guns. "We hand each other loaded guns. That type of trust is tangible in the dark." Here, letting go means a wild vulnerability, but one that builds and rebuilds a gender hierarchy.

As with many evangelicals, Pablo often imagined himself in dialogue with a skeptical secular voice. God's presence seemed shadowed by a constant dread, what I have come to call "ontological anxiety"—a deep-seated urge to definitively prove that God is ontologically, meaning actually, real.[8] Pablo's response? His confidence comes from experience, not primarily from scripture. "When the truth is your own truth and you've lived it, it's very hard to convince you differently." He couldn't, however, completely evade the nagging worry of mistaking his surrender for manipulation. "I do understand there is sometimes a programming that can go on in church." But then, he trusted his senses. "But your experiences and your relationship, that's why I've said, 'Me? I'm a believer.' I've seen it. I've seen demonic possession up close. I've walked and experienced the blueprint of my life at 11 years old up to 47 that has shown me over and over and over and over again the truth of God."

The process by which evangelicals distinguish God's work from other processes, what they call "discernment," is complex. "In my knower, I know for sure. Can I be wrong? I can be 100% wrong." I pointed out that as he spoke about confidence, he was holding his hands to his chest. Pablo explained that his certainty was internal and bodily: "In my knower, in my soul, in my chest, in my heart. I've felt darkness. I've felt the cold. I've also felt the warmth." Sensation played a pivotal role in shaping his conviction.

Ultimately, charismatic prayer inspired in Pablo a profound sense of empowerment. "Like I was a superhero, it feels like metal in my veins, almost like the X-Men. I can't even explain it; it's almost like I'm having too much energy in my body." This feeling of power has propelled charismatics out into the world with a story to tell and the confidence to express it.

Charismatic Release

Charismatic evangelicalism is an oral tradition and a highly charged practice, not a spiritual tradition that works comfortably with lists. So, building a taxonomy of charismatic release is a bit untidy. The central premise of experiential surrender might transcend most conceptual frameworks. Maybe a domain on the edge of words. Certainly a challenge to write. Like this book.

Maybe this is because charismatic practices are rooted, to a degree, in a Black prophetic tradition relying primarily on storytelling and personal experience. One that nurtures a highly improvisational ethos. Think Jazz. A wealth of sophisticated charismatic theology explores ethical considerations and details the importance of the spirit. But, we find very little writing on inner states, let alone the intricate connections between the inner and outer realms (I did come across a collection of training manuals during my investigations—see Chapter 3).

This scarcity of written guidance may come as a surprise in a tradition associated with an unwavering belief that the words in the Bible are best read as literal and precisely accurate depictions of history and ethics. But while Buddhist traditions have produced volumes chock-full of lists enumerating the various states of mind during spiritual practice, the charismatics' sacred text—the Bible—focuses on matters of ethics and narratives of worldly action rather than inner experiences. Sections of pure poetry, like the Song of Songs, might be the closest charismatics come to categorizing their inner feelings. So, while the language of letting go loosely ties to biblical stories—especially that moment of speaking in tongues at Pentecost—charismatics largely work with a fluid folk taxonomy that shifts and adapts with time. Less is written on paper or stone.

Endora: Letting Go of Thoughts and Feelings

I watched Endora, a small and stout grandmother with short-cropped hair, as she traversed the crowded church atrium as the tiny hands of her two grandchildren pulled themselves close to her hips. Tattoos covered Endora's neck and back, the only visible sign of her past. When we finally sat down together, she seemed excited to tell her story. Endora had lived a life entangled in drug addiction, headed a drug-dealing gang, engaged in battles wielding knives and guns, and, at times, taken lives. Yet she felt that surrendering her anger to God had transformed her existence. She told me how she had cleansed her home, distanced herself from her gang associates, and converted her former drug havens into spaces dedicated to prayer.

Five hours of conversation revealed a profound and simmering anger—a fury that seemed fully reasonable given her tumultuous past. Having grown up in a brothel run by her grandmother, she was left vulnerable to the whims of aggressive men from a tender age. Her childhood was marred by the abuse of an uncle who subjected both her and her older aunt to forced sexual acts. She shared with me the profound rage she harbored toward her uncle, toward her grandmother for punishing her when she dared to speak of the abuse, and toward her aunt for knowing about the ongoing ordeal and allowing it to persist. Reflecting on her past, Endora seethed,

> He would come and get me when he was out of the army, and I already knew what to do when he took me to buy a dress or something. I just didn't understand why they let me go with him. If my aunt knew what he was like and she experienced what he did to her constantly too, why didn't she stop him?

Endora's anger was palpable and understandable.

Throughout her turbulent journey, God became a beacon of hope and meaning. He provided her with solace and a sense of security in the midst of a life engulfed by violence. When the voices of her traumatic past haunted her, God offered a private sanctuary within herself—an inner core she could repeatedly return to. She shared, with poignant honesty, "When I was being raped, not just molested, but truly raped, I wanted it to be over. I wanted him to be finished and gone, every single time. And I would hear God saying, 'You're going to be alright.' Even though I felt utterly alone externally, there was a sense of safety within me." Within the depths of her being, shielded from physical violence, a space emerged—a place of tranquility, gentle guidance, and nurturing care.

In spite of, or perhaps because of, the violence around her, God's voice became a regular part of her everyday life. Throughout what Endora called her "gangbanging" days, he reminded her of the life she thought she should be living. The message was twofold: first, things will be alright, and second, she should follow his ethical path. The latter took a while to sink in. On rare occasions, she heard prophetic visions of the future as a warning. She reported a time when, at what seemed like God's urging, she counseled her sister not to travel to Santa Cruz, only to later discover that the car they were planning to drive was severely damaged and an accident was likely. However, more often than not, God's voice served as a guide for living—a conscience, one might say.

"It's just this gift that guides me and it's telling me right from wrong. Say I want to have a beer and I already know to get right back on that wagon again. I can hear him say, 'It's not for you and I'm with you.'"

I asked if those words from God were audible. She responded, "Yes, 'I'm with you.' I hear it."

"Does that usually sound like a man speaking?"

"Yes."

"Do you hear it inside or outside of your head?"

"I would feel it's all in me." Then, as if on cue, as we talked, she started to hear a voice. "Even now, because speaking about my life is not easy, but I want to be a help to someone. I want to bring others to him, to let them know that they are not lost if they are anything like me. He is telling me 'this is right.'"

"You're hearing that right now?" I asked.

"Yes, 'This is right.'" She described the tone. "Soft but powerful, like, 'This is right.' Almost like your real dad."

"Where are those words coming from?"

"In me, all me."

"In you? You're pointing at your chest."

"Yes, it's my own voice I have. All I can tell you is it's not comparable to anything else; it's Him, because that same voice has followed me since I was five."

Abuse victims often develop internal voices as a means of regulating their suffering, a well-known phenomenon among therapists. This is the imagination as therapist. Anthropologist Tanya Luhrmann, among others, argues that establishing a connection with an unseen entity also requires some capacity for imagination.[9] In certain religious practices, this ability to imagine becomes sharper and more palpably real. Perhaps the cognitive processes that facilitate communion with God bear similarities to the imaginative work undertaken in certain forms of family therapy. In these therapies, people are encouraged to identify elements of their inner experience and personify them, giving them names, clothing, and personalities. By creating personas for their inner experiences, patients in family therapy gain a means to engage with and ultimately heal those experiences. This approach allows them to establish a degree of separation from the critical voices within their heads. Similarly, for Endora, the personality of God serves as therapeutic material—an avenue through which she can navigate her internal landscape and find solace.

For Endora, prayer was undeniably about healing. "I spoke in tongues when I started going to the apostolic church as a kid. I was about 12 years old. All I wanted was my dad and my mum to get well, to get sober, to take care of us. I put all of me in it." The Holy Ghost took the space inside of her where she imagined there might otherwise have been a healthy, undamaged sense of one's body. "I never felt my body right. I've never felt I could be a kid, a child, and so I got the Holy Ghost there." This inner tenderness and vulnerability persisted despite the harshness of her street life. "In the streets I'm hardcore. I'm known to be ugly, very hard. I carried guns and stuff. So, I find it crazy because inside now it's different. I've always been mushy. I cry easily. I break easy." Her inner softness was revealed through prayer.

Endora worked hard to let go of her anger and show her soft side. "You know what has been my hardest really?" We paused for breath. "Not hating the relative that did what he did to me. The forgiveness for him was tough. Boy, it's tough." The practice, as she described it, involved entrusting her anger and the desire for retribution to God for safekeeping. It was not always successful, as she admitted. "Sometimes I'll try to take it out of the King's hands and I start to get angry again." But that feels awful. "I know it's the King's because he's the only one that can make it feel better, by saying, 'Leave it to me.'" Endora could even let herself feel the anger, as long as it dissipated before she acted on it. "I'll find times where I just have that tantrum and it's okay, but sin not." Her new husband went through a similar process—out of the gangs, into the church. "We gave up on that anger and gave it to Him and prayed and He took it." Letting go of thoughts and feelings is far from simple; it can be super difficult. It has me pondering what distinguishes one thought as tenacious and difficult to release, while another seems fleeting. And then, what transpires within us when we do let go?

Similar to Pablo, Endora's relationship with God both melted and molded her sense of self. "I feel like I lose me," said Endora.

"You lose you?" I asked.

"I feel like I'm with him; I'm out of my own place. His is a safe place. A place where I can let go. I can't really explain it. No one else can go there." The body was something different. "I have sold it. I put drugs in it, and I let anybody use it. I have let gangs use it. I let them tattoo me. I didn't care about this body because I didn't think it was worth anything after what had happened." In other words, the body and the "me" were separate. They were both, in her assessment, dirty and damaged and yet always open to healing, for they were inhabited by, in relationship with, and occasionally controlled by the Holy Spirit. As she explained, "I have always cried out to God. In gangs where I could have been shot, because my house has been shot up, or I'm doing dirt, too, or shooting up drugs; I would cry out to him because I just felt he always followed me. It was like a voice that never let me go." And the body could be recovered. "I was five and he never let me go, and now I'm here today and I'm protecting this body."

This interplay of internal realms poses a fascinating puzzle because we in the West are accustomed to thinking of the interior as a unified thing, and yet here Endora describes several interiors—the bodily, which is dirty and cleansable; the Holy Spirit or God as a voice of calm and safety; and then perhaps even another that is the person's own spirit. It could sound quite chaotic, something akin to what psychologists might call dissociation. Yet together, all three realms, in an overlapping and interrelated manner, make up the experience of Endora's self that was being released and refashioned through a relationship to God. Moreover, recent studies on psychedelics indicate that while dissociation has often been regarded as an indication of psychological distress, a very similar experience often called ego-dissolution is typically linked to positive outcomes. The distinction can sometimes be difficult to draw.[10]

Endora's interior, soft and safe, was the most private and self-oriented place imaginable, not the superficial "me" that Pablo referred to. Nor was it her fleshly body. Within this thing she called a "self," one could find a body, a conscience, a safe interior, and, at times, the Holy Spirit. Some combination of these was surrendered when she connected with God.

Interestingly, much of the activity within this tripartite self does not appear to be under Endora's control. Tongues speech, for instance, arises without obvious prompting. "I don't even know what happens when I just start doing it, but it just happens. I can't tell you when it's going to start." Just to be clear, many charismatics can control its onset. But, for Endora, connection with God, understandably, transcends ordinary control. His voice was neither audible, mental, nor purely bodily. Instead, it fills her senses. "I feel it in all of me. It could start in the mind but I just feel it at the same time, it's all through me really." In this fullness, she found herself unable to direct the unfolding process. "It takes control of me."

Ultimately, what Endora calls "a language of love" sends her airborne, both spiritually and bodily. "When I'm praying I feel like I'm free. I feel like I'm flying. I don't have that pull in me. I'm not who I was at all. I'm what he's made me. I'm just flying. It just takes me into the air. I visualize a dove just gone, or a butterfly just going." The freedom experienced through release, the inner possibilities akin to an inner butterfly, can emerge once she entrusts God with the inner turmoil. However, she must first articulate her thoughts to facilitate the process of release. "It was so hard to let him have it." For a religion in which the central narratives have Abraham letting go of Isaac and God letting go of a son, perhaps letting go of anger and forgiving a rapist may sit on the edge of plausible.

A quick aside. A friend read this chapter and told me the first two stories— Pablo and Endora—both came across as working class, perhaps poor. She worried if I might be, however unintentionally, rehearsing that old narrative: religion as the opiate of the masses. People have said that before about charismatics.[11] Some do invert the story and imagine class as the source of their vast power.[12]

And yes, the data show some truth to it. On average, charismatics are less educated than the norm in the United States and they include millions of deeply impoverished people outside the US.[13] But we're talking about over 500 million people across the globe. Many are middle class, and not a few are wealthy. The connection between economic precarity and charismatic experience exists, but it is neither sufficient nor necessary to explain the phenomenon. To think about how religion works with class is important, but people don't speak in tongues merely because the rent's due. To reduce that to hunger or hardship would be to miss the point. We might miss the people too.

Releasing Thoughts: God's Backpack

So, to get back to it, the stories charismatics tell about letting go seem to narrate something about how thoughts and bodies work together. They suggest that there is something different when we hold our thoughts tightly, or, instead, loosely. Thoughts can take on different qualities. Elusive and transient, or substantial and clingy, they bubble up within the confines of our consciousness, each possessing varying degrees of clarity, wholeness, coherence, and retrievability. Yet, paradoxically, the tighter we clutch, the less we seem to hold on—and that doesn't really make sense anyways, because thoughts can't be truly held. Still, we keep trying to grasp, and also to release. Memories, too, can cling stubbornly; the harder we strive to forget, the longer they seem to linger—often the same goes for desires.[14] The failure of fundamentalist abstinence, as seen in the restriction of sex education materials among young people, highlights this phenomenon. While it delayed the onset of intercourse by about nine months, it paradoxically led to a rise in teen pregnancy. Sometimes, the act of clamping down on the mind only serves to invigorate thoughts, rather than stifle them.[15] And yes, please notice that I am describing differences between fundamentalists and charismatics—they are often not the same.[16]

In sharp contrast to abstinence or renunciation, the practice of letting go offers a fundamentally different approach to self-management. It asks us to attend to and connect with our thoughts and feelings, but it means noticing them without grabbing onto them. The quality of attention is key. By allowing God to tend to our thoughts, we might learn to hold them with a gentler touch, or perhaps even relinquish them entirely, they suggest.

For Endora, releasing thoughts supports her efforts at coping with the aftermath of abuse.

In this case, you could say that God's presence is simply a psychological contrivance, an auditory hallucination designed to cope with pain. However, as she specifically contends, God could very well employ hallucination as a tool for healing. That her most poignant experiences of God emerged at the pivotal moments of her abuse might signify confusion, dissociation, and fantasies of safety. Or, they might serve as a testament to the resilient faculties of her psyche, her adaptive flexibility to endure and resist suffering. Such pliancy could even be evidence of a divine responsiveness—an indication that God, sensing her need, manifested in a manner that defied dismissal. Perhaps trauma, in its shattering of our beings, paves a pathway for the spirit to permeate our fragmented selves.

The kind of hurts that charismatics hand over to God can be big or small. As one churchgoer, Jean, explained, "I was 16, just broke up with my boyfriend and was facing all these crazy things and abuse in my family. And I was just screaming all this pain out and I remember laying on the floor screaming. Like every anger I ever felt. And just letting go of it." She attests that this act of release shifted her pain. Through earsplitting articulation of her anguish, her thoughts metamorphosed into tangible entities that Jean could then release. Charismatic communities rarely focus overtly on the mind except to control and discipline nefarious impulses. But in this case, the release of thoughts to God offers one tool for introspection.

Mark, a pastor at Glad Tidings, was tall, pale, and broad-shouldered, and importantly, the number two, always by the pastor's side. He recalled a conversation with the pastor—an exchange that revolved around the delicate art of controlling one's thought life. "I was like, 'What do you mean? It's your thoughts. How do you control your thoughts?' Since that time, I've learned more and more about how to be able to do that. I would say it's not so much getting rid of the thought, but maybe putting it on a back burner, or compartmentalizing it." Or sometimes handing it to God, "If it's something that I'm obsessing about, that I can't stop thinking about, I'll say, 'God, I'm going to take this thought, and I'm putting it in a box, and I'm putting it at the foot of the cross until such a time as You can deal with it.' Sometimes that helps. Sometimes that's harder to do than others."

Once again, this has us leaning into the world of therapeutic methods, where naming thought patterns can help people release their grip on a single idea. "The more I recognized my position in who I am to God," explained Valentin, a black-haired pastor at Glad Tidings, "the more I was able to have distance from the hyper-analyzing of my day or how I blew it or who thought that I was a failure." Prayer allowed her a separation from thoughts; these thoughts then became metaphorical objects that she could pass on—like items in a backpack, as she put it.

> God started taking things out of that backpack and saying, 'You were never meant to carry this. You are not a failure.' In this way, I was able to experience healing from God, from pain that I had been through as a kid and just the regrets I had for my own actions. I started writing letters to people to ask their forgiveness. It wasn't just my dad. I wanted to have a clean slate to be free to just love on other people, right? I had been too busy carrying my stuff. We all have stuff. But it doesn't incapacitate me like it used to. I used to just replay stuff all the time and have a lot of angst. Life is too short.

Valentin's prayer practice gave her access to inner thoughts. She could then pack them up and hand them over.

Submission and (Some) Lack of Control

But to release control requires openness, as Shavon explained. "Until I was 28-years-old I was pretty much closed," she said.

> I know it all. You can't tell me. I'm not willing to be vulnerable. Vulnerability is open, right? Now, I'm okay if I sit here and start crying in front of you. I'm not going to feel embarrassed. I'm vulnerable, I'm open in front of the Lord, in front of you. If you think I'm crazy that's okay. Vulnerable, open, aware, humble.

The way Shavon talked about it, I began to think that this ability to submit translates to all sorts of encounters in the world. Or maybe it only works with God?

Letting go is not always simple. Somehow, people seem inclined to clasp tightly. Charismatics often describe an internal battle between their desire to release, to be in God's company, and an impulse to control their own bodies. "Why should I raise my hands?" asked Valentin. She was talking about the signature evangelical prayer posture with hands open and raised, almost as if inviting a soft rain. "That feels like surrender. I don't wanna' surrender to anybody. I've got this covered."

Perhaps we sometimes understand letting go best by looking at its opposite—what we might call "holding on." People often resist the urge to release. "I used to fall over all the time and I would fight it. I try to stop it because I want to be in control." When Abigail finally let it go—"I was like okay, I give up control"—the experience shifted from words to something deeply physical. "It was powerful. I was just shaking more than I ever have and it was fast and frequent. Like electricity in my body. I felt like fire in my hands."

Maybe, as psychiatrist Wilhelm Reich wrote, the deep need for control stems from the "armoring" of bodies—an affliction born of the ills of modern society.[17] Reich suggested that beneath this superficial armor lies a reservoir of healthy energy, waiting to be freed. Charismatics often express a similar yearning for release. Abigail felt like her tongue was stuck inside her mouth. All she had to do was let it out. "The funny thing is, I remember distinctly feeling as if there was something inside of me that wanted to come out from inside my throat, like wind wanted to come out." Then, it did.

Remarkably, the act of being vulnerable and surrendering thoughts can inspire the feeling of being loved. As one charismatic, Cassie, put it,

> I can't describe it. It's too glorious. I don't need words, I just feel secure or loved. I have never felt love like that from anybody. When you hold a baby and you look at that child, there is something that happens in the heart. You're not thinking. You see the baby, so I don't know if the brain is working along with the heart or what, but I have that same glorious feeling inside that I know the Holy Spirit is with me. There is a confidence; I don't have to think. I just know I am loved. He hears the voice in my heart. My heart is speaking, and I am just soft, I feel soft.

In that moment, letting go of reason brought a kind of softening. The hard push of thought fell away. In its place came something gentler, something she could almost feel. Maybe even thoughts can turn soft?

Release can feel like freedom, as I have been told. Alison explained, "When I do speak in tongues, it's like you're free." First, she submitted. "If you let go, you know, if you're like, 'all right, God, I'm gonna just do whatever you want me to do.' Then I can just feel the Holy Spirit come through me." This process rapidly became bodily. "Sometimes you shake, I've experienced that. Sometimes one body part is just shaking and you're like, what is this? You can feel it shaking but you have no control. It's a beautiful feeling. There was one time when I was at the altar and I was just shaking for maybe two hours." Unlike the rigid tenor of fundamentalist literalism, where each word in the Bible is tested for its exact precise meaning, Alison's release evoked an attitude of openness and an acceptance of and even desire for uncertainty. "This happens when there's something that you're not in control of or something that you can't predict. That's what we pray for. That his presence would just walk in and that people would feel it because he's so powerful that if he walks in the room, you're just dismantled." She came to rely on submission to an all-knowing God. "He can do anything, right. Like, whatever you're praying for." And it felt like freedom. "It's much more than what you could ever imagine, freedom and just like dancing."

What might seem strange to outsiders is that this process is both profoundly willful and also, at the very same moment, very much about submission—a submission so absolute that the worshipper becomes only a conduit for God's project on Earth. "God is just using us as vessels. We're just people, we're—I mean there's nothing special about us." Yet, if they open themselves, they believe they can be filled.

Submitting the Body

In many ways, speaking in tongues stands as a classic model for spiritual release, moving from a tradition that shapes a metaphor and theological concept into sensation. But just as often, the looping works in reverse. The body can be the catalyst. Sensations inspire experiences that are mediated by theological metaphors, where physical practice shapes, and is shaped by, the discussions within the church.

In the fall of 1899, preacher Charles Parham had been reading the Bible in a somewhat new and unusual way. He had come to feel that tongues prayer was imperative for personal spiritual advancement in the twentieth century. He saw January 1, 1900, as a turning point. Parham longed for a spontaneous eruption of the Spirit instigated by God. This became the framework that people translated into action. He became one of the founders of charismatic evangelicalism. Indeed, sometimes release begins with an idea.

Likewise, Bright, a highly active member of Glad Tidings, described the act of releasing her thoughts and seeking cooperation from God. "I just ask for it, like, 'Lord I need help, like I really dislike this person or they get on my nerves,' I'm like, 'I have judgmental thoughts toward them; I don't want that.' I'm surrendering this 'yuck', right. It's as if I'm holding a bunch of stuff, and setting it down before God," Bright gestured, mimicking the act of placing an object down. "I'm giving you a vision."

"That's what it feels like?" I asked.

"Yeah, in the spirit. Take these things off of my heart, take these things."

"You feel like you set them down?"

"Yeah, releasing them."

"Releasing them? And then what happens?"

"A lot of times it's not something that is instant, like 'oh it's gone.' A lot of times we pick it back up. That control that we want as human beings, or if this person is still bothering you, you metaphorically pick it back up, right?" It might be about social anxiety, she explained. "In order to flop, you cannot care about who is around you." And then, after letting go of control, judgment, or anxiety, on occasion, there came peace.

I have a stillness of mind, sometimes. It's kind of like you're in a bad neighborhood, even if you don't hear gunshots, you're just kind of aware. I try to quiet the awareness. That's my pursuit of focus and single mindedness, so I can enter in this cooperation with God, because it's very hard when you have all these other challenging thoughts.

Her metaphors acted as a fragile bridge between thought and sensation, allowing her to move between the two.

Yet, at times, the act of letting go began with the physical. When I met John, he had just rejoined Glad Tidings from a stint with an AG rehabilitation program. "Letting go to me just kind of looks like this," he explained, lifting his hands as though confronted by a police officer with a drawn weapon.

With my hands raised. I heard someone say this once, that when you have your hands raised it's a sign of surrender. But it's also a sign of praise. It's a sign of worship to God, and that looks like letting go for me. With that, I am also letting go of whatever I might be going through, whatever I might be dealing with, whatever I might look like, we're all doing that because in moments like that I'm fully in tune with the fact that again I am still here after there's been countless times where I should have died. I'm praising him and I'm worshipping him, and I am not thinking about circumstances or job or school or frustration or anger or anything like that. I am more focused on who God is. To me that's what letting go looks like, just full freedom. If you won a million bucks. It's like you don't care about anything but receiving your prize.

In John's narrative, the body was the trigger for attention toward God that could fill his mind, leaving little room for everyday worries.

Like the mind, the body responds to letting go with tremendous shifts. One of the more outlandish practices they call being "drunk in the spirit," a form of bodily letting go if there ever was one. Here people laugh and cry and sway as if drunk, and they seem to love it. "I feel a joy and I start laughing, and you can't really control what you're doing or saying. But it's good," explained Joy. In the past decades, several revivals inspired hundreds of drunk moments. The other side of being drunk in the spirit is crying in the spirit. While letting go can sound lovely, like flying or floating, the reality is often a bit less pristine. "I'll just start praying for my family and my sister and next thing I know, it's like five hours later crying, snot everywhere."

As the body learns to let go in a close loop with submission to authority, physical movements can stop feeling like technique or practice; it feels like the body has a mind of its own. Speaking in tongues means saying words you don't understand, giving yourself over as a vessel for spirit. But to make it work, the surrender has to reach the body. You give up control of the tongue, open to whatever comes, and meet God there. The release matters more than the sense the words make, they say. Each register of release, bodily and conceptual, seems to permeate the others, giving them more traction and more flow.

"Logically I don't know what these words mean," said Alison, "but I'm believing that when I pray in tongues that you're praying through me, that you're doing the interceding." She alluded to the classic biblical formulation from Romans 8:26 that encourages "groans that words can't contain." Imagine the groaning supplicant in prayer, working far beyond the rational. "I'm not praying with my mind. There aren't clear and distinct thoughts accompanying the tongues. There can be a state where it's like my spirit is just communicating with God and I'm not governed by the thoughts in my mind," she said.

Yielding the Self

The feeling of giving up the self—what some psychologists call "ego-dissolution"—runs through mystical states and psychedelic trips. It's now one of the most prized goals in psychiatric work, tied to healing posttraumatic stress disorder and depression. But among charismatics, who shy from words like "mystic" and anything that suggests collective manipulation or hysteria, their commitment to releasing the self can be ambivalent.

From my interviews, however, it sounds like many charismatics can't help but feel a form of ego-dissolution. "I feel like I lose me," as Endora put it. For Pablo, the process of "dethroning" the self involved relinquishing control over every element of life. He released all his resistance to the guidance he felt emanating from God and discovered a childlike "raw self" beneath it all. As he explained, "I think the bottom line is really how much are you willing to give up? Are you really willing to die to yourself? If you want change, do you really want change or do you want minimal change or do you want a partial change? How much change do you really want?" This sounds a lot like ego-dissolution, ego-death is a related term. For Jennifer, the loss was complete. "There is no awareness of self," she explained. "When the Holy Spirit pours out or comes on you rapidly, there is no awareness of self for me. It's all focused on him and his presence and goodness."

Researchers studying psychedelic substances often describe a shift in the perception of time as a crucial component of shedding the self. Time may slow down, speed up, or even become irrelevant. Michael talked about something similar in prayer when he let go of control, "If He [God] takes over for a while then the prayer time goes longer. All of a sudden you realize, 'I've been on the roof for like an hour,' or something like that." This reworking of time is one key for scholars who are trying to compare the ways the self-dissolves across practices.

Charismatics do occasionally describe losing their sense of self, but more frequently, they speak of being an individual in solitary communion with God. This is a whole other kind of experience. The world falls away, not the self. What is left after is not clear to me. Perhaps more unmediated connection to God? Bright expressed this simply:

> When everyone else is singing, I am worshipping in tongues. I definitely feel like I've had an experience where even if I'm in a crowded auditorium, I'm the only one there. Sometimes that is a choice where you're like, 'I am focused on God. I'm not focused on who is around, what is happening,' but I have definitely had that experience. That is why it helps me personally to close my eyes and close out all the distractions to experience.

It does seem that there is something about the 1:1 with God that is powerful and unusual. Shavon found it very appealing, "My desire would be to be alone with him because there's so much going on in my life, right? I need that time where I'm just in his presence. I don't always feel alone when I'm in a group of people. I'll want to. I don't want to see you and everybody." Is this merging with God? Or is it simply quiet time together? Maybe this is why charismatic movements seem so compatible with capitalist expansion: they both nurture the sense of being an independent individual. There is a whole literature on this story with the argument that something in the specifics of the 1:1 connection with God promoted by evangelical worship leans away from a collective sense of self to something more individual.[18] Maybe the dissociative experience here is about losing a sense of the world around us, and instead of dissolving the self, they dissolve the messy human community for a moment?

But, of course, sometimes, letting go can be a collective endeavor, although how people come out the other side (more or less individual) is a whole different question. Most people do assume that I am describing a group activity when I tell them I study speaking in tongues. It often sounds to me like they carry the old warnings about crowds, emotions, and manipulation in such situations. Later chapters of this book explore the relationships between the release into speaking in tongues and its effect on the mind. But it is important to recognize that the vast majority of participants who return to the church do so willingly. They know what is expected, and they want it. Researchers have increasingly acknowledged the importance of expectations (what they call expectancy) in contemplative practices, but for charismatics, the key lies in expecting to expect. They consciously cultivate a sense of anticipation. Expectancy plays a role, albeit a purposeful one.

During one of her short-term foreign mission trips, Alison described an experience that seemed to turn on the power of being in a group. "The whole team, 90 of us, went down to these 500 kids, and they were in an assembly line with people just praying in front of the line and then whole line would just fall out." Fall out means to be slain in the spirit. "And then kids were speaking in tongues and they didn't even know anything about the Holy Spirit, they had never heard of anyone speaking in tongues. They don't even know about God. … And that's when the Holy Spirit just fell. And it wasn't about anything that we did, it was just God wanting to help these kids."

These collective experiences were frequently described as especially powerful. Heidi struggled to find words to describe the intensity, saying, "When there's unity, there's definitely like a 'boom' moment, he's here and we all recognize it, everybody knows what to do. It's like a 'boom' moment. Boom!" she told me. Her words carried a felt sense of awe and power.

She talked about "unction," a biblical word that generally slides between meanings: consecration, sometimes with oil; religious fervor; and exaggerated earnestness. In this context, it captured the sense of being called or driven to take action.

> It's like that same unction feeling, it's like your purpose, your call, such joy, revelation, power, all come inside of you like an eruption and it's just— boom, everybody in that room knows it. I would stake my life on it that every single person in that room knows when that boom hits and it's an amazing feeling for all of us.

When we began to ask more explicitly about the experience of ego-dissolution during prayer, we found that a vast majority of sixty-six participants agreed that the more intense the prayer, the more they felt merged with God and as if their self had dissolved.

A Continuum of Control

Yet a complete surrender of self or absolute loss of control remains rare. Charismatics talk instead about a sliding scale, holding onto a thread of awareness and control as they pray. Most often, they are not fully entranced, and they can initiate or halt the process at will. Lori shed light on this, explaining, "I think I could stop it if I really wanted to." And having done roughly a hundred sessions with brain scans, I can attest that at least those folks could turn it on at will as well. Lori explained that letting go is easier when they feel safe and know what's happening. "Its more about being comfortable, knowing what's coming and being okay to release." But when they feel responsible for others they can't fully surrender. "There have been situations on mission trips, where I feel less comfortable giving up all my own personal control, maybe because I'm tasked with an assignment to hold everyone's passports." If they sense they might lose control at the wrong time, they might actively stop themselves from letting go. "If there's a moment where I feel like that control is going to be lost maybe I will force myself not to." For Lori, real faith means not being the one in charge, even though that's deeply uncomfortable for them.

I'm releasing control, which is hard for me to do. I'm not allowing myself to make the decisions that I would normally. It's a removal of the fear, pressure, or whatever, to just have the faith that the best thing is going to happen. It's not me in the driver's seat. I'm in the passenger seat, or maybe even in the back seat, I guess, is a good way to describe it.

And yet, even in this release, there is a moment of choosing. "I feel like for me I can't be in the middle. I have to be in or not be in."

"So, there's a little bit of will that goes in as you're dropping?" I asked.

"Exactly. I can feel God's presence if I'm praying for someone and I'm not fully dropped in, and I could be able to pray for that person and be in that moment, but I am going to control myself enough to know that I'm not going to release it all, because I don't want 50 passports to go missing." Even so, there are, on occasion, times when it is too far along to be contained. "But if I'm fully dropped in then no, I don't feel like there's times where I have control over that aspect."

Through this unique choreography, at times graceful and sometimes quite awkward, charismatics navigate a delicate path, constantly shifting between control and release. This dynamic balance becomes the fulcrum upon which their journey unfolds, balancing between their own immediate needs and the call of spirit, oscillating between a state of receptive openness and the instinct to safeguard their innermost thoughts and feelings. In this intricate dance of release, they find themselves embracing both tender vulnerability and self-preservation.

2

Training: Both Caught and Taught

Fresh out of divinity school, Heidi returned to the church as a youth pastor. She spoke to me about the connection between faith and release and helped me visualize the charismatic step into uncertainty. "I usually get very frustrated when the advice given to me is, 'Just let go,' and I'm like, 'How do I do that?'" She protested. "And they never give an answer or practical steps for how to do that. The image I keep getting is stepping out of the boat onto the waves where Jesus is, you know? That's the best way I can describe it, it's literally like that—Step on water and see if it works." Heidi was asking for training. And if you think about it, training might make sense as one step in a loop between theology and experience.

***

When I tell people that speaking in tongues could involve training, they look surprised. Some laugh, saying they knew it was fake all along. Charismatics themselves find it hard to talk about training. It seems to suggest that human effort, not God, shapes their experience. There's anxiety in that idea when they say it.

People, however, assume that training is needed for most everything else—dance, sports, music, and relationships. Yet, when it comes to spiritual practice,

---

Elements of this chapter were published previously as: Brahinsky, "Cultivating Discontinuity."

training feels strange. It clashes with a Protestant vision of religious experience that comes from grace, not effort. There's also a sense of contradiction in the idea of training real hard so you can let go. It sounds counterintuitive. Letting go is the opposite of effort. Maybe?

But after a few decades of this research, I can say with some certainty that this kind of religious practice often—although perhaps not always—requires work, and, yes, training. The ancestors of today's charismatics were called Methodists, named for their systematic approach to building church communities, spreading the gospel, and cultivating spiritual experience.[1] Maybe it is easier for some to call it "seeking," which is how they described the special "Flood Gate" weeks at the United House of Prayer, a church studied by anthropologists in the mid-1960s.[2] My colleague, anthropologist Felicity Aulino, once described a church in Thailand where people were very explicitly taught to speak in tongues. They would start by repeating the words "shoulda' bought a Hyundai" over and over until it became automatic. I, for one, do not think this is a problem. Not for people who believe this experience is divine or for those who think it is about releasing control of the body or mind. As Tanya Luhrmann, often says, developing unusual experiences of the divine may be, in some ways, like becoming a skilled athlete: practice, repetition, pushing past the familiar until the mind can actually inhabit a different space altogether.[3]

The following stories of training come mostly from young AG missionaries who were just about to enter the missions field, as well as from professors of theology, evangelism, and missions, and then finally, from published training manuals.

***

"Method, think method!"

I was sweating in a missionary training class. It was October, and it was hot in the Santa Cruz Mountains. I sat on an uncomfortable wooden chair desk in a classroom at Bethany University, listening to a lecture on mission logistics in South Africa. The professor, Dr. Stewart, had lived there as a missionary for much of his life. Beware, he told me, even the missionaries stifle. Their systematic approach, he explained, seemed to shut down spiritual expansion.

"Where we have missionaries, the works aren't growing. Where we don't, they are exploding. Sometimes God moves people's hearts best when there isn't that orchestration." Dr. Stewart sounded like a classic charismatic—a man who loved freedom. And yet, there he was, teaching us to plan. A course on missionary methods had us reading texts and discussing strategies. It seemed like a bit of a contradiction.

Dr. Stewart spoke of tactics and stratagems, an approach that may seem a bit too precise for something as elusive as spirit. At the same time, the not-so-hidden thesis was always that it is best to "yield" to "the Spirit." He repeated it again and again. This tension between spontaneity and systematic method was, to say the least, perplexing.

In charismatic circles, letting go is considered superior to relying on trained responses. But it's hard to deny the reality of methodical practice. Charismatics, especially teachers, tend to discuss this tension openly. One day in class, Dr. Chandler, the other missions professor at Bethany, challenged me in front of everyone. He spoke to the ten-person class, "One of the things I hope Josh comes to in his research is that this is not human effort alone. From the beginning, this is supernatural. More caught than taught."

He might be right. When people first try to speak in tongues, many fail. Some give up altogether. Charismatics sometimes pretend to speak in tongues, actively making nonsense syllables. But it can feel fake, they say. Of the scores of people I interviewed, the vast majority simulated tongues prayer for a while, some for weeks and months, others for only minutes. Eventually, many of them gave up, believing it's impossible. They stopped trying. That's often the turning point. When they give up control and let go of their need to succeed, something happens. It's what many call "openness." When the guard is let down. And then, the tongues come on their own—or so it seems. But this rarely happens without the training and effort beforehand.

For all the talk of spontaneity and freedom of the spirit, charismatic culture is structured at almost every level of experience. Think of a charismatic's week—it's a lesson in methodical spirituality. Christians meet every Sunday. Many have Wednesday prayer sessions too. Add to that classes, small groups, and one-on-one meetings; there is a tremendous variety of systematic modes of connection and spiritual awakening. On top of that, there's careful instruction on how to create the right atmosphere in church during prayer, how to meet and welcome new people, and how to lead in song and call-and-response. And then there's the training in prayer itself—pastoral guidance on daily prayer, Bible study sessions, times when others pray over you, explicit calls to release the tongue, and other collective efforts to induce tongues speech. I found myself constantly surprised by the systematicity at the heart of charismatic spiritual release.

***

It was early for a rock concert. At 9:30 in the morning on Sunday, the speakers started rumbling. Deep bass, squealing guitar, and boom-bap layered over the straight-ahead feel of gospel beats. Then the five-minute countdown began; a digital clock on the giant screen ticked seconds until takeoff. The volume rose as the band kicked in. The crowd swayed, hands raised in the charismatic salute. To me, it seemed surprisingly physical for a denomination where dancing had only recently been forbidden. Even so, the sway quickly turned to bounce, and as the music sped into a frantic gospel pulse, people started jumping— up and down, up and down. About 500 filled the hall; the energy was just starting to overflow. The line of greeters by the doors left their posts to join in, to sway, sing, jump, or clap. Preachers broke the singing with occasional bombast. Fundraising took a good twenty-five minutes, supplemented with videos and a carefully orchestrated appeal to the pragmatic, the visionary, and the compassionate.

Then it was time to sing along. Line by line, the pastor taught us a 1940s gospel song to complement rock ballads from the Vineyard and Bethel Church that had started the morning. The lyrics appeared on the screen, typed in slowly. We read them as they came—the timing was off; the lyrics were coming late. We mumbled to fill the gaps. The head pastor was a quiet man, slumped a bit, almost shy in front of such an energetic crowd. Every few minutes, he asked for "connection," for us to "raise your hands," "lift your head," "give me your attention."

Finally, time to raise the spirit. Sudden silence. His testimony began slow and deliberate. He paused, broke the thread, and asked for more spotlight. His focus today was on compromise—there must be no compromise with the world, certainly not with the churches that lack the spirit and were caught in ritual, he said. But it was carefully balanced—we fall down, we get up, he said. As he spoke, his slump sloughed away, the voice grew stronger, and his hands began to guide. The crowd responded, and the band worked toward a crescendo. Quiet again, and then the call: "let the spirit fall."

One small Asian man started speaking—his voice rising above the rest. I couldn't catch the words. He was speaking in tongues. Incomprehensible to the uninitiated, translatable by some, and—as the pastor would later suggest—perhaps a foreign, but earthly, tongue. The tongues speaker repeated the same line four times until the pastor paused the service. "Who will interpret?" he asked. Candace spoke up, culling a line from the Bible, but the pastor immediately stopped her. "I believe you Candace, but not today. Today is for someone else." Not every move of the spirit is spontaneous, it seems.

We sat again in silence. He guided us toward open-handed waiting: "If you are shy, speak. If you feel the impulse, let it out. Come to my side, we can do this together." We waited. Silence. The band started. It was the wrong song. The pastor stopped them, once again gently correcting. They began again, a slow, mournful ballad to pull the spirit closer. As it wound down, he called again. We waited. Silence. I felt anxious for him and the crowd. He may have heard my thoughts, for he told us, "It's okay." One day, he reassured us, we will grow in God so we can all take that step, worry less, and let the spirit move us.

That morning at Glad Tidings stunned me, partly because of the loud music, but more because of the apparent lack of concern for spontaneity. There was no pretending that the music, the setting, and the direction were separate from the process of encountering God. Music inspires, obviously. There was no imagining that our hands raise on their own. The preacher told us to raise them. We were learning the song together, the song for prayer and the broader skill of prayer. This was not a polished ministry dazzling us with the flash of power. It was raw, blunt, and clearly step-by-step instruction made for our participation.

The pastor's seeming humility felt exposed and awkward amid his total control. Just as the lights responded to his command, so did the screen, the music, and the crowd—all carefully managed elements of incitement. The prompts—for lights, for song, for a new song, for raised arms—were all visible. Nothing hidden, no polished veneer. He literally stopped a song in the middle when it didn't flow for him. He told someone that it wasn't their day to interpret. He made us wait in silence. In many ways, this was wildly controlled. Like the building we sat in, where the exposed pipes were both an artistic and budgetary choice, the underlying structure of maintenance, seen in the awkward shifts and turns of the techniques of inspiration, was part of the performance.

At the same time, the practice also felt open, collective, and cooperative. We saw. We followed. We chose to raise our hands, to sing out loud, and to call in the spirit. And we felt something in the process. Pastor asked, and we yielded—by choice. Maybe that was freedom, in the midst of what could easily feel like control?

***

My puzzle here is the relationship between training and spontaneity and how this tension shapes charismatic worship. Many are simply swept up by the presence of God. Others reach the supernatural through a kind of pretend. But, before I go any further, I want to be clear that by "pretend" I am suggesting that imaginative effort is intriguing and important to charismatics. It's a tool for charismatics, a way to bridge the gap between doubt and belief. It doesn't prove that God isn't real, or that he is, for that matter. For some, pretending works in a secular context to enable the person to feel more confident that God is present. Others rely on "fake it till you make it," learning to speak in tongues through repetition. In both cases, the imagination is a support for finding a way to a confident sense of God's presence.

All this involves cultivating an attitude of openness. For some, pretending can be a deliberate training of the mind, a means of attuning and refining thoughts to focus them more firmly toward God, despite the doubt they feel.

Lisette explains it well—a small, young, round-faced woman, upwardly mobile, working her way through graduate school in psychology. She is very much in the world of everyday secular experiences but also in constant contact with what she takes to be divinity. Jesus is with her always—while eating breakfast, on the bus, and in class. Her primary outreach tool is imagination. She calls it pretending, but also not pretending, because to her, Jesus is real.

"I just imagine when I'm driving, that Jesus is in the passenger seat," she explained. I ask her if it gives her a sense of God's presence. "Sometimes," she says, "when I remember to do it. Yes, [call me] crazy lady, but I'll talk like he's there, and when he's not, I'm looking up because I'm constantly in conversation." Lisette aims for uninterrupted pretending that Jesus is with her. I asked her if Jesus is really there or if it is just pretend. "Both," she replied. "I pretend that Jesus is there, but I'm not pretending."

This is an exceptionally clear depiction of what Tanya Luhrmann calls the "double epistemological register" of US evangelical thought.[4] Lisette both asserts and denies the pretending. She moves through the pretend to experience what she feels is the real. And sometimes, the pretense fully lifts. "Sometimes I feel like I'm pretending that he's there, but then I just throw that out. I don't need to pretend [anymore] because he *is* there." The double register collapses into one.

When people learn to speak in tongues, many do something similar. Speaking in tongues is an expression of syllables and phonemes that sound like a language but, as far as we can tell, most often lacks the structure of a language.[5] Charismatics call it a "gift," something given by God. It feels automatic, unchosen, they say. Yet almost everyone I talked to described a time when they made nonsense sounds on purpose. They "pretended."

Most folks told me privately they had faked it at some point. But I have never heard an evangelical say this publicly. This may be because most of them also described a moment when pretend turned into something that felt real. Like Lisette with Jesus, people fake speaking in tongues and, in doing so, train themselves to let go and to open up to the experience. Crossing from doubt to what feels like genuine experience means learning to let things flow, in the mind and in the body.

Bethany University

Eleven students stood in a circle, each speaking in tongues. It was a systematic project, a practice of love, they explained, but also a way to reach God. They did it regularly, with a serious intent, following a careful plan. In the center, a girl, nearly a woman, was crying, struggling to keep up. She had been trying for weeks but couldn't catch the rhythm of tongues prayer. Her friends were patient; they had all been there. She gave up, tears in her eyes. That, it turned out, was the trick. She let go, and the babble came. Once she stopped trying, she began to speak. It was nonsense, outside the semiotic frame, free of any linguistic laws. If there is pure freedom, this is it, she said. If there is a place in mind and spirit that breathes its own life, it is here. She glowed, filled with the energy of motion and a "spontaneous" connection to the Holy Spirit. They celebrated.

If you take one picture from this part of the story, let it be of these young people: yearning, richly aspiring, yet systematic, meticulous, and persistent—this is charismatic cultivation. Like farming, it demands tremendous effort and tremendous structure. Then, once the rows are laid out and the seeds planted, it slips from their control. It becomes a submission to the transcendent—to the weather for the farmers, to God for the Christians, to something bigger for both. Charismatics gather, aligning their tremendous energies to feed an openness to spontaneity. These gatherings are shaped by history and culture and, more immediately, by the training developed throughout the AG.

I found Bethany University, my first and most extended field site, by chance. It was 2007, and I was new to California. I was scrounging through the archives at the Graduate Theological Seminary in Berkeley. I came across a reference to a Bethany College in Scotts Valley. I knew the area. I was a student in Santa Cruz, just 10 miles away. I had a six-month-old son at the time and was anxious to find a site close to home; I was not ready for lengthy fieldwork across the globe. This seemed incredibly fortunate, or what my informants might call God's intervention.

It turned out that Bethany was the first-ever AG Bible college, and had been the organizational hub of central California. I went to visit. Nestled in the hills of Northern California, deep in the redwoods near Santa Cruz, this small Bible school brought together young, charismatic evangelicals from all over. It linked the conservative religious culture of California's Central Valley to the more esoteric Christianity of the coast. Bethany was a cultural hybrid: students of varying ethnic and cultural backgrounds with ripped jeans, tattoos, and eyebrow piercings, together with the occasional suit and tie. The rough wooden structures of the 1940s and 1950s still dotted the campus, though porches had begun to tilt down steep redwood slopes. They say construction was on the cheap because rapture seemed imminent. Rustic, modestly built, and falling down—more a summer camp than a university. The outdoor theater was stunning, surrounded by towering redwoods and arced by a small bubbling stream. Later construction, the modernist simplicity of concrete dorms, blended the aesthetics of summer camp and prison. By the time I finished my fieldwork in 2012, the most impressive new building, the dining hall, was half-finished. It was a deep pit filled with concrete and iron rods, its promise unfulfilled.

The Bethany approach to managing a university was unusual. There was almost no focus on fundraising. Instead, there was patronage and odd perks: free houses, meals, offices for relatives who weren't on staff, and big childcare discounts—at least, that's what a group of administrators told me when they were angry. I don't know how true it all was, but it made a good story.

In the AG, Bethany was well known. Almost everyone I spoke to in AG's central office in Springfield, Missouri, had gone there. It was the oldest-running AG Bible college, began as Glad Tidings Institute in 1919 and later adding liberal arts education and accreditation in the 1950s. Over the decades, the faculty blended a mystical sense of openness with sophisticated academic scholarship and deep faith. The teaching that developed took the sense of crisis inherent in charismatic practice, layered it with critical theory, and made it a tool to prepare young Christians facing the secular world.

The president, Reverend Shelton, gave me access to any classes with professors who agreed and to willing students. I spent the next three years sitting in missions prep, theology, and church history courses. I talked with students during lunch on the grass after the morning chapel, which I attended occasionally. Most students were second- or third-generation charismatics; a few were converts, and some were other kinds of evangelicals. I interviewed Shelton and other administrators. I designed an online survey for Bethany alumni, and 150 responded to the 42-question survey. After focusing on Bethany, I expanded my research to find alumni in the mission field. I called and interviewed fifty of them. Then I traveled to Springfield, Missouri, for a week of interviews with the AG missions department faculty and professors of local seminaries. These were sites of training. Although more important for me, these interviews and conversations laid the groundwork so that when I came to Glad Tidings Church a few years later to see if folks would work with me on an anthropology-psychology study of speaking in tongues, I came with glowing recommendations, or so they told me.

Bethany Cultivation

Modern religions often draw authority from the sense that God's work is spontaneous, which may be a signal that it is not easily faked. At Bethany, these moments of spontaneity rarely came without effort. Some students described simple tools they were taught, "Relax," and "Let God have you." Others mocked the tricks passed around, "repeat those words twenty times fast and pray real loud." Even so, many faked it on their way to authentic spirituality. They might have pretended for a day or months. Only later did they come to the experience with the ease of a skilled athlete, sure of its spiritual promise.

Daily chapel at Bethany was mandatory, a guided devotion where students honed their own abilities and learned to guide others. An ID reader tracked attendance precisely, and there were penalties for skipping. Between 100 and 200 students and faculty "swayed" to contemporary Christian pop played by a rotating cohort of student bands. Eyes closed, arms raised, and faces turned upward in supplication as the simple, four-chord pop washed over them. They spoke of music pulsing through their bodies, the desire for transcendence in their hearts, and the struggle to participate properly—with integrity, true spirituality, and within limits. Youth pastors urged them to "give God your tongue."

One pastor led a "study" of the gifts of the spirit. He sent home a flyer with Bible verses. It was the topic at youth group and at home for weeks—some parents were suspicious. Finally, when the group decided to "go for it," the pastor circled the room, laying hands on foreheads. "The room exploded!" a student told me. Kids were flopping all about the floor. When it was time to invite the spirit, some said the unspoken out loud: that students should make nonsense noises, loosen their tongues, and yield to God.

Over lunch, a few undergraduates shared stories of friends or neighbors surrounding them and speaking in tongues, hoping to spark the same. Others dismissed their own efforts as simply "gibberish." They knew faking it was common; maybe it was a way to fit in, or perhaps simply rehearsal. Sean told me, "In school it was what everybody else was doing and a way to show your closeness to God. So, we all faked it." In fact, nearly every student and faculty member I interviewed admitted to pretending before they experienced something they felt was real. Maybe pretending is part of learning, I thought.

It had me wondering why effort is considered fake, and why it seems so odd that effort and letting go are so deeply connected. One student began speaking in tongues by what he called "babbling." Then, at some point, it became real. "I prayed for myself and had others pray for me. And what do you know, it happened." It took a while for me to understand what "it" was. My best sense is that this is where the evangelical story of connection to God and tongues speech without effort meets the neuroscientific story of moving in and out of trance. The shift from effortful to passive action where something—the mind, the spirit—takes over. In our later research, we saw a full range of release times: when folks were completely in control and others when they were at a loss even to think coherently about the previous moment.

Even so, many felt that acknowledging this process of training undermined its legitimacy. Amy put it bluntly, "The preacher says 'raise your hands, receive this, repeat after me' and it always pisses me off." Valid religion, she might say, shouldn't need anything beyond believing.[6] Or maybe simpler: real faith shouldn't take effort. Yet Amy's education didn't stop at the irritation. "Then in chapel, it just came out."

"Spontaneously?" I asked.

"A feeling of peace. It wasn't that I couldn't stop speaking, but why would I?"

Steve also developed a practice that felt like yielding. "The backstory is, I said I don't want it. It's not for me. I just thought it was weird. But at youth camp they told me, 'You've given God your life, why not give Him your tongue too?'" He decided to try, but "effort" doesn't capture what came next. It was more like a dare. "I said, 'God, if you want this, then give it to me now.'" And it worked.

Many described something like this: Steve hoped to speak in tongues, but of course, God was the referee. "I don't control it. It's something God gives

you—peaceful—I am speaking to God in a language only he understands,"
he explained. Yet he still approached tongues like any research project. "I
am trying to get a deeper grasp on it. I've done studies on it—praying for it,
reading more about it." And the experience changed. "It gets easier—before
I'd pray 'God let your spirit fill me' but, sweet, I don't have to pray anymore.
Now it just happens." Once he learned to let go, his systematic method began
working.

When psychologists tried to dismiss tongues speech as mere performance,
they had a point.[7] As many interviewees explained, there are many times when
tongue training is very much about showing off or proving oneself to the folks
gathered around. As a child, Bethany's professor of theology Dr. Espinosa
struggled to meet the expectations of his AG congregation. "There was pressure
to speak in tongues. Social pressure: it's what all the cool kids do. You want to
be on fire for the Lord. That was the controlling message." Speaking in tongues
was seen as a sign of inner spiritual health, creating a powerful motivation for
those who couldn't do it yet.

And many fail in their training. Daniel, a Bethany alumnus, told me, "I do
not believe in speaking in tongues. For many years I 'tried' to speak in tongues
and thought I was not Christian enough because I didn't do so." Daniel had
been through intense training. "I have had people try to get me to speak in
tongues. My pastor wanted me to speak in tongues, but I was uncertain. As he
prayed, he put his hand on my forehead and spoke in tongues. He said, 'Try
not to fill your mind up with words. Try to accept it. Try to have your mind
empty.'" This was hard for Daniel. "My mind is always thinking of something."
Stray thoughts made it difficult to focus on God. The AG's emphasis on tongues
prayer became a sore spot. "I would go up to the altar specifically to have that:
to speak in tongues. The AG, they believe that that's your spiritual baptism." He
came to disagree. "I'm not sure that everyone needs to speak in tongues. There
are other gifts—educational, pastoral, leadership."

Daniel could describe the technique for learning to speak in tongues, but he
still fell short. And according to Dr. Everett Wilson, "More fail than succeed." I
didn't meet many who did not succeed, probably because I was talking to folks
in a charismatic community. Daniel, though, was left with a deep mistrust in
the whole process.

Containing Excess

The other side of training as cultivation is training for containment.

"She goes off the deep end. A 'charismatic experience,'" Dr. James Stewart said, his voice lilting with what I thought was maybe subtle sarcasm—it was at least an in joke. Dr. Stewart was a missionary, a professor at Bethany, and a pastor. He was also a white South African critical of racism. "She was speaking in tongues—but not doing anything that made sense. Fully on the ground, screaming like a banshee. In her church the wilder you are, the more spiritual you are. I stepped in and said her name 'Olibile.' And then, 'Didi Mala! Didi Mala!'—That means, Shut Up! Shut Up!" He paused, waiting to see if his students caught the acute absurdity of the situation. "'I'm telling her to shut up?' A white missionary silencing a local who is caught in the spirit?" Even so, he continued. "This is heresy. I said, 'I want you to sit up.' 'What's going on?' 'You've been taught that God comes and takes over and throws you on the ground. That's not God. Maybe evil spirits do that, but that's not God, maybe Demons.' In her church being spiritual is not about being spiritual but about yelling loud," he explained.[8]

I sat in Dr. Stewart's missionary communications class, listening to his tales of African missions. He had reached his limit with Olibile, a young Black South African convert. He thought she needed guidance. The story was meant to be funny, but it was also a lesson in setting boundaries for future missionaries. And if you step back, his reaction made a kind of sense—movements need structure. You can't have an "anything goes" policy if you want credibility.

Even with these guardrails, charismatics are regularly mocked for their excess. Secularist, fundamentalist, and mainline critics all agree: charismatics are chaotic, crazy, and too much. In response, charismatic leaders do a lot of self-policing, which they call "discernment." Dr. Albrecht, a leading Pentecostal philosopher and professor at Bethany, explained that this process is essential because "the mystic left alone spins into all kinds of heresy." But he also talked about the need for openness and change. Dr. Stewart mixed these ideas well. "When you think you got God squished into a box," he said, "cut the sides off. God will only move freely when he's got the freedom to move." But then he pointed to the other side of the story. "Some see charismatics swinging from the chandeliers and all that good stuff … Watching folks running in the aisles, the pastor's wife jumping across the pews." Or, as Dr. Albrecht said, "Wacky things can happen, and you've got to admit that it's not the Spirit. It's some emotion. It's something else." Not the spirit—it's emotion? And at the same time, he warned, "Be careful in discernment that you're not saying things are inauthentic." It's a dance back and forth across the line of acceptability. "I think I'm gonna' say, 'you know that person's a nut!'" Dr. Albrecht finally said. Dr. Espinosa set the boundary a bit more gently. "If you have your Bible and go out in the woods, enjoy. Just don't stay there." Enjoy the break from the everyday, he said; just return to regular life afterward.

Students struggled to find their own boundaries. When I first came to Bethany, the last pastor had just been ousted in a haze of discontent. His replacement, Brad, stirred new controversy by emphasizing tongues speech. He spoke in tongues publicly and translated other people's tongues prayers. He told students they should try it. Even though Bethany was a charismatic university, several students came from noncharismatic evangelical churches. Some felt uncomfortable. Some felt pressured. One said other students gave her "flack" for her more restrained prayer practices. The whole situation generated anxiety. Tongues prayer "scared the heck out of me," one woman explained. Some felt unsure. "These fruits of the spirit, I am really skeptical about, super skeptical."

Faced with doubt, Onella admitted her experience of tongues prayer was not fully spontaneous. "It's not like I can say that there was just this one night and I fell over, but honestly it began out of the understanding that there was that gift and praying for it." Her explanation seemed aimed at an imagined critic—someone questioning the integrity of her practice because it was learned and thus maybe not from God. Perhaps my sober Jewish anthropological vibe reminded her of the secular world out there, just waiting to pounce. She turned to me and made it clear, "I really felt that my prayer was true." The words, she insisted, were not her own. "I was not just making it up. I don't really feel like

I ever made it up. I don't like just doing it to do it—I think that it's definitely real. The best way I can explain it, is that it's not contrived." Not contrived is a somewhat defensive way to say "genuine." Given the history of mockery, it probably makes sense to be defensive. It also makes sense that this worry permeates charismatic storytelling.

Andrea had her own response. Tongues felt contrived unless she could connect it to the Bible, she explained. Her first time: "I had never spoken in tongues. I know people who claimed they have. Pastor Brad is the only one who I've felt comfortable with. He came to the front and said the Lord is giving me word as far as what this tongues prayer means. He said it was a Bible verse." The spirit now had a frame to fit within—we anthropologists would call this looping between theology, practice, and experience. Andrea showed how a theologically grounded translation of tongues solidified her sense of acceptability: "earlier it seemed like they were just saying things and then making something up, but this felt more solid. Even if it wasn't exactly that translation, we were going back to the Bible and that is the foundation for our beliefs." With tongues tied to text, her confidence grew.

Tongues prayer is shaped by AG leaders—both encouraged and constrained. They control it through various mechanisms, including interpretation and decorum. In many AG churches, praying in tongues publicly without an interpretation is not acceptable. This wasn't the case in most of the churches I visited, but the idea that interpretation lends credibility was important to some, especially among missionary students. They often cited Paul's admonition to speak in tongues only with an interpreter.

Chet was skeptical of the idea that speaking in tongues always showed spiritual growth. "I've seen people abuse the gift, use it to show off. To claim to be superior to others who don't have it." But interpretation helps him feel like it is grounded in his tradition. "With no interpretation it meant someone was speaking out in disorder, more like conflict. Interpretation shows some sort of validity to our belief." But like many AG pastors, he distinguished personal from public prayer practices: "I practice mostly by myself. But I think that tongues in a group needs interpretation."

Texts Teaching Gifts

After a few years in the field, I had heard plenty of stories of people striving and studying to receive the gift of tongues, I could see that worship sessions were aimed at cultivating an atmosphere that would lead people toward release, but I was still caught off guard when I found actual training texts for preachers to teach their flock exactly how to speak in tongues. These were basically scripts, with step-by-step plans for rousing the Holy Spirit. All the following citations are from texts published by AG's Gospel Publishing House through their Evangelism Commission's annual Holy Spirit emphasis. They have titles like *The Youth Ministry Institute Manual, Helping Others Receive the Gift, When the Spirit Speaks, Hungry?,* and *A Study in the Baptism in the Holy Spirit.*[9]

The texts weren't all the same, but they shared some basic ideas. The language of submission, letting go, and yielding dominated, though the very existence of these booklets suggested that method might be just as important. Look closely, and you'll see a struggle—charismatic churches trying to hold training and spontaneity together, the balance of encouragement and control shifting over time.

"Relax … worship God … seek the Giver, not just the gift," they write. After relaxation, focus on language. "Leave your native language so you can speak a new language … trust that you are getting what you asked for." The tongue is key for speaking in tongues, but it's also seen as a gateway to something deeper. "The tongue is the most unruly part of the body (James 3:3–6). … And yet like the rudder of a large ship, it can set the direction for our entire behavior." The ship, in this metaphor, is steered by release, not control: "Speaking in tongues is an act of submission, indicating that we have given our entire beings to God."[10] God is the agent.

Even so, these texts share a step-by-step guide to attuning believers to the presence of the Holy Spirit: (1) set the atmosphere, (2) describe the process, (3) call for decisive action, and the Spirit will come.[11] Pastors invite participants to "align themselves so they are ready to receive."[12] They describe developing an atmosphere that encourages tongues speech. This involves people working together. "Develop consensus in the room."[13] Pastors are given exact phrases to guide the group. "'You might hear words in your spirit' or 'you might feel a tension in your tongue.' Encourage [participants] to ... open their mouth and release the language."[14] These manuals work with the community feeling generated during collective worship.[15] Sometimes, individuals lay hands on seekers. Perhaps in the right atmosphere the energy moves without direct action. "Radical worshippers set an atmosphere and environment that is charged with the anointing and people just get baptized."[16] With children especially, seeing another child receiving the Spirit can inspire.[17] The group imprints on individuals, rendering them more open, and perhaps more capable, than before.

Once the atmosphere is set and the plan in place, newly able practitioners are called to act decisively: "Now, just speak in tongues."[18] "Speak, even if only a few syllables."[19] As one author wrote, "It takes a bold, deliberate step."[20] Or, "You will never speak if you keep waiting for the Spirit to put you in some kind of trance and do it all for you. It will be your mouth, your tongue, your voice—but His words."[21] Like Christian rebirth, Spirit baptism involves choice—choice in the making of the atmosphere, choice in the method, and choice in the moment of yielding. "The Spirit doesn't just overpower a person's will. We cooperate with him and invite Him into our lives ... God does the baptizing, but you're responsible for how you proceed."[22] So, act decisively, "Leave your English ... altogether."[23] In other words, after an atmosphere is developed, the texts ask for a moment of intense, directed will.

There are specific physical directions too—especially for the mouth and tongue. "I usually mention that I've never seen a person filled with the Holy Spirit with their mouth closed. People need to relax, open their mouth and give praise to the Lord, and expect they will speak in a language they don't understand."[24] It reminds me of research showing how bodily posture shapes the emotional experience of prayer.[25] Tongue training texts ask for close attention to micro-level sensations in the body. These sensations provide an impulse to act. "You will get to the point where your tongue feels like it's too big for your mouth, and you want to say something."[26]

Texts Constraining Emotion

While these texts encourage release, they also include a cautious undercurrent, a warning against excess and "hyper-emotional" devotion. This might be a response to critique from outside the church, but past revivals have also shaken AG and caused tremendous conflict. A friend of mine in the AG hierarchy was sent to Bethel Church in Redding to see if its highly energetic revival was of God or of the devil—should they be welcomed within the church hierarchy? The Latter Rain Movement (1950s) and the Toronto and Brownsville "laughing" revivals (1990s) all expanded AG's doctrines of tongues and healing. The Toronto Revival, for instance, was known for endless laughter and loud animal sounds—people squawking like chickens and barking like dogs. The participating churches were disciplined. These internal rebellions were flush with a variety of physical experiences deemed spiritual by participants, but their more expansive sense of what was okay faced immediate censure from within and without AG.

Discerning what is of God and what is not is crucial to AG's internal process. From the start, AG structured itself to both encourage and contain such insurgencies: its leaders balanced the idea of loose "fellowship" with clear doctrine explicitly to regulate enthusiasm. Many of the early institutional battles were about controlling churches—often Black-led ones—that were considered too enthusiastic. As I read through the training manuals, these concerns over excess popped up regularly. As one manual put it, "These manuals aim to describe adequate teaching on how to encourage, guide, correct, and respond to these gifts."[27] Encourage, guide, correct, and respond—the instruction runs the gamut from inspiration to discipline.

Warren Bullock, author of *When the Spirit Speaks: Making Sense of Tongues, Interpretation, and Prophecy*, proposes a thorough process to ensure proper decorum when speaking in tongues. He asks churches to position elders throughout the room to guide the gifts of the spirit. He suggests they first collect requests to speak in tongues. The pastor should be alerted to volunteers and then fit them into the program.[28] For Bullock, the dynamic between believer and spirit requires order. "The Spirit does not 'possess' or 'overpower' the speaker," he writes. "[In fact,] what the Spirit has to say will be said in an orderly and intelligible way … He speaks through the controlled instrumentality of the believer's own mind and tongue."[29] For Bullock, tongues speech is a careful joining of human and spiritual agency. Similarly, at times in Glad Tidings, Pastor Beiser would ask if someone wanted to speak in tongues. He then chose who stood up to pray. Later, I visited a church in the Sierras where people submitted requests to prophesize to church leaders on the floor. If accepted, they could speak, but even then a transcription was sent to an advisory board for certification. If accepted, it would be sent to the person praying and the person prayed over. I found myself the recipient of a ten-minute sermon that was uncannily prescient. It cut straight to a grief I hadn't spoken of—about a close friend who had just died. My coworkers had similarly provocative experiences. We have the emails with the transcripts. They are warm, welcoming. But also, the products of a close hand, built to keep the church message coherent—or perhaps to control it, one could argue. I wondered what made some things feel like support and others control—I have been asking this kind of question a lot as my son turned eighteen.

Emotions must not determine the reality of an experience, argue the training texts. The evidence of baptism in the Holy Spirit, according to the Scripture, is that the believer speaks in other tongues. It is not about the emotions displayed, they say. Some suggest that when people cry, feel like they've been hit by lightning, or experience a quiet, peaceful feeling, none of these should be considered significant. Instead, "the reality of what people experience is not based on what they do or do not feel. The evidence is in speaking in other tongues."[30] All the texts agree, "the baptism is not the result of emotionalism ... keep your head."[31] Charismatics have long used technical language to describe tongues as "scientific evidence" while regarding emotions as far more ephemeral.

Tongues, prayer, and healing, what church leaders called the "evidence of the spirit," were physical signs broadly accepted by charismatics in the early twentieth century. But in one-on-one interviews, charismatics describe numerous other bodily sensations that they attribute to gifts of the spirit. Because of this, when reading these manuals, I struggled to understand what was okay and what was forbidden. A few texts legitimized specific physical sensations outside of tongues prayer, especially when they were described as similar to tongues or as especially biblical. One youth training manual cited the Bible to support a more expansive interpretation: "Some physical things may happen," the authors wrote. "Stammering lips, tears of joy, and trembling or shaking ..." (cf. Isaiah 28:11; John 7:38, 39). However, they also set very clear boundaries. "Remember: Goose Bumps are not the baptism."[32] In one interview, I was told that it was important to ignore goose bumps, though in many others, this sensation was very much part of what made the experience feel so potent.

Wesleyan Methodists

The idea of organized effort toward spiritual and physical release wasn't new to twentieth-century charismatics. Their predecessors were called Methodists, and for good reason. John Wesley, an English cleric and theologian in the mid-1700s, led the Methodist revival, which by all accounts included an extraordinarily systematic approach to experiencing the Holy Spirit. Wesley formed his followers into twelve-person bands of closely monitored practitioners. They encouraged and tracked regular home visits and daily regimes of prayer, and they carefully constrained everyday practices—eating, teatime, reflection, and conversation all became spaces for the cultivation of spirituality. Wesley paid close attention to the smallest details. As he wrote, "studious persons" required "about eight Ounces of Animal Food, and twelve of Vegetable in twenty-four Hours," good amounts of water, and two to three hours of physical activity a day.[33] Elders within the bands kept a careful watch on spiritual development, visiting members in their homes weekly. These networks were supported by itinerant circuit riders who rode from town to town encouraging conversion and whole meetings of local members every few months. At the quarterly "convergence" (conference), those who showed proper spiritual development received tickets of spiritual certification, and those who didn't—both enthusiasts (folks deemed too uncontrolled) and formalists (those unwilling to let go and live a little)—were expelled.[34]

From the outside, Methodists were widely known for extremes of emotion. These were the people falling on the floor, moaning at camp meetings, and singing and shouting the Lord's praise until the wee hours of the morning. Methodists had refined the tension between the methodical and the emotional. And they grew fast, from 2 percent of US church membership in 1775 to 34 percent in 1850.[35]

Pentecostals took these Methodist practices and refined them further. Instead of Wesley's vague call for sensory experience, by 1914, AG leaders defined very specific modes of feeling—tongues, prayer, and healing—as central to spiritual growth. They came close to making physical experience a requirement for spiritual progress. Through intensive striving and practice, the heart could manifest very specific bodily sensations, they thought. What emerged was a distinctively modern, and highly rationalized, but wildly enthusiastic, form of religion. They also managed to grow by hundreds of millions of people in just a few decades.[36]

Early Tarrying

Early charismatics had a word for the effort it took to bring about spiritual experience: tarrying. Nearly everybody in their churches did it, they say. In the late 1980s, Margaret Poloma, a charismatic Catholic sociologist, interviewed a group of older charismatics who remembered those days. They spoke of an "overwhelming desire for power" and "a conviction that the only way to receive it was through prolonged, constant and persistent prayer, sometimes called 'tarrying' or 'waiting' upon God."[37] It was a practice with a definite shape, repeated in testimony after testimony. One participant recalled, "at that time, people thought they had to tarry. And people tarried for hours—days ... We'd go early in the morning and we would be there all day. They would have food on the table in case we got hungry. I think I must have tarried for about three months."[38]

This has changed. As one participant explained, "in my day ... no one got it [baptism of the spirit] by the formula they use today! You had to work, toil, struggle." It was collective. "People would help you get it." And when you got it, that was the break between the old you and the new one.

Training and Breakthrough

The idea of a sudden and total break with the past is crucial to the charismatic ethos, and to put it mildly, this kind of rupture sounds a lot more like spontaneity than a concerted method. As Devan put it, He (God) "flipped a switch and instantly I changed." This kind of breakthrough was a common refrain. It probably helps that it is almost taken for granted in Western culture that authentic experience comes without constraint and guidance. This is obviously absurd if taken as a rule of thumb, but somehow a core belief.[39] When I mentioned something that sounded like training during interviews, the conversation sometimes got uncomfortable. Many charismatics found process-oriented understandings of their practice mechanical and even distasteful.

I may have been lucky, though. I spent time with a few charismatic leaders who saw their training as somehow different from both the moments of explosive transformation and also distinct from something more routine. For them, training was a fluid process that shaped people along the way. It could mean encouraging a breakthrough, but it also meant building a capacity for change. Professor Dan Albrecht stood out among Bethany faculty for his positive use of the term "ritual." He explained that for many of his colleagues, "ritual" meant "unspiritual." Ritual seemed external, repetitive, mechanical, and profane. But Albrecht insisted—and he taught me—that charismatics learn, and repeat patterns, using what he called "ritual" as a path to spiritual breakthrough.[40]

However, Dr. Wilson, former president of Bethany and scholar of Latin American Pentecostalism—and Albrecht's friend and boss—challenged me when I used the term "training." He was willing to see the effort involved, but my language didn't sit right with him. In my attempt to understand this balance, I suggested we use "rendering capable" as a concept that might bridge training and sudden transformation. Wilson was a brilliant man and a friend. But he didn't go for it. There was a gap between me, the anthropologist, and my informant—maybe a space generated by what anthropologist Pierre Bourdieu calls the "scholastic fallacy," which I think of as a fancy word for not listening closely enough.[41]

Later, at Glad Tidings Church, Pastor Beiser and Pastor Tim made no secret of using lights, sound, and language to control the atmosphere and encourage the Holy Spirit. When Beiser said, "Let the spirit fall," or Tim asked the crowd to create the "atmosphere of the Spirit," I felt like they were recognizing the link between inner experience and the outer environment. In the process, they challenged decades of charismatic worries about having too much agency as compared to God. But also, they helped me to see the ethnographic gap differently.

At first, it seemed simple. Maybe I was right to call it training. Or maybe it was truly spontaneous, and I just didn't see it. I wasn't a charismatic, after all. But my charismatic friends pushed me to think this through. I began to feel that the gap wasn't in what was happening. It might be in how we looked at it: in the perspective, not the content. Comparing a rush of feeling to a long, careful shaping might be a mistake. They move at different speeds, live at different scales.[42] If that was true, then maybe we were all correct. Culture shapes what we feel and how we see. It trains the senses. These moments feel different, and more important, than everyday training. From Paul to Martin Luther, Protestants have focused on breaking with the past, the crack that lets the Spirit in. These feelings about breakthrough become part of the learned landscape. Over time, they become material, settling into the body by shaping comportment and even physiology. Charismatics may be trained, yes. But they're trained to let go and seek spontaneous breakthrough.

Careful training to be able to release thoughts, feelings, and control? It sounded a lot like other forms of meditation. And yet, speaking in tongues looks so different.

3

Attention, Arousal, and Release: To Spiral Toward God

When asked if she felt that a specific place in the body enables her to sense God, Shavon pointed to her belly.

Yeah, right around here, there's this. I know in the Bible, it's called Rivers of Living Water. Flowing from your Belly. It really feels like rivers. I mean it is just cleansing rivers, redeeming rivers, healing rivers. During worship, Pastor Tim was saying, "Bubble up, let it bubble up." It's when the Holy Spirit comes up. It's like a rushing wind through your belly, at least it is for me, and it comes up and I end up muttering tongues, I have no idea what they are saying.

This sounds very much like a typical charismatic experience—the kind of stirring, embodied sensation that grabs notice. Nothing like the somber focus appropriate to a serious meditator or a Catholic monk.

The feeling then travels through the body, Shavon explains.

From the belly [points to belly] all the way through here [points to head], but it doesn't stop there, because it overwhelms you. You start speaking and then it goes through your mind and your head and you start having these, what do you call them? They're not chills, but it's like they are the opposite of chills, you get these sensations all around you—tingling.

At this point, the sensations seem generalized throughout the body, sensations that play a crucial role in thought, as well. "You get the tingling all throughout your head and it even blocks out negative thoughts. When I am in that realm, it blocks out any negative thought that my flesh would want to bring up." Perhaps since bad thoughts can be associated with the flesh in charismatic theology, it makes sense that exciting the flesh can fill that space. And through practice, this capacity to block thought with sensation becomes more available. "I have been in situations where I'm like, 'I don't want to think about that.' And it doesn't happen. It's like something is blocking it. Shaking the body can focus our attention and drive out bad thoughts."

"Focus our attention and drive out bad thoughts." Attention—as a tool for clearing the mind.

There it was. In the thick of what seemed like high intensity, highly somatic, emotional, and even chaotic, Shavon found something else. Attention. It wasn't the quiet, deliberate focus of meditation, but it sounded like attention nonetheless. I wondered, can attention still be attention if it is wild and passionate?

Whenever I mention that tongues prayer might change the mind, someone asks if it's similar to meditation. The answer seems obvious, at first.

Speaking in tongues and meditation appear worlds apart. The meditator sits still, calm, outwardly serene, and inwardly focused. They follow a quiet path laid down by the ancient teachings of the Buddha, their minds trained to lock onto the breath, to stabilize in equanimity. It's a practice of stillness, of quiet stability. For the most part, it appears calm. Tongues prayer—that's quite different. The people who speak in tongues don't sit quietly. They shout, cry, laugh. They move. They let their bodies sway with the rhythm of the Spirit. Their practice is built from brief verses of the New Testament, passed down orally with historical roots in the Black Church,[1] told and retold until the worship sings through their bones. It generally seems raw and spontaneous. Meditation and tongues—one can't be mistaken for the other.

But then, look closer. Beneath the noise, beneath the movement, both practices share something; they both bring together intense attention and some form of release. It's just that the charismatics wrap theirs in emotion, in heat, in passion. Their focus isn't quiet; it's fierce. It burns. Speaking in tongues might be a kind of contemplative practice—only it starts with the fire of attention on God, and from there, the flames of arousal take over, rising higher and higher until the practitioner lets go.

I have started to think of it as a spiral. Attention sparks arousal, and arousal feeds back into attention. The harder people focus, the more they heat up. It gets easier to pay attention as it gets more pleasurable. The ease suffuses the experience, focus grows sweeter, more natural feeling. Letting go becomes easier. Attention, arousal, release—round and round it goes.[2]

In this chapter, we'll look at how this works in tongues prayer. Up until now, we've spent lots of time on release, on letting go, and on training for it. Now we'll look especially at the other two—attention and arousal.

Desire Focuses the Mind

Attention in tongues prayer begins with passion. Picture the fervent longing of a devoted churchgoer, striving with every fiber of their being to encounter God, yearning to make contact, to be recognized, and to recognize. This again is "tarrying." To stay up late, sometimes for days, waiting for that moment of connection. In ancient Christian traditions, this desire is often expressed through the language of love and fervor. Think of Saint Teresa of Ávila. And this might be a bit counterintuitive because it doesn't look like attention: charismatics are not monks in somber robes, nor are they Llamas immersed in attention for days at a time. This is not quiet contemplation of breath or on a fixed point across the room. Yet even the most exuberant forms of desire for the Lord involve deep, focused attention.

Abigail called it a hunger—a hunger for the word of God. "I really want to dive into the word. I'm just getting more hungry for it. It's crazy. He's given me that hunger." Valentin talked about "a sense of urgency [in worship], that makes you more alert." Candy described it simply: "It's like I want to touch him, so I use my fingers and I rub them as I am feeling this in my heart." "I don't know, I just want to touch him. I rub my fingers like I am trying to feel him, or I want to see him." Urgency, hunger—these are not the words we associate with attention.

Charismatics desire the gifts of the Spirit so intensely that the wanting and searching become a tool for sharpening their attentional capacities. Donald's quest for the Holy Spirit led him to St. Louis. "I went on a spiritual journey, and all I could think was, 'Holy Spirit, Holy Spirit, Holy Spirit. What is the Holy Spirit?'" His attention was laser-focused.

There were tons of churches. So, I went to this church and it was closed. Another wasn't open yet. I tried to go into a bunch of different churches and nothing really worked out. So, I was like, I'm just going to walk back to the youth hostel. Then this family pulled up. "Hey, do you know where there's a Taco Bell? I'm starving," I asked. "No, but we just started this church, do you want to come in?" So, I just walked in. I'd never been to a Pentecostal church before. After the church service, this little old lady said, "Have you ever been baptized in the Holy Spirit?" I'm like, "No." She said, "Do you want to?" "Sure!"

And here is where the attention becomes especially visible.

Because that's all I was thinking about, the Holy Spirit, so the lady says, "Hey, everybody, this guy wants to be baptized."

They circled around me, were praying for me, and they said "Just start speaking in tongues." I didn't know what they were talking about. I just remember closing my eyes and they were praying and then those weird kinds of sounds started coming out. I guessed this was speaking in tongues because I've never done it before.

Donald's story broadens the charismatic idea of attention. Desire can infuse daily life. Charismatics bring focused attention into their everyday routines. "If you stay where you're conscious throughout your day of His presence, it's super easy to get into his presence."

There's an obvious parallel to sexual desire. This analogy might unsettle some, but it's useful for noncharismatics hoping to understand the potent draw. Our interviews didn't directly ask about sex, but after hundreds of hours, it inevitably came up. Jeremy explained, "There's a huge difference. They are both fulfilling. But sex is fulfilling to the flesh." He clarified that flesh could include the experience of winning a sports tournament or following an intensive yoga class. "I compare experiences with sex and alcohol or the high you get from any of that stuff, with God. But, you know, candles to a sun." Both are fire, but one burns brighter, they feel. We are, however, in similar terrain.

Charismatics believe God is always present, always listening, always communicating. They just need to pay better attention. They strive for finer sensory awareness, discerning divine messages in the subtlest experiences. Through prayer, their senses become more vivid and attuned. Sensations that once seemed vague grow sharper and more meaningful. As Amy explained, "I feel like just now that I'm getting closer to Him and he is starting to show me things with more clarity." What was once blurry becomes distinct as a finer set of sensations emerges on the edge of consciousness.

This kind of passionate focus contrasts sharply with the folk understanding of attention I grew up with. "Paying attention" meant focusing on a particular element. It was an elementary school basic, where distraction loomed as the ever-present adversary to this focused awareness. Emotions were also distracting. Attention was like a beam of light—isolating and illuminating. Quiet was essential, a distraction-free space fostering concentration. Teachers valued this consistent, almost forceful, engagement that they called attention.

My teachers were in good company in this conception; the prevailing theories of the time (this was the 1970s) likened attention to a "spotlight" on the mind's stage.[3] Even when I think of attention today, I turn to the tranquil, focused thought patterns emphasized in Western mindfulness practices. These were modernized and then westernized to lose much of the cultural baggage previously attached to meditation, including the emotions.[4] Here, attention is a solemn and composed experience—marked by structure, intent, and singular focus. Charismatic practices, by contrast, color this spotlight with emotion, intensity, and internal struggle. They create a vibrant, chaotic mosaic of feelings and thoughts—an open, fluid, and passionate form of attention.

This chapter, then, becomes a project of anthropological deconstruction. Broaden the cultural lens, and our concepts can stretch, sometimes even to the breaking point. If attention is a spotlight, it's easy to imagine passion coloring its lens—maybe pink, red, or blue. Attention can handle emotions.

Scholars outside of anthropology have thought a lot about this. Cognitive scientists talk about something called "affect-biased attention."[5] Affect here describes the physiological underpinnings of attention. When you feel scared, your system heats up, almost the same as being excited. Affect-biased attention is the idea that emotions shape what we notice. You easily notice your neighbor's cat because of the warm feeling you had petting it before. You notice their dog because it once terrified you. For me, it's bigger than that. Perhaps it is my anthropological training, but while the dog is especially frightening, it also seems that all attention must be shaped by emotion, even if the emotion is relatively mild. And even more broadly, this seems a subset of the thesis that attentional styles and psychological tendencies more generally are shaped by cultural expectations of all sorts, not simply emotional ones.[6] So, strong feelings about God, or anything else, ought to shape what we notice, even in ways we don't realize.

To Be Aroused

Passion may do more than merely color attention. The feeling of fierce focus shapes bodily experience as well. When asked why she used the word "fire" to describe her sensation, Rhea explained, "That's the word I know to use." She didn't mean real flames. But it wasn't just a metaphor, either. She told me she felt heat in her body. The words and the feeling worked together.

She quickly moved on to point to other metaphor-sensory connections: "There's been times where it felt like my hands were hot and there's other times where I felt like electricity. Like there was this really weird instance where this guy was like 'here, put your hand right here [points to her chest] and start praying'. 'Feel it?' And I felt energy. It was trippy."

For Sam, a literal form of heat emerges from attention.

All of a sudden, your body's just like "It's hot in here." It's usually when you're pressing into God. Pressing in is inward. It's the simple way of taking my heart and saying, "God, no matter how I feel right now, or what things look like right now, I love you and I'm going to worship you." So that's pressing in, it's an aspect of prayer. It's not about how we feel. It's about knowing who he is which causes us to say, "You know what, God, you're worthy and I love you."

Jane used the image of steam as a metaphor to demonstrate both the fiery nature of the Holy Spirit and its capacity to still her mind and body.

I could feel almost a vapor on my hands. Think of steam coming out of your hands. There is just a gentle feeling when you can sense the Holy Spirit. The other way that I know that God is present, is that nothing matters at that point. Oh, actually this is how I would describe it, when you are in a steam room and you can feel the sweat beads running down your cheek and you don't want to move. You're so hot, you're enduring. That is how it feels. It's like you don't want to even move because his presence is just running over. Oh, it's hot … You just want to let the process happen. I am paying close attention, I am focused on what is happening with me and the spirit, or just adoring God. I think it's your heart is filled, your perspective is changed, your outlook, your stance. You get filled with this inner strength and peace, whatever it is.

The heat dissipating from her body shifted her emotional state, she thought. "I am just going to go with those words, strength and peace. Coming out, you have the energy, the love, the perspective for the circumstances around you but also to pour out into other people." But was the metaphorical heat actually hot? I wondered. How far does this loop travel? From concept to experience, yes. But to physiology too?

While many practitioners accepted fire as a fitting metaphor, there was a tendency to avoid making these powerful emotional experiences the main goal of the practice. Church leaders consistently emphasized that, while such intense feelings can be part of the journey, they shouldn't overshadow the core purpose of speaking in tongues—encouraging submission and connection to God. Conversations often started with stories of strong emotional experiences and ended with a reminder that, though the feelings were intense, they were just part of the atmosphere in an encounter with something much greater.

Filling the Mind

Returning to Shavon's story, I noticed another distinction between speaking in tongues and other forms of meditation. Some other meditation practices aim to empty the mind. Tongues prayer fills it. Mindfulness seeks emptiness. Charismatic prayer saturates the mind with God, pushing other thoughts away. Both jettison everyday worries and desires, but they do it differently. Shavon put it this way, "Focusing on the Holy Spirit would be the same as letting go of your own thoughts." In other words, focusing on one releases the other, culminating not in emptiness but in a sense of spiritual fullness. She elaborated,

> focusing on the Holy Spirit would be trying to let go of my own what we would call flesh, right? My fleshly desire wants to pray for me. But the Holy Spirit might want me to pray for something else. So, in order to get to what I feel like the Holy Spirit wants me to do, I have to let go of my own thoughts, meaning my own prayer in English.

Cheryl said, "the house is full." Which seemed a succinct way to say that the tongues prayer can help with managing emotions and unwanted thoughts.

English prayer by contrast, for Shavon, is about earthly desires. It doesn't play the same role. It may be too cognitive. Instead, "I have to speak in tongues so that I can transition into whatever God wants me to say."

"What are you focusing on?" I asked.

"God."

"Is there a quality of God that you focus on?"

"I would say it's a feeling."

Rather than clarity of mind, speaking in tongues provides a feeling of focus on various sensations. "In the middle of focusing, there might be some feeling that appears. That's what I'm always looking for. That's what I always want."

"What's the feeling?"

"Sometimes it's intense peace, which happened today. Sometimes I could feel a shift as if I'm pivoting in my mind. Once I felt something spiritual in my workplace. I just can feel something different."

Shavon's approach to prayer and spiritual focus spans a vast range of feelings, markedly distinct from the serene attentiveness to one's breath or a static object of meditation. "I start speaking in tongues because I need to know what to pray for and all of a sudden, it could be within two seconds, it could be within two minutes, I feel a person's name. I pray for that person." She highlights a focus imbued with uncertainty and a willingness to follow. "I don't know what's happening. The Bible says the Spirit comes and the Spirit goes but you don't know what direction it's taking, so you just have to be awake to whatever the spirit wants you to do." And in spite of this diversity, this is still a practice of focused attention. "When I say focus, I mean I am trying to focus on God. I am not looking for anything, I am just wanting to know what he wants."

Through focus, Shavon strives to align her thoughts with those of the Divine. "Have you ever heard somebody who lost something saying, 'What would my mom do with her keys? Let me get into my mom's head.' It's kind of like that. You're thinking, 'What would God want me to do right now? What would Jesus do?' I mean, WWJD?" Or, perhaps, what would Jesus think?

Jeanine, who had experience with mindfulness meditation, clarified the difference between emptying and filling practices of attention. "Christians speaking in tongues are very different, because when we speak in tongues we're actually trying to fill our mind with God. You are not trying to focus on your physical presence or your emotional state or the things around you, but rather you are actually instead focusing on something which I can only describe as a higher entity." She saw the dangers of Buddhism in terms of its relationship to an empty or full mind.

A lot of the so-called emptying your mind and emptying your body and so on is supposed to allow other spirits to enter your body, when you go to the really high levels of Buddhist meditation. This is how you usually get things like the powers of fortune tellers who actually tell fortunes very accurately. That's why this is not something I pursued very seriously. I have come to understand that the Holy Spirit is powerful but there are also a lot of very powerful counterfeits who are out to harm you or to harm the people around you. The biggest harm of all in Christian belief is actually being separated from God, so of course if I go for these other spirits instead, I'm cutting myself off from God.

While the connection to God can fill the mind and push other thoughts to the side, sometimes these thoughts intrude. Then begins a process of acknowledging them and explicitly pushing them away. Joy told this story of a

Glad Tidings church service: "I could sense that the Holy Spirit was just so present." The service had run late, and she was caught in prayer.

> I didn't want to move because I didn't want to get myself out of it. There was a slight thought somewhere that my child is still at childcare and I should probably go and get him but I didn't want to be interrupted or distracted or pulled away from his presence. It was like a thought that floated. As a mother I remembered my child.

The thought drifted by, and then she refocused. This happened often. "There are times when it's difficult to pray because of your fleshly desire or rebellion or where your focus is. It's when I am focused on me and my circumstances, instead of focusing on God."

Ananda described similar distractions. "It's too cold in here, it's too hot, I'm hungry." Her initial strategy was to exert effort. "Once you press through that point and feel like God shows up then you can also show up." But also, she suggested just letting go. "Just kind of forget about it. Just like, 'Stop it, I'm praying.' Be focused on it and just keep going. It's kind of like noticing it and letting it go, but I notice it and then I say, 'Jesus, take that.'"

This broad and overlapping set of techniques seems to be available, in part, because of a primarily oral tradition built in the Black Church; charismatics have put little theological work into parsing their inner modes of attention. As a result, their genres are easily mixed and matched. Bright, for instance, uses both "focus" and "surrender" to describe modes of attention.

> When I'm speaking in tongues, I don't think about what people are thinking, I don't think about if I'm too loud, I don't think about my laughter. I think all those things are distractions, and if those distracting thoughts start trying to infiltrate—I focus and surrender. Surrender in my prayer, like I don't want to be aware of other people's judgement or their thoughts, or whatever they have, because I feel like that's my time with God.

For her, much of the intrusion comes from self-conscious thoughts about others observing her prayer.

> I have to drive out the thoughts that anyone is watching me. I'm just like, "Lord, still my mind so I'm not aware." Still the thoughts, like competing

thoughts against—I don't want to be focused on those things, I just want to be focused on the time I have with God. If I have a bad attitude or I'm upset with something or someone, surrendering that to Him, in my prayer, like, "Lord I know I have this really bad attitude, help me. This person is working my nerves, help me." So, those are the things I'm surrendering.

No, you may have noticed the stilling of the mind here. And this is counterintuitive, at least at first. But charismatics often describe stilling their minds, even in the midst of passion and chaos. The white noise fills, and in some paradoxical way, it also stills. Think of the burbling sounds of a child's sleep machine or a heavy summer rain, and it may sound restful in a similar manner.

Refocusing the Mind

Charismatics have developed a diversity of techniques for refocusing attention when the mind wanders. Often, they work together.

Mike talked about "pushing through." Prayer doesn't always come easy, he said. Some days, even with all his attention on God, it's a struggle. He described a technique for working past this kind of difficulty. "Let's say you wake up in the morning and your back hurts and your head hurts, and you start to pray. At first, you're not feeling it. Your attention might wander and wane for a little bit." For Mike, the answer isn't to let go but to push. Push through the messy tangle of everyday thinking so as to focus on God. "Sometimes I had to push through. I had to push through my thoughts, I had to push through the busyness of the day to get into his presence." He has tools for this. "There's scriptures for that. There are certain things to pray and stuff that will help you quiet your mind. And then sometimes you're walking in a place in your life to where it's easy." Amanda spoke of it similarly. "The first ten minutes are probably hardest, harder than the last ten minutes, to press through the distractions. 'I'm not going to worry about my stresses, I'm not going to worry about today, or the fleeting thoughts.'"

Sometimes it's not about letting thoughts drift away. It's about clearing them out, one by one, making space for God. Rhea called it "washing." Before she prays, she thinks about her mistakes and repents. She cleans her mind. "I'll be like 'Jesus. I pour your blood over my mind, over my heart, over my eyes, over everything.' That's how I start off to just get focused, otherwise, I'm just sitting there thinking about everything else."

Mike knew this washing, too. "It feels like you're washed clean because you've been in the presence of God. You're hearing from God more easily, so you're going to be aware of your thoughts a little bit more." Bright likened it to sweeping.

It's almost like you're clearing out, you're sweeping. Let's say these benches exist but they're littered with leaves everywhere. You're clearing all the leaves and then you're able to notice, "Oh, look at these beautiful benches. I didn't notice them because all I saw was leaves." It's already there, I just don't have the mind to see it because my mind is busy thinking about other things, or seeing other things, or other things are weighing in.

The metaphorical cleaning of the charismatic mind comes in many flavors.

For Anselm, it wasn't about words or thoughts—it was about movement. Pacing back and forth helped him focus. "I'm not thinking about anything else except what I will pray to God about."

"How do you get yourself to think about nothing else?" I asked.

Decide what you're going to pray about. It's something that you work on; everything takes work to get to where you want to get, right? It's like yoga; you don't go in the class and just know what you're doing, you've got to find out how you get in the mode, like breathe in, breathe out. It's not hard breathing in and breathing out, but you've got to get into a mode that makes you comfortable.

He usually prepares by walking—which, as you may remember, made prayer in the MRI quite difficult. "For me, I just walk back and forth and I think and get myself into the situation that I'm praying. I use my mind to imagine the situation that I'm asking God about, because if you're in that situation, it's much easier to express yourself." When effective, it feels as if he is talking to a person right close by. "It becomes as if talking to God is like I'm talking to you."

Listening Meditation: Stilling the Mind

Charismatic practice can also be described as a form of listening meditation. Here is where the stillness really plays a role. In mindfulness, the goal is to focus on thoughts, then let them go—to "be here now." But for charismatics, the task is different. They quiet their minds to listen, not for their own thoughts, but for God's. The end goal isn't silence, but a stillness that allows them to hear the quiet voice of God. As Melvin described it, "I feel like the Lord is talking to me all the time, that He's with me, that He has a direction that He wants this or that. I think it's a question of how often I'm going to really, be able I should say, to really shut down all the other voices and all the other thoughts and hear."

Even in the intensity of tongues prayer, some find moments of stillness. After several years of sitting with charismatics just following highly energized collective worship sessions, I was surprised. I'd expected noise and energy, but they kept talking about quiet. A tranquil mind, like a still pond. I asked again, and they told me stories of complete stillness. "Utter calm" as ripples from the smallest rock resonate throughout the pond. It's the "small quiet voice of God," they said. That was the clue to the role of quiet contemplation, even in the midst of an energized trance.

Jeremy shared a similar story: "There are times when I will lay flat on my face, like on a yoga mat and I will just listen. The goal is to listen and be receptive to what he has to say once you pray." Mike explained that listening means looking closely at your own internal processes.

When you're in the presence of God your antennae are up, your feelers are up because you're always trying to be attentive to any perceivable shift of anything. You want to hear from God and you don't want to miss anything. So, you're always going to try to be hyper-aware of anything you're thinking or feeling. He might open your eyes, he might draw your attention. He could be speaking to you in any number of ways, by something that you hear or something that you see.

Tongues prayer seems particularly suited for this kind of close listening. "Tongues has been a tool of clearing for me so that I can hear," Shavon explained.

You want to hear from God. The way I've successfully heard from Him is to quiet my mind. Tongues quiets my mind. Because my only sole focus is Him, there, right? I'm speaking in tongues, I'll do it right now. [She speaks in tongues for ten seconds.] I feel peace. When I speak in tongues, everything else, the kids, are not on my mind. My husband's not on my mind.

"Even just now, when you just did it," I asked, "it quieted your mind?"

"Just right now, I got chills, yes." The arousal of chills overlayed the experience of quieting.

"And that was after about ten seconds?"

"Yes."

Stilling the mind here is different from the fully quiet version in other meditations. Instead, stillness emerges out of the white noise that fills the mind. It's a quiet that relies on the storm. But both enable a listener to hear the voice of God. And sometimes they are entwined.

Instead of waiting for the presence of God to still me. I'll still myself. My Shavon mind can go at a million miles a minute. I'm not a person that just is naturally sitting in peace. I'm a doer. I want to go, do, be, go, go. That's what I do. But God doesn't necessarily want me to go do, go, go, go. He sometimes wants me to stop. I'm stilling for him, the stilling is the notice that I need, the feeling of more of him and less of me. So, the stilling could be in a walk, the stilling could be in a run, the stilling could be during a meeting with my boss. The stilling could be in a presentation with people at my firm. It could be anywhere.

Stilling can take will and action. "Because there is self-control, I decide to quiet myself. I have to decide to let go. It's not that He makes me let go. I have my free will. I can do whatever I want."

"You've described quieting," I say. "You've also talked about letting go?"

"Yes. Quieting is letting go. Right? I was thinking about this jumping off a cliff, right? Doing a bungee jump. Okay, well I can jump to my death. Thinking about all the statistics. How many people have died in this? But if I quiet that thought and just say, 'Jump,' that's what I'm talking about. 'Just do it. Just go.'" And quieting makes sensation available differently. "I feel like I'm seeing different. Yes, I guess you can call it seeing. Seeing, sensing. Everything else is quiet. Meaning I'm not concerned about work emails, things like that. I'm aware of the sounds of the heater above us. I can hear that *shh*."

A Model for Attention, Arousal, and Release

Together, myself, neuroscientists Michael Lifshitz, Jonas Mago, and Mark Miller, along with meditation teacher Shaila Catherine, tried to write about what happens in the mind and body in high arousal practices like speaking in tongues. It started with Jonas and me telling each other stories from our interviews of tongue speakers and another study we worked on of Jhana meditators. We had heard people describing the way that attention seems to heat them up and then how things got easier and easier until they could let go of control more comfortably. The strange thing was that this seemed true of both meditation and of speaking in tongues.

Jonas and I started drawing in the air with our arms, a swirling that we thought might describe the relationship between attention, arousal, and release, until he put the spiral on paper and we stared at it smiling—I know this seems silly, but it was quite exciting at the time. The way we envisioned it: you start by focusing on something, and that focus makes the object of attention sharper and clearer. Your brain starts to feel more certain, and with that certainty comes pleasure, pleasure in the mind but also the body. It begins to feel like you are warmly engaged, maybe even loving the object. In the case of speaking in tongues, folks already have plenty of positive feelings toward God, so they start the spiral a bit ahead. These positive aroused feelings make attention easier, they draw us toward the object—we become attracted. This creates a cycle where attention feeds arousal and arousal feeds attention. The pleasure grows, focus becomes easier, and attraction grows. Throughout, practitioners consciously work to surrender individual thoughts, self-oriented desires, and personal control, a process made easier by the emerging sense of effortlessness fostered by the broader cycle. They surrender. The pleasure makes it easier. The arousal gives it a draw that we can fall into—why do they call it falling in love? And as the spiral tightens, we're drawn deeper and deeper until all that's left is God or the meditation object. We call this the AAR Model—Attention, Arousal, Release. We imagine it as a spiral. If you want a more technical version of this story that tries to tie this to neuroscience, you can read the paper we wrote.[7]

The spiral of attention, arousal, and release can lead to quiet stillness. Is it the same equanimity that meditators find when focusing on the breath? Does it bring the same effects—relaxation, prosocial impulses, and more? Or is it something entirely different? As this study evolved, I have begun to examine more closely how speaking in tongues affects mental experience, or more to the point, how it shapes the blurry line between mental and bodily experience. It began to remind me not only of meditation but also of other altered states of consciousness, where sensory experience is expanded rather than simplified.

4

A Feel and a Say: God's Hug

"Sometimes when I'm praying for people, say at the church, and I look at them. I can feel like something shifts in my tongues. I felt it a second ago. Literally, I feel in what I call my spirit [points to belly]. In my 'well of living water' I could feel a shift in my body going [snaps fingers]." It was Shavon speaking.

"What does that mean?" I asked.

"If you can imagine your child, you know when your kids come up to you and they love you? They come over to you and they hug you and they hug you hard? That's how it feels for me."

"You feel hugged?"

"I feel hugged."

"You feel hugged?"

"The reason it could feel like a hug for me is because a hug is an embrace, right? A hug is knowing that you're loved. So when I feel the presence of God, that's almost like an encouragement, like a love, like, 'This is the love.'"

"So you're praying, there's a shift?"

There's a shift, a snap for me, Warm hug, and then a shift. I'll give you an example. Imagine I'm speaking in tongues, I'm praying like this and I'm saying, "Father can I just pray for Josh right now? God, give me the words to say over him. Oh Lord, okay I'm coming against fear. Father of God I come against fear right now in the name of Jesus," Right now I'm feeling that hug, right? So I'm feeling that hug and as I'm talking and I'm speaking over you. I can feel the prayer escalating and then deescalating. So, there's a breaking point that happens. I feel like at the tip of the escalation. I can feel the different urgency in my prayer. It will come up and I will start speaking in tongues [she spoke in tongues for twenty seconds], and then I can feel again the snap, and then I can feel, "Oh something's been broken." I'll still keep praying because I don't know what else God wants to do or say … For me there's a rhythm, I'm learning his voice, right? Even still, I'm learning his voice. When I feel his voice, I can feel a warmth, the warm hug thing. It's probably a "feel and a say," feelings and words at the same time together.

***

Shavon called the hug "a feel and a say." I took this to mean that the feelings and the words were somehow part of the same thing. The warmth of the hug, the love in it, the physical touch—it all came together in one moment. We can't be sure how this all works. But we can guess. Being hugged by God is one way that charismatic worship connects metaphorical ideas of love and care to what people actually feel. It may be that through this kind of metaphor-experience loop, practice can actually get under the skin. I had never heard "feel and say" before or since, so I don't know how common it is. But it's certainly a lovely way to describe something of the relationship between mind, body, and heart that anthropologists, psychologists, and charismatics are trying so hard to understand.

A hug might be the perfect lens for this study, as a hug from God was described across many interviews, yet with many different meanings. Charismatic worship brought forth a range of warm, cuddly sensations. Many connected to a sense of being deeply loved and lovable. Some felt warmth in the chest and even a distinct sense of being embraced. These differences might come from a mix of natural ability and training—what charismatics call "gifts"—and from "leaning in," or how connected that person feels to God.

It makes sense to me that a hug touches the mind, body, and heart all at once. What's surprising is how the lines between them blur. Sometimes, it's hard to say if a person is talking about a physical sensation, an emotion, or a thought. The way they shifted back and forth was striking to me. But maybe it shouldn't be. All thoughts probably carry some level of emotion, and all emotions have a sensory aspect—at least that's what neuroscientist Antonio Damasio believes.[1] Yet it's not something we notice often. When the sensory element of a warm feeling shifts from a warm chest to a sense of being touched, it crosses a line that can be hard to grasp.

For charismatics, the feeling of release and connection comes with physical sensations, often believed to be God's presence. These experiences are framed in metaphors—openness, submission—but they are also simply felt in the body. After many interviews, I began to have some insight into the finely grained details of the spiritual experiences that accompany these metaphors. Paying close attention to thoughts can push them into the world of the senses. Likewise, paying attention to physical sensations gives them emotional and intellectual weight. In charismatic worship, the act of paying attention might mediate the relationship between thought and sensation. And we know they are paying close attention.

But this raises more questions than answers. Why do some people feel more than others? Is it natural, learned, or cultural? Is it God? At Stanford, our research team found that people who can immerse themselves in their senses are more likely to have spiritual sensory experiences.[2] That's an example of a trait, or a stable ability of a person. Different cultures also use their senses in different ways. Anthropologist Steven Feld said that the Kaluli people in Papua New Guinea describe their world through sound, while in the West, we emphasize sight. From reading the literature of the past hundred years, historians say sight has overtaken smell as the main sense in the West.[3] More directly, Tanya Luhrmann suggested that prayer works with each of the senses: "The person praying is seeing in the mind's eye, hearing with the mind's ear, smelling with the mind's nose—imagining an interaction with the mind's inner senses."[4] From the charismatic perspective, this means attending to the still, quiet voice, touch, or smell of God. Researchers might see it as paying close attention to the edges of consciousness, searching for an external connection. And both charismatics and researchers likely agree—the more you attend, the more you experience.

God's Hug

When Shavon felt God's hug, it wasn't just an idea. It felt real. She felt the tactile sensations of a person hugging her; it wasn't just a metaphor for love or a warmth in the belly. Her experience sat at the far end of three continua: concept (it was imagined as a hug), emotion (it was deeply emotional), and sensation (it provided a full-on sensation). The concrete physical sensation of being touched by another body, body to body, is a sensory experience that covers a large expanse of skin and comes also with powerful associations of intimacy and its many kinds of baggage, both sweet and scary. These associations can involve warmth, just heating up the body. Sometimes the hands, sometimes the belly. Via another reading of this multidimensional diagram, the experience of God's hug is emotional. It might be vaguely associated with connection to God, but it is not the same as the tactile sensations that feel like hugs or direct touch. As Emily, a GT practitioner said, "in my mind I'm like, 'Man. I feel like the Lord's putting his arms around me.' I just feel like someone's hugging me." But, in this instance, she is clear that it's not physical. "I know I'm alone, and if it is taking place, it's taking place in the spiritual realm. It's unseen. It's not a physical thing."

Nikola, also a GT, had a similar experience: "We were recently in South Carolina for our godson's baptism. I think that God was there in that moment and I felt that feeling of hugging someone you love." Nick was quick to clarify. "It's not a physical sensation but just there's a feeling, like when you know that you are loved, and someone is there. It's an emotional thing."

"So, you're standing there, at this event, and you're feeling the emotional part of the hug?" I asked.

"Yeah. That sense of security and love that we're all there and surrounded by God's love."

Sometimes it's hard to tell the difference between an emotional feeling and a touch. Charismatics seem to hold a folk theory of mind-body connection in which emotion and sensation are often entangled.

"Do you know what it feels like to be loved?" Melvin asked me. "We were on the phone, Covid-19 had just hit, and we weren't taking chances by meeting in person." He felt hugged by God. "If you've sensed that before, you've felt there's something other than you." He then linked emotions to bodily feelings.

You feel it inside of you, there's that sensation. When I'm connecting to God and feeling his spirit and his presence, I can tangibly feel it. There's something physically on the inside. People who pray say, "You can feel it in your spirit." You can feel something, there's a joy, a peace. Something just perks up inside of you. Just really like his love is what I feel like I'm normally feeling.

For the most part, the feeling is simply warmth and sweet emotions. "The love of God sweeps into you and there's a warmth. Joy, love, peace. All these emotions in a wave sweep in. Physically in the body I would say in your chest, in your heart area. I feel it there. It's normally in the chest."

In some ways, this isn't remarkable. We all know emotions can bring on physical feelings. It's only when those feelings become sharper and more like tangible touch that we step into something more striking.

Sometimes hugs come with a word from God, often when most needed. Holly's story started at a difficult moment.

I was sexually abused as a kid and because I was very sheltered I blocked it out. And because I blocked it out and it was very traumatic it kind of led me down a road to do different things; body image issues, self-esteem issues, the need for a guy, you name it, it really led me down a dark path.

I remember I was just at a very, very low point; it was like an ultimatum with whether I wanted to be a Christian or not, if this was for me. I was a sophomore in high school, and my parents were on a date night one night. I just finally started expressing everything that I'd kind of pushed down for years. It's kind of embarrassing, but a lot of it was like yelling and just crying, I was finally feeling and telling God what I really thought. Even though I knew he was real, I was just more like, "I'm angry that you would let this happen and I'm even angrier at what I've done to myself for the past couple of years, the roads I've gone on." I was just very angry. That was the first real encounter I had with God.

I'm in my room. I'm on the floor. There's stuff all over the place because I'd thrown stuff. I'd pounded the floor. My hair is a mess. I'm sweating; I remember my face is completely soaked in tears, and then it's like all the chaos in my mind and outside of my mind, all the noises—because I'm in the middle of the city—just silenced. I felt him in the room and I felt like a warm embrace. My body started to heat up, and it was like an embrace. It was like someone was just kneeling next to me on the floor hugging me. I don't know if that makes sense. I just felt him speaking to me. It wasn't like an audible voice. It just was more like him justifying the fact of what happened to me wasn't right and he weeps over it too, and he's not okay with it either, something like that. A lot of what happened I can't really put words to it, it was more of the moment. I just finally felt a release—I just needed to know that he wasn't okay with it, you know? I needed to know that he was upset too.

Endora described something even more clearly physical: "When I pray sometimes I feel him all over me. Like if there was really someone all around me, like holding me. Just holding me and saying that I'm special to him."

"When you say that, how is it different or the same as a person holding you?"

"I don't see him."

"You don't see him. But do you feel him?"

"It feels safe."

At this point, I wasn't sure if she was describing a hug, merely warmth, or an emotional connection that felt like a hug. I asked if it felt like there was a body against her.

"Mm hm," she replied.

"Do you feel a chest against your back?"

She nodded, affirming that this was sensory, not merely emotional.

"How is he holding you?"

"Sideways. So warm, so safe, like nothing in my life before. I feel that warmness. I feel it in here [points to chest] and everywhere in the wrap around me."

"You're putting your hand on your chest."

"They wrap around me like, 'You're safe. You're free. I freed you. Quit trying to put those cuffs on yourself.'"

Here, again, I was unsure of the degree to which this was literally language or more like an impression. "So you hear those words as if they are words in your head?" I asked.

"Yes, sentences."

"And you feel this warmth around your body?"

"I feel his arms wrapped on me."

"Specific arms?"

"Yes, I feel a holding, a grip on me, that it's his arms around me." She was then careful to explain that this was not visual—God is invisible. "Now I'm not going to tell you I see his hands or anything. I just feel a holding." She is clear that this is not a visual hallucination. But it does sound fully physical.

Looping and Confusion

That sensory experiences fall on a spectrum became clear when I noticed how often stories landed somewhere between feeling and touch. People moved back and forth between the idea of a hug, the emotions of being hugged, and the physical sensation—sometimes settling on one but often shifting between them, as if the line between these experiences wasn't clear.

From an evangelical perspective, this in-between experience might be due to a person's uncertain connection with God. Maybe demons are interfering, or maybe it's just a matter of inattention or bad luck for beginners. From a research angle, it makes sense that people aren't always clear about what they've experienced. Memory can blur across the senses, especially with supernatural experiences. This ambiguity often came up in interviews after we would probe. We'd hear something was audible, but after digging deeper—asking if they turned their head or whether the sound was inside or outside their head—the voice was often remembered as internal. But not always.

This fluidity makes sense when you think of charismatic prayer as a way of training attention, a slow process of learning to experience God. Smell, in particular, was unstable. In one case, a spiritual embrace—a hug—triggered smell, then sight. As Emily described it, she was listening for God and "just smelling." The memory started very concretely, but immediately she receded from the senses to describe emotions instead. "I have these moments of incredible joy, it's like you just feel the presence of God and you feel Jesus there." Then it returned to sensation. "You know he's there and he's embracing you." But she questioned the physical reality. "Maybe not physically but you're like embracing him in the spirit." Finally, she used a mixed metaphor, blending smell, sight, and the mind to describe her connection to God: "It's like a sweet fragrance and in my mind's eye, I might see a light."

The movement between smell, emotion, touch, and sight could be because smell isn't a sense most people in the United States are attuned to. It might also be that this particular smell was mostly metaphor, making it easier to interpret loosely. Maybe Emily was experiencing synesthesia. Maybe God works through multiple sensory routes. Or maybe, she just couldn't quite remember.

A broadly accepting approach to mental states in the charismatic oral tradition allows people to move freely between thought and sensation, between different modes of experience. As Rhea explained, "When I don't know what to pray, I'll pray in tongues to help me know what to pray about."

I asked her, "so it's almost like the tongues comes before your ideas?"

"Yeah, it's not in your brain. It's kind of like it just comes out." And then it rebounds back as a physical sensation.

I noticed she was gesturing to her chest. "Do you feel like it's coming out of your torso?"

"Yeah. Sometimes when I'm praying really hard I can just feel heat there and experience power experiences."

It is sometimes possible to follow their attention from thought to sensation, and often back again. Charismatics are aware of this link between ideas, physical sensations, and emotions. Some even find the ambiguity fascinating. Valentin struggled to explain her experience of God's hug as purely mental. "There is a mental part of that, but it's—you can't say that a hug is mental." She paused, searching for the right words. "People might say enveloped, you feel enveloped by His peace, by His love, or blanketed. The Bible says, He's like a mother hen that takes her chicks under her wing." She was quick to add that not every connection with God feels like a hug. "I would say the opposite is true, too. He is my father in the sense that He also corrects me. That correction doesn't always feel like love enveloping me."

We learn two things here. First, that experience with an unseen other can range. It goes from faint feelings and soft sensations to full, flesh-to-flesh contact steeped in unconditional love. Second, more often than not, the experience lies somewhere in the middle. It's caught in the space between warmth and touch, between the feeling of being hugged and the physical reality of it. And this balance between thought and sensation shifts—while it's happening, when it's recalled, and when it's told.

These shifting experiences suggest that things aren't always as they seem— or as they seemed a moment ago. They aren't always as they are spoken about, either. But that doesn't mean they're fake or illusions. Memory changes, especially when emotions run high. Think about an argument—you might remember the feelings, but the details get fuzzy. You'll be honest, sure, but the truth gets slippery. And spiritual experiences? Maybe even more so. Scholars often say they're ineffable, meaning too great to be put into words.[5] They are also riddled with emotions, which seems a recipe for unclarity.

Trying to map out something close to inexpressible is a challenge. Maybe it's impossible. But from our interviews, we've seen that across the senses, there's a shifting, uncertain, and yet incredibly powerful range of experiences with the invisible. They can feel more or less real, more or less external, and more or less clear. But we can at least begin to trace their outline.

A Range of Experiences

The idea that people experience an unseen other in varying degrees of clarity isn't new. Late nineteenth-century doctors knew that patients with psychosis often blurred the lines between perception and thought. And while I am not at all trying to say that prayer is like psychosis—I find the continuum of experience helpful. Hallucinations varied in how clear they were, whether they felt internal or external, and whether the patient believed they caused them. Tanya Luhrmann and Nev Jones reference G. T. Tuttle (1902), who described a spectrum from mere thoughts, to a voice in the head, to an external voice. Tuttle spoke of "shades of difference," from thoughts that don't feel like they belong to the person, to words that have no sound, to words that take on sound. In a recent study, Luhrmann and Jones found that more than half of their schizophrenia spectrum patients described a similar range of auditory experiences. One participant described trying to "distinguish (or explain the difference) between real voices, 'hallucinated voices,' thoughts in my own head, other people's thoughts, thoughts that might be circulating in the air, and then even the extent to which anything exists other than thoughts."

But again, these stories come from people deemed pathological. From what we've learned, I think it's safe to say we probably shouldn't worry too much about comparisons between charismatic experiences of God and pathology. It's true that charismatics feel God's touch, hear His voice, and sometimes even smell His presence in ways that seem to go beyond what's around them. I have a few responses to this. First: in our study, we did what is called a Structured Clinical Interview for DSM Disorders, which is a diagnostic tool used by mental health professionals to assess and diagnose mental disorders based on the criteria outlined in the Diagnostic and Statistical Manual of Mental Disorders (DSM). Our practitioners were relatively normal compared to the overall population.

Second, if we look around, we might find that hearing voices simply fits into most definitions of normal. This feels like a bold claim. Recently, a cultural movement has been growing, one that says hearing voices is a normal human experience, not necessarily pathological. Their argument includes claims that this is quite common, but also the idea that removing the stigma of voice hearing in some cultures lowers the need for medical treatment. It's not certain, but in communities where hearing from God is normal, those who hear voices may be less likely to be seen as crazy.

One website is warm and welcoming: "If you hear voices, see visions or have similar sensory experiences—you're not alone. The statistics vary, but somewhere between 3 and 10% of the population have experiences like these (increasing to about 75% if you include one-off experiences like hearing someone call your name out loud). Despite being relatively common, many people who hear voices, see visions or have similar experiences feel alone. Fear of prejudice, discrimination, and being dismissed as 'crazy' can keep people silent."[6]

In some non-Western cultures, something close to what we call schizophrenia or bipolar disorder can sometimes be seen as a sign of spiritual insight or connection with the divine. For instance, the Shona people of Zimbabwe might interpret schizophrenia as spiritual possession or communication with ancestors. This cultural framing provides individuals with a social role and community support, which has been associated with better long-term outcomes for people with these symptoms.[7] Similarly, in some Native American tribes, visions or auditory experiences are considered spiritual gifts rather than symptoms of psychosis.[8] If symptoms of mental illness are seen as spiritual gifts and not medical issues, can that lead to better outcomes? Or does it mean people don't get the help they need? In contrast, Western medicine tends to view mental illness strictly as a pathology needing treatment, which isolates and marginalizes people.

In church communities, a similar dynamic could play out. Hearing voices or having visions is often seen as a divine encounter or spiritual warfare, not pathology. This may reduce stigma and provide a supportive community, which can protect individuals from suffering. Perhaps religious belief can provide a framework for understanding experiences in a way that provides purpose, which has been linked to better mental health outcomes.[9] It may also be that fewer people in these communities suffer from harsh, loud, and overbearing voices from an invisible other. These make daily life hard.[10] In charismatic communities, spiritual practices, prayer, and social support may help mitigate the suffering often associated with mental illness by reinterpreting it as part of a broader spiritual struggle rather than an isolated medical condition. Or it may not.

The DSM has adapted to this growing awareness of cross-cultural differences and the biopsychosocial factors at play. The latest editions have moved to a dimensional approach to illness, factoring in functional impairment alongside symptoms. This means that the key criteria for diagnosing illness is how you manage life, not if you hear a voice or feel a touch when there is no physical being there to interact with. In other words, schizophrenia and other mental illnesses are now defined, in part, by the suffering and impairment they cause. This is a shift from earlier editions that focused more on clusters of symptoms and less on how they affected someone's life. Now, the DSM-5 says that "mental disorders are usually associated with significant distress or disability in social, occupational, or other important activities," placing personal suffering at the center of the diagnosis.

I did some digging and found that studies show that between 5 percent and 15 percent of people have heard voices at some point without having a psychiatric diagnosis.[11] People who have experienced trauma, especially childhood trauma, are more likely to hear voices, even if they don't develop psychosis.[12] But, among those who hear voices, only about one-third report distress significant enough to seek psychiatric help.[13] Auditory experiences are the most common, but others (visual, tactile, or olfactory) are also reported.[14]

The challenge is that these statistics don't tell us the source of the experience. It could be hallucination, it could be God, or something else entirely. This means we can explore how training, personal tendencies, and culture shape the sensations people feel or recognize, regardless of the source.

Bodily Sensations

In our interviews, we found a range of bodily sensations apart from a hug. They went from a faint impression, barely more than an emotional sense, to something a bit more clear and all the way to moments of full-on touch.

Janine gave us one of the clearest examples of the far end of this spectrum, where the experience is more idea than feeling.

> I actually sensed that somebody was placing their hand on me and praying for me, but I knew that nobody was there. It happened several times over a few months. There was no tactile sensation but it's kind of like there was a sense and I kind of like knew that there was somebody praying over me. It was kind of like, "Someone's there," but I did not feel an actual touch, which is how I knew that there was no one physically behind or in front of me.

Other times, the sensation has more shape. It starts to feel like a hand—sometimes with fingers, sometimes with a push. Norman explained that he'd felt a hand on his back. "There have been other people that have had this too, but I felt his hand on my back."

"Hand on your back? Doing what?"

"Just a warm hand."

"What gave you the sense that it was a hand?"

"It just felt like a warm hand … I knew it was Jesus."

This particular account was short on detail, so it could be challenged quite easily. But more detail doesn't always mean more accuracy. It could just mean more effort to prove it's real. Also, tactile hallucinations and real sensations both come in a range—from sharp and clear to fuzzy and vague.

Often, there's doubt, even skepticism. As Mark reflected,

I can think of once where I felt a hand. Then I looked up and I'm still not even sure if it wasn't someone just walking by and praying for me, but it struck me as supernatural at the time. It felt like just an encouraging hand. A warm hand and then it was gone. Now it's not to say that somebody couldn't have been there, but I had that sense like maybe it was God, you know.

"You didn't turn around?"

I didn't want to find out because it felt good. I felt reassured, encouraged, and I thought I'm not going to mess this up, like ask "what's going on here?" Because I have done that, where I think God wanted to do something supernatural and I just couldn't turn my brain off or get my head out of the what's happening here. I was so busy trying to explain it that I couldn't experience it.

Jeremy had no such compunction.

A few months back, we were standing in worship and the fire was there and I felt someone, I kid you not, put their hand on top of my head and just rest it there. I kind of looked around, just to make sure I wasn't crazy, you know. And it felt like your hand would be resting on top of my head, it was just there.

"It really felt like a hand?"

Yeah, it was just there. Then within about a minute and a half, it lifted. I get home and I felt, and I have never felt this again, something resting on my chest and then this stirring from my belly, it was so intense. I am crying, I am sobbing, I am laughing, it's all these sensations of joy. I am laughing uncontrollably. I was literally on the ground trembling under the power of this overwhelming love. It was like my body couldn't handle what he was doing to me. When it was done, it was like, I just felt peaceful.

Valentin also felt a hand,

I don't exactly know why, but I still can remember what it felt like to hold Jesus' hand. Just like the best kind of dad's hand. Just bigger than mine and secure and sure and that whole thing where you know that somebody else's got you. I don't remember the temperature of the hand. I just felt like everything was just right about it.

Audible Continuum

In my first set of interviews, one question aimed at understanding whether people had simply thought about God or actually heard His voice. Many answered right away, saying, "I heard God out loud." Yet, a whole lot of shifting and changing followed. Our probes often revealed that when people thought a bit more about it, many decided that they had experienced an inner voice that they felt was from God, but it was probably not audible. Many had never really considered the difference before. A good test was asking if they turned their head to hear the sound. If they did, it was a sign their body registered it as something from outside. Some, although by no means all, then decided that they had initially felt an impression of God—not a sound—that they later put into words.

Through this process, we sorted out different kinds of communication-like experiences. Some were as clear as spoken words. Others were inner voices that sounded like speech. Some felt something like speech but were probably concepts derived from impressions without tone. My favorite line in all of this came from a woman who said, "God is a baritone."

Often, it was hard to tell if the voice was audible. The clarity of the experience, the invisibility of the speaker, or perhaps the power of modern secular thinking made it vague. Norman told me he heard God speak out loud, but he quickly clarified. "Actually, that might have been an impression. I just stood at the very back of the church and all of a sudden there was the lull, where the music is quiet, and my heart was just beating out of my chest and it was just—that wasn't audible, it was like, it was very rare. It was almost audible."

At first, you might think that "almost audible" seems a logical thing to say. But what does that mean? I think it captures something key about charismatic experience—sometimes things sit on the edge of being sensory. The line between the senses and the mind isn't always clear.

I asked Norman, "what do you mean by almost audible?"

"It was like it was just in me, coming out of my head and my heart." He explained,

> God said, "I have loved you with an everlasting love and I join you with chords of loving kindness." That's the scripture from Isaiah. It was uncontainable. It was like I knew I was supposed to say it. Then Pastor Forrest stands up and says, "Somebody has got a word." My heart was like, "Err, you've got to say it." Forrest was like, "I'll wait." I thought, "Ah, you've got to say it super loud." Then Forrest goes, "Alright, I feel like the Lord is saying, 'I have loved you with everlasting love.'" He said this. I did not say it.

For Norman, a Bible verse became God's message on the threshold of sound. This was especially potent because of the timing—Nathan thought he ought to speak it just as Pastor Forrest called for the same phrase.

Jeanine also talked about something like this when she asked God about the irrigation ditch on her parents' land. It was working well, which was unusual. She asked, "Why doesn't this happen all the time?" and God's response was, "Perseverance." Here again the sonic content was ambiguous.

"When you heard that, was it a word?" I asked.

"Yes," she clarified.

I probed further. "Was it your own thought, or did it sound like a voice?"

"Not necessarily an audible voice that we could hear but it was a conversation I knew I was having. I can't say that I heard any voice, be it outside or inside, but it was an impressed conversation, so maybe just thoughts." It was almost audible.

English doesn't have a good way to describe communication that isn't heard but comes in the form of concepts or phrases. Mike tried to explain it. "It was a voice, but not a voice. More like, 'You need to be kinder.' It wasn't even a full sentence. Just this sense that that's what God was saying. That's how I'd describe the inner voice."

To clarify the experience, I often asked people to compare God's voice to a memory of a conversation with a friend. How was it different? Nathan said it wasn't just the sound. It was something felt in the body, something that pushed out every other thought. This reminded me of Cheryl's full house. "There's like life on it. It's just like every part of you reacts to it. When you hear the internal audible, which I've only heard twice, it's loud. It drowns out every fear, every thought, every worry, all happiness. Everything. It drowns it all out and all you can think is, 'I really need to respond to this.'" He called it "internal audible." Its key flavor was vitality, life. Even so, it sounded male gendered and like a real voice. "It sounds like a voice. It's like alive, but gentle."

Rhea's experience of God's voice changed over time. She often received messages from God, but not in an audible way. "When I was younger I would write my prayers out. And I would just write 'cause I love to write and it's one of my hobbies. And then, I would stop and I would just start writing and it would be like God's response to me. The words were just coming." Recently, the voice came during moments of quiet in the midst of intense prayer. "Now I'll just be in prayer and pushing and pushing and then I'll sit back and be like okay, 'I don't know what to say anymore.' And he'll speak directly." But again, it was internal, not audible.

I hear it inside and it's a calm, strong, gentle voice. It makes my heart feel still and calm and takes away the anxiety. I feel like it's changed for me. Before it used to sound like the leader that I was under. But now it's just a very familiar voice. It's just; I don't even know how to explain it. I'm trying to—it's gentle but strong.

She recalled one time she heard an audible voice.

I've only heard him audibly one time, and it was the scariest thing in my life. I was seven and I read my Bible every day and prayed every day and one day I decided to color and not read my Bible. And I heard this out loud audibly, I remember, and I told my mom. He said, "Rhea, why aren't you reading your Bible?" And I freaked out. And it was not a dominating, strong voice but it was just an I have authority voice. And I was like mom, I heard a voice.

Conclusion

Their culture of sensory practice makes charismatics mind-body theorists in their own right.

You're talking about senses, about the fine line between what's audible and what isn't, what you are hearing in your mind. Is it a thought? Is it a sentence? You're stepping into an amazing space. Biologically, it's complex—how God made our minds and bodies. You want to dig in and ask, how are you hearing God? What's a word? What isn't? You look at that and think, "Wow." God can certainly make you hear it in your ear if He wants to. Or maybe there's more people connected with their hand, or something. Another person might say, "It's a sense in my mind."

That was Norman.

Charismatics seem to be very aware of this uncertain space. They value hearing God's voice out loud, but they're flexible about it. They've got a working folk theory that God's communication ranges from impressions to clear audible words. Norman explained, "I had that encounter and I didn't hear the words, 'You're my son and I still love you.' But it was an overwhelming impression which later I interpreted to be that."

These experiences—tactile and auditory—raise more questions than they answer. How does it happen? Is it simply God's process, or is this, to some degree, shaped by the person's inner state? By how we pay attention to what's happening? As a researcher, my first thought was that practice brings clarity. Research on mindfulness backs this up, focused attention sharpens sensation. But as we've seen, letting go is just as important.

When charismatics fall in love with God and let loose their tongues, they release their emotions, and maybe they loosen their minds too, becoming open to sensory contact from God. The spiraling relationship between surrender and the release of emotions, bodies, and thoughts—connected to attention and arousal—is the perfect place to see that sensation, emotion, and thought are deeply entwined. The boundaries between them blur. A feeling might be an emotion, a sensation, or a thought—or all three. Charismatic practice works at the intersection of these experiences, where they overlap and blend together.

5

The MRI:
Or, Is It Real?

Surrounded by the intensity of experience described by people speaking in tongues, I often found myself pondering the bodily dimension of release. Clearly, this was a profoundly physical practice, far more than a thought game. But what exactly was happening? What did the body do when it released control, when it let go? You could ask this about almost anything, it's true. But, I wondered, what did the brain look like in the midst of spiritual surrender, down to its firing circuits? Could we find a physiology to letting go? Perhaps naively optimistic, I imagined an MRI would clear this up quickly. (Magnetic Resonance Imaging (MRI) measures brain activity indirectly by looking at the ways blood flow responds to a magnet. It is the first of several brain scan techniques we will discuss later on.) I remember that the question itself felt straightforward, as if the answers lay just beyond our grasp. By the way, parts of this next chapter are written from the perspective of "we," which is because a team of researchers, including neuroscientists Michael Lifshitz, Jonas Mago, and anthropologist Tanya Luhrmann, study.[1]

***

Amy Hollywood distinguishes between the "real" (something experienced) and the "true" (third-person verified). I am using real in her sense of the word true. Hollywood, *Acute Melancholia and Other Essays*

When someone asks you a question that makes you wonder if everything you're doing is truly worth your time and energy—maybe that's when things are really moving, for better or for worse. One evening, we sat at dinner with a group of anthropologists, psychologists, a neuroscientist, and a few others. The food was on Stanford. It was good—piles of meat and vegetables; there was all I could want. It was about as ideal an academic experience as one could imagine. The talk turned to Chabad, a Jewish tradition with a mystical emphasis, and whether their practitioners might open up and tell us more about their practice.

"The Chabad folks are shy," someone explained. "They don't want to share the intimacies of their faith practices."

Another joked, "Terminally humble."

Then someone asked: "Would they be up for praying in an MRI machine?" It got a laugh. We'd only just started asking charismatics to do that very thing—pray in English and then speak in tongues, all while we watched their brains at work. At that point, Anna Corwin, a linguistic anthropologist and colleague, asked a simple but cutting question. "Why are we thinking this would be useful? You have years of ethnographic data and hundreds of hours of interviews about spiritual experience from charismatics. What could we learn from an MRI that we don't already know?" It was friendly enough, but it touched a nerve.

This, I now think, was a very excellent and helpful question. At the time, it was unsettling. I could feel in my gut that the answer should be obvious. "Hard" data—the data that comes in numbers and images, that takes shape on screens and graphs—that was what felt solid, real. Not subjective accounts and anecdotes. Part of me thought that it was clearly a far sight better than the subjective mush I was used to collecting. I was, however, embarrassed with this internal response because I was no stranger to the critiques of "positivist" hard science's blind spots, as it tends to barrel past nuance and ignores those on the margins of society. I could even tell you why hours of interpersonal interactions and thick description might be considered better than MRI data: it wasn't tainted by reductionism; it could be more holistic, built on long-term relationships of trust with people engaged in the research process; it could acknowledge local practices and beliefs on their own terms, and might reveal more about the intricacies of human behavior and social interactions; such a culturally sensitive research process would be responsive to the changing needs of field research and would allow us to be honest about our biases. I could go on. I was trained as an anthropologist, remember?

Yet, part of me still thought that hard, quantifiable data was superior and more real. Wasn't it? I certainly wished Dr. Corwin had been there to ask this twelve months previously, back when I was just signing up for the study.

Our MRI study had launched with a plain idea: that numbers and scans might somehow help us define "realness." The MRI captures brain signals, tangible and unmistakable. It's not just talk or discourse—it's there on the screen, a visible pulse of truth. But the longer we lingered on it, the slipperier the notion of "real" became. It was always pretty clear that the weightiest realness question—the ontological inquiry: does God exist?—lay far beyond the scope of our study. Whatever data we pulled might well be evolution's handiwork or God's design or both, and no imaging technique could pin that down. Beyond that, as I learned of the debates that preoccupy the field of neuroscience, clear truth appeared farther and farther away. But we hoped, at least, to see if people praying in tongues were doing something beyond pretense. More than make-believe. After years of watching, listening to their stories, and feeling that power in the room, I certainly thought so.

In a sense, I was actually searching for two distinct versions of the real. First, there was the question from my informants, very much like the neuroscientist version—does this experience change the mind in tangible ways? Secondly, as an anthropologist, I was drawn to map what Daniel Dennett would call the "real patterns"—the structures visible in subjective experience, in the body, and in the spaces between.[2] I thought that these patterns were likely to loop across registers of experience and maybe we would be able to see how brains, bodies, and cultures were shaping each other. Somewhere between the neuroscientific, the experiential, and the cultural, I hoped to find some inkling of what we call "the real."

This contemplation led me down a meandering path. It went something like this: is the act of letting go pretend? If it's not pretend, is it mechanical—something forced and without depth? And is that even the right question? What's so good about authenticity anyway? Aside from the mechanical, how much of this experience changes the body or brain? And if it does, are those changes lasting? Then also, are they healthy or harmful? Finally, do they loop back out into the society that they emerged from and in turn shape how charismatics think, act, and build community? For these questions, though, we needed an MRI study that would give us meaningful data, which is not as easy as it may sound.

In designing an MRI protocol, it can be helpful to compare. You need something very close to the object of study, so you can see what is unique. Otherwise, you get a vague sense that something is happening. So, what is tongues prayer similar to? Is it like seizures—unbidden and uncontrollable? Would tongues show up as temporal lobe bursts like some epilepsy?[3] Or more like a runner's high, something that could be called up again and again? Is it tied to releasing frontal lobe inhibition which seems intuitive,[4] or maybe the split frontal lobe of jazz musicians and hip-hop artists, whose expansive artistry is shaped by a formal musical structure—this shows up in the brain as partially activated and partially inhibited.[5] Would we find the especially changeable brain connections sparked by psychedelics?[6] Or was it closer to certain forms of hypnosis, where the motor areas are especially involved?[7] Or perhaps tongues in the MRI would show us a unique mix—a flicker of intense focus followed by a release, maybe a rise in the frontal lobe that quickly ebbed. We were after something elusive. We wanted to know if charismatic prayer defied the "normal" lines of brain activity and what that might mean.

Given that tongues prayer moves through focused attention, arousal, release, and tranquility, and that prayer involves a mix of sensory processing, social engagement (with God and the church community), and a whole host of emotions, we expected that the neural signature captured in the MRI would be especially complex. We would have to break the experience down to bite-sized chunks and analyze them piece by piece before exploring the whole. This process proved to be quite an undertaking.

Realness

So, is it real?

When Christians speak in tongues, they often describe losing control over the muscles in their mouth, as if the sounds they produce are not entirely their own. Observers have puzzled for decades over whether people truly give up control or whether they are purposefully pretending in order to fit in with their church community.[8] Some critics say they're faking it—deliberately and determinedly using their tongues to speak as if in a foreign language, but all for show.[9] We chose to do an fMRI study, in part, because we believed this method could help us to distinguish between the two interpretations, the simulated and the genuine. Previous research shows that brain circuits activate differently depending on how much control, or "agency," someone feels.[10] We thought that if this experience truly altered their sense of agency, it would be visible in the brain.

The study of tongues prayer has a rough history among academics. Psychologists William James and Carl Jung were unusual in that they were intrigued by the potential in charismatic prayer to access something deeply subconscious or spiritual.[11] James saw passivity as central to spiritual experience. But most early observers painted grim portraits of people barely in control of themselves. They saw tongues as aberrant—a kind of mental breakdown. Interestingly, some of the harshest critiques came from Christians. Some fundamentalists called it devil's speech.[12] Mainline churches felt threatened by the charismatic revival among Catholics in the 1960s.

One prominent voice against tongues was John Kildahl, a Lutheran clergyman and psychologist who toured the United States and interviewed dozens of practitioners. In his reports, Kildahl argued that tongues prayer wasn't divine or therapeutic but a form of hypnosis gone wrong. Yes, he admitted, it might make people feel loved, but it also led to what he called "psychological regression," a loss of "reality constraints," and "community disruption." To Kildahl, tongues was a descent into chaos.[13]

But in that same year, 1972, linguist and anthropologist Felicitas Goodman turned Kildahl's frame on its head. She spent time in churches across Mexico and the United States, where she observed rhythmic speech patterns, heightened arousal, and involuntary movements in tongues prayer. It induced confusion and reduced recall, just as Kildahl said, but Goodman saw value in it. To her, this loosening of the mind wasn't disorder—it was an opening. It offered a way for people to escape the tight grip of society, trauma, or both. Goodman believed that tongues prayer created a trance state, a deep change in consciousness, which she even began to teach to non-believers.[14] She would have appreciated today's studies on psychedelics, which provide new tools for exploring the loosened mind.

Goodman's ideas, however, didn't go unchallenged. Also in 1972, linguist William Samarin disagreed with her altogether, but on different grounds.[15] (For some reason I have not yet fully uncovered, 1972 was clearly the year of speaking in tongues research—probably a response to the massive growth of the hippie Christians). Samarin saw no sign of trance. To him, tongues was simply a performance—a dramatic display to say, "We're one of you." Samarin went as far as to call Goodman's findings "erroneous, speculative, contradictory, [and] incredible, because of her relentless hold on an idée fixe."[16] The idea was trance. Goodman, for her part, argued that Samarin was missing the point.[17]

Psychologist Nicholas Spanos and his team then jumped in the fray with a study titled "Glossolalia as Learned Behavior," the exact title of Samarin's earlier piece, as if to hammer home their point. Spanos had taught non-believers to speak in tongues, showing that people could effectively mimic the sounds of tongues prayer "fluently" without entering a trance. These participants kept their eyes open, experienced no disorientation, and showed no unusual bodily movements.[18] It was a tremendous take-down of Goodman's argument. Spanos concluded that tongues prayer was a learned performance, plain and simple. If he was right, our MRI study might turn out futile or, at best, a bit dull, capturing a ritual of social signaling rather than anything deeper.

I did hope we would find something else. I wonder if that is ok to admit— but I think all scientists hope for a breakthrough. Which makes me wonder if maybe I was becoming a scientist.

The Brain on Tongues

Goodman and Spanos had seen the same thing, but with different eyes. Science is full of these tensions. Some stay unresolved, forever pulling in opposite directions. Others force a reckoning, one side disproving the other. But in our case, we now think, both may be right. Perhaps there is enough variety within tongues prayer to support both views? Some prayers could evoke a genuine trance, while others leaned more on the social side, maybe even a performance. We knew from my prior interviews that some folks faked it—at least in the beginning. Either way, if there was a real altered state, an MRI should show it. We expected it would reveal a pattern distinct from social signaling, a telltale sign of surrender if anyone could reach a trance in a cold MRI scanner. But what would that look like?

Early neuroscience leaned heavily into the idea that certain parts of the brain worked specific skills or traits. Before the advent of brain scans, the only way to see this was in people who had damaged the brain. In 1861, French scholar Pierre Broca did an autopsy on Louis Victor Leborgne, who was nicknamed "Tan" because that was the only word he could pronounce clearly. Broca discovered that Tan's inferior frontal gyrus, a small region located above and in front of the left ear, was damaged, and over time, studies confirmed that damage here impaired speech production. We now call this Broca's Area. Sadly, Broca's fascination with the brain's physical traits ran deep, and he tangled this discovery with ideas of racial hierarchy, trying to "prove" that European skulls were superior to African ones. Though his racial theories have been thoroughly debunked, his work on language endured, with Broca's Area associated with speech and language production. Much of early neuroscience followed similar thinking—mapping behaviors to distinct brain regions.

The temporal lobe was the initial contender for the seat of religious experience. During the late 1800s, John Hughlings Jackson studied patients with partial epileptic seizures that began with sensations of déjà vu, vivid memory-like scenes, or sudden emotions. He called these "dreamy states." I suspect I know what he means—my epilepsy produces something similar on occasion. These states are quite uncomfortable, disconcerting. In a famous case, "Dreamy state #2" Jackson's post-mortem on a patient who had lived with dreamy seizures showed damage to the temporal lobe. Other dreamy prone patients had olfactory or gustatory hallucinations, which Jackson had already suspected (from other lesion cases) were also localized to the temporal region. He came to see the temporal lobe as a high-level representational area, integrating memories, emotions, and perceptions—he described a seizure there as something like a twitch in the muscles that would release fragments of these memories and emotions.

These temporal lobe seizures seemed to mirror mystical states: a sense of detachment, visions, and strange voices. Some speculated that the experiences of God among historical figures like Joan of Arc and Teresa of Avila were just temporal lobe epilepsy. In the 1940s, Walter Penfield was doing surgery on epileptics and wildly—they were fully awake. These folks had intractable seizures and Penfield was in search of the regions involved. He used their and self-observation to try and connect the experience of the seizure to brain activity—it was an early effort at neurophenomenology. A seizure beginning with a burning smell or dreamy state might originate in the temporal area. One beginning with a jerk of the right thumb could involve motor areas, he thought. Penfield and his team would numb the scalp of epileptics, remove parts of the skull, and put electrodes on their brains to look for what they called epileptiform spikes—bursts of abnormal activity that were often associated with epilepsy. If a region repeatedly showed these spikes or if the patient's habitual seizures began as they monitored that region, Penfield tracked it. Avoiding areas critical to function, they would then remove small parts of the brain—and some folks did stop having seizures. But perhaps most importantly for our purposes, when Penfield touched the temporal areas, patients described unusual experiences: "I hear voices or music," "I see myself as a child," or "I feel as though someone is here." Because these "experiential hallucinations" only happened when the temporal lobe was stimulated—and not with other lobes—Penfield came to connect the temporal lobe to a "sensation of presence" and "memory replay" that he described as numinous. Notice here that the criteria was mystical experience, not agency release. That becomes important later on.

Psychologists of the late twentieth century went further, describing the "Geschwind Syndrome." Among patients with temporal lobe epilepsy, Geschwind and Waxman described traits like irritability, compulsive writing, hypersexuality, and "hyper-religiosity"—labels as socially loaded as they come. These were patients "intensely concerned with ultimate questions." Later, scholars proposed the idea of a "temporal lobe personality," suggesting that those with this condition were inherently "religion-prone."[19]

The quest for a specific "God Spot" in the brain peaked in 2002, when neuroscientist Michael Persinger had nearly 1,000 people wear a specially designed helmet that sent weak electric signals directly to the temporal lobe. Astonishingly, 80 percent of them reported feeling a palpable sense of the presence of an invisible being. The media dubbed it the "God Helmet," sparking debates over whether spirituality was just brain mechanics. Some saw it as refuting the existence of God (i.e. "it is all mechanical") and others read proof of God's profound physiological effectivity.[20]

The first-ever brain scans of tongues prayer began to shift the story towards the puzzle of control, or letting go. In fact, a study resembling ours has been conducted, albeit on a small sample of only five people. Andrew Newberg and his team scanned five people using SPECT, a technique that involves injecting a radiotracer to capture 3D images of the brain. As a control, the researchers used worship singing, another religious practice involving vocalizations and a high degree of arousal; however, the worship singing was in English rather than nonsense syllables and seemed less likely to involve a change in the feeling of self-control, hopefully allowing the researchers to isolate these unique features of tongues prayer.[21] The scans associated tongues prayer with reduced activity in regions tied to self-regulation and executive control. Newberg described it as the surrender of volition.[22]

Newberg's effort to associate prayer with regional activation was, if nothing else, badly timed. As early as 2004, neuroscientist Pehr Granqvist and colleagues at Uppsala University in Sweden attempted to replicate Persinger's God Helmet study using a more rigorous double-blind design. Their findings? No effect at all when participants weren't expecting something mystical. The results pointed to the power of suggestion, not neural stimulation of the God Spot.[23] It was a strong testimony to the power of placebo, but not great evidence for the importance of temporal lobe activation. Additionally, numerous scholars argued that while temporal lobe activation might have us thinking that religion was mostly emotion, in fact, religion looked more like social engagement with an invisible entity and involved careful, rational thought. When people prayed or meditated, their brains lit up in the areas for talking to friends, not in the places for feelings. It was like they were having a conversation with someone real who wasn't there. This was supported by fMRI studies showing that brain areas activated during religious activities were associated with social connection, rather than emotional experiences.[24] This made sense to me—prayer seemed largely about engaging with an invisible being and the emotions come from the passion and submission in that relationship. That would mean that the brain patterns for relationships, emotions, and submission could all be a part of the MRI story if we looked carefully.

Even more challenging, in the years following, the idea of a specific location for any given neural capacity was usurped by the recognition that most experience involves complex neural networks and dynamic relationships between activation patterns across the brain. The idea of a "God Spot" or particular region in the temporal lobe faded fast.

To be honest, when the tables did begin to turn once again, we didn't catch it, at first. In a 2016 study with over 100 participants, neuroscientist Irene Cristofori and colleagues found that lesions in the temporal lobe do indeed correlate to more reported feelings of unity, sacredness, ineffability, joy, as well as a sense of transcending time and space, and an intuitive belief that the experience is a source of objective truth about reality—what they described as mystical experiences.[25] And a growing collection of research proposes that temporal lobe stimulation or inhibition results in hallucinations, feelings of "strangeness," and other experiences that seem to correlate with spiritual experience.[26] More to Persinger's idea, it has also been shown that stimulation or damage to the right and left temporo-parietal junction (which is within the temporal lobe) can induce an out-of-body experience,[27] an illusory shadow person felt to be looming slightly behind the participant's body,[28] and also the feeling of a presence in daily life.[29] And to thicken the intrigue, Persinger has continued to insist that Granqvist's methodology in debunking his study was flawed, and one new study now says they have replicated the God Helmet study.[30] But the hidden key in this in this debate over mystical states was the emerging literature on agency and agency-release—scientific language for 'letting go'—which suggested these processes may also be rooted in temporal-lobe circuitry.[31]

Our project was inspired by Newberg's interest in control, but now with more than five subjects, a better brain scanner, and refined tools for analysis —but also, as we will see, it very much builds from this broader puzzle about relationships between social, emotional, and volitional elements of prayer and their variable neural signatures. We weren't looking for a God Spot or a neural map of belief, though. We wanted to know something simpler: what does a brain look like when it lets go?

In 2020, we got a hint. Yoshija Walter and a team of neuroscientists in Switzerland took up Samarin and Goodman's debate. They scanned thirty seasoned tongues speakers—not while they were praying, but while they rested. Just as Goodman might have expected, Walter and his team found a strong link between years spent speaking in tongues and the shape of these individuals' brains. There was more gray matter in two non-linguistic regions, and they took this as proof that tongues prayer isn't mere performance—it does involve neurocognitive specialization, but not about language.[32]

The findings aligned roughly with earlier work on long-time meditators. Over decades, Richie Davidson and others revealed that people with thousands of hours of meditation had brains shaped differently from the rest. But there was a catch—a big one. At first, Davidson couldn't tell if these unique brains drew people to meditation, or if meditation caused the changes. It was only through longitudinal studies—data collected over time, before and after meditation—that researchers started to see that the practice itself was shaping the brain.[33] We're now at a similar crossroads with tongues prayer. Walter's findings show differences in the brains of experienced practitioners, but the question of causality—what came first—remains.

Control: The Other Side of Letting Go

To understand the brain's way of letting go, we could start by looking at the flip side—how we plan and prepare for action, what happens when we're fully in control. Take something as simple as flexing a finger, or wrist. Turns out, this small act involves a lot of preparatory activity in the brain. Back in 1983, neuroscientist Benjamin Libet expanded on earlier work by Hans Helmut Kornhuber, who had found that before we move, the brain slowly ramps up electrical activity prior to the action. Kornhuber had called it the "readiness potential."[32]

Libet's experiment had people sitting with their arms relaxed, ready to make a small spontaneous movement like flexing their wrists whenever the urge struck. As they did, he tracked their brain's electrical activity using EEG. Libet also had them report the exact moment they became aware of wanting to move, using a clock to time it precisely. He found that the EEG showed activation, the readiness potential, about half a second before movement, but the shocker for his study was that conscious awareness of the intention to move came significantly after the readiness potential kicked in. This gap between brain activity and conscious intention suggested that the brain initiates action before the conscious mind even decides to—a finding that stirred up a firestorm of debate around free will. Maybe we simply believe that we use our "will" to generate activity when in fact the brain has already chosen to act?

In the years that followed, researchers pinpointed the core of this electrical activity in a small region near the middle of the front part of the brain, just beneath the surface. It was called the pre-supplementary motor area, or pre-SMA. Simplified vastly, this area, right in front of the Supplementary Motor Area (SMA), seems to do the planning, while the SMA sends motor commands.[33]

I've always been wary of comparing tongues prayer to hypnosis. Too often, people think hypnosis means manipulation from outside. But Michael Lifshitz, a neuroscientist and colleague, pointed out that both hypnosis and tongues prayer sometimes carry a feeling of unintentional motion. It struck me that an act can be unintentional in one moment yet chosen in another. Like when you step into a church or kneel down to pray, opening to what may come. You choose to be out of control. So maybe a hypnosis study could be useful to think with.

There's a trove of studies on hypnosis, but Lifshitz suggested we examine one that used fMRI on nineteen people who were put into a hypnotic state and told to imagine they were being controlled externally, to engage in "automatic writing," the kind that flows in a trance. When researchers compared this to regular, voluntary writing, they found that trance writing came with a dip in activity in the left SMA, which includes the pre-SMA.[34] Maybe something similar would happen with speaking in tongues. This gave us a rough hypothesis to start. Perhaps there was a real release of motor control that we could show in the MRI?

MRIs of Tongues Are Impossible

So far, this may have sounded a bit easy. But, actually, every time I broach the idea of an MRI of tongues prayer to experts in the field, they say it's intriguing, but nigh impossible. High-arousal prayer isn't neat or quiet. It's full of movement, wiggles, and head turns, the kind of activity that an MRI picks up far better than it does brain activity. They figured our data would reflect the neural jolt of head motion more than anything spiritual. It would be full of noise. And with MRI time costing around $500 an hour, it'd be a super expensive way to chase shadows. Then there was also the belief that charismatics wouldn't even go for it. They'd heard enough from studies that painted them as psychological misfits. And, finally, as the experts reminded me, MRI studies lose all the nuance. They're reductionist. The richness of experience slips away.

This is partly because MRIs are nowhere near as definitive and clear as suggested by the allure of the little colored pictures of brains that we have all come to know and love. For once you navigate countless confounds and establish sufficient power to show clear distinctions between the states of mind you hope to compare, the process of interpretation remains profoundly messy. One highlighted area might mean multiple things. The same network that kicks in for noticing another person's capacity to think—what folks call "theory of mind"—also fires up when someone is simply spacing out. These two activities literally stimulate the same network of brain regions, and that doubling is quite common.

Broca's Area, as we said, is famous for its effect on speech. But neuroscientist Russell Poldrack did a meta-analysis showing only a 69 percent link between Broca's damage and speech loss.[35] This means that more than 30 percent of the studies that looked at damaged Broca's Areas show no impact on language function. So, if we find Broca's lighting up in a scan and we don't get the person's direct experience, we're stuck guessing. When investigating something far messier like speaking in tongues, this uncertainty is tremendous, and daunting.

That's just part of it. Turns out, psychology more broadly has been hit hard with doubts over its reliability. They call it the "replication crisis." It started in the mid-2010s, when folks began retesting major studies and finding them shaky. A big-name study in *Science*—one of the top journals—went back over a hundred famous psychology experiments and found only thirty-nine held up. The rest crumbled on retest. It was a hard hit. Even the classic marshmallow test, where a kid's ability to resist grabbing the first marshmallow so they could get two in the end, didn't hold up fully under scrutiny.[36] So much for my faith in "hard" data.

And here's the kicker. How do you replicate the feel of a church in an MRI lab? Ecological validity (the scientific way of saying that certain things are normal in their regular contexts) asks whether you're close enough to the real thing for the results to mean anything. What could be further removed from the ambience of a church setting than the MRI's cold metal tunnel? (The tunnel that folks describe in near-death experiences is often imagined as spiritual, but that is a bit of a stretch and not much of a selling point to volunteers—"come experience the near-death tunnel.") Think of the clinical hospital environment with its blue paper gowns, the MRI itself, which is kept quite chilly and echoes with the tremendous din of the magnet in motion (very far from the pop-rock background of most charismatics worship), individuals on their backs rather than standing or kneeling in customary prayer postures, where they have to whisper and barely move, and finally, in our case, where they pray in front of non-believers who stare at their feet and scrutinize them anxiously the whole time. (Several potential volunteers canceled their MRI when they thought their prayer might be heard and recorded by non-believers.) Either way, it's about as far as you can get from a church service. Really, in any MRI study, ecological validity would be compromised, making any collected data questionable.

As luck would have it, a new way of studying the mind has been cutting through the challenges of reductionism and the vulnerabilities of hard science by linking the strengths of neuroscience to other methodologies. Folks call it "neurophenomenology." It starts by imagining the mind as more than our thoughts in our brain but also what they call extended, embodied, embedded, and enacted—in all "4E cognition." This basically means that our thinking transcends the brain. When I line my books up by theme, the shelf itself does some of my thinking, letting me reach for what I need. A note: my brilliant anthropologist friend Felicity organizes her hundreds of academic books by color, which leaves me deeply curious about how her thought processes work. But the crux of the matter is that our environment and our body make up important parts of our mind. Neurophenomenology blends neuroscience and phenomenology (and for us, ethnography) to look at first-person accounts of a phenomenon combined with its neurobiology.[37]

The 4E perspective challenges the idea that brains do all their thinking within an individual's head. It starts with small but potent claims around things like emotion: Antonio Damasio, a neuroscientist, found that without emotions, people make different choices. In some sense, this is obvious—how often do you react to something from your ex with some extra oomph? But

Damasio had a stronger claim. He says that without the sway of feeling, people can barely decide at all.[38] They're cut loose from the world. For Damasio, thoughts and emotions are a single, living network, imprinted by life's scars and supports. And then, when you buy the thought that emotions are part of cognition, you can add the bookshelves, our relationships, and more.

In our work, neurophenomenology meant years of groundwork— ethnography, interviews—before we even touched an MRI. This is called "front-loading" our neuroscience.[39] For years, we'd been studying prayer and tongues through ethnography—firsthand stories, hours spent talking to people in churches. Then even more years of close-up interviews. Only then did we set foot in the MRI room. This book's structure follows that approach, moving from the outside world of experience to the inside world of the brain, and back out again. Those years spent at Glad Tidings, talking to people and witnessing spiritual experiences firsthand, this was front-loading that convinced the National Science Foundation (later joined by the Bial Foundation and Mind and Life) to support our study on the neurophenomenology of speaking in tongues.[40]

This was also why we had folks willing to try the MRI. We found participants in large part because of the previous time spent building trusting relationships. This success may be the most powerful argument for interdisciplinarity: neuroscientist Michael Lifshitz, Shavon Gartrell (a leader at Glad Tidings), and I sat down to design the MRI study together, and we had had the whole plan approved by Pastor Tim. When people tried it, some saw it as a test of faith. Some found the MRI's hum soothing. A few found it nearly unbearable. And we asked this again and again—is it working? People did seem to feel confident in telling us if and when they had connected with God and when they had failed. The failures gave us more confidence in the positive reports. Most succeeded.

Our Study

At first, brains in the functional MRI (fMRI) look a lot like soup—ours was yellow when we first ran the data. Not even minestrone, where you can differentiate the noodles and the vegetables, but soup after the stick blender has all but destroyed distinctions between elements. My mom makes a mushroom soup that looks just like a single person's fMRI. Everything's mixed together, soft-edged, the colors washing together. It is absolutely delicious. But not especially informative.

The fMRI is supposed to measure the blood flow in a brain—when you have a thought, you use up sugars, and the blood flows to those areas to replenish and heal them. But this is wildly hard to follow. Blood flows slowly in the brain, like any liquid, and brain scans capture where it's going four to twelve seconds after the brain does its work there. So, real-time fMRI looks like a sea of blood flowing about. Very unclear. Sometimes beautiful. The brain scan pictures you see in glossy magazines? With all those pretty colors? They're averages, usually built from hundreds of scans. I remember that Michael Lifshitz told me that a good rule of thumb for our kind of study is to aim for at least 100 moments of comparison between two very closely related brain activities. Funny thing is, I learned this, repeated it, took it as truth. When Michael read this chapter he had no memory of the conversation, or of the rule. He explained that it really depends on the length of the trial and the effect size. So I may have made it up. But, it is a good way to understand the idea that it takes lots of trials to figure this stuff out. With that reiteration of the comparison, we might get to what statisticians call significance—95 percent odds of being more than a chance occurrence.

So, we set up three experimental conditions to explore the neural core of tongues. From interviews, we guessed tongues involved at least speech and then also social interaction, improvisation, and letting go of control. Uffe Schjoedt, a neuroscientist from Denmark, had shown that prayer activates brain regions involved in social cognition, like talking to a friend. His work compared prayer to God to talking to Santa Claus—two conversations with invisible figures, but one believed to be real, the other fantasy. Compared with the pretend engagement with Santa Claus, in prayer, regions involved in real social interaction—the medial prefrontal cortex, the temporo-parietal junction—lit up.[41]

Then there's improvisation. Tongues seems free, a bit like jazz, maybe a kind of sacred improvisation. This comparison between jazz and speaking in tongues also points to their shared roots in Black spiritual traditions. Charles Limb, another neuroscientist, had found that jazz improvisers enter a specific brain state when playing: some parts of the frontal lobe activate, others quiet down.[42]

It's control within freedom, maybe the mind half-watching itself as it makes something new. The way the brain balances freedom with structure was a likely predictor for the flow of tongues, we thought. And finally, what we figured would be the deepest change: the release of control, where we expected to changes in the SMA and maybe especially the pre-SMA—remember Libet's area?

So, our study compared three forms of prayer to see what fell away when tongues fully let go. We had people recite the Lord's Prayer, a structured, familiar prayer—here we would expect speech and social cognition, but no improvisation. Then we had them try improvised prayer, still in control of their words but looser, inventing as they went. And last, tongues prayer, where they would more fully let go of control. By comparing these, we hoped to see the neural signatures of release.

We put that hypothesis down in a formal document called the preregistration. It's meant to keep us honest and cut out bias. A preregistration sets down the goals, the methods, the whole plan in a timestamped record, and it makes it hard to change course after the fact. Once you see the data, it's easy to start bending the hypothesis, shifting things to fit what you've found—what they call "HARKing" from Hypothesis After the Results are Known. But not with the preregistration in place.

In the lab, our participants whispered each prayer to keep their heads as still as possible, first the Lord's Prayer in one-minute blocks, then two minutes each of tongues or improvised prayer, order reversed for half the people. All along, we worried they might not be in a true prayer state—maybe the atmosphere was all wrong, or it was just a bad day to pray. So, we ran what we called "experience checks." After each block, we'd ask, "From 1 to 10, how much did you feel God's presence?" In theory, it would tell us if they could still feel God, even inside the MRI. We figured this whispered prayer might weaken the connection to God and make it hard to find what we were looking for. But somehow, they felt Him. We trusted this because, like Anslem in my opening story, they didn't hesitate to tell us when it didn't work. No shyness about it— they'd say outright if they felt nothing. That honesty gave us confidence that the moments of connection we captured were the real thing.

Because we were studying control in the brain, we also asked, "From 1 to 10, to what degree were you in control, and to what degree was God in control?" There were a lot of opinions about how this should work. One woman kept saying 50/50, no matter the block. "It's a partnership," she said. "We share control." Another explained that "It's not pagan. I'm never fully out of control." Another told us:

> you're always in control of what you do. You can stop at any time. You never lose control. But He definitely meets you. And I would say you're not in control of whether He meets you or not. That's all on Him. But you don't lose control. It's not like a mystical thing, like a horoscope or a tarot card reading or anything like that.

It seemed possible that the data could be more about people's preexisting expectations than experience.

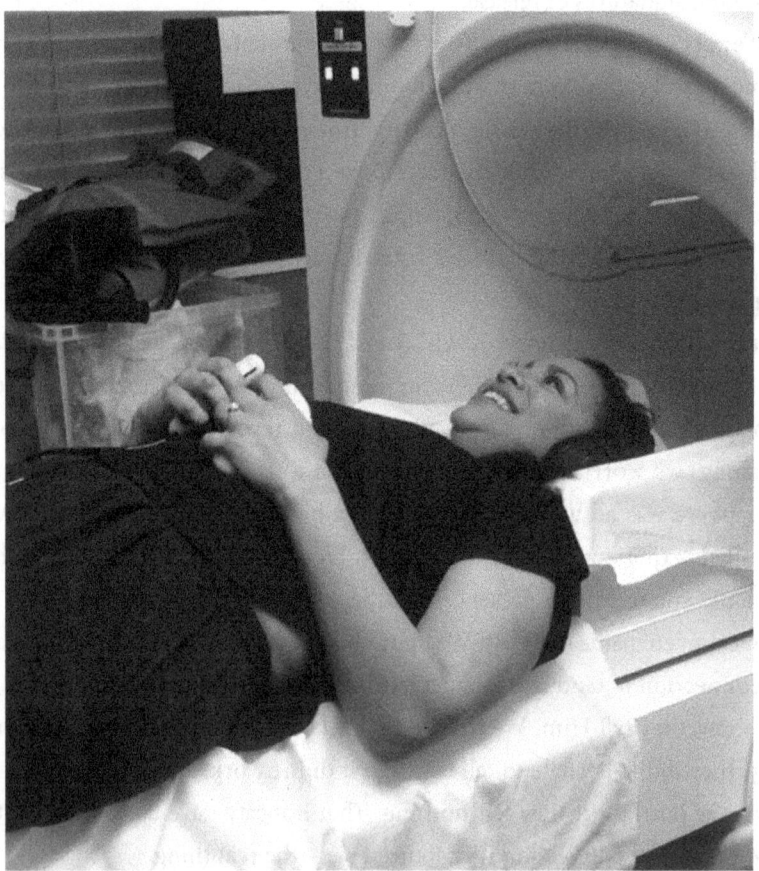

Figure 5.1 *Shavon in the MRI at Stanford's Center for Neurobiological Imaging.*

Even so, the self-report data came out just as we'd expected. In tongues prayer, people reported feeling less in control and more presence of God than in either the Lord's Prayer or improvised prayer.

And the brain? It's hard to put into words what it feels like to pull something meaningful from such a mess of data. We'd been at it for years. Sixteen years interviewing charismatics, and because of Covid, five years on this MRI study. Our brilliant graduate student and friend Jonas Mago had gone over the data again and again, recleaning it, writing code in Python and other languages to double- and triple-check the findings. Only about 60 percent of the scans were usable, the others were ruined by overzealous motion. We ran a few analyses, comparing each condition (tongues prayer, praise prayer and Lord's prayer) by looking at the whole brain, and then also using a special kind of analysis, called a region of interest (ROI), focusing in on the SMA, like holding a magnifying glass to one part of the brain. Neuroscientists only do this if they have a well-established hypothesis, as we did.

Then the images came up. And sure, they are usually wrong the first time, some glitch or fluke. So, I was ready for the drop. But I couldn't help but feel a bit thrilled. And this time, they stuck. When people speak in tongues large areas of the brain shift, it is a complicated behavior. But, although it was not alone, we could see that the pre-SMA was especially deactivated, with a p-value under .05. That's 95 percent odds that this was more than luck.

In addition to the pre-SMA, in the back of the brain above and behind each ear we saw what neuroscientists call "blobs"—yes, that's the term many use, although you could say "clusters". Those blobs showed deactivation during tongues prayer compared with the lord's prayer and were especially visible at precisely the junction between the temporal and the parietal lobes. This region, the temporo-parietal junction, involves two distinct areas—left and right—that sit at a crossroads in the brain, linking multiple sensory cortices, and are known to activate during social engagement—perhaps making them ideal sites for the sensory experience of a social interaction with a seemingly sentient God. Between the start of our study and the eventual data analysis—delayed several years by COVID—new meta-analyses had identified the temporo-parietal junction as involved in the sense of agency.[43] In our study, this area was even more strongly deactivated during tongues than the pre-SMA. The blobs were adjacent to the Temporal Lobe and overlapped it some. This suggested to us that that Penfield, Jackson, and even Persinger may have glimpsed a truth, and by shifting the focus from the seeming mystical aspects of experience to what we thought was the underlying mechanism—the act of letting go—we were, in effect, recalibrating and reawakening the story of the temporal lobe as religiously entrained. This meant that in the end, we had found evidence of deactivation in not just one, but three hubs positioned where we might expect the neural convergence for something like the feeling of submission to God. By the time you re reading this book, the neuroscience article is likely to be available online and you can look up the details if you want more.

Before we celebrate this as firm evidence of a brain-experience linkage, it's worth pausing to remember—as Cliff Saron would remind us—that neuroscience is to some important degree an art. So this is an inkling, an idea, a possibility. Not a truth. But also, so much fun.

The takeaway? Maybe people weren't just saying it. When they spoke in tongues, they were really letting go. Just like they said they were.

I liked that idea. And I am telling you that I liked it in part because unlike neuroscientists, we anthropologists get to, and are even asked to, share our feelings. It is more trustable, we think, to make transparent what is always there anyways.

Conclusion

When I talk or write about this research, something strange happens. The MRI takes over. Eighteen years of fieldwork, the hours spent in churches, the scores of four- to seven-hour-long interviews—they all start to fade. Because what could be more captivating than a look behind the curtain, a glimpse into the hidden world of the brain? And how cool that the MRI data aligns with the charismatic emphasis on the body. It's no surprise that the MRI, with all its rational sheen, holds a stronger pull for most any crowd. However much I like my storytelling, that much is obvious.

But I was surprised by the sense of mystery the MRI brings—almost a spiritual quality. The data showing motor deactivation hints that the body is central, that it's the axis everything turns on, yet it remains just that—an inkling. A small dot, literally. And it turns out that brain data is so ephemeral, so uncertain. Which is, in some ways, a perfect representation. The layers of bodily experience, of release, of the way it all plays out in charismatic life, are so much bigger and wilder than anything we'll find in brain data. In this way, the MRI as a mystery parallels the undeniable truth that prayer and release are impossible to fully understand—my charismatic friends are indeed correct.

Even with an MRI, we can only touch on the body and its capacity for release, never fully revealing its many layers. But maybe that's enough. Perhaps we don't need more clarity or hard data to be intrigued? Maybe the unsolved puzzles of release—how it takes hold of the body, what it ties to in the real world, how charismatics handle its mystery—can continue to drive this book forward.

So, let's come back to this question of letting go.

A True Story

We all know the fluid feeling generated by good music. Something permeates the body, loosening and juicing fibers. Perhaps the volume shakes our bones, instigates a nervous system shift, a mode of sensual pleasure. Or maybe the crowd inspires collective effervescence, togetherness, a single trajectory among many bodies.

On this day, we've been in the chapel for several hours—it is Spiritual Emphasis Week at Bethany University, in Scotts Valley, California, with classes cancelled to make room for collective devotion. The band plays for a good forty minutes; a few hundred students stand and sing, swaying in place, many arms outstretched in signature charismatic worship. Preaching soon adds a second layer to the music: words insistent and passionate, staccato and pointed, contrast sharply with the continued roll of a highly flanged electric guitar.

At first, the message surprises me with its relevance. The previous evening, a friend asked about my spending all this time among charismatics without feeling the tug of faith, thinking I was bound to convert—she was a bit concerned. And when the preacher begins, "What you behold, you will become," I am struck and a mite anxious. I am in a crowd of converts, a few hundred people so devoted to Jesus they spend their days in an all-Christian college and participate in daily repetitions of ritualized devotion and commitment.

The message—where your attention goes, so does your self—seems especially primed for an outside observer like myself.

I soon realize, however, that the message is aimed not at me but at the insecurity of every person around me—in response to the deep-seated sense that God's reality is being questioned every day outside these walls, the preacher is offering a story of confidence and stability. All these folks are already safely beholding and thus becoming Christian. The preacher is actually pointing outside, telling his flock to be less attentive to pop culture and its temptations: sex, drugs, partying, and again, especially sex. It sounds like a typical fundamentalist narrative. Yet in the two years that I intermittently attended services, there had been little mention of discipline, hell, or sex. I did recently hear that Reverend Shelton is on a campaign to quell partying. I guess this is the first step. Instead of release, yearning, and passion—all so well manifested in the lyrics posted on the screen—this service joins intimate ecstatic devotion to its counterpart in ascetic discipline and biblical single-mindedness.

I am not buying the message, so what happens next is certainly not intellectual acceptance. The pastor calls for community participation. All eyes close. He asks us to seek ourselves in his story of desperation. Heads bow; many touch and comfort neighbors. One student puts his hand on my shoulder. I do not reciprocate. He retreats.

In the next moment, when the lights dim further and singing resumes, I feel a burning in my thighs down by my knees. A flamethrower has been aimed at my legs, and a fiery heat rises through to my hips, belly, chest—I am drenched in an all-out sweat. This is not familiar. Years of epileptic paresthesia have prepped me for strange sensations, and in fact make them suspect, but this heat is new, not erotic or athletic in any usual sense I am familiar with. It feels both separate and within. I can understand how it would seem an outside force.

Our brain scans show that charismatics can learn neurological patterns, and I wonder if I am learning. The truth is I hadn't done so much to earn my way into the charismatic culture of sensation—their sensorium. Yes, I had been sitting in on services, but I didn't raise my hands to ask for speaking in tongues, or pursue any of the other routes to physical conviction. I just stood there, maybe rocked back and forth in time to the music—for years. I didn't even sing, although that has changed. On the one hand, I was psyched to feel the burn—what incredible research data! But on the other hand, and more intensely, I simply wanted it to go away—a wish made more poignant by my ever-present fear that I might be on the verge of an epileptic seizure. Yet, even my cynical body somehow responded to the call to let go and feel the heat.

6

Prayer Loosens the Tongue and the Heart, Does It Also Loosen the Mind?

Watching charismatic worship, you can't miss the sheer physicality of the experience, a deeply visceral letting go. Charismatics describe it as a release: emotions cascading out, bodies yielding to a flow that seems less driven by intention than by surrender. From the outside, you see it in the way people stand, in their gestures, in how they let their voices carry. Sometimes in how they fall to the ground. There is a profound submission, a loosening of the usual grip of self-control. And our brain data seems to agree: what we are seeing is more than a rehearsed performance or a conscious effort; it is real physiological release.

Yet a question lingered in my mind: does this release go beyond the body and the outpouring of emotions? Is there, I wondered, something in the thinking parts of the mind that lets go too, similar to the way thought patterns unravel in meditation or psychedelics? They talk about feeling renewed, as if their mind is refreshed by prayer. Could this cognitive release be one key to enabling charismatics to feel God's touch or hear his voice, an openness that allows them to meet something greater, to pull the divine in close?

Driven by these questions, and with a touch of luck, we took our lessons from the MRI into our next study. The precision of the MRI protocol had pushed us to notice things we hadn't seen before. Speaking in tongues, it seemed, held another quieter shift. Shavon called it a drop-in. This suggested an even deeper submission—perhaps a way of loosening thought itself, a door opened just a crack, enough to let new ways of seeing and feeling slip in. It was territory we'd been curious about. In the end, drop-ins turned out to be crucial. But, at first, we simply wondered if we could show that bodily and emotional release combined to release the mind as well.

Awe

The letting go people feel during tongues prayer often comes with a rush of emotion—awe, wonder, love, and peace, they say. Dacher Keltner, a psychologist at UC Berkeley, understands this kind of emotion in a very hands-on kind of way. First, he's one of the warmest people I've met, and even on Zoom, during those first pandemic years, that warmth came through. When I finally joined his lab, spending two years there to develop our second study on tongues prayer, I saw it firsthand. There was a genuine kindness in that lab, an excitement, a sense of joy in the work they did. It wasn't all soft edges and easy smiles, though; they were doing real science, precisely measuring emotions and digging into the way our minds open up.

But in Dacher's lab, science and kindness had a way of blending, each one strengthening the other. I loved that they combined emotions research with studies about the influence of wealth and power on people—they are famous for the study showing that more expensive cars are especially likely to run you over when you are crossing the street.[1]

Dacher sees emotions as more than poetic notions. He believes they're distinct measurable states that change us, our body and mind. Awe, for instance, comes with a sense of vastness, a feeling that you're part of something much bigger, he says. A mountain range that stretches beyond sight, a sky brimming with stars, a piece of art that grips you—all these things can make you feel small in comparison.

To explore the effects of awe, Dacher and his team led a group of fifty-two at-risk youths and seventy-two military veterans into the wilderness where awe might come easily—on one-day or four-day whitewater rafting expeditions. Each evening, participants reflected on their thoughts, emotions, and experiences from the day. One week after the trip, folks reported a significant boost in well-being, with awe on the trip emerging as the strongest predictor of this positive shift.[2]

In a related study, researcher Michiel van Elk sought to capture the profound effects of nature's grandeur. He showed participants awe-inspiring videos of vast landscapes: towering mountains, expansive vistas, rolling oceans, graceful birds in flight, and cascading waterfalls. As participants entered states of awe, van Elk's team used fMRI scans to observe brain activity, seeking to uncover the neural imprints of standing in the presence of something larger than themselves.[3]

What they found was striking. In those moments of awe, the Default Mode Network (DMN)—the brain's seat of self-referential thoughts, the inner chatter that reminds us of our worries and goals—quieted down. For some neuroscientists, this suggested that the self itself had dialed down, loosening its usual grip. And it also turns out that the videos don't have to be beautiful. Terrifying images also inspire awe and similar brain patterns.[4] People who feel awe regularly, and are open-minded and wonder-filled in how they approach life, also showed deactivation in important parts of the DMN.[5]

Dacher wanted to know if this openness shaped social interactions. He also had participants watch awe-inspiring videos of grand natural phenomena. Images were chosen to shift a person's focus from themselves to the larger world. Afterward, participants were asked to do tasks to measure how they might act differently. In one task, they were given money to split with a stranger and had the choice to keep more or share evenly. In another, they had to work with a partner on puzzles, where cooperation would make the difference.

What they found was simple but telling. The ones who had felt more awe were more generous with their money, more patient with their partners, more likely to help the group as a whole. Participants said they felt open, in a way they didn't feel in the everyday rush of life. It reminded me of the way charismatics describe the experience of God. They felt "small" but in a way that made them feel more alive, part of something greater, as if the world outside had grown larger.[6] It was that last part that hooked me—a smaller self that didn't close in on itself, but opened up to the world outside, ready to explore, to learn, to see life with fresh eyes.

Dr. Keltner has now spent decades building measures of emotional states. He taught them to me. To track emotional response during prayer, we recorded video and audio of thirty-three pairs of people praying—in tongues, and also in English praising God. We wanted pairs to see if prayer changed us more when it was shared. It meant I spent hours studying the faces of people in prayer. It was strange. Sometimes haunting.

The emotions of prayer aren't simple. I watched people weep from joy. They were smiling in sadness—a complex cocktail of feelings that reminded me of grief, where intense emotions overlap to produce both sorrow and joy in tandem. Watching them sometimes made me cry, too. Some of the tongue prayers, with their rhythmic cadence, made me want to dance. We'd find ourselves swaying behind the EEG monitors.

But more than anything, the prayer was wildly beautiful. The interplay of emotions—the raw expressions of care, fear, and hope. They moved me. They

Figure 6.1 *Two Participants in the EEG Study Speaking in Tongues.*

shook me, in a way I can only attempt to describe. I wanted to show everyone I knew, to let them see what I saw. But I couldn't. Now I am telling you. It's the best I can do.

Neural Plasticity

As awe loosens the mind, it points toward a unique kind of changeability; in the experience of a small self and the quieting of the Default Mode Network, we might release the brain's hold on habitual, deeply ingrained patterns, what neuroscientists call "top-down priors." This idea is at the heart of today's research on neural plasticity. Certain experiences seem to make our brains especially pliable, less bound by previous frameworks. Psychedelics can do this, maybe through the feeling of awe itself, or maybe via another route. Even small doses can shift the senses, pushing auditory and tactile changes, influencing emotional[7] and social processing,[8] stirring the imagination,[9] and shifting one's sense of self.[10] Larger doses take it further, as time and the self-fade until they're hardly there at all. Especially since 2006, dozens of papers have mapped these inner landscapes.[11] And the key for me, stories of psychedelic experience mirror what practitioners of tongues prayer describe—a feeling of release, of being caught up in something that renews us.

In 2006, Roland Griffiths and his team at Johns Hopkins gave psilocybin, the drug in magic mushrooms, to folks who had never tried it. The results were staggering. For many, that single experience stirred an enduring sense of unity, sacredness, and awe. Nearly 70 percent said it was among the most meaningful events in their lives.[12] This was just a science experiment! Their vivid shift, perhaps a "born-again" moment, bears a curious resemblance to the transformations often reported in charismatic worship, where similar feelings of release and renewal unfold with each practice, each moment of surrender.

The terms researchers use to describe the central element of change they experienced—ego loss, ego-death, ego-dissolution, ego-disintegration—can be somewhat confusing.[13] Defining "ego" isn't easy, let alone its death. Is the ego our awareness of self, our tactile sense of our body, or maybe just our feeling of control over what we do and think? There are literally dozens of ways to see it. But for now, let's go with what many researchers use: the ego is that felt sense of being a single, separate person with boundaries.

To measure ego-dissolution, we can ask a series of questions. Do you "experience a dissolution of my self or ego" or "experience oneness with the universe." They ask about feeling unity with others, about reduced emphasis on the self. This merging with others, and with the world, has long been a mark of mystical experience. Keltner's study on awe found similar results. He called it a "small self"—skipping the word "ego."[14] But then I wonder again, what is this self, and how does it get so small?

Both psychedelic and awe researchers see ego-dissolution as loosening the brain, a kind of openness that can be tracked behaviorally through creative thinking tasks and in the brain through the degree of randomness or "disorder" in the neural system, which neuroscientist Robin Carhart-Harris measures as "entropy." More entropy means more unpredictability in the brain's circuits, and that freedom shows up as richer experience. Of course, full-on entropy means the brain cannot function—too much of a good thing?[15] But increased entropy, up to a point, correlates with creative thinking since the prior patterns of thought are loosened up. If speaking in tongues opens up experience in the same way psychedelics do, then we might see creativity there too, we thought. Goodman may have been right to think trance—tongues included—can open new doors of experience.

Speaking in tongues shares many of the characteristics of psychedelic experiences. At times, the body feels totally, or somewhat, out of control. Emotions like awe flood in, and the mind opens up, ideas and self-concepts shifting and evolving quickly. Peace often comes at the end. In interviews, I asked people if they thought they felt their ego dissolve in prayer. The answers were mixed. Some embraced it, others resisted and instead suggested a very particular balance between control and surrender. But when we systematically asked if they felt ego-dissolution right after they prayed, almost all sixty-six from the EEG study said yes.

I have to say, at first, I hesitated to compare tongues prayer with psychedelics. I felt on tenuous ground. Many Christians I met found the comparison a bit ugly. Psychedelics have been associated with hippies, drugs, sex, and rock and roll. They don't seem very Christian. Somehow we always forget the hippie Christians at times like these. But, for me, the paths to release seemed so different. Tongues prayer is an act of letting go. Psychedelics force that release through chemicals, or so I thought. Then, I found a reflection that said letting go is crucial to both. In an essay titled "Learning to Let Go: A Cognitive-Behavioral Model of How Psychedelic Therapy Promotes Acceptance," psychiatrist Max Wolff and colleagues argue that the freedom people feel on psychedelics doesn't come merely from the drug. Therapy shapes it. And then also, each person needs to actively *let go* to make it work.[16] It was fun to see this laid out in plain language. Release is key to the psychedelic process, just as with speaking in tongues. I came to think that a comparison with psychedelics might be useful in helping to model how speaking in tongues generates increased brain plasticity. I just needed to deal with my own and my informant's biases.

The Story of Predictive Processing: Or How Neuroscientists Think We Can Loosen Our Brains

I like to tell it like this: Once upon a time, in the world of cognitive science, a question emerged that would reshape everything scientists thought they knew about the brain. Does the mind sit back and take in the world, or does it guess, anticipate, even shape what it perceives? This is the story of predictive processing, and it leads us nicely into thinking about how we might loosen our minds.

The tale begins with Hermann von Helmholtz, a nineteenth-century German physicist and physiologist. Helmholtz was taken with how people sensed depth and motion, even when the signals were faint or misleading. He looked at how we fool the brain into "seeing" things that weren't there. Take a flat picture, for example. Shadows and lines trick the eye into believing it has depth, and the brain buys it because it expects depth. We foresee the depth we experience, he thought. Perception then seems more like solving a puzzle than looking through a window. You hear a rustling in the trees, and your mind says, "A bird," because that's what it's used to finding there. This idea—that the brain interprets rather than simply sees—was unusual at the time. Most people thought the brain worked like a camera, just taking in things as they were. It took years for Helmholtz's idea to stick.

In the 1960s, Horace Barlow, a British neuroscientist, added to Helmholtz's theory. Barlow studied how neurons respond to motion, especially in edge detection—the way we spot lines, shapes, and boundaries. Barlow found that our brains are good at cutting out what's less important—shadows, background noise—and locking onto what matters, like the outline of an object. He thought that the brain makes a guess about where the edges of an object are and keeps adjusting as it gets more visual data. That's why we can recognize things quickly, even in low light or blurry pictures.

Imagine looking out over a field of rustling leaves. Your brain doesn't notice every leaf. But a sudden movement, an animal darting out—now that is picked up. Barlow believed the brain expects leaves to sway in the wind (it has a "prior" that says this), so it ignores them, focusing instead on the things that break the pattern. This use of past information to understand new data laid the groundwork for contemporary neuroscientists like Karl Friston and Geoffrey Hinton to describe the brain as a "Bayesian machine"—from Thomas Bayes, an eighteenth-century statistician whose theorem gives us a way to update beliefs based on new evidence.[17] To Barlow, the brain does this updating of our prediction all the time—adjusting and shaping what we see in a dance of expectation and surprise.[18]

Neuroscientists David Hubel and Torsten Wiesel built from Barlow's findings in their work with anesthetized cats and monkeys, whose visual systems are like ours. They placed electrodes in different parts of the visual cortex and recorded how the animals responded to shapes and lines on a screen. They saw that some neurons, which they called simple cells, fired when a line was at a particular angle. A simple cell might respond strongly to a vertical line but not at all to a horizontal one. Deeper in the cortex, they found complex cells. These responded to lines moving across a wider area, not fixed to one spot. Some cells even responded only when lines moved in a certain direction. Hubel and Wiesel guessed that complex cells gathered input from simple cells, letting them respond to patterns over larger parts of the field. They called it a hierarchy.[19] The concept of hierarchical processing raised a critical question: what distinguishes different levels of the hierarchy? This line of inquiry eventually opened the door to a new idea—that higher levels of the brain actively predict the sensory inputs processed by lower levels. By anticipating incoming information, the brain can streamline perception, making future processing more efficient and adaptive. But this same mechanism can also backfire—creating entrenched patterns that limit flexibility and distort new experience. That is where momentary disorganization might be helpful.

On a bit of a tangent: I have to say, as a social scientist, the idea of the brain organized into a hierarchy makes me uneasy. It feels like layering social metaphors onto biology, and I don't trust it. I am drawn instead to the metaphors in the work of Olaf Sporns, a neuroscientist mapping the connectome—the brain's complete network of connections. Sporns and his team describe the brain somewhat differently, less like a hierarchical ladder, but organized into modules instead, clusters of densely interconnected regions and hubs. Each module can handle its own job, like sight or movement. In Sporns's model, visual processing doesn't move in one direction. The lateral geniculate nucleus (LGN) in the thalamus, for example, connects to both higher and lower visual areas, creating a feedback loop that sharpens basic sensory processing. This loop helps the brain recognize objects more quickly, even as things change. The cerebellum and basal ganglia also work as hubs, adjusting movements based on what's happening in real time. Movement planning isn't just top-down; it's also a flexible, adapting system, he suggests.[20] I find that model more appealing, but it's not really up to me.

Either way, both hierarchical and network models do well with the idea that the brain works through predictions: Neuroscientists Rajesh P. N. Rao and Dana H. Ballard took predictive processing a step further. They suggested that higher-level brain regions—those involved in interpreting objects, for example—send predictions about expected features down to the primary visual cortex (V1), the part of the brain that processes basic visual details like edges and contrasts. Imagine you're looking at a familiar object, like a coffee cup. Higher brain regions, drawing on your experience with coffee cups, anticipate specific features—a handle, rounded edges, a certain shape. These predictions are sent to V1, which detects the actual lines and edges. As you look at the cup, V1 processes the sensory data, comparing it to the prediction. If there's a match, perception flows smoothly; the brain's guess was right. But if there's a difference—maybe the cup is broken or partly hidden—a prediction error brings information back to higher levels of the brain, adjusting the model and refining what you see.[21]

Rao and Ballard's model lets the brain work through complex sensory worlds without getting lost in every detail. It focuses on what's new, letting the familiar slip by. In this loop of prediction and error, the brain doesn't just take in information; it shapes what it sees, updating with each new bit of evidence. This is how it saves energy and keeps attention on what counts.

The model also paints a picture of abstract thinking at the "top" and sensory experience at the "bottom." And again, they inadvertently echo the old hierarchies where those "fit" for planning were put above others set to physical work. But despite this, Rao and Ballard's work gives us something crucial about how the brain really works.

Neuroscientist Karl Friston added energy conservation to the story of predictive processing. He argued that by minimizing surprises, the brain keeps perception efficient, allowing only unpredicted information to move through its channels. According to Friston, the brain's primary role is to minimize "free energy"—a term borrowed from thermodynamics that represents surprise or uncertainty. Friston said the brain constantly predicts and corrects so as to reduce this free energy, keeping us stable and aligned with the world around us.[22] Others took this idea further. To neuroscientist Andy Clark, the brain is like a surfer, always riding the waves of sensory input, adjusting to keep its predictions close to reality.[23]

Some skeptics called this whole thread of thought reductionist and solipsistic; some thought the theories were too neat. Perhaps they leave out the brain's creativity and intuition, turning rich experience into nothing but "errors." For these critics, predictive processing missed the depth of human perception and all that gives it life. And for others, the predictions mean that we are basically in a dialogue with ourselves, not the world.

But I do find predictive processing an appealing story of the brain as an active, anticipatory organ, making its own sense of the world instead of simply taking it in. Here, perception is a process of constant estimation, relying on priors—our memories, patterns, all that we've learned. Perhaps predictive processing could model how we think, feel, and even create.

For our research, if we could show that entrenched brain patterns—these priors—were loosened or released, we might find a neurobiological explanation for the experience of letting go, for the profound sense of renewal, and even the intense journey that leads us there. Yet, we quickly found that we were not quite ready for this question. To truly understand plasticity in charismatic prayer, we first needed a finer understanding of just exactly what is this thing called speaking in tongues.

Planning the MRI: What Is a Drop-In?

Preparing for the MRI taught us something about speaking in tongues we hadn't expected. After years of interviews and firsthand accounts, we were steeped in the charismatic world, deeply familiar with the stories, practices, and language. But when we met with Shavon to set up the MRI protocol, the central question, besides feasibility, was whether what we called speaking in tongues was one thing or many—was our object of study defined well enough to study with MRI technology? Now this may seem minor, or silly. Of course it is one thing. But then, of course it also is many things. I studied philosophy. I learned that everything can be divided or unified in our minds. I am Josh. I am also sad Josh. Happy Josh. I am also the millions of bacteria in my gut. I am one, and I am many. I could go on. But just know that the data from MRIs are so messy that good studies need to find relatively tightly bound categories to study, or else we end up with mush. So, we probed to see just what was in this category called speaking in tongues.

Shavon first explained that speaking in tongues felt entirely different from speaking normally. "When I'm speaking in tongues I'm not thinking about what I'm saying at all. It's very spontaneous. When I'm speaking in English, I am trying to make sure I pull all my words together, that I am articulating my thoughts correctly to you. In tongues, I don't care." But it's purposeful, too.

I feel like speaking in tongues is allowing me to be in the presence of God and to make myself mindful of what he wants, not what I want. I'm praying for something I don't even know what to pray, but God then is praying through me, and something spiritually is happening around me, and something is clearing. You're speaking in tongues; you don't know what the heck you're saying. I just can feel something different.

Also, there was the "warming up," a concept we'd seen before in Goodman's work. Worship often began with long, song-filled sessions, slowly shifting into new perceptions and trance.[24] So folks might need to warm up before they get in the MRI.

We thought that was complex enough, but Shavon went on to describe a form of tongues that we hadn't previously encountered, something closer to everyday speech. "I start speaking in tongues because I need to know what to pray for." In other words, when she feels at a loss for words, she speaks in tongues. Here, Shavon presented a vision far more in line with Samarin than Goodman, where tongues seemed less a trance and more a tool—a way to bridge her own uncertainty, almost like a placeholder. A way to start.

Shavon also described moments when she seemed to shift her state of mind entirely, flipping from this more routine form of tongues, practiced and familiar, into something almost out of control, and full of heat and sensation. She called this "dropping in." This was a new concept. The idea that there were at least two versions of tongues prayer and that they often came in sequence with a rapid shift between them was unlike what we had previously heard from informants, and we had not yet come across it in the scholarly literature.

We then asked a dozen probing questions to distinguish between these two kinds of tongues. Shavon explained "dropping in" more fully:

> I am praying in tongues. And all of a sudden, it could be within two seconds, it could be within two minutes, I feel a shift. Sometimes it could be literally like today, when I was praying and I felt peace. Previously, everything felt chaotic, but just now, at that moment, everything ceases to pull, and there's just a sense of clarity.

We asked what she meant by "ceasing to pull."

> When I say pull, for me, I'm busy, I oversee three offices for a finance company and I oversee a team of seven people. I've also had the responsibility of

ministry at church and I'm a mom and a wife. And I am the sole financial provider for our family. So there's a lot of things pulling at me. But when I drop in, everything stops. All of a sudden there's a ceasing of that.

She described releasing attachment to everyday worries and desires. In the quiet that follows, she could listen. "Everything stops, and all of a sudden I'm waiting for God to speak. He's either about to say something or he's empowering me to do something else." Sometimes dropping in involves sensations as well. "Today, I felt my body start to shake and I welcomed that. The shaking was losing control. If I was standing up, I would have fallen down." She saw this as a deepened connection with the Holy Spirit. "Dropping in," as she called it, captured her experience of "letting go." It often came with a response from God, felt as a physical or sensory shift.

It struck us that a session of tongues might include multiple layers of depth—and this would make it very difficult to know what we were looking at in an MRI. In church services, we had noticed that tongues prayer seemed to shift over time, both in the congregation and in individuals. Jonathan, another MRI participant, described multiple ways tongues prayer was used. When we read the literature again, we found some scholars had noted this diversity—tongues prayer with more trance, or less.[25] In 2003, historian Grant Wacker suggested that charismatics could control the entry, depth, and exit of trance during tongues speech, using it as a ritual that sometimes led into trance.[26] Yet, when Newberg and his team did brain scans of tongues speakers, they had described only one state during tongues prayer, seemingly a trance state.[27]

Our initial study design had us comparing speaking in tongues to regular improvisational prayer and the structured recitation of the Lord's Prayer, looking at three prayer styles with different levels of control. But Shavon's description of drop-ins raised red flags. MRI studies need a clear contrast between specific states. If tongues included multiple states—dropped and undropped—could we tell them apart in the MRI? We changed our approach. Along with comparing types of prayer, we decided to also look closely at the moment of letting go, where practice meets surrender. We'd follow Newberg's study but focus on how participants felt their control shift.

As we pushed participants to describe these experiences, we saw that dropping in during tongues often had three elements, though not always together: (1) a shift in control, (2) an experience of God's presence, and (3) a sense of receiving something from God. We included self-reports for control, presence, and response, right after each scan. We added a component where participants would press a button when they felt a drop-in and again when it faded. Afterward, they described each drop-in, rating their sense of control, God's presence, and any response they felt.

All twenty-seven MRI participants, and the sixty-six who later joined the follow-up EEG study, confirmed their own experience of "dropping in." Though many hadn't heard the term, they knew the feeling. When asked if they ever felt a shift during prayer, a drop of control or effort, they all agreed. Some saw it as the natural ebb and flow of prayer. Laura shared an experience like Shavon's. "I think it's a release," she said. "It's letting go of control. At those moments, I'm not deciding things like I normally would." She went on, "It's letting go of fear, pressure, whatever's holding me back, and just trusting the best thing will happen. I'm not in the driver's seat. I'm in the passenger seat—or maybe even in the back." We began to suspect that "drop-ins" might be useful in our search for brain plasticity related to release of control—and they were, though not exactly in the way we'd expected.

Divergent Thinking: Study #2

After gathering our MRI data, we knew that tongues prayer brought about a shift in the mind related to agency release. It wasn't necessarily faked or performed. But what sort of change were we really seeing? Hours of interviews told us that people felt renewed, opened, and humbled. It sounded like the awe Dacher Keltner studied or the psychedelic effects Roland Griffiths described. So, we decided to look at the plasticity of brain and behavior to see if tongues prayer could actually affect them.

The design was quite simple, built closely on our MRI study. Participants switched between English prayer and tongues, each for eight minutes. Afterward, they filled out surveys including experience checks and emotional reports. They did this twice, English and tongues. Before, in between, and after, they completed a divergent thinking task. This measures creativity. We hoped to compare the changes in creativity wrought by tongues prayer to the changes from praise prayer.

Psychologist J. P. Guilford described divergent thinking as the key to creativity.[28] It was in contrast to convergent thinking, which aims for one correct answer. Guilford's studies asked people to come up with as many uses as possible for something common—a brick or a paperclip. He measured how many ideas they generated quickly, how varied they were, and how original. This kind of test seemed like an ideal way to understand if prayer loosened practical elements of the mind's functioning. But these tasks were time-consuming, often scored by hand, and open to bias. We had only a few minutes between prayer blocks and couldn't risk breaking the flow of prayer.

Luckily, Michael Lifshitz had been in school with Dr. Jay Olson who had developed a quicker way to measure divergent thinking. We met with Olson and learned to use the Divergent Association Task (DAT).[29] Simple enough: participants list ten nouns as different as possible. They might start with "house," then move to "fish," each word as distinct from the last as possible. It was quick and simple, and it turned out that the results correlate very closely with the more cumbersome divergent thinking tasks we were planning on using.

The DAT uses a big database that assigns "semantic distance" between words. Semantic distance describes how unrelated two words are. Greater distances mean a wider search for ideas and less leaning on what's familiar—a sign of creative thinking. "Cat" and "dog" are close in meaning; "cat" and "ocean" are worlds apart. Words like "sun" and "moon" or "river" and "ocean" are closer. "Computer" and "mountain" or "love" and "hammer" are much farther. Words with similar meanings are located closer together, while words with different meanings are farther apart.

With the DAT, we could quantify the diversity of participants' thought patterns before and after tongues prayer, using a swift, reliable method that wouldn't interfere with their prayer experience. It was a tool that might allow us to map how tongues impacted the mind's ability to reach beyond the familiar. Our DAT data showed the average distance between the words a person lists following each prayer type. A higher score meant the person came up with words that were more varied.

We expected people to show higher scores in divergent thinking after tongues prayer than after praise prayer. This would confirm that the altered state of tongues prayer included a cognitive release alongside the physical and emotional effects we had already seen.

But when we analyzed data from sixty-six participants, there was no difference in divergent thinking between praise and tongues prayer. It looked like the study had missed something, maybe something big. I was close to deciding that we were simply wrong. There is no connection between physical, emotional, and cognitive release, or at least not in our data.

Then our participants surprised us. When we looked at their self-report forms, many people had reported drop-ins during praise prayer, something we hadn't expected. It looked like a fluke. You see, we had thought drop-ins were part of tongues prayer—a peak moment when participants surrendered fully to God. We didn't think it would also happen during the praise prayer that was already more structured simply because they were speaking English. But when we created the self-report sheets, we accidentally left a space for drop-ins on every sheet. We didn't remove it from the praise prayer sheets, thinking it wouldn't be relevant. It was a simple mistake and it shouldn't affect the data we were interested in.

When the data showed no difference between tongues and praise prayer in overall divergent thinking, it looked like we'd come up empty—which is quite common in science, but still disappointing. But now that we found the drop in data across all prayer types, we had another shot. So, we compared all prayer blocks, both praise and tongues, by the duration of drop-in reported. Participants had marked the start and end of each drop-in on their forms, so we could calculate the percentage of each block spent in drop-in. The results were a bit stunning in their simplicity: the more time spent in drop-in, the more that divergent thinking increased from before to after the block.

In other words, mental flexibility wasn't tied to tongues or praise prayer; it was simply shaped by the depth of surrender—how much a participant felt released into God's presence, regardless of prayer type.

So, we were wrong, and also partly right. Tongues prayer alone was not the main determining factor. Instead, the feeling of letting go during prayer was very likely linked with letting go in the mind. People in prayer were having experiences like those who feel awe or take psychedelics, where their usual thought patterns (the "priors") were loosening to allow a freer flow of ideas. The more they surrendered to God, the more their thinking opened up. This was in some ways to be expected, but in others—it was pretty far out. We had shown that emotional release, bodily release, and now also cognitive release were all a part of charismatic worship.

7

Certainty: Ontological Anxiety and the Body

Now we know—release is learned, it has real effects, is tied to attention and arousal, and, as it turns out, is reflected deep in the brain. Letting go is real, says the MRI. It has real effects on creativity, says the DAT. Right? Enough. The quest is over. Time to end the book, time to rest.

But, it turns out that it isn't that simple.

I began this project by looking at the outward signs of charismatic worship, tracing them from what we see and hear through the felt experience to their roots inside the body. We went in deeper and deeper until we got to the brain itself. And even though the brain pictures are, at best, educated guesses, they are informative, and they are pretty. But now, I need to loop back outward. An experience so potent ought to be visible in the social world around it. The world makes the experience, but does the experience make the world?

It turns out that tracing the effects of letting go can take us far beyond the brain. These sensory experiences, shaped by language and practice, do seem to echo out into the world. What's inside pushes out—bodily release might drive anxiety, also confidence, a sense of agency, and the possibility of changing the world. To trace this effect, these next chapters focus on core questions that anthropologists muddle through: first, ontology—what is real to people, and how does that sense of reality shape their experience? Then, agency—how do groups experience the feeling that they can affect the world around them? And finally, power—how does this inspire action? I like to think of it as a complex dance between brain, practice, and community.

The ambivalent role of the body in charismatic life is a central part of the story. Charismatic practice is focused on the body, yet Christians often talk about spirit and flesh as if they're at odds. This often confused me. How do these two opposing forces—the celebration of the body, and its seeming denigration—sit side by side? The phrase "body logics" became my shorthand for understanding this tension. Charismatics may say the flesh is "of the devil," but at other times, they nurture bodily experiences and see them as signs of God's presence. These sensations, this physical evidence, help them face a skeptical world. The body becomes one of several internal tools, measuring the reality and truth of their faith.

Bodily sensations are hard to ignore. They're immediate, undeniable, and they fit into a charismatic schema for understanding the relationship between mind and body, what anthropologists call a local theory of mind.[1] In the West, we often separate the two—mind and body are seen as distinct. But charismatics need the mind to be porous, open to the divine. It's easier for them to believe in the supernatural when they feel it in their bodies. Intense physical experiences help break through the Western barrier between mind and world. This means they think about how to break that barrier.

When anthropologists talk about a "local theory of mind," it is because we know that across the globe, people imagine the mind—the locus of thoughts, feelings, intentions, beliefs, desires, and other mental "stuff"—in ways that are culturally particular.[2] This means also that cultures differ in the ways we envision relationships between our minds and the rest of the world, including our bodies. After all, models of minds are tied to models of selves, spirits, and bodies.

Philosopher Charles Taylor (among others) says that in North America, or even in the West more broadly, the mind is seen as fully bounded, matching the self. Taylor describes a sharp boundary between self and other, individual and society, subject and world, mind and body. For charismatics, God is on the other side of that line. To experience Him, the line must be crossed. The charismatic evangelicals I came to know shared a rough version of Taylor's separation between mind and body—but they see the mind as porous in specific ways—open to God, the Holy Spirit, and, sometimes, demons. When asked directly about the possibility that our thoughts could travel out from our minds, they responded that this was absurd: everyone (within this secularish model of the mind) knows it is impossible. But they do pray for the Holy Spirit to enter their innermost selves.

Worship is, in many ways, about making space for God. Pastor Beiser would call out, "Go for it! Let God in!" But there was also always the fear of letting something else in, something dangerous, like a demon or angry thoughts. The mind may be open, but maybe only at certain times—during church, in prayer, or in specific, intense moments of life. Most of the time, charismatics live within the everyday assumptions of scientific causation. Because of this, they constantly worry about whether their experiences with God are real. Many felt doubt, though some were hesitant to admit it in our interviews. Some saw doubt as betrayal, but others saw it as a healthy response to the world they lived in.

There's a line from the Disney movie *Mulan* where the father says there is no courage without fear. Perhaps similarly, I suspect that there may be no faith without doubt. In the United States, 80 percent of adults say they believe in God, 28 percent say that they talk to God—and God talks back.[3] At Glad Tidings, and other charismatic churches, many feel God communicating with them daily. Yet, doubt is common. The stories I heard of encounters with God were filled with caveats about how "strange" and "crazy" the encounter was. The storytellers worried quite publicly about how to hold onto faith and skepticism at the same time. Narrative details seemed intended to show that there were no plausible explanations other than the reality of the supernatural. In addition, these stories were often presented as believable because of hard-to-deny physical experiences that forced practitioners to set aside their doubts. Because of this understandable reaction to secularism, I started to think of charismatic evangelicals as "anxiously supernatural." They live in a world where supernatural and secular forces collide, unlike in Europe, where secularism is more straightforward, or in Ghana, one country where our research showed that the felt realities of the spirit are well established. Charismatics in the United States respond by expressing doubt.

Perhaps ironically, their strong commitment to the divide between an ephemeral inside and a concrete outside seems to mean that for charismatic evangelicals, the outside—the body—comes to play an especially important role. While some evangelicals argue that evangelical bodily practices provide a holistic approach to mind, body, and spirit,[4] I found that the mind-body split still matters in their practice. Anselm, one of the charismatics in the MRI, said, "I know God through my senses." His words echoed a broader charismatic idea—that the physical and spiritual experience of tongues prayer is "evidence of the spirit." The people I talked to spoke often of their bodies—what they felt, how they reacted. If they felt something in their bodies, they were more likely to describe the spiritual experience as real.

This chapter focuses on how US charismatics cross the barrier between their minds and the supernatural—through emotion, speech, bodily sensations—all strategies for breakthrough. I explore how charismatics wrestle with the line between the real and the unreal, between nature and supernature—as they are especially ontologically anxious (concerned to clarify the fundamental nature of existence, i.e., is God real). They are deeply concerned with what is real, and with discerning God's presence. Throughout, I switch between interviews with charismatics at Glad Tidings and at a small charismatic church in a tiny Central Valley town of Madera, California. This chapter is also one of the few places in the book where you'll see mention of the comparative work our research team at Stanford University conducted to compare evangelicals around the world—US evangelicals are a bit unique, it turns out.

Strategies for Crossing the Line: Emotions

Emotions might provide one path across the buffer between the world and the inner self. Charismatic evangelical practice is certainly intensely emotional. When they talk about being "drunk in the spirit," for instance, they mean you are so happily giddy you can't stop laughing. Many of the people I interviewed said they were regularly overcome, bawling like babies—evangelical churches are among the few places in the United States where men can cry and still keep their sense of masculinity.

At the close of Glad Tidings' services, Judy, who always attended on Wednesdays, came to hug me and check on my spiritual progress. Through her warm smile, I saw a face streaked with tears. She walked with the relaxed gait of one who has just finished a good cry. It hadn't been a powerful service for me, but Judy was a seasoned worshipper. She often left looking as though she'd been run over and then gently picked up off the ground—exhausted, but eager. Drained, yet inspired.

Nash, another regular at Glad Tidings and part-time carpenter, recalled an evening when he lived in a Christian-run alcohol rehab center and experienced what he called "true" worship. "There was this band—the prophetic worship band—and I was on my face, just praying at the altar and all of a sudden, people started speaking these words from Matthew, 'I have prepared a place for you, that you know not of, at my father's house.'" The words hit him hard. They felt like they were meant just for him. "It was so piercing and so for me at that moment I was crying, but it was different, it was not like weeping, it was more like literally when I looked down, it was projectile tears. It was projecting off my face. I had never had that happen before." Crying changed something deep inside of him. "I felt like my whole body was being turned inside out and I heard an other-worldly scream that I thought was coming from across the room. There was a second of realization that it was me. It was crazy." The sense of complete emotional release, of being turned inside out and losing control of his actions, was, for Nash, in some sense terrifying. But later, he said it gave him something else—a raw, unshakable sense that God was right there with him.

Strategies for Crossing the Line: Speech

"The Bible says there's power in words," David told me, his voice steady, full of conviction. For many charismatic evangelicals in the United States, words matter. Spoken words, especially. He explained how, in his view, the Bible and science were in agreement. "In [scientific] studies, positive language changes how people behave or act," he said. To David, both scripture and science confirmed the power of audible speech to shape the world.

For charismatics, words are more than sounds—they're a way to cross the barrier between the mind and God. You can see it clearly in faith healing. Donald, one of the men from Glad Tidings, told me about the faith healing sessions he attends every Saturday. "When someone says they are sick, another person is like, 'All right, I'm going to pray for you right here,' and then they use, 'In the name of Jesus, I command this person to be healed.'" The simple statement "you are healed" spoken in a moment of devotion affects the world. Like when you say "I do" at a wedding, the words themselves are not just observations; they *make* things happen. They are what linguist J. L Austin[5] calls speech acts—a form of speech that acts all on its own. The right context—a church, a prayer meeting—gives the words their power. And when they come from an authoritative voice—a pastor, a deacon—they carry even more weight. The key, it seems, is that speech happens outside the mind-self. Evangelicals do often believe that even silent prayers can be effective, but when there's a real battle to fight—against illness, against evil—the spoken word is the tool of choice. This is true for exorcisms as well.

Halley, who had experience with demonic exorcism, shared a story from one afternoon at Glad Tidings. A woman up front was causing a commotion. "During the altar call, they're screaming, screeching, all this stuff," Halley said. The woman was clearly distressed, and Halley led her behind the band, beneath the stage, down to a long room where pastors often performed exorcisms. Possession was more common during mission trips, Halley told me, but even San Francisco had its share of demonic forces. There were often staff in that room ready to help.

The challenge, Halley explained, is knowing when it's possession and not something else—mental illness or just someone deeply upset. The signs are usually physical: vomiting that seems unprompted, agitation when God's presence is strong, sudden strength, changes in posture, shifts in personality, and even strange shifts in physiology, she explained. "I've seen people's eyes turn completely gray."

This woman's strength convinced them it was possession. "We had five of our strongest guys trying to hold her down. She'd throw them off with one arm. I'm watching it with my own eyes, thinking, 'Am I in a movie?'" They struggled to restrain her. The men held her down for a while.

Deliverance came through loud, audible prayers, calling Jesus to act. Halley shouted, "In the name of Jesus, I drive you out. Demons, be gone!" The woman's body went slack. It seemed to work. But within seconds, she sat up again, and a new, angrier presence took over. A fresh demon. Her voice changed—deep and guttural at first, then high and raspy, her tone shifting from angry to taunting and later to sly and seductive. Over several hours, the team prayed, moving her through six different demons until she was freed.

Glad Tidings participants called this "spiritual warfare." It rests on a worldview made especially visible by charismatic thinkers like C. Peter Wagner. From this lens, the world is a battleground where demonic forces compete with God and with Christians for control.[6] Charismatics fight these demons through exorcisms, through prayer, through asking God to cleanse their spirits, their cities, their country, and the rest of the world. Halley explained that demons can't just slip into our minds. They need an opening—a mistake, a moment of weakness. And once that door is cracked, they can manipulate us. The best defense is spoken prayer, sharp and loud. Just like a curse that only works when spoken, to push demons out, the words have to be said out loud.

Strategies for Crossing the Line: Breakthrough

At Glad Tidings, almost everyone I spoke to told a story of feeling something powerful, something they said washed through their bodies like a wave, leaving them renewed—closer to themselves, to God, and to the world around them. As many scholars have noted,[7] this kind of breakthrough, this immediate shift, is at the heart of charismatic evangelical practice. But, also, it's not a one-time thing. From baptism and conversion to being born again, charismatic evangelicals worship through a never-ending series of small ruptures (little rebirths) that they call "gifts of the spirit." Some describe the initial submission to God as a baptism by water through Jesus, with speaking in tongues a baptism by fire through the holy ghost. Speaking in tongues, faith healing, being "slain in the spirit"—each moment is like Paul on the road to Damascus, struck down, changed in an instant.

These ruptures occur most visibly in the body. The body reacts—suddenly, powerfully—and something shifts. Some call it hitting a "wall" and then breaking through. Sometimes God speaks. Sometimes they just feel His presence. But the breakthrough nearly always comes on with a bang. It's God "breaking in," piercing the barrier between the human and the divine and confirming that He is real.

Since the days of Jonathan Edwards and his "hellfire-and-brimstone" sermons in the 1700s, evangelicals have seen everyday life as involving powerful ups and downs. That oscillation is what makes the transition to godliness possible. Shane, a farmer and missionary, told me about one of his moments. "I was at a really broken spot in my life you know, super broken." He came back to church, and the flood of emotion he'd been holding in broke free. He could feel God's love in that release. "I literally started bawling and I could feel peace come on me." He felt freed from the despair that had brought him back to church. "I wanted to stay the night in the church, it felt so good, you know? I felt like I was being set free." It was a massive shift, the lowest point of his pain turning into the highest point of his faith.

A prime example is being "slain in the spirit." It happens when a person feels the force of the Holy Spirit so intensely they fall down. I saw it for the first time at a Vineyard Church in Scotts Valley. A woman was jumping, shouting her love for Jesus. Then she stopped, stared at the wall, and fell straight as a board. She would've hit the concrete floor if another worshipper hadn't caught her in time. At Glad Tidings, most people I interviewed had been slain at least once, many several times. Some worried it was just the pastor's touch that made them fall; they were just being compliant. But the sensations were real, they said—partial consciousness, intense heat, tingling across the skin. Shane described what it was like to support someone being slain. "As soon as I put my hand on him, he instantly falls down, boom, boom. Boom!"

The "boom" is the key. This isn't subtle. This version of Christianity is high-energy, high-emotion, and change comes in bursts. Jimmy, a young lawyer, told me about one of his breakthroughs. "I was in my car driving home, and I just felt the presence of God, overwhelming. He must have been resting right on top of me, in my car or whatever. It was so powerful, it was hard for me to drive the car." Once home, he could fully let go.

I get on my knees and I just fall to the ground. I say, 'God, have your way' … I have never felt this again, like something resting on my chest and then this stirring from my belly, it was so intense. I am crying, I am sobbing, it's all these sensations of joy. I am laughing uncontrollably. It was so powerful … It was like my body couldn't handle what he was doing to me. When it was done, it was like, I just felt peaceful.

Each of these moments reaffirms the realness of God. It takes power to break through the bounded mind.

Strategies for Crossing the Line: Body Logics

As a persistent and (hopefully only) slightly annoying anthropologist, I tend to repeat the same question over and over: "What makes you think your God is real?" It would often get a perplexed look, but then some of the most fascinating answers. At Bethany University, a few students talked about logic—the complexity of the world pointing to a creator. Others mentioned how faith changed people for the better; this was a social good. But those answers got lost in a flood of stories rooted in the body, in physical experiences that felt supernatural, yet undeniably real.

The consensus among my informants was that assurance resides in the five senses, with touch the most convincing. "The reason I still am a Christian is I've felt God and I know he is there," one student told me. I couldn't pin down exactly what he meant by "felt," but the message was clear—he trusted his senses above all else. Aldus, another student, was more specific. The feeling was brief, but convincing. "I fell back. I felt I had been shot with electricity. Whether or not I had been manipulated, I don't worry about it. At that moment, I decided to come to Bethany." Even though he recognized the possibility for something less than genuine, perhaps manipulation, the power of what he felt won out.

For Bethany students, to merely agree is good but to feel or to see someone else feeling is far better. "One kid spoke a word in tongues and this other kid starts interpreting it. The guy then said, 'Who just touched me?'" No one had. "When you touched me, I felt a physical sensation, tingling, or a warmth." Each sensory element added a layer of potency—the more feelings, the stronger the conviction. Another student described a moment in a doctor's chair. "I thought I was going to die. I started praying the Lord's Prayer, and I heard the words 'Do you really mean it? Do really mean what you are saying?' I said 'Yes.' immediately. Then I physically felt a warmth. Like somebody wrapped one of those hot blankets all around me." That warmth stuck, even during our interview. "I walk around feeling that," he said.

Some students tied the sensory and the pragmatic. "I felt him inside. I heard him talk to me. I felt the warmth." Then, almost as an afterthought, "I've seen a difference in my life." One student called it a "tangible understanding." Another described times when the heat of worship turned her hands red during church services. "It's because the Spirit of God is covering me," she explained. The heat confirmed it for her.

Healing too, was a common source of certainty. Dr. Stewart, the missions professor, told a story about Robert Fiero, a healing evangelist. "He was paralyzed for 25 years and miraculously healed. Like, he was thrown out of his wheelchair. You can imagine what that does. People's faith goes skyrocketing." One student added, "I've had encounters with God. The most clear. The most factual. I've seen miracles. Saw someone's leg grow. People healed from cancer." Angela, another student at Bethany, shared similar stories. "Why believe in God? I've been delivered from depression. I've seen my mom delivered from chemical depression. She doesn't have to take pills. She was bipolar. I've seen extravagant things. I've talked to people who have had physical healings." These stories often ended with someone tossing their meds in the trash. "Father looks like he is dying. They got no money for a doctor, no money for anything. But grandma's a woman who has always read the Bible and says 'I believe in you and I don't have anything else. Would you heal my husband?' And he gets well. She throws all the drugs away." A professor of theology at Bethany, Dr. Albrecht was breaking down the power of the narrative piece by piece. Yet, also, I am pretty sure he believed it himself. Pills in the trash are a clear sign, he explained.

Healing isn't the end, though. It's just the start. For Aldus, the warm, melting feeling that rippled through his body during a prayer session on a freezing afternoon signaled the presence of the Holy Spirit, but it was more significant because it inspired action: it was time to get more involved in his church. The body played a similar role at Glad Tidings.

I asked Mark if there was a specific moment when he became absolutely sure that God was real. "Yeah," he said, "I knew when I was lying in bed, and I felt God's presence."

"What made you sure in that moment?" I asked.

"All my senses were engaged. My emotions, my physical body. The way I connect with the world. That moment was all I could think about—God was there."

Jeremy's story was much the same. "I got baptized when I was eight, nine, ten years old, something like that. A week later, I received the Holy Spirit. I was trembling and all that. I knew from that point on. The day I got saved." For Jeremy, the sensations kept coming. He told me he often feels a rush of spiritual power, like a force running through his body. "Every time I encounter the Holy Spirit, yeah. If I don't feel that, it's not really an encounter, as far as I'm concerned."

Ontological Anxiety: Worrying if God Is Real

Ontology is the philosophical study of the real. It's how people draw lines between what is and what isn't. I love asking my students to try and prove that world is more than my or their imagination gone haywire. It is a slippery slope. But, for the charismatics I worked with, this line was super important. It seemed as if they were always asking themselves—and others—if God was real and trying to prove it, not just to skeptics but to themselves. Their constant questioning, this worry about the boundaries of the real and unreal, I called "ontological anxiety." It was a kind of tension we didn't see much in other places we studied (we compared charismatic experience across Thailand, Ghana, China, Vanuatu, and the United States), even among other charismatics. In Thailand, for example, people didn't seem as concerned with such clarity. There, as my colleague Felicity Aulino noted, there was more of an openness to multiple realities—a kind of "ontological pluralism."[8]

For US charismatics, these explosive bodily events—speaking in tongues, faith healing, being "slain in the spirit"—may be ways to deal with their ontological anxiety. The physical experiences confirmed God's presence, bypassing the mind's doubt. When your body feels something so intense, it's hard to argue with it.

But there was another strategy too: rational argument. Some talked as if to bring God into the realm of secular certainty, to describe the supernatural as logical, even scientific. The strategy does not always work to calm the anxiety. Often, they described being uncomfortable, recognizing that their beliefs about God breaking into their minds didn't quite fit with their intuition that the mind is a closed, bounded thing.

When people say, "I know it when I see it," they are performing what scholars call "Common Sense realism." It's the belief that what you see, hear, and feel directly is the foundation of all truth. It's a kind of democratic knowledge—everyone's senses are equal. This was popular in the late 1700s in Scotland and made its way to America in the 1800s. For Historian Charles Marsden, the Common Sense realism of mid-nineteenth-century theorists was central to the beginning of what eventually became evangelicalism, partly because it posed a direct challenge to more theoretically based approaches to scientific rationality.[9] Common Sense realism is an often cranky but down-to-earth approach to understanding the world from inside the trusted body.

The evangelicals I spoke to often talked within a framework of scientific inquiry and causal logic that cast their own miracle and conversion stories as sounding at first a bit crazy, but then scientific logic proved the truth of it. They cast themselves as especially skeptical, not at all prone to emotionalism or fantasy. Their stories often sounded like police reports—"just the facts, ma'am." When they got a bit wild, narrators introduced multiple caveats, and they very explicitly searched for confounds—my newly learned psychology term for reasons their experiences might not be what they seemed. But usually, they couldn't find any.

This may seem obvious in the United States—if you tell a story about demons or spirits, you have to answer to the skeptical people who are listening and prove it is real to them. People in our other field sites around the world were not nearly as anxious about the very existence of spirits—they seemed more concerned about meeting or not meeting their specific obligations to particular spirits or worried about what spirits might be thinking or doing.

But in the US, take Phil. He'd traveled west from New Orleans as a young Christian rapper, then came back a few years later as a youth pastor. He is now married with several kids and works at the local high school. Like many of the charismatic evangelicals who used this common-sense, fact-based strategy, he prefaced his stories of the supernatural with the rational. He is clearly all about the nitty-gritty of the real. Phil was highly educated, had been to college, and studied history. He knew that what he believed didn't fit the secular mold. "I'm going to tell you my craziest Jesus story," he said. He'd gone to a revival led by an evangelist who played the biggest drum kit in the world. People said you'd smell this beautiful fragrance during worship, like roses. Phil was skeptical. Then his friend handed him a baby, and the kid threw up all over him. In the bathroom, Phil tried to clean up, but the smell of vomit stuck to him. But when he turned his focus to God, the smell changed. Roses. At first, he thought it was a trick. "Okay, so what did they do? They put something in the vents, some perfume?" He checked, but there was nothing. Each time he stopped praying, the vomit smell came back. So, like a scientist, he tested it. Back and forth: God→roses. No God→vomit. "I did it twice and I'll never forget. It smelled really like the most fantastic smell you've ever smelled in your entire life. It was just a total moment of things and I've never been able to explain that."

As he finished the story, he brought it back into the secular frame, "I don't share it a lot because people think you're a nut job when you say this kind of stuff." It is exactly the kind of magical tale that a reasonable person would check multiple times. In the end, for Phil, discerning God's presence is about fact, hard and solid, not emotion, and not fantasy. "I can't justify your emotions. I can only justify what is fact for me, what I've felt." For him, God's reality had been verified by his senses.

Anxiety about what's real and unreal becomes especially visible in the ways charismatic evangelical participants demand coherence—of themselves and the world around them—even as their belief in the supernatural makes this difficult. In interviews probing how people link thoughts, feelings, spirits, and imagination, we started with a simple question: can emotions like anger, care, or envy affect someone else if they're kept hidden?

Charismatic evangelicals began by answering in straightforward, rational terms. To them, the mind was a closed space; thoughts stayed inside and didn't touch the world. When asked if thoughts alone could change the world, nearly all answered with a firm "no," sometimes with a laugh at the absurdity. Yet, they held a deep belief that prayer could heal, and curses could harm. As the conversation went on, this tension grew. As the interview unfolded, some practitioners seemed to notice that prayer and cursing were somewhere in the general world of mental causation. This seeming contradiction unsettled them.

Jean, a single mom and deeply religious woman, noticed the pattern when I began asking about envy. At this point, after questions about care and anger, she understood that the survey was testing whether the mind could affect the world. "Woah," she exclaimed, "where is this going?" She guessed that I was asking how thoughts might travel across space, and had hit upon the idea that God's thoughts and spirits were also in this same general category. She asked me to pause. We talked through the difference between prayer and mental causation. Jean believed the mind was closed off, that thoughts couldn't travel. But she also believed that God's communications, and even spirits, could break through that barrier. She hadn't worked through this distinction before, and it made her uneasy, thinking that there might be an inconsistency in how she understood the world.

It has to be tough being both a Westerner, raised with all our underlying rigidity around the wall between mind and body, and then living as an evangelical, where experiences challenge that boundary all the time.

Discernment

How do you know if the voice you're hearing or the feeling in your body is from God or from somewhere else? For charismatics, there's a process for figuring that out. They call it discernment. First, they ask if what they're hearing or feeling is unusual. Next, they check if it lines up with the Bible. And finally, they ask if the pastor approves.

"If I never thought that way before, then I test it." Valentin explained. "I don't just say, oh, it popped into my head. It must be something that God wants me to do or say. I ask, 'does this sound like the character of God?' I want God to guide my actions, I mean, all the time ideally."

"Do you remember the feeling or the quality of the thought?" I asked her.

"Surprise?" she replied. "I think just surprise, like 'huh. Where did this thought come from?' I just use caution. 'God, is this really you?' If it is, He'll show that He's in it in some way."

"Do you ask Him directly, 'Was that you?'" I asked.

"Oh, yeah. For sure."

Mark told me about checking with his pastor. "Hey. I felt like the Lord was saying this to me. 'What do you think? Pray about this with me.' He'll come back and say, 'I agree' or 'No. I think that was just the pepperoni you ate the night before or whatever.'"

Often, the body is the first signal that kicks off this process of discernment. The folks I interviewed tended to be skeptical of the role of the senses in discerning God's presence, but many described empathy for fragile humans with few other tools for assessing spiritual connection. Norman put it this way, "Now, I don't look for those experiences. Early in your faith you are just really wanting those experiences. I think later on, it's not about the experience. If God wants to give you an experience that's great, but my relationship with God is not based on just the giggles and the shakes that he gives me sometimes."

He then told me a story. "I was praying and a pastor laid hands on me very lightly. When I got up from the floor an hour later. I was ten feet behind where I started. So, my body actually flew backward. That's pretty crazy," he paused and turned serious. "If God didn't give me any of those experiences then his grace would still be sufficient. I wouldn't say that the experience is shallow. But I would say if that's the motivating factor of your faith, that's shallow. I think it is shallow to feel like you need a physical touch." He did leave space for the role of sensation in the charismatic community. "We are weak human beings. Sometimes we just need something."

Discernment is something charismatics talk about all the time. They see themselves making mistakes, getting confused, and constantly learning what is clearly a difficult task. Abigail talks about developing the skills for discernment. "I'm learning to discern. It's like an antenna, trying to put that in. There are times when you're super sure, I think this is the voice of the Lord. And then you ask 'Is it just me, is it just me making this up?'" And many have stories of mistakes. "I've seen a lot. Sometimes it's just you, it's just your flesh, you know."

No matter how clear the sensation, there's nearly always some doubt. God is hard to put a finger on. "I think in the walk of God, you can never really get out of doubt, you know, because it's a faith walk." But feelings help—perhaps faith is a feeling?

You can't really see, you can't really say 'oh, I saw God standing next to me.' It's more like faith, like, I did feel it, you know. So, there are times when I would feel doubt and sometimes it could be from the enemy telling me, 'oh, that's not real,' which I've experienced, or it could be from God trying to sharpen me. But I don't think you are a real Christian if you don't doubt.
As Mark put it, "He who has not wrestled does not really believe."

Norman said one piece of discernment is consistency.

"I think the further I go in my journey, the more I think it's a little bit easier to tell whether it's the Lord speaking. Not that I know when it's God and when it's not. Sometimes he knows that I'm stubborn and I ... "

"Need it to be repeated?" I finished his sentence.

"Exactly."

And, sensation can help.

At the beginning of my prayer time, God and I are talking about my sister, and then in the middle of that, she somehow comes back into my mind. Then at the end she comes back again, and I think, it's weird for me to think three times about Angela in the same prayer meeting, so maybe God's saying something here. That's when I'll ask God. 'Lord are you trying to say something?', and if it's God, I'll feel this confirmation.

"Tell me about that."

"That would feel a physical feeling"

"Physical feeling?"

"You may feel a chill go down your spine. You may feel goosebumps. That would be a confirmation. Now there's also the possibility that I just happen to walk under an air conditioning vent. I might immediately look up to make sure there wasn't one above me."

External sensations and internal feelings are different, at least in someway. "There is also an internal feeling. It's not necessarily physiological. I think it's more emotional. I would say it's in the same vicinity of when you know that you're falling in love. There's this part of your heart that when you feel that infatuation beginning to form or that genuine love that's beginning to form in a relationship. I think it's a human feeling and I think people feel it differently."

Sometimes, however, the feeling is more ambiguous. "When I pray for China, I feel this tinge in my heart and I feel this, I don't know how to describe it. It's not a sick feeling. It's not like a bad feeling. It's kind of a good feeling but I may even feel sadness, and like 'oh, maybe the lord wants me to spend more time on this.' I don't always get goose pimples. I don't always get the chill down my spine. I don't always get that feeling of falling in love."

And again, discernment often fails. "We get it wrong all the time. Maybe that's part of the reason that God uses physical things to help us understand where we're on the right track—Usually, to be honest with you, I don't feel anything."

Still, sensory experiences are hard to ignore. Norman told me about an unusual one. "I've seen the matter of thought," he said.

He was telling me that his thought was actual material—talk about a challenge to the theory of mind! And he knows his experience was unusual: "That was weird. It was the weirdest thing, guys. I remember Pastor Forrest speaking something and he said, 'Our church, we're going to have a revival service. There's going to be 1,000 people here.' And I saw soundwaves coming out of his mouth, and I was like, 'Hold on a second, what am I seeing?' This was when I was like 29 years old. This is in the peak. This is when I was doing lots of prayer and lots of reading. And I saw little dots. Everybody was made up of, 'Let there be light,' and then there was. It was like, 'Oh my God, it's all made up of sound, it's all made up from you God.' And I was sitting there, and the thing that I said, I saw soundwaves, and … I remember saying, 'That's going to come true,' and it did. 'That's going to come true.' The things that Pastor said that I saw soundwaves with, those were the things that came true."

I couldn't help blurting, "That's cool."

"I know," he said grinning. "That's how I know there's a God. Come on, who doesn't want to experience this stuff? Superheroes, what? I'm telling you, it's crazy."

Conclusion

In anthropology, the question of what's real—ontology—is key. Many of the cultural differences I just described hinge on trust in the supernatural. Anthropologist Evans-Pritchard wrote about the Azande.[10] When a house collapsed, they knew termites had eaten through it. But why did it collapse at that moment, on that particular person? The answer, for them, was witchcraft. Malinowski described something similar among the Trobrianders.[11] They used skill to navigate calm waters but called on magic for the rough and unpredictable seas. At other times, ontology is about the ways an object fits into a broad cosmic order. Mauss saw that among the Kula, when you gave a gift, part of yourself stayed in the object. It wasn't just a thing; it was inalienable.[12]

Charismatics, too, believe in the supernatural. But, in the United States, they aren't that unusual, which has me wondering why Evans-Pritchard described the Azande as so far from the norm, but regardless, let's continue. Remember, about 80 percent of Americans believe in God, and many believe He shapes their lives. Even so, charismatics feel different. They feel set apart, marginalized by secularism, by science, and often even by other Christians. This sense of being outsiders is at the heart of the charismatic movement. It shapes their daily lives in several ways. They are engaged in a cultural battle. They tend especially to wrestle with the secular view, seeking evidence to prove their reality. This manifests as a constant anxiety over what is real, a need to tell stories that make them seem reasonable.

One of their strategies is to return to the basics of experience. When they feel something in their bodies, it counts for a lot. It's hard to deny. It's compelling evidence of something beyond what they can see. When their belief in the reality of God meets the imagined gaze of a secular world, it creates an unusual pattern of argument, what I call "ontological anxiety."

Anthropologists have long noticed that ontology is shaped by culture. I am showing that these assumptions about reality are unstable and fraught with emotions like anxiety when they are challenged by other worldviews inside and outside their community. These tensions shape cultural logics—like how charismatics think about their bodies, how they describe what they know in scientific terms.

In previous chapters, I talked about experience. But in describing the importance of the body and ontological anxiety, I am taking a step back from experience and talking about a community of experience, a culture—much more like a regular anthropologist. I have been asking how charismatics turn their spiritual experience into culture, or something in that vein.

So, that is how they deal with the real. But charismatic practices also give them unusual approaches to the feeling of agency and power, because this is not all in their heads, bodies, or churches; charismatics live in the outside world too.

8

Letting Go Brings Power: The Feeling of Agency

" Because she has let go of herself, she is perfectly fulfilled."
—LAO TZU, *TAO TE CHING*[1]

"Trust in the Lord with all your heart and lean not on your own understanding; in all your ways submit to him, and he will make your paths straight."
—PROVERBS 3:5–6, *THE BIBLE*, NEW INTERNATIONAL VERSION

I've always wanted to start a chapter with cool quotes. This was my best bet. So, I went for it. And this kind of thinking extends from ancient texts all the way through to contemporary new age thought. As Eckhart Tolle, puts it in *The Power of Now*[2] "What the ego doesn't know, of course, is that only through the letting go of resistance, through becoming "vulnerable," can you discover your true and essential invulnerability."

When you read these—and read them closely—you may notice that these writers tend to imagine letting go as doing more than release. It makes you fulfilled, straight pathed—maybe more clear-headed, even "invulnerable." And please notice that this is actually quite strange, this proposed connection between release and activity. Because at first, letting go sounds like losing control, like vulnerability, unease, or even fear. You'd think it would make action harder. How does one act while submitting? But often it seems, the opposite happens. When people let go, they may fall apart, but also, things can fall into place. Sometimes, it feels like a stronger force takes over, guiding things to their natural flow. This force might be God. Maybe it's in our minds. Maybe both. But either way, if we believe the charismatics I spoke with, letting go can put us back in control. It gives us a sense that we can shape the world around us, what anthropologists call a sense of agency.

For charismatics, after prayer, something changes. They feel enabled to act differently. They feel it physically, emotionally. They call this "power." But what's odd is that this power comes from letting go. It goes head-to-head against the modern idea of controlling to achieve. Through prayer, charismatics can release their need to climb, to battle for success in work or play. It's confusing at first—how can you achieve something by letting go of the need to achieve? But that's what seems to happen. Letting go is both empowerment and resistance against the constant pressure to perform.

This led me to think that charismatics practice a unique form of agency—one that breaks some of the usual rules of how we control things and get things done. So, I looked for it. I found that charismatics speak of agency in three ways, all of them tied to letting go. First, there's the immediate freedom that comes with breakthrough. This one was all over the place, in texts, sermons, and my interviews. The next two were harder to see. There's cultivation—planting seeds and nurturing them, not through control but through joint effort with God. And finally, patient listening only appeared at certain moments. None of these forms are about force or willpower. This may be surprising, especially since American evangelicals more broadly (including the charismatics) have become the epitome of rugged, "get-it-done" agency. The American cowboy is often cited as their cultural model.[3] But if my data is accurate, it suggests that charismatics shift between different modes of agency—and that this capacity for code-switching (a term typically used to describe moving between two or more dialects or languages within a single sentence) directly or indirectly challenges the dominant US vision of agency.

A quick note: This is the most philosophical chapter in the book. I'm looking at ideas from scholars, philosophers, social scientists, and cognitive scientists who spend their lives studying the enigma of agency. I explore various theories, and many of them contradict each other. I'll also show how evangelicals contribute to this conversation with their own unique views on agency. Agency itself is a strange concept. Like letting go, it's hard to pin down. I will try to make it clear. But, if you want to skip this philosophy chapter, you can, and it will all make sense anyways—perhaps more lighthearted, perhaps less deep. Either way, don't worry too much about it and see how it lands.

The concern that we lack agency has troubled Western thinkers for centuries. Many have tried to prove that our sense of individual freedom is real, that we are truly making choices. They are anxious about agency. Therapist parents like mine are well known for inspiring anxiety, or at least its awareness, in their children—so maybe that is why I often use the word "anxious" as an analytic tool. But I do also think it helps us see cultural patterns that might otherwise go unnoticed.

Charismatics worry about agency, too, but differently than the traditional Western philosophers. They aren't afraid humans lack it—they're afraid we might think we have too much. Charismatics fear that pride might drive us to meddle in God's work. But charismatic beliefs grew up close to secularism, so they also echo the Western struggle with what it means to be fully human. They express multiple versions of agency. This comfort with multiple versions of agency might explain their unusual ability to grow their group and simply get things done.

In the next sections, I'll walk through centuries of philosophy (condensed, of course) to show how Western minds have wrestled with agency and its shadow, determinism—the idea that all is preordained, by God or by fate. I'll also show how charismatics define their sense of agency, sometimes in tune with secular views, and sometimes against them.

Agency and Anxiety: A Brief History of Philosophy

I like to suppose that the philosopher Immanuel Kant was anxious, a man of strict habits and intense concern over his own morality. His big concern in the mid-1700s was whether human actions and thoughts were truly free or somehow controlled. Historian Isaiah Berlin explained that Kant wasn't alone. He was just one of many Western thinkers who spent their lives trying to prove that people make real choices, not ones predetermined by outside forces. "Although it was particularly acute for Kant," Berlin writes, this worry about agency "has dominated European thought, and indeed to some extent European action, ever since. It is a problem which obsesses both philosophers and historians in the 19th century and, indeed, in our own [20th] century too." Let's trace this anxiety over agency across some areas of Western philosophy.

Modern thought celebrates human creativity and control, but at times it feels like we're trapped in the gears of modern life. Philosophers like Max Weber, Michel Foucault, Karl Marx, and Martha Nussbaum have all tried to explain this. They called it "rationalization" or "discipline," "alienation" or "objectification." They were trying to explain why there's a gap between the promise of freedom in modern life and the felt reality, and they suggest that this gap might center on our sense of agency.

Modern anxiety over agency runs in two directions. First, we tend to wonder if we are just products of an endless chain of causes? This is what neuroscientist Robert Sapolsky argues.[4] He thinks we should be more empathetic with each other because, for the most part, we can't help what we do. The second question is a bit different: How much does society control us? This is particularly important in modern life. As fewer people came to truly believe in God, the old idea of fate—of a life determined by something beyond—started to fade. In its place came a simpler story, one of cause and effect. Without the supernatural to lean on, freedom felt thinner, harder to grasp. It seemed more likely that we were just machines, a set of responses shaped by the world around us, by a society that held the reins. Modern philosophers pushed back against both forms of this "agency-anxiety." They imagined consciousness, emotions, or fleeting moments as tools for agency.

One common idea is that our consciousness frees us. Step back, think, and view the world reasonably, and that is freedom. Kant described it as transcendent reason—a way of thinking that he thought could escape the chains of causality.[5] I'm skeptical, I must admit. But Sigmund Freud also suggested that deeper self-awareness could be the basis for resisting cultural repression.[6] As historian Michael Gillespie notes, this idea of an autonomous consciousness, untouched by past experiences, allows for a kind of knowledge "altogether independent of experience" even of our sense experience.[7] In this view, the outside world and our senses are less important than our inner lives— very different from charismatic theories. Our conscious self here becomes the key to freedom that can sidestep the control of history or society. I find this odd—how are thoughts protected from the causes around us? Just because they are hard to see?

When philosophers Jean-Jacques Rousseau and Michel de Montaigne told us that pre-modern peoples were more free than modern humans, they proposed a very different vision of agency. Their well-meaning, albeit racist, story depicted a "noble savage" who was uninhibited by modern life, running healthy and free. Rousseau extended this idea by criticizing the dehumanizing effects of owning property. And his thinking inspired others—Friedrich Nietzsche, the Romantics, the neovitalists, and even evangelicals—who embraced the idea of freedom through emotional expression, not reason. In their view, emotions were more authentic and genuine. Neuroscientist Edward Slingerland said something similar: emotions seem unfakeable, he said.[8]

This strikes me as true—emotions are hard to fake—though I would be surprised if my emotions actually free me. Or at least not always. I do have moments of openness where joy or sorrow seems to make the world anew, like walking across town after a good soaking rain. But at other moments, it feels as though they're doing the opposite—surging through me, filling and directing, less freeing than controlling.

***

Imagine you're in a prison. The guards can watch you all the time, but you're never sure if they actually are. What would you do? Philosopher Michel Foucault argued that eventually, you'd act like they were always watching. After a while, no guards would be needed. You'd regulate your own behavior.[9]

Foucault saw our modern society as this kind of prison, called the Panopticon. We internalize society's rules until they become our own. He argued that sexism, violence, racism, and homophobia, are drilled into us by society. They become simply *who we are.*

In Foucault's view, we have little or no real agency. Not because we're trapped by a chain of causes but because we're the product of our conditioning.

There is no true self beyond what society makes us, he thought. He rejected Freud's idea that we are naturally agents repressed by society. Instead, Foucault argued first that sexuality, and then pretty much all of culture, comes from social power. There's nothing natural or free about it.

By this logic, Foucault erased the idea that we could have a conscious self outside of culture. Our consciousness, he argued, is shaped from within the structures of power. It's just as controlled as everything else. It was a bleak view. Foucault was influenced by the revolts of 1968 and felt disillusioned when the leftists lost.

Yet, while Foucault's pessimism did become one of the most influential concepts of the late twentieth century, it also inspired a massive search for agency, even for Foucault.[10] The philosophical response to this increasing agency-anxiety was, in some sense, brilliant.

When I was a child, my father told me a story about Mulla Nasrudin, the wise fool. The king had declared that anyone who told a lie would be executed. Nasrudin arrived at the village gate and said, "I will be executed." This created a paradox. If it was a lie, he should be executed, but then it would become the truth. In the early twentieth century, mathematician Kurt Gödel developed a proof using this same paradox—the Liar's Paradox. Godel's uncertainty theorem showed that any coherent story would, of necessity, be left incomplete, and anything complete could not help but be a bit incoherent. This left no room for full-on determinism. The fully determined world that Foucault seemed to suggest wasn't possible, Godel thought. There's always some space for incoherence or incompleteness, where human agency might slip through. The future, then, couldn't be entirely predictable.

This idea of uncertainty spread throughout philosophy. Philosopher Judith Butler described the uncertainty generated when we repeat a phrase. Each time we say something, we can't help but subtly change the original phrase. The new moment and new context make perfect repetition impossible.[11] Say the same thing again; it is necessarily different. For Butler, this unpredictability is a kind of freedom. The chain of causality is broken when we speak, we are more than machines, perhaps.[12]

Another thread followed Rousseau's interest in emotions to argue that the body, its energies, and the aesthetic impulses stirred by art could escape the mechanical grids of modernity. Throughout the twentieth century, this was played out in art, poetry, jazz, philosophy, and politics. Modernists sought to break free from rationality with the irrational. Pablo Picasso, for example, borrowed from African art, believing it tapped into a non-modern part of ourselves. Others, like The Incoherents, explored freedom in blank canvases and absurdity.[13]

This idea of uncertainty as freedom is more intuitive to me than consciousness or emotions. Or maybe self-aware forms of consciousness are formed in moments of uncertainty, kind of like the loosening of prayer. But, I am not actually trying to solve this puzzle of freedom. That would be some serious hubris. I simply want us to notice that Western thinkers are deeply concerned with agency. This matters because charismatics, too, are preoccupied with agency—but in distinct and creative ways.

A Charismatic Philosophy of Agency

For charismatics, the question of agency is altogether different. They flip the Western anxiety of having too little agency. Instead, they tend to worry that modern people believe they have too much power. They aren't surrendered enough to God's plan.

My favorite example comes from an early AG revival which, in this case, might have been polite language for a revolt. Revival-revolt was actually encouraged to some degree within AG. There is something about catching the spirit that sparks the impulse to break away. Small rebellions sprouted up nearly every summer after AG's founding in 1914. By the mid-1940s, AG leaders set new rules about how and when people could speak in tongues— they limited the frequency, required translation, and designated times for tongues prayer. The Latter Rain Revival in 1949 was a popular response to those rules. It spread across several states and inspired thousands. The rebels of the Latter Rain Revival argued that with the new rules, AG leaders were controlling access to the Holy Spirit. People wanted a direct connection with God, and they believed they should take it.

Hundreds split off, forming their own networks, churches, and journals, letting the spirit guide them. AG's general council pushed back hard. They denounced the revivalists for placing too much faith in human influence rather than God. The council diatribe spoke against "the extreme teaching as advocated by the 'New Order' [the revival] regarding the confession of sin to man and deliverance." Revivalists, they thought, had claimed "*prerogatives to human agency which belong only to Christ*."[14] AG leaders were anxious about the revivalists, fearing they were shaping their spiritual world too much on their own. And ironically, the revivalists felt the same about the leaders.

In charismatic lore, the Western view of agency—where people actively try to change the world and then succeed or fail—is seen as dangerous and also mistaken. A 1944 issue of the *Pentecostal Evangel* (AG's monthly newsletter) shared a story of a preacher with a temper. He tries to sweep clean his soul, apparently a bit too actively. It's a dirt floor. Sweeping produces only a growing cloud of dust. "You see the mistake the preacher had made," AG author F.M. Bellsmith wrote. "He was trying to sweep his own heart clean." Instead, he should have let God do the work for him—"I will cleanse thee" was God's response.[15] Bellsmith turns the Western concern on its head. Instead of worrying that we can't affect the world, he warns that we try to control too much.

"Words of Counsel from Daddy Welch" in the 1936 issue of the *Pentecostal Evangel*, put it simply: "Never neglect the cultivation of every talent you have, but keep them under the Blood, on the altar, and consecrated to God." There is but one anxiety. "The *only* danger is when natural talents cause one to be *self-reliant* [emphasis added]." Instead, "rely on the power of the Spirit always and let Him use you."[16]

I imagine Kant rolling over in his grave. Don't be too self-reliant? Charismatics can reject the Western ideal of agency as profane. Yet, they push back against the idea that they have no agency at all. When I ask charismatics if they fully let go during spiritual moments, they're quick to clarify. They aren't in a trance, they don't lose all control, and their ego isn't completely gone. Those are things for mystics, they say, not for them.

In reply, charismatic practice brings multiple interesting twists to the idea of agency. Some are found in texts and conversations. Others are implicit in the practice itself. As I see it, charismatics code-switch between three philosophical traditions. First, they are the founding thinkers of a theory of social change built around breakthrough, one that philosopher Alain Badiou and others have openly credited, borrowed, and expanded upon.[17] Second, charismatic say that the world is guided and controlled by a higher power with a long view. This allows them to use the metaphor of gardening: they work in the garden; God shapes the crops with his weather. Finally, if God is the prime agent, then simply waiting and listening can become an act of agency. Charismatics code-switch between these three modes of agency depending on the context. For simplicity's sake, I call these three forms of agency "breakthrough," "cultivation," and "listening."

Charismatic Agency as Breakthrough

Charismatics experience sudden, deep transformations. They call it being born again, but the brilliance of charismatic practice is that for many, little ruptures are experienced almost daily.

Take Jeff, one of the men I interviewed. He hit rock bottom. He stole from his parents and got kicked out of the house. Then, the homeless shelter tossed him out because of his addiction. That's when it happened. He heard a voice say, "Now go and be a man of God." He looked around, thinking someone had spoken, but no one was there. The voice shook him. It was clear, loud, and real. As Jeff told me, "Those were the exact words ... I can hear them clearly in my head today ... I just felt like it was a voice that pierced through all the doubt and stuff that I had in my mind about who I was, completely shattered the wall."

That voice—the one that felt as if it came from outside his head—helped him believe. He now knew God was real, and he knew he was changed. In that moment, his story flipped. He wasn't the broken man anymore. He was renewed and flying upward, freed from the chains of doubt and en route to an intimate relationship with God.

That's often how charismatics experience God. These moments of transformation are like lightning strikes. They wake you up and make you act. The famous preacher Oral Roberts' 1964 essay, *The Baptism with the Holy Spirit and the Value of Speaking in Tongues Today*, outlines charismatic agency so clearly that I think it should be subtitled "A Charismatic Treatise on Agency." He calls it "power." As he writes, "The keynote of the Baptism with the Holy Spirit was to be power." And power comes from release. "We are really getting release, or true edification … power release." He describes a break with the past—an explosion that enables the participant. "The word 'power' in Acts 1:8 denotes dynamite," he writes, "explosive power, the power of enablement … not only to become, but to do and to be like Jesus with the force of an explosion." Later in the book, I think more about what kind of action is enabled by this form of power. But, in this chapter, I am especially interested in the way it comes on—with a boom.

For Roberts, it's all about breaking free from the past. He wasn't subtle about it. Power, built from release, is explosive and immediate. When people speak in tongues, it's like dynamite going off. They can tap into that power every day. It's not just a moment—it's a revolution in your life. He wrote, "An inner power that becomes an outward force … this is one of the most revolutionary experiences that can happen to a believer."[18]

A breakthrough is often experienced as surprising. Planning gives it the feel of something more incremental. Even the most meticulous and systematic scholars of charismatic training insist on its spontaneity. AG missionary theorist Grant McClung describes a "theology of immediacy" in his essay "Spontaneous Strategy of the Spirit."[19] Russell Spittler, another charismatic thinker, said the ideal is "spontaneity in personal conduct as well as corporate worship." A message in tongues "comes unplanned, unprogrammed."[20] Even Donald MacGavran, a scholar known for blending sociology and theology, called charismatic practices spontaneous: "[The] principle of spontaneous action under the control of the spirit of Jesus as revealed in the scriptures lies at the heart of the Pentecostal faith."[21] Perhaps this is not surprising in a tradition where the founding missiological—missions theory—text is Roland Allen's "The Spontaneous Expansion of the Church: And Causes Which Hinder It."[22]

In this tradition, everything starts with the event—the moment of surprise that transforms you. McClung described it as "the priority of the event,"[23] and Paul Pomerville, another AG theorist, said this event does more than change you in the moment—it sets the stage for everything that follows. "The great commission [to evangelize] derives its meaning from the internalizing event," he wrote. "The Pentecostal event is decisive for understanding the role of the Spirit in mission."[24] If you find this interesting, and you like extended philosophical treatises, read Alain Badiou's *Being and Event* or *Saint Paul: The Foundation of Universalism.*[25] He found charismatic visions of agency highly appealing and turned them into a broadly applicable philosophy of breakthrough.

Charismatic agency, however, works on many levels. First, there's the raw experience of immediate transformation. This is all about the now, stripped down and pure. No preparation, no planning, no looking back. That single moment changes everything. It marks a shift in the whole direction of a life. But, then shifting scale, looking at the whole life, or at seasons or decades, other forms of agency sometimes pop into view as just as important.

Charismatic Agency as Cultivation

In contrast to the immediate event, cultivation describes the slow, deliberate process of building change over time. I use the term "cultivation" because charismatics often use this metaphor to explain how people gradually develop sensibilities, dispositions, and habits. Rather than seeing habit as a rigid obstacle to agency, as in Western liberal stories of freedom or charismatic stories of dramatic events, habit formation can be viewed as a form of intentional doing. It is just an action that takes a season.

I first encountered this idea of cultivation in charismatic missionary training courses. The teachers spoke of striving for conversions, but rather than emphasizing the active work of systematic outreach, they believed they were following God's seasons and contributing, or cultivating, along the way. They likened the conversion process to growing a garden—God did the converting, while they were merely "sowing the seeds." This analogy makes sense: gardening takes human effort, but it also includes a healthy dose of nonhuman support, with seeds, soil, and sun playing tremendous and decisive roles.

This kind of agency, where a person shares control and follows God's lead, isn't the modern idea of individual freedom as pure autonomy. It makes some sense that a metaphor rooted in agriculture might blend the drive for action with a need for submission. Though this idea aligns with some visions of humans as part of nature's balance, white charismatic politics today often hold little room for the Gaia-like agency of the natural world.

Cultivation offers a way to reconcile two seemingly opposed impulses: methodical effort and the charismatic practice of letting go. Charismatics are extremely diligent and methodical in shaping bodies, dispositions, and values. This systematic approach extends from intimate spiritual moments to mission pamphlets and the management of billion-dollar organizations. Yet this modern, bureaucratic mindset constantly wrestles with the belief that true human agency requires yielding to a higher power—any plan, fully human-driven, will fail without receptivity to God's intention. And that wrestling shapes the idea of cultivation.

In 1929, the *Pentecostal Evangel* published "Fallow Ground," a metaphorical reflection on evangelism. "Before the ground which has become fallow can be used for cultivation it must broken up, plowed deep, harrowed down … There are some who … never dig below the external and superficial in their hearts … either because they do not want to know it, or perhaps because they are afraid or do not know how." Life's hardships serve as tools for self-observation and transformation. "But there are instruments necessary to accomplish the plowing up of the ground. Bitter trials, deep sorrows, galling afflictions which God permits to come are plow and harrow." Trials make us tender, able to yield and open to a new form of being, "willing at any cost to be conformed to the image of his son." The final exhortation: "Break up your fallow ground."[26]

Cultivation here aims at the individual psyche. But it can be more than ripe fruits and springtime buds; it also includes dry spells and droughts. Farmers often take a tough-love approach, willing to cut and shape intensely. The cartoon figure shown reads, "They who would bear fruit, must bear pruning," and offers a tree with God pruning off the branches of temper, indifference, laziness, selfishness, pride, and self-glory. It is tempting to see this pruning as a violent mechanism of control. "Every branch that beareth fruit, he purgeth it." It certainly doesn't sound especially gentle. It was the 1930s, so perhaps these folks had not yet heard of the teddy bear God—before the softer depictions of God emerged in twentieth-century evangelicalism.

But, for charismatics, cultivation is neither a rigid system of control nor a breakthrough event outside of history. Instead, it involves holding firmly to God's plan (unknowable), the whim of the Holy Spirit (unpredictable), and to human intervention (fallen). Agency here is unknowable, unpredictable, and flawed. Human action alone is undesirable, as W. E. Moody's question in a 1940 *Pentecostal Evangel* asked, "Have You Become Entangled?"[27]

Agency, Repetition, and the Brain

Cognitive scientists often define agency as the feeling of control over your own movements or the world around you. They say you feel agency when what you expect lines up with what happens, or when you think you're in charge of your own thoughts.[28] But this sense of agency is fragile, fleeting. Scientists have found ways to trick it. Set up a computer so that when you move the mouse left, the cursor drifts right, and suddenly, people think they're making decisions they're not. Some even mistake their own hand for someone else's.

Agency, in this sense, may only last a moment—a brief awareness of initiating action or changing something. And because it's so brief, it can easily be shaken. In fact, when scientists study agency in the moment of action, they often conclude we don't really have any at all. Remember neuroscientist Benjamin Libet's study. The moment we believe we choose to move might just be our mind catching up, explaining an action already set in motion by the subconscious. Maybe our subconscious is really in charge. Libet's work has been backed by some and questioned by others, but it changed how we think about free will.

Some modern neuroscientists take a broader view, closer to what charismatics believe. These scientists think that agency isn't just about single moments of action or thought. They argue that what matters more are the habits, moods, and dispositions we develop over time.[29] In this view, fleeting moments of agency might not be as important as the deeper, more lasting ways we structure our lives. We are creatures of habit as much as moments of inspiration. And maybe it's the habits we build that define our true agency.

I spent the last several years studying at the crossroads of anthropology and psychology, especially around this question of agency, and the results surprised me. Classic social psychology has long emphasized the power of immediate situations, and research into automatic behaviors only made that case stronger. But as I dug deeper, I started to see things differently. So I came to ask: Does agency live in the moment, or is it cultivated over time?

Counter-stereotype training is an example of this tension. One study I share with my students often shocks them. It showed how people react unconsciously to images that flash by too quickly to be "seen." In the United States, people had stronger emotional reactions to Black faces than to white ones, even when they didn't consciously perceive the faces. This was true even for those who claimed to be anti-racist, and even for Black participants. It's an automatic fear response, a form of cultivation shaped by society. But also, it can be changed. Psychologists found that if people train themselves to say "no" when presented with a stereotype, their automatic reactions can shift.[30] We can retrain our deepest responses. That's also cultivation—changing the way we react at the most instinctive level.

Another example is what they call "if-then" plans. If you decide in advance how you'll act in the future—say, you decide to smile at a neighbor—you're more likely to follow through. Even if they scowl at you, you are more likely to smile because you already made the choice. These decisions, called "implementation intentions," create automatic responses to situations you've prepared for. You made a conscious decision earlier, and now your reaction feels almost effortless.[31] I've been trying to make if-then plans so I respond with less intensity to my son's teenage expressivity. I'm not sure how effective it is, although it does seem to give me a reminder that I have choices about how to respond at any given moment. Either way, that is also cultivation.

This idea—that cultivation is a form of agency—is growing in neuroscience. Neuroscientist Antonio Damasio likes to talk about "dispositions." Dispositions, the tendencies to act a certain way—like automatically smiling at someone intimidating—are key to how the brain stores information. Without these tendencies, our brains would be overwhelmed by the complexity of life. We need habits to make sense of the world. Damasio calls these habits "space-saving mechanisms for information storage." Far more than simply cognition, he tells us, dispositions control the release of hormones, contract muscles, and hold multiple forms of information.[32]

A growing collection of neuroscientists argues that consciousness itself evolved to create and solidify these patterns. Merlin Donald, for instance, explains that the power of human consciousness lies in its ability to automate complex skills, whether it's driving a car, playing an instrument, or speaking. These skills take years to master and only become automatic through long practice. Consciousness supervises and installs these patterns, turning them into habits.

Donald challenges the short-term thinking of many neuroscience experiments. He argues that consciousness isn't just a momentary spark. It's an extended process, guiding us over a lifetime. He calls this "cognitive epigenesis"—the slow building of knowledge, skills, and habits that shape our lives.[33] This echoes the charismatic idea of cultivation. Habits and structures aren't less creative or alive than chaotic systems. They're just another way of being in the world, a way that may realize more agency than we realize.

Charismatics move between these different registers of analysis, code-switching from one to another with ease, from the immediate breakthrough to the cultivated season. They speak about agency in many ways, across different scales.

Charismatic Listening as Patiency (A Mix of the Words Patience and Agency)

Picture Shavon, after her fierce prayer, sitting by the quiet lake of her mind, listening to the stillness. This is agency at its simplest. Now return to Chapter 1 and remember the moments of letting go. How it shifts the mind, loosening old thought patterns. Think of the peace that follows—soaking in the spirit after worship. Feel that reversal, where filling the mind brings a release, emptying us of every constraint. And in that moment, letting go doesn't leave us weak. It fills us with power.

When I take the charismatic call to let go of human agency seriously, it seems to me that this dominant idea of agency is wrapped up in what may be a Western tendency—to act enables us to feel fully human. But within every culture, there are people who challenge the dominant ideas. William Mazzarella and Donald Gell, two anthropologists, give us a different model for agency, but also within Western philosophy. Mazzarella talks about "patiency," which I suspect is as appealing for its silly play on words as its potential philosophical intervention. At least, to me. Mazzarella tells of Giordano Bruno, an Italian philosopher, mathematician, and astronomer who, in the sixteenth century, argued that life demands both the power to act and the power to be acted upon. Mazzarella then takes us to what philosopher Martin Heidegger calls "releasement," which means, as Mazzarella puts it: "We are to do nothing but wait."

At first glance, patiency might seem like another among many contemporary calls to chill out and drop the Protestant work ethic, to step back and relax. But that's not it. Mazarella points instead to an overlooked tradition in Western thought that values waiting, watching, and experiencing over immediate action. This thread flips the scales. It doesn't rank action higher than inaction. Instead of seeking agency through individual will, Mazzarella suggests we change the way we value things entirely. Let us prize inaction, he says. Mazzarella reminds me of the charismatic path from stillness and release into power.

When we look up close at the breakthrough, or step back to see cultivation, or then explore relationships between release, stillness, and action at different scales, agency looks altogether different.

Thinking about Scale

Discussion about scale as a philosophical construct can seem quite dull. Maybe it is just a way of saying, "Look at everything from different angles so you don't miss anything." I suspect, however, that scale matters more than that. It may even be a way to fight off the feeling that we are fully controlled by the world around us. It definitely helps me deal with my own anxiety about agency. Let me explain.

When you walk into a forest, what do you see? The trees, the whole forest, or maybe just the leaves? It depends on how you look. It depends on what scale you use to see with. Each scale tells a different story. You can mix them, or shift between them, but they give you a new way of seeing things. I think that's how cultures work too. We are trained to focus on one scale over another, depending on what's at play. (Oddly enough, this may also be rooted in the brain's prediction mechanisms, because we save mental energy by predicting what we will see, and this means we choose some scales to prioritize over others.)

Our particular ways of looking at things, of paying attention, shape how we experience the world. This is important to charismatics when they scale their analysis of agency. At one scale, it is immediate, at another, it is a season. It depends on how they look at it. By shifting scales, they gain access to multiple ways to understand themselves as effective actors in the world. This seems important.

It turns out that relationships between scales are often uncertain, and they don't just add up one from the next. This seems surprising. It seems intuitive that on a closer look and a broader view, we ought to find the same stuff, and they should be compatible. But, there is at least some interesting evidence that if I study something at one scale, then shift to another, what I find may not match up. This is super confusing, so give yourself a few pages to work it out with me. Here's the basic idea: according to some philosophers and scientists, things don't always act the same way at different scales, and one scale doesn't predict the next. Look at one car and you can't predict traffic. Pool balls might follow Newton's laws, but the atoms inside them don't. Knowing the atoms doesn't mean you can predict how the balls will behave on the table. Different scales don't cause each other in neat, linear fashion.

Neuroscientist Michael Gazzaniga wrote a whole book on this scale issue— *Who's In Charge?* It is about free will and the brain. Gazzaniga dives into the idea that things act differently at different scales. Let's explore this a bit and see how it connects to charismatics, both in terms of their sense of agency and the common idea that they misunderstand their own economic needs, often dismissed as false consciousness.

We can start with Eve Marder. She spent years studying spiny lobsters, which seems a lovely way to start an exploration of human agency. Marder mapped out every detail of lobster nervous systems, tested 20 million combinations of neural networks, but even with all that data, she still couldn't predict how the lobsters would behave. As Gazzaniga says, "You'd never predict the tango if you only studied neurons."[34] Similarly, some ants and termites are really, really boring. They just make tunnels and eat and sleep and do regular ant things. That is at one scale of their community. But when their communities reach a certain size, those ant communities jump scales, and they suddenly start generating huge tower-like structures. At one scale, they're just ants. But at another, they're architects.

Gazzaniga explains that different scales come with different rules. Each scale is its own world, with its own laws and logic. One scale may come from another, but you can't predict it.[35] If each scale has its own logic, then the spaces between them might be where we find agency, he thinks. Geographer Nathan Sayre saw the same thing in biology. When you shift far enough across scales, the dominant processes change. Things don't just get bigger or smaller. They change altogether. And here's the key—every analysis depends on the scale you choose.[36]

This understanding of scale offers a way to break the chain of cause and effect. If scales don't line up, if the rules change as we move from one to the next, it's hard to imagine that everything fits into a simple, linear path. Then, to bring it down to the level of culture: scale shapes what we see, and what we see shapes our attention.[37] Our attention shapes our experience. That's how scale influences how we understand the world.

This idea might give us a more generous way to think about things. If we accept that scales are actually different, then we can value different perspectives. When philosopher Brian Massumi talks about the freedom from the chaos generated by our subconscious emotions—what he calls "affect"—he's looking at a very small scale. Antonio Damasio, on the other hand, looks at larger-scale patterns, "dispositions." Scale lets us see the thinking of both researchers as important.

But scales don't always complement each other. For example, the liberal focus on the individual often clashes with a focus on the collective. It makes us ask if the most important way to see our lives is as individuals or as part of something larger. Maybe the real agent is the family, as many argue. These aren't just differences in tone—they reveal a power struggle at the heart of society. Scale matters, and in ways that might surprise us.

Charismatic Scale Battles: False Consciousness

It's common for secular liberals to talk about evangelicals, especially charismatics, as if they're missing something. The story goes like this: charismatics are emotional, confused about what they need, so they vote for Republicans who are interested in state subsidies to big corporations that are both "too big to fail" and they are uninterested in the basic needs of working people.

Political theory calls this *false consciousness*, the idea that people are blind to their own self-interest. But scale effects suggest something else. Maybe it's not confusion—instead, it could be a disagreement over what is the right scale to focus on. When evangelicals argue about the role of the state versus the family, maybe they're really debating the proper scale for social intervention.

Let's break it down. One day, I was sitting in a small Indian restaurant near Springfield, Missouri, not far from the global headquarters of the Assemblies of God. I'd been spending time in the AG archives, digging through files for days. Darrin Rodgers, the head of the archives, met me for dinner. We had talked for hours, so now it was time to push a bit, see where our differences lay. I asked about neoliberalism and its effect upon the poor in Springfield—what did he think about the disintegration of state support as the Springfield tax base was privatized?

Darrin was quite sympathetic. He connected taxes and inequality to race with an incredible story of the racial reconciliation that he had facilitated within the city (FYI, he appeared white). On the very day in 1906 when the Azusa Street revival in Los Angeles ignited the multiracial charismatic movement, a white mob lynched a Black man in Springfield. Black families fled, and ten years later, when white charismatics in the Assemblies of God left their Black brethren to form their own church, they chose Springfield as their headquarters—a city that had become almost entirely white.

Now, a century later, the white charismatics in Springfield were finally reckoning with their ancestors' actions. Darrin spoke about prayer and reconciliation, but I pressed him—would this reconciliation include economic support for the Black community? He shook his head. No, the real solution wasn't economic. It was about building strong families. Black families, he said, needed help with creating a culture of safety and hard work. He didn't see the problem as something to be solved by addressing neoliberalism or deindustrialization. The issue wasn't at that level. To him, the problem—and the solution—was at the scale of the nuclear family. And the state wasn't the answer to a family-level problem. Uplift here comes through removing sin and a personal commitment to God, not from systemic change. This is classic white evangelical social theory.[38]

Here was a battle of scales. Charismatics had focused their attention on one scale—the family. Voting Republican, for them, often meant choosing the scale that mattered most in the moment. The family, in their worldview, is the most important site of agency. This belief is reinforced again and again, not just in testimonies but in the institutional support of charismatic churches. The family becomes the key. And although it's just one way of seeing the world, because charismatics have fought to claim a particular scale, what they focus on shapes their experience, with real consequences.

***

For those of us raised in the United States and outside the charismatic world, it can feel quite natural to imagine agency in the individual, rooted in a single moment of choice or feeling. We're used to thinking this way—it's a hard habit to shake. But charismatics invite us to code-switch, to step back and widen the lens. They show us that agency works on many scales. It emerges from breakthrough, through tradition, in the habits we form, and even in the quiet patience of listening. Agency can be dispersed across all these layers.

When we accept that scale effects mean that cause and effect aren't always neat and linear, we can see that life doesn't always fit into one clear narrative. The world is messier. The connections between different levels of experience are full of noise—what happens at one scale doesn't always predict what happens at another. Our view shifts. The story changes. The future isn't locked in. There's room to breathe. And to disagree.

This may be another charismatic insight.

9

Activism: The Spider-Man Principle and Spirit-Filled Activism

As we near the end of the book, I must turn to the elephant in the room, hiding in plain view: I like to think of it as the connection between spiritual life and social action. Every few days, people ask me about this link. They sense that charismatic worship—the highly skilled practice of bodily, emotional, and cognitive release—has something to do with politics, with the pressing issues of justice, power, and social change. Put this way, it certainly sounds like an odd linkage. But people keep trying to make that connection for me. It turns out, this is for good reason.

In the downtime after an MRI session, one of my informants, Shelly, explained that some churches use their power to hurt people. She didn't like it. She talked about the "Spider-Man Principle": that with great power comes great responsibility. She wanted churches to pay more attention to their effects out in the world. The radical power of charismatic worship can be a force for incredible good or, sadly, destructive harm, she thought.

This is a difficult conversation both within and outside the charismatic movement. For all my talk of bodily, emotional, and even cognitive flexibility—for every moment of hope, every story of newfound agency—there are plenty of accounts of wildly harsh social and political inspiration, coming right from the center of this movement. It doesn't take much attention to notice that for every pastor like Heidi Baker, known for giving out massive support to poor people, there's a Sean Bolz, who copped to overtures described as sexual harassment and was also accused of using social media data mining to manipulate people by crafting prophecies that seem to come from God. I've heard from charismatics and non-charismatics alike that while many churches generate brilliant forms of care and compassion, others inflict tremendous suffering in the name of Jesus and the Holy Spirit. The same fervor that inspires healing can sometimes drive actions that are, at best, troubling, and, at worst, deeply damaging. That may seem counterintuitive when we remember that all this is tied to an experience of loving God and of God's love. But, it is no fringe idea that some churches do harm with their love.

How can this love, this care, and this damage come from the same fabric, I wondered.

As I write this, white evangelicals, especially charismatics, are often seen as the shock troops of the Republican Party. It's easy to then assume that this kind of worship naturally leans toward extreme right-wing radicalism or supports the idea of a Christian nation built on narrow interpretations of scripture. And yes, there is a grain of truth in that view. But it's not the whole story. Far from it.

The same kind of spirit-filled worship that drives these movements has also inspired very different kinds of social action. Black charismatics today are largely aligned with the Democratic Party and civil rights organizing, for instance. In the early twentieth century, a large swath of the charismatic movement was led by radical social progressives, many were pacifists. The flames of spiritual renewal have sparked wildly different political and social fires. But, and this may be the through-thread, they were all intense fires. Very little of this movement is slow or quiet.

It often sounds as if there is something about the very experience, the feeling of power, or of warmth in the heart, that inspires people to be active in the world, to be engaged in changing it. Shavon describes the impulse as "subcultural." And Jesus was certainly that with his challenge to wealth and power. For Shavon, it is a refusal to accept the world as it is because she has felt and seen a different possibility in the inner recesses of her heart and mind. Here, perhaps inner experience shapes the outer? Or is it the reverse, does the outer shape the inner? Maybe the effect of worship emerges from the values and practices of the church community? Even more likely, is it some mixture of the inner and the outer? How does the looping between culture and spiritually infused bodies play out when it comes to social action?

From my interviews, it sounded as if charismatic worship can inspire a profound sense of freedom and possibility—a feeling of being renewed and open to change. And, that in turn, can inspire urgency toward action. Empowered to act, people come out of worship feeling renewed, radicalized, and capable. The direction that this power takes—whether it's toward justice or oppression, inclusion or exclusion—now that depends.

Power and Urgency

From my first interview, it was clear: charismatics talk about their bodies. Sensation was their favorite language for describing their connection to God. They talked about training that capacity. A bit later, I found philosophy of agency: they talked about breakthrough, also cultivation and even waiting, it was a fresh way to think about the Western conception of will. Maybe they experienced a deep, subconscious build-up that, in a moment, bursts through. Interesting, yes. That sums this book up to now. But how does this all become real-world action? That wasn't so obvious, and it took a bit of translation.

Nearly every text on the charismatic movement talks about power. Along with power, fire. Flames, burning. *The Fire Bible, The Word on Fire Bible, Black Fire*, an endless stream of sermons and scholarly texts with the word "fire" in the title—this book has good company. To me though, the words power and fire seemed to describe strong emotion. Metaphor, nothing more. At first, they didn't sound like what I'd call power. I thought of power as a means to affect things, to change them around me.

But as the interviews piled up, I began to hear these words differently. People told me how prayer changed their patterns of thinking. They sometimes had thoughts that didn't seem their own. They experienced a kind of clarity that was missing previously. This, they said, brought the courage to stand up in front of a church, or to march out into the world and fight for change. It seemed that there was more to this than simply release. Maybe the release of social constraints enabled activity? Release generated heat. The words "fire" or "power" weren't merely describing the intensity of worship. They described something that propelled people. Along with release, this heat was shaping actions and thoughts. They were feeling pushed to go out and act in the world. The feeling of freedom, of renewal, seemed to carry with it the will and the capacity, and even urgency to do something.

For some, it's that easy. Jeanine told me, "It's simple. When I pray, I feel the power to go out and change the world. And then I do it." At the time, she was involved with a campaign with poor Latino youth in Los Angeles, her home community. She described God's presence as both peaceful and urgent. "I hear people talk about how getting high is all about relaxing, not caring about anything. That's not God's presence for me. For me, God's presence is peace, yes, but it's also this urgency to do something meaningful with it."

Jimmy spoke the same way.

It's more of a groaning, an urgency, like a flow. You've probably heard it described as a river. It's like a rushing river, not just in a biblical sense. It's a force that has to get out. If you don't let it out—if you don't speak in tongues—it's like you're holding it back. But when you let it flow, that urgency takes over. Maybe that's why people speak in tongues the way they do—loud, with different tones and intensities. Some probably sound better than others, but it doesn't matter. It's this urgency in your spirit. For me, speaking in tongues is life. That urgency doesn't bring anxiety, though. It brings peace, deliverance.

John was teaching courses at Teen Challenge, the Assemblies of God's detox program. He talked about giving up control and feeling something else take over. It was a release into power, he said. "It's like a force running through me." Words then came out that surprised even him. "Some of the things I said in that class, I don't even know where they came from. I was thinking, 'Wow, John, where are you getting this stuff from?'" He described it as a certainty, a surety, like he knew something beyond himself was speaking through him. "I can feel the power in my words as I say them," he said. William James described the certainty and clarity gained from spiritual experience—he called it the "noetic feeling."[1]

When Williamson, Pollio, and Hood[2] did their analysis of Christian serpent handlers, they noticed a similar feeling of power that enabled people to take risks they wouldn't usually. As one participant described, "It had a feeling of power of knowing that the Lord would give you the power to do things like that. It really gives you a feeling of power that He gives me—That devil's subject unto you. It just makes—It's a feeling of power." That word—power.

I had imagined that letting go meant falling—like being slain in the Spirit. But that wasn't the end of the story. What struck me later was this: release doesn't necessarily drain power. Sometimes it inspires it. Sometimes it helps power burn. Remember the spiral—attention, arousal, release? This combination of new thoughts and joyful feelings generates confidence and clarity that may drive people toward action.

Radicals

That release inspires power is exactly what charismatic history tells us. The earliest charismatics were not satisfied with prayer; they were advocates for social change, and not simply minor social revisions, they saw their practice as straight-up rebellion. The 1906 Azusa Street Revival—led by a half-blind Black preacher William Seymour—brought together men and women, Blacks and whites, in a raw and extravagant celebration of the "infilling of the Holy Spirit." Radical impulses held the day. One of many prophecies that emerged from Azusa spoke with little caution:

> The time will come when the poor man will say that he has nothing to eat and work will be shut down. That is going to cause the poor man to go to these places and break in to get food. This will cause the rich man to come out with his gun to make war on the laboring man ... blood will be in the streets like an outpouring of rain from heaven.[3]

There's nothing held back there.

And that was the movement's spirit. Azusa Street started with a Black man leading a mixed-race church. It spread worldwide, with the experience of the Spirit pushing people to reject the norms of the world they lived in. They ignored the rules around race and gender, wailing through the night, crossing lines that would seem crazy to most of America back then.

The Spirit gave them a kind of freedom. As Pentecostal historian Cheryl Bridges Johns said, "It was a subversive and revolutionary movement, not based upon philosophic ideology nor totally upon critical reflection. It was a movement that experienced through the Holy Spirit, God's divine liberation."[4] With that spirit, charismatics fought against corporate greed. They challenged big-box stores, went after wealth inequality, some even challenging the very idea of the nuclear family.[5]

In Chicago, charismatics turned their power toward tenant movements. Historian Walter Hollenweger, in *Pentecostalism and Black Power*, wrote about Arthur Brazier, a Black Pentecostal evangelist whose The Woodlawn Organization, run by Black people in the Chicago slums, regulated local markets, checking for overpriced stores exploiting the neighborhood. They used the press to expose landlords who charged too much, organized rent strikes, and formed youth groups to stop violence in schools. Hollenweger believed the Gifts of the Spirit led to political action. "In addition to the charisms which are known in the history of Pentecostalism, such as speaking in tongues, prophecy, religious dancing, prayer for the sick, they [at Woodlawn] practice the gift of demonstrating, organizing, and publicizing as another kind of prophecy." Hollenweger said the activism in charismatic practice came from its African roots, born in the Black churches of the 1800s.[6]

Similarly, in "Why Scatting Is Like Speaking in Tongues: Post Modern Reflections on Jazz, Pentecostalism and 'Africosmysticism,'" Stephen J. Casmier and Donald Mathews compare tongues prayer to jazz scatting. They argue that both reflect African forms of creativity that help people break free and challenge the social order. Others tie this tradition of rebellion to the First and Second Great Awakenings, which were the European channels into the charismatic movement.

But by the mid-twentieth century, this rebellious energy was redirected as the Assemblies of God and other Pentecostal formations began their lean toward fundamentalism. Early charismatics were fluid, spiritually and culturally, and their fundamentalist neighbors criticized them relentlessly. Over time, charismatics adopted the fundamentalist theology and the social rules that came with it.[7] As the curator of the AG research library, Darrin Rodgers explains, by the early twentieth century, charismatics had embraced fundamentalist norms, rejecting "pacifism, interracialism, feminism, and environmentalism—all these radical interactions with the world" that had once been core to their movement. AG became increasingly identified with the conservative movement, finally rejecting even faith-based pacifism during the Vietnam War.[8]

Yet, even as US charismatics joined forces with Republican elites, the drive for transformation stayed alive. Historian Mike Davis, in *Planet of Slums*, called charismatics the new proletariat. "Marx has yielded the historical stage to Mohammed and the Holy Ghost. If God dies in the cities of the industrial revolution, he has risen again in the postindustrial cities of the developing world ... Pentecostalism is the first major world religion to have grown up almost entirely in the soil of the modern urban slum." For Davis, charismatic evangelicalism holds radical potential to drive real change.[9] I suspect that many charismatics are still radicals, only their radicalism shifted poles, from left to right.

A lot of people have noticed that charismatics were revolutionaries; it wasn't just me. Only, I think most of us—myself included—tended to see tongues as more of a metaphor than a real blueprint for social change. I've spent years gathering these references to the "metaphor" of tongues. Philosopher Michel de Certeau called speaking in tongues a "vocal utopia," something beyond rationality, untrained, spontaneous, with no clear direction. Author Norman O. Brown thought the chaos of tongues could be a model for human liberation. He asked us to imagine "Pentecostal freedom, Pentecostal fusion. Speaking with tongues; many tongues, many meanings ... The Babylonian confusion of tongues redeemed in the pentecostal fusion."[10] Brown wanted to unleash the chaos of tongues against the discipline of society.[11] Feminist theorist Donna Haraway called for "a feminist speaking in tongues to strike fear into the circuits" of the new right.[12] Author Gloria Anzaldua's Chicana women "speak in tongues like the outcaste and the insane," and it is a revolt.[13] Philosopher Mary Daly suggested "speaking with tongues of fire" as a way to resist patriarchy.

Philosophers like Alain Badiou, Slavoj Žižek, and Giorgio Agamben added their take—the organizing success of evangelicals caught their attention, so they came to imagine a new radical approach to life, one modeled on evangelical Christianity. Badiou, in particular, saw Paul's conversion as a blueprint for radicalism.[14] The radical break in charismatic worship might open the door to subversion or rebellion, they thought. And these philosophers were right, only this was more than metaphor, and rebellion, it turns out, has many forms.

The Christian Right today frames its politics as a rebellion. Against modernity, against abortion, against what they experience as the twisting of social norms. Charismatics among them are still fighting the good fight; only their allies and enemies have shifted. Most aren't standing in solidarity with socialists or communists like they were in the 1880s or 1930s. They're still in resistance, still driven by moments of power and freedom, just aiming at Democrats, cities, and "wokeness." The Tea Party and Trumpers—they're radicals in their own new way.

Outside the United States, charismatic politics are complicated. It's beyond the scope here, but it's worth noting that global charismatic churches also mix resistance to modern life—whether it's seemingly new ideas about gender, sexuality, or labor—with resistance to older systems like Catholicism and a striking relationship to paganism where charismatics had tremendous success because unlike previous missionaries they accepted the reality of existing spirits but switched the assessment from positive to negative as local spirits were renamed as demons.[15]

Now, after all this talk about fluidity and resistance in charismatic practice, we should remember there are some depictions that make the charismatics appear mostly rigid, even reactionary. Sociologist Christian Lalive d'Epinay saw charismatic practice as creating good workers for US economic interests, and in the process, defusing their revolutionary impulses.[16] Then there's the Ugandan right-wing and its anti-gay movement, rooted in charismatic churches, which pushes for the death penalty for gay sex.[17] Or you can look at the close ties between charismatic evangelicalism, prosperity doctrines, and neoliberalism.[18] The same fiery passion that drives transformation and resistance can work as accommodation.

But the point here is that, to a large degree, charismatics see themselves as, and might actually be, activists for radical change.

This Is How Social Change Works

Wait! No!!

Social movements aren't religious!

Social movements are run by radicals challenging society, not the churches that uphold it.

Aren't they?

The right answer would simply be: Nope.

If you don't have that initial voice in your head, fine. But it's been at least a murmur in mine throughout my life. Admittedly, it was an odd thought for an activist Jew whose own social engagement feels very much like a form of worship. I was simply dead wrong to imagine that social change was primarily a secular thing.

In the United States, according to sociologist Michael Young, the whole idea of a social movement was born in the mid-1800s, right in the thick of evangelical prayer meetings.[19] Abolition, anti-vice campaigns, temperance—all those moral reforms—they all got their power from the church. As did the Civil Rights movement.

Here is where we get to one place where my research is somewhat unusual. Religion breeds movements in many ways. Getting folks in a room weekly gives you numbers, and there's the collective feeling of worship. And certainly some of this brain shift we are outlining is in a loop with being together—the safety of the group may very well help us release. But I think there is more here than collectivity. The experience of a renewed mind, of a fiery soul, can feel like a rejection of everyday norms, a kind of defiance that lets people turn spiritual passion into political action, something that often does not appear especially sacred. Prayer practices do this, I think.[20] We know they open up new ways of thinking and living. And maybe those ways spill out beyond the church, beyond the given prayer, out into the world.

But what kind of new thinking and being? That's the heart of the book. The question puts us back at the dinner table with my parents, wondering how the inner life relates to the outer world. We've circled back to a central puzzle: if charismatic worship can spark radical personal and social change, why does it look so different in different times and places? What kinds of changes come from the practice itself, and what depends on the world outside? Or how do these loop back and forth? How does the inner fire reflect in the outer life? Or maybe more to the point, who do you resist?

Loosening the Brain and Relaxation

When we talk about the loosening of the brain that comes with this kind of prayer, there is the inevitable question of manipulation. Many scholars view high-intensity prayer as a sign of vulnerability, a trance-state that leaves followers open to manipulation by church hierarchies.[21] I think they may miss the fact that most charismatics invite this openness. Charismatics know they're making themselves flexible and exposed, but they're choosing it in a context they believe in. Charismatics could easily respond: Of course, we're making ourselves available. We open ourselves to a tradition 2,000 years old.

For the most part, this book turns that critique on its head. For even when charismatics are understood by their most extreme impulses, they are also the progenitors of an incredibly sophisticated set of mind-body training techniques that combine a humble sense of yielding the mind, body, and self to a higher power and a series of overlapping and often highly subtle practices of attention—both fiercely active and intensely quieting. In many ways their minds are quite expansive, perhaps even especially open to change and to radically different ways of seeing the world.

Sometimes the radical change from surrender is very personal. Of the first five preachers I met in the United States, four were ex-cocaine addicts. The Assemblies of God runs a rehab program called Teen Challenge, with around 1,000 residential centers. I wonder if the high from drugs and alcohol gets swapped for trance-like prayer experiences, now experienced as gifts of the spirit?

When I interviewed Sam from a church in the Sierras, he told me straight up that he swapped his meth addiction for worship. "They're exactly the same," he said. He explained that the pleasure from drugs was so close to the pleasure from worship (though maybe worship was a touch better, he said). Either way, though, one high destroys you, and the other puts you in a community where you can live a full life.

From our research, we now think that charismatics cycle between release of body, emotion, and mind. That's at least what our creativity data suggests. Thinking about addiction—and it's still early to know for sure: first, we've seen pre-SMA deactivation during speaking in tongues, and a similar result in lesion studies is tied to reduced addictive behavior;[22] second, higher creativity scores during release suggest loosened mental priors, which may be also linked to better outcomes in addiction recovery.[23] We know also that Alcoholics Anonymous came from the Oxford evangelicals, who weren't just about prayer but about surrender—of mind, body, and emotion. Think of the Serenity Prayer: "God, give me grace to accept with serenity / the things that cannot be changed, / Courage to change the things / which should be changed, / and the Wisdom to distinguish / the one from the other." If that isn't letting go, I don't know what is.

In the past decade, researchers have started to think more about the effects of practices that enhance brain plasticity. Michael Pollan spent years diving into the world of psychedelics, trying to understand why they're sparking so much interest. His book, *How to Change Your Mind*, paints a picture of great social possibility. For Pollan, psychedelics offer solutions to massive problems—political polarization, environmental crises. As he sees it, these substances open up the brain, creating moments of intense plasticity where old ways of thinking give way to new patterns, ones that might heal us deeply.[24]

This plasticity, Pollan suggests, is where real change happens. Old habits shift, and in their place come new thoughts, often gentler ones, he thinks. Some say these new configurations lead to compassion, empathy, and trust. Psychedelics, they claim, generate "feelings of trust, empathy, bonding, closeness, tenderness, forgiveness, acceptance, and connectedness."[25] And these changes shouldn't just stay within the self—they are all about how we treat others, what researchers call "pro-social attitudes and behaviors."[26]

Maybe this kind of prosocial behavior will change our society. In a review of fifty-four empirical studies, Henrik Jungaberle talks about how psychedelics offer social mechanisms to spark both personal and social change.[27] More and more, the idea is taking root: psychedelics might just be the answer we have been looking for—not just a replacement for SSRIs, but the foundation for a new kind of society.

These altered states seemed a lovely model for our research into speaking in tongues—these findings could explain why it feels so good to pray, why folks are energized, why churches can be such warm, welcoming environments, maybe even why prayer can heal bodies. But this is just one piece of the charismatic story: charismatic worship involves high arousal release, for sure, but also a kind of relaxation.

Remember, after and sometimes in the middle of worship, there can be a moment of calm. It's a quiet within or after the storm of the lalling of tongues. Soaking in the Spirit, some call it. This calm might have benefits. Maybe relaxing the body can bring a kind of peace that helps people respond gently to the world around them. If inner experience actually drives the outer, maybe both or either of these feelings—the aroused release or the calm—can lay the groundwork for a different society, for people who can change the world. There's certainly some evidence that prayer, like meditation, engages the "relaxation response," good against inflammation and to calm the nervous system.[28] There's also some research showing that the quieting of the mind during charismatic prayer lowers cortisol, a stress hormone.

In a small town in New York's mid-Hudson Valley, anthropologist Chris Lynn took saliva samples from worshippers on a busy Sunday and then also on a quiet Monday to measure cortisol and alpha-amylase—two biomarkers that show when a person is more or less stressed out. During the lively Sunday service, both levels were high, showing stress and arousal. But by Monday, they dropped sharply. That is unsurprising. But here is the key—the drop was especially pronounced for people who often spoke in tongues. Maybe, this study suggests, tongues prayer helps us become more flexible with our stress response, which is another way to say that it helps us to modulate stress—offering a kind of relief from the weight of daily life.[29]

This kind of relaxation is exactly what people say is the heart of mindfulness. Since the mid-1970s, when Harvard researchers first showed that meditation can change the mind, this research has exploded; now over a thousand papers are published every year on the benefits of mindfulness. I definitely want to complain on some other day that this is way more attention than prayer ever gets, but more important to note right now is that it took three decades to build up the science to say mindfulness changes us—not just for a moment, but in a lasting way. It is not just a temporary change. It changes our lasting traits, the parts of our personalities that stick around for the rest of our lives.[30] We are in the very beginning of this kind of work on prayer.

For mindfulness, some suggest that the calm we feel inside after meditation can ripple out into society, making us not just healthier but kinder. Think of the title: *Mindfulness: A Better Me; A Better You; A Better World.* Here the authors join a chorus of voices who link personal transformation to social change.[31] It makes sense in a way. If we're healthy inside, why shouldn't that spill over into the world around us? The research on meditation hints that there's a connection between mindfulness and kindness out in the world.

Researchers at the Max Planck Institute tested this. They looked at how people responded to graphic violence before and after an eight-hour loving-kindness meditation.[32] Before the meditation, when folks saw others in pain, they felt it—it activated brain circuits that mirrored suffering. But after the meditation, when participants were shown people in pain, a different set of circuits lit up, the ones associated with a parent's love for their child. Researchers felt this suggested that mindfulness can make empathy more potent.[33] Psychologist Erik Wallmark and his team found something similar: mindfulness made people feel less personal distress when they saw others in need, but more empathic concern. They called it an "altruistic orientation." In short, there's real evidence that mindfulness fosters empathy.[34]

Then there's also generosity. In economic games where people were given money and a chance to donate, those who had just practiced mindfulness gave more.[35] Karl Frost and his team ran an experiment where people played a game following a calming meditation. They found meditators cared less about their in-group's success, and they cooperated more.[36] In other words, mindfulness doesn't just make us kinder within our own circles—it might blur the lines between "us" and "them."[37]

In study after study, mindfulness shows itself to be both calming and healing, linked to prosocial feelings like empathy and altruism. The evidence points to this: those who practice mindfulness, and religion for that matter, are often more compassionate and generous. But, as I studied this more closely, things got messier. Here we go.

Like prayer, meditation can be practiced with the intent to care. Just as one prays to God for healing, people meditate to cultivate compassion. They call it "metta," or loving-kindness meditation. And the story here is easy enough to grasp: if you meditate with compassion in mind, there is evidence that it leads you to compassionate thoughts and then maybe or maybe not to compassionate actions. But what about the practice of relaxation itself? Without all the cultural trappings and intent, does relaxation work on its own to generate prosocial emotions or behavior? Does this cultivated neurobiology really push us toward social impulses?

Some researchers claim compassion begins with the relaxation, the attention training, and the better control over emotions, not only the direct intention toward compassion.[38] The ability to focus and refocus can help broaden one's capacity to regulate emotions, making the mind more open to the suffering of others, they think.[39] It makes sense—if you're less reactive, maybe you can be softer, more gentle. That seems right to me.

And, there is some good evidence that mindfulness, even without the visualizations of kindness, can promote empathy and prosocial actions.[40] It can reduce biases and soften the lines between groups,[41] perhaps by enhancing attentional habits that tune us in to the needs of others.[42] Contemplative practices even change the body's autonomic functions, like raising heart rate variability (HRV), which has been linked to greater compassion and prosocial behavior.[43]

No matter the mechanism, meditation seems to spark a deep form of empathic concern, and that's key for prosocial behavior.[44] Those with more empathy are more likely to engage in selfless actions, even when it costs them dearly.[45]

Empathy?

But here's the kicker: maybe the change can go multiple ways. The inner shapes the outer, sure, but the outer—your hopes, your expectations, and the social around you—well, that might shape the inner just as much. So, while religious faith can certainly build solidarity and foster in-group kindness,[46] in some situations, when the outer world is shaped differently, say we are focused on our conflict with our neighboring country as we become more plastic, it can also lead to hostility toward outsiders.[47]

And in these contexts, it turns out that empathy itself doesn't guarantee kindness, at least beyond your close circle of friends. At first, that surprised me. But it makes sense when you think about it. Take the Israeli military or Hamas fighters, for instance. Research shows that both groups are capable of deep empathy toward insiders. But that doesn't extend to people outside their group.[48] In fact, there is evidence that, in certain circumstances, the more you love your in group, the more you hate the others. Put that way, it seems a bit more intuitive. So, empathy isn't just a simple thing. Context matters. When empathy is bound to your in-group, it becomes what Cikara and her colleagues call "parochial empathy,"[49] or empathy that is tightly bounded.

Mindfulness also may have a dark side. Some argue that instead of promoting the social good, corporations have co-opted mindfulness, turning it into a self-help tool that makes people work harder, faster, without benefit other than corporate profit. It's also used by the militaries to make soldiers aim better when shooting to kill.[50] Whether you see that as good or bad depends on your view of the military, but it is not easily framed as kindness.

Psychedelics too. Not every trip is a smooth ride. Some trips inspire; others lead to panic or paranoia. Timothy Leary talked about "set" (mindset) and "setting" (context) as key to shaping a good or bad trip.[51] Researchers now agree—set and setting, and how you process it all afterward, are what determine whether brain plasticity leads you somewhere healthy, or somewhere dangerous.[52] This is clearly another way of saying that cultural forms and expectations shape our brains. Because of this, psychedelics aren't always the path to peace. Neo-Nazis, Proud Boys, and other extremists use moments of psychic break for their own revolutionary goals.[53]

So, what I'm saying is that there's no contradiction between empathy, calm, loosening the mind, and extreme unkindness. We know that charismatic practices, like mindfulness and psychedelics, bring calm and cognitive loosening accompanied by deep experiential and behavioral changes. These could inspire social change—and they do. But what kind of change? Again, that depends. We can measure health and prosocial impulses in mindfulness, psychedelics, or charismatic worship. But then we must take them out of the lab, let them loose in the world, and watch how they weave—and loop— through the social forms we've built.

These moments are fluid, but they don't exist in a vacuum. They're shaped by where and how they happen. Charismatic prayer doesn't just manifest in the brain. It's shaped by the community around it. And that varies—maybe it's occurring at home, in a field, in a Black church, in a conservative church, in a progressive church, in the United States, or elsewhere. Because people become especially open, different contexts can yield different, but unusually potent, results. And that is where the Spider-Man principle comes in—when someone opens themselves up fully, the context drives the outcome even more than when that person is protected. And sometimes, that outcome is powerful.

At times, charismatic worship becomes a petri dish that nurtures social change. But then we need to ask ourselves: how is that change shaped? In other words, how do personal experiences of transformation become social change? How is the sense-based moment of freedom shaped into social interaction?

Of course, charismatics knew this already. Plasticity of this sort is an attitude and a potential. It is not politics. At least not at first. The moments afterwards, what charismatics call soaking and what we call reintegration, that is where directions are set.

Re-Integration

It took a while for anthropologist Victor Turner to learn this same lesson: that reintegration is where the change can be measured. At first, he was focused on release. He studied the Ndembu in Zambia, where he noticed gatherings that sparked warm, almost electric feelings of connectedness—he called it *communitas*. These rituals generated the feeling that change is not only possible but imminent; as the grip of the everyday loosens, people become ready for something new, he thought. For those who followed his work, Turner's ideas promised freedom—a way to shake free of life's set patterns.[54] This sounded revolutionary to some.[55]

But as years passed, Turner saw something else: the freedom he'd celebrated could be quite temporary. The fluidity flickered and then often gave way to a process of reintegration, through which change was often dulled or reversed altogether. His later analysis echoed scholars who'd examined festivals like Carnival, where social roles were temporarily upended—where the rich might play the poor, men might dress as women. These ritual inversions hinted at a glimpse of something different, of power flipped on its head. Yet, when the music ended and the masks came off, questions lingered. Did these moments of role reversal foster reevaluation, or were they merely a release, a bit of steam shot into the sky before things went back to normal? Did the rich come away humbled, or the poor emboldened? Or did these rituals simply defuse social tensions, allowing power to stay firmly in place? In the end, even *communitas*—the freedom Turner had first celebrated—might act as a kind of control, as much a tool for preserving the old order as for forging a new one. Loosening was key, but when things resolidified, that was where the real measure of change sat.

Spider-Man

When I first saw charismatics worship, I was struck by the sheer intensity of their release, their rigid bodies softening, their postures collapsing. It reminded me of psychiatrist Wilhelm Reich, who believed that a person's ability to let go was a sign of emotional and social health. For Reich, neuroses showed up in the body as "character armor"—tension held so deeply it molded people physically. Therapy, he argued, could release these tensions, unlocking emotions like sadness, sobbing, and even rage.[56] Reich believed that the hard and soft in the body had social parallels—that people who could be flexible emotionally would also tend to be kind and gentle socially. On the other side of things, in *The Mass Psychology of Fascism*, he links rigid bodies to the psychological character of Hitler himself and to the willingness of millions to follow Nazi and also Soviet totalitarianism.[57]

I wonder what Reich would make of charismatics in prayer. Would he see them as letting go? Or would he, like my skeptical ex-mother-in-law, call it a shallow release? Ironically, many charismatics themselves critique today's worship as just that.

As we work through these questions, I am beginning to think that while the difference between the gentle and harsh outcomes of prayer has something to do with how deeply we let go, it might be shaped even more profoundly by the way we shape ourselves when coming out of that state of profound vulnerability. In those moments of deep prayer, people give themselves up—to God, to the Holy Spirit—and they release control, quite literally, over body and mind. And the strange thing is that this surrender first brings an overwhelming sense of peace, a quieting of the self. In that peace, constraints and worries fall away. But then the quiet begins building into a kind of power, and an urgency that presses toward action. Charismatics have built a whole way of life on this experience—one that celebrates the body, that feels alive with the chance to shape the world, and that asserts an unusual sense of agency.

In many moments of prayer as well as meditation or psychedelics, there's a softening, a loosening of who we are, a letting go of the edges we hold onto for dear life. Psychologist Alison Gopnik told me it's like being thrust into a fire, the kind that softens metal, makes us pliable, bendable, ready for change— she called it "annealing." The potential can feel limitless. But it doesn't last. The fluidity, the openness—it's transient, sometimes just a flash. As we cool, the structures we tried to leave behind come back, pressing in, hardening us again. Charismatic freedom flows like a river, but the banks are carved from centuries of Christian faith and the hard edges of modern culture. The world always returns to a form, it seems.

But, I suspect that it's not only us who change within these fires. The world shifts too. The seemingly immovable frameworks of society respond to our brain plasticity and the actions it sparks. Even the broadest social structures— the institutions, norms, the scaffolding of everyday life—can yield ever so slightly, altered by our inner revolutions. And if we do it together, the push is that much stronger. It's a continuous back-and-forth between what's inside us and what's outside, between the small revolutions within and the larger frameworks of society, and then also between the big revolutions outside and the selves we have built over our lifetimes. Sometimes, the old riverbanks overflow, and entirely new boundaries emerge. In those moments, my therapist father warns, the world may shift, but will our inner selves be flexible enough to let the change take hold? Or will our own internal rigidity pull everything back to the familiar, something in our comfort zones?

This process—softening, then hardening, yielding, and solidifying—is the rhythmic looping between the self and society. Neither ends up the same. Each time we enter these states, each time we open to change, we create a crack—an entryway for new ideas, new influences. This is the quiet power of charismatic worship: it lets us change in ways few things do. It is, very simply, powerful. And that is why Shelly reminded us: with that great power comes great responsibility.

Bibliographic Essays

Bibliographic Notes for Prologue

For people who simply want to read more about Pentecostal and charismatic movements, there is a tremendous literature from anthropologists and sociologists,[1] anthropology of Christianity more broadly,[2] people from inside the movement,[3] philosophers,[4] the Black church,[5] the religious right, on psychological research on tongues prayer,[6] and lots more I am not aware of. But this will certainly get you started.

For years, I studied prayer through ethnography—collecting firsthand stories, spending hours talking with people in churches, and conducting close-up interviews. That took me from 2005 to 2018. Only then did I set foot in the MRI room. From there, I went back to rethink my ethnographic and phenomenological data. This book's structure mirrors that journey, moving from the outer world of experience to the inner world of the brain, and then looping back out again. And looping is key.

My use of looping is inspired by Ian Hacking's essay "The Looping Effects of Human Kinds," a central theme of this book both in method and substance. Years of observing spiritual practitioners and listening to them describe their experiences confirmed for me that experience often arises from the interplay of expectation, cultural invitation, social practice, and bodily response. In this case, we have a theology of submission, a community conversation about submission and letting go, a practice all about letting go of the tongue and releasing the thoughts and emotions to God, and a neurophysiology that shows that bodily, emotional, and cognitive release are all a part of the story.

These are the cultural, phenomenological, and physiological elements that are looping back and forth and inspiring each other.

There are many terms for these kinds of loop: Seligman and Kirmayer call it "bio-looping,"[7] Csordas "the somatic mode of attention."[8] In a series of articles, Laurence Kirmayer articulates this approach in systematic detail, emphasizing how mind and culture co-emerge (Leung et al. 2011; Seligman, Choudhury, and Kirmayer 2016). Drawing from Bateson's ecology of mind, Kirmayer maps biocultural feedback loops that extend cognition through cultural practices, tools, and social interaction. His work integrates theories of embodiment (Varela, Thompson, and Rosch 1991; Gallagher 2005; Chemero 2009), situated cognition (Clark 1997; Clark and Chalmers 1998), and enactivism, which views organism and environment as co-constituted (Noë 2005; Di Paolo and Thompson 2014).

Kirmayer explains that there is strong evidence that looping between cultural understanding and mental experience has significant embodied consequences. Social epidemiology, for example, has shown how social context profoundly influences health outcomes.[9] You can see this in psychiatry, where conditions like anxiety, depression, hallucinations, and delusions which are often viewed as biologically fixed, actually slip in and out of the bounds of normalcy depending on context. Illness here is not only a matter of neural misfiring, but of social meaning piled on.

Anthropological and cross-cultural studies affirm both the shared architecture and the malleable facades of mental illness (Kirmayer 2006; Larøi et al. 2014). Kleinman (1987) describes pathogenesis and pathoplasticity: the former, the biology of disorder; the latter, its cultural costume. A hallucinated voice may be experienced as a god in Accra or a government agent in Ohio (Gold and Gold 2014; Larøi et al. 2014). Tanya Luhrmann shows that American voices in the head accuse while Ghanaian ones may comfort. Disorders of selfhood, like dissociation, bend to local expectation (Seligman and Kirmayer 2008). Psychedelic experiences, often seen as self-generated, still tend to reflect individual narratives and cultural themes. In Canada, religious psychedelic users sometimes report visual and auditory phenomena associated with local Aboriginal spirits, showing how personal and cultural contexts shape even seemingly autonomous perceptions.[10] In other words, language does not float above the body—it grows from it, shaping and shaped by the rhythms of breath, muscle, and metaphor (Körner, Topolinski, and Strack 2015).

Philosophers of embodied cognition like Alva Noë,[11] Andy Clark,[12] and Mark Johnson,[13] take looping as a foundational principle (see also Csordas, *The Sacred Self*; Jackson, "Where Thought Belongs"; Stoller, *The Power of the Between*),[14]–for them, it is the basis of 4E cognition. These enactivist perspectives in cognitive science suggest that our experiences and expectations—shaped by the narratives, symbols, bodily practices, and scripts of specific social and cultural contexts—fundamentally influence thought processes, affecting attention, sensation, and perception.[15] Thus, no thought is entirely free from these situational dialogues, no matter how spontaneous it may seem.

Kirmayer links enactivism to culture through predictive processing: the brain actively anticipates sensory input through generative models, enabling both perception and imaginative, culturally embedded cognition. These models guide action and incorporate social affordances, forming feedback loops where culture shapes cognition and cognition, in turn, reshapes cultural environments. This book adds to the biocultural framework which outlines "culture as patterned practice"[16] and joins anthropology to cognitive neuroscience. I am trying to show concretely that cultural practices are characterized by particular social patterns, and that patterns of social practice (e.g., prayer) shape patterns of cognitive and neural processing (e.g., maps of the sense of release, power, and agency.

Of course, biocultural approaches are not new; they extend some of the thinking of medical anthropologists, where mixed methods have become more common as these scholars engage with and respond to medical scientists. Such scholars (like Arthur Kleinman, Byron Good, Kim Hopper, Neely Myers, Janis Jenkins, Rebecca Lester, Thomas Weisner, and others)[17] publish in both anthropological and medical journals. These citations reflect the interdisciplinary focus of this research, that speaks to the intersections of anthropology, psychology, medicine, and sociocultural factors. The use of mixed methods research specific to the anthropology of religion, however, is relatively modest. Rebecca Seligman,[18] Jeffrey Snodgrass,[19] Rita Astuti,[20] and Christopher Lynn[21] all used mixed methods to explore spiritual experience.

I do believe the time is ripe to expand this enrichment of ethnographic methods. Scholars increasingly describe religious experiences as brain events. We now know that certain kinds of spiritual practices (such as meditation and prayer) have concrete and seemingly lasting effects, many of them somatic. Several scholars—among them Richard Davidson,[22] Cliff Saron,[23] Andrew Newberg,[24] and their colleagues—have demonstrated that meditation practice leads over time to a wide array of neurophysiological outcomes. A collection of emerging subdisciplines—cultural neuroscience, the cognitive science of religion, sociocultural neuroscience, and neuroanthropology—all share the insight that religious practices impact bodies in deeply physical ways.[25] These fields would benefit from work that uses the ethnographic method, and the anthropology of religion would benefit by adding mixed-methods approaches that would enable the work to be read across the different fields. Now one could try and distinguish between these different versions of joining culture and the body, but I am inspired by an openness to multiple starting points.

Aside from simply describing how I try to do this, I do want to offer one theoretical opening that at times feels mundane—and at others, a bit like insight. The brain has been described as an oscillation machine—swinging, pulsing, like a vast playground of a thousand swing sets. As neuroscientist Buzsáki puts it in *The Rhythms of the Brain*, these brain oscillations are linked with broader metabolic rhythms.[26] There might be a loop between them, scholars suggest. I wonder also if something similar might be true of the social? And then could these loops be the kind of reiterated patterns that create relational stability—perhaps even, as Karen Barad and other relational ontologists suggest, co-emerging patterns of being?[27] Or maybe they function as stable attractors that make room for emergent complexity? It sounds banal to say that our relationships hold us together—of course they do, and of course relationships between bodies, social facts, and institutions do the same. Yet, from another angle, it feels strangely profound.

In this book, the research itself begins in ethnography. One beauty of anthropology is its ability to capture both the vagaries and indeterminacy of human experience and the ways that cultures and bodies intersect to shape our possibilities and affordances. From here, the ethnography expands, becoming increasingly psychological, until the mixed methods of

Chapter 5 place me squarely in the realm of neuroanthropology or cultural neuroscience—perhaps neurophenomenology.[28] I do attempt to hold to my cultural studies roots, for even as the MRI becomes important, I am regularly in the process of trying to dissolve its authority, although I suspect that I fail here. After that, we move back out into the social sphere.

But the ethnographic intuition is the overarching frame and the place I return to again and again when confused or just needing to reset: early on, I heard that for charismatics, bodily sensation creates a profound sense of cultural direction and forms a central component of their self-articulation. I first wrote about this in a 2012 Cultural Anthropology article, where I describe the centrality of conversion and certainty of the portable sensory dynamics— "body logics"—embedded within the charismatic sensorium.[29] As time went on, my informants continued to insist that the bodily component of faith was deeply felt, and I came to suspect that these body logics were more than symbolic or idealist conceptions but instead were one node in a circulation between practice, neurophysiology, and social articulation within charismatic communities. This was especially controversial because some argue that speaking in tongues is primarily a performative practice that confers social status; any seeming physiology that points to "trance" or an altered state during tongues prayer is simply a pretense, they argue.[30] If I could show that there was a neurophysiological component to the experience, I could then ask if it correlated with the kinds of somatic configurations associated with other altered states of consciousness. I decided to try and more fully trace the looping between what I saw and experienced during participant observation, what I heard in phenomenological interviews, and what might appear in the neurobiology of practitioners. This research goal pushed me to extend the work on the anthropology of the body and senses by scholars like Constance Classen and David Howes, integrating insights from anthropological phenomenology and biocultural anthropology.[31]

In bridging ethnography, phenomenology, and neuroscience, my research extends the methodological framework of "front-loaded phenomenology."[32] This approach suggests that studying complex, culturally embedded experiences requires combining phenomenological self-report methods (interviews and questionnaires) with cognitive science techniques (behavioral tasks and brain recordings) for more informed data collection and analysis. My approach adds years of ethnography to the "front-loading"—an innovation I enjoy. Also, please notice that the mutual and reciprocal constraint described as the core of neurophenomenology by Varela and colleagues describes how the MRI is shaped by the front loaded ethnography and phenomenology, but in the case of the drop-ins, it is truly reciprocal, as the MRI then shaped our phenomenological understandings and future interviews.[33]

The methodological and theoretical tools of what we are now calling "ethnographic neurophenomenology" allow us to reach into the fabric of experience in ways that neuroscience (and even mainstream ethnography) may miss. In the process, I hope to demonstrate links, both practical and philosophical, between a "critical phenomenology" as theory[34] and Tanya Luhrmann's phenomenological interview method that enables me to work closely with neuroscientific and psychological research methods.[35]

Phenomenology here is less a complex continental philosophy and more the "radical empiricism" of William James.[36] I aim to observe richly but as much as possible without judgment.[37] By joining this empiricism to the excitement that Jason Throop[38] brings to close observation, our team at Stanford developed the intensive phenomenological interviews that are key to this research. These in turn have provided the data that inspired the hypothesis that spiritual practice enhances the capacity to surrender agency and that release empowers people into action. A central part of this insight also came from approaching our subjects as theorists in their own right.

In practice, "phenomenology" here manifests as extremely careful interviewing about the details of felt experience. Many of our probes emerged from the literature about "core" experiences.[39] More arose out of many, many conversations with participants. We wanted to know not whether someone believed in God, but rather how they knew that God was present. By "radical empiricism," we mean following James, with a dogged attention to the details of what a person has felt.

This mixed method responds directly to ethnographies of Christianity which have thus far emphasized social context.[40] *Tongues of Fire* offers to explore how social context shapes experience. Thomas Csordas, Jon Bialecki, and Tanya Luhrmann are probably my closest compatriots in this project.[41] I also address a gap in the anthropology of the body, wherein previous scholars have suggested connections between culture and bodily transformations[42] but have not demonstrated them as explicitly as my research does by combining brain scans and psychological scales with interviews and participant observation. That part is simply to say, there is more converging forms of evidence here.

***

From a critical theory perspective, I have often been asked if it might not be more informative to simply look at the ideological formation of these movements. People submit to God, and it's the idea that God is powerful that shapes their experience. The emotions and the release aren't especially important, they suggest. I do think there's something important here; ideology matters—but I also believe that reducing people to the ideas that shape them, or the power structures they inhabit, misses crucial details. In some sense, this book aims straight at the famous Chomsky–Foucault debate: is human action structured primarily by discursive power systems, or by contrast, by biological systems?[43] To what degree does discourse matter? And, implicitly, to what degree does the neurobiological side of the looping I explore here matter?

Sociologist Debbie Gould offers one answer: affect matters in the building of movements.[44] There are certainly human patterns of emotion and release that shape how we interact. Charismatics crowd-source some of these capacities through very specific practices—and make good use of them. I'm relatively confident that without these embodied tools, they wouldn't be the movement they are today.

There is also a compelling argument on the other side of this divide, when you notice that the expansion of evangelicalism supports—and is supported by—a neoliberal sense of the self.[45] In that view, the global charismatic movement's growth coincides with the expansion of capitalism. So, it could simply be seen as an ideological tool for enclosure. I find this plausible— although the word "simply" is doing too much work there.

My own argument is also simple, and admittedly avoidant: the divide between minds and bodies, ideologies and biologies, can be muddled and fuzzed over, they can be linked and joined in a million ways. There are many instances when we can't see the division clearly. Yet, for myself as a researcher, this divide is actually quite useful. I want to study things. Things have boundaries. I can't study everything at once. I need a method for noticing the ways they are separated and joined in a given complex with traits.[46] Looping is that method. It might be an effort to turn Spinozan monism into a practical strategy for studying the world. Or for recognizing what Foucault might have meant when he said discourse includes bodies. In this story, minds and bodies are shaped out of the innate holism of being and recognized as elements within loops. We can explore how they interact and how they have moments of seeming independence. We can ask if the bodily component is 10 percent or 80 percent. My own personal experience suggests it's often pretty high up there—individual people and specific movements differ in that regard. But the bottom line is that I think they are both always in play, and significantly so. Learning about either structure (affective or ideological) is useful and interesting for those who want to understand how humans behave. In this book, ideology becomes part of the set and setting that shapes the expectations and integration of neurobiological experiences. But these social forms work to some degree because they rely on biological patterns that humans are capable of enacting—including the capacity to temporarily loosen our cognitive strictures.

* * *

To the field of religious studies, this book might be perplexing. It's not a critique of religion, nor am I fully adopting the perspective Ruth Marshall advocates, where we aspire to see the world entirely through a tradition's lens.[47] A recent discussion about Amy Hollywood's *Acute Melancholia* got me thinking about what it means to "take seriously" a practice or tradition. For me, taking something seriously doesn't mean believing it's true. It means engaging with it thoughtfully, as something worth caring about. That involves asking questions, recognizing critiques—whether from the tradition itself or from outsiders—and asking, "Is that right?" We know religious people can be as critical and thoughtful as anyone, but also as confused and mistaken.

Eduardo Viveiros de Castro suggests anthropologists often see only themselves, and he has a point. But rather than abandoning the attempt to write about others, I want to write about my relationship with them. This book, then, is about my engagement with real people—people who both argue with and agree with me about many things. It's about how we learn from each other. Yes, I taught them things—though probably not as much as they taught me, which creates an asymmetry. Piled on top of the also asymmetrical balance between researcher and subject, it's a bit messy. Still, I was a teacher as well as student; I directly influenced their world. For example, I introduced the concept of a "drop-in" to many who hadn't heard of it before. Even this writing is an intervention if my informants decide to read it, which several already have.

I'm not here to "debunk" anyone; I assume my informants are not dupes, at least any more than I am. And I remain grounded as a person engaged in the real world with this community. My approach is not methodological agnosticism. Nor is it Thomas Fearon's "methodological Gnosticism," which suggests fully immersing in experience (though I did some of that inadvertently). Instead, my approach is about curious engagement and actual interaction.

In other words, I hope to take charismatic practice and people seriously as partners in the world, recognizing both their beauty and flaws. Many in this community are brilliant and passionate, yet still human. I'm not just studying them—I'm interacting with them in real time. Through research, sharing, and co-designing studies, I'm not only exploring how they see the world, but how their practices and worldview shape their experiences and surroundings. As Jim Clifford and Donna Haraway taught me,[48] I can't remove myself from the story or pretend to understand from on high. So, I aim to notice where I am, to be as open as possible, keeping my biases in mind as I ask questions that help me translate this for others. It's a translation through myself.

This book, then, exists on two levels: it's not just the traditional anthropologist uncovering culture, nor simply a reflexive narrative in the Cliffordian sense, nor the ontologist dividing multiple realities as separate. I am a person, they are people, we met, influenced each other, and that continues. That's the story.

Bibliographic Notes for Chapter 1: Letting Go

It seems to me that letting go is a commonly spoken term. I see it everywhere I look these days. This may reflect recent Buddhist interventions into contemporary culture, or my own obsessions.[49] I do think, however, evangelicals bring a spin to this conversation that is unique and underappreciated. In the process, they help me recognize the strange blend of will, desire, and releasing of intention that permeates all of our existence.

One of the more extensive philosophical interventions in *Tongues of Fire* is a joining of Buddhist, enactivist, and feminist constructivism in thinking about the ways that evangelical thoughts are built to let go. I see evangelicals framing and consolidating specific thoughts as objects that can be given up to God. This is the backpack story I referenced. This process seems close kin to feminist scholar Gayatri Spivak's depiction of what she calls "strategic essentialism," which is a social process of defining oneself in relation to the powers that be.[50] The definitions here are temporary and yet potent. Likewise, some Buddhist accounts of the oneness of the universe provide a similar story of bracketing out the objects we work with for the purpose of everyday function.[51] This comes even closer to evangelical practice when seen through the lens of enactivist accounts of the complex entanglement of our mental processes.[52] Each of these approaches recognizes the reality and importance of even transitory fixedness that allows us to see and feel parts of the world.

I am also inspired by Mike Murphy's radically synoptic empiricism to build a taxonomy of release. He says that by following the technique of Linneas and building extensive taxonomies we do less explaining away of the edges of life and more accepting of the ambiguities and possibilities of human experience.

This chapter, especially and the book more generally, relies to a large degree on Tanya Luhrmann's development of an intensive phenomenological interview method, what she calls a semi-structured phenomenological interview. For us, they were three- to seven-hour interviews that involved hundreds of specific questions, but were most striking for a process we called "probing." Basically, when a participant would describe an event, we would then go deeper, asking about the context, the sensations they experienced, their thoughts, their meta-reflections, and their emotions, hoping to wring out as much detail as possible. This meant that a 30-second event could produce half an hour of interview material. For instance, when a participant said they had heard God's voice, we asked first if it was out loud or in their head. If they said out loud, we would probe further: Did you turn your head to hear it? How did it sound? Was it similar to my voice? To a friend you heard earlier today? Gender? It was in one of these interviews that it was explained to me that God was a "baritone."

Here is an excerpt from one of my interviews at Glad Tidings.

Me: Have you heard God out loud, where you heard him with your ears?

Respondent: Yes. I've only heard God speak clearly once. It was an audible voice; I can't even explain the voice, it was just a voice that I heard in my head.

Me: You heard it in your head or outside your head?

Respondent: I don't know. I can't tell you for sure … I just had my eyes closed … and I heard, "Now go and be a man of God." Those were the exact words; I can tell you this happened six years ago. I still remember them. I can hear them clearly in my head today.

Me: What did it sound like?

Respondent: I don't even know how to describe it. It just said, "Now go and be a man of God."

Me: Did it sound like a person speaking?

Respondent: Yes. It sounded like a person speaking. It wasn't like a big, Godlike voice.

Me: Was the person a man?

Respondent: No, it was firm, like, "Now go and be a man of God," I would say it was a man, yes.

Me: Can you hear it in your mind's eye right now?

Respondent: Yes. If I say it, it just sounds so clearly, "Now go and be a man of God."

Me: Okay, can you think back to a conversation you had earlier today. Can you imagine that?

Respondent: Yes.

Me: What's the difference between that and this voice?

Respondent: I feel like the difference in this was just when you're speaking to someone it's like you're having a conversation with somebody, it's pretty casual, right, like how you and me are talking right now. This time for me, I just felt like it was a voice that pierced through all the doubt and stuff that I had in my mind about who I was, completely shattered the wall, because I was convinced that my future had nothing in store, and this voice is telling me to go and be a man of God. The way that it was said, it was just like, "This is who you are." There was truth in it.

Our phenomenological interview protocol was developed in the United States and then translated (and back translated) and used in each of our sites across the globe. It is a close kin to the micro-phenomenology of Petitmengin and Hurlbutt.[53] In my research in the two US charismatic churches, the interviews were connected by extended participant observation.

Bibliographic Notes for Chapter 2: Training

In this chapter, I describe a carefully directed pedagogy, as anthropologist Thomas Csordas would say, "culturally taught, socially expected, and deliberately deployed."[54] Anthropologists have often been interested in the ways that religion involves learning.[55] Charismatics are deeply involved in this kind of process. Even though this was originally an oral culture and there is little attention to the mind in its theology, I was surprised to find that the bodily training they use has been written down and distributed via training texts that are made available in missionary training classes at Bethany University, in prayer weekend intensives, and online catalogues. This extensive training that enables practitioners to speak in tongues and to experience spiritual breakthrough complicates the debate between anthropologists who argue whether continuity, rupture, or some version of their interplay accounts for charismatic inspiration.[56] These training texts and practices literally sit between, and help to link, the structure of the church and the newness of revival. They are the link between continuity and change.

Because it is such a messy mix of training and letting go, charismatics worry constantly about the balance between inspiration and method and how it affects their organizational health. What makes prayerful experience legitimate? How to nourish the good and discourage the bad? Some argue that they need more freedom and spontaneity. Earlier generations of charismatics in the United States apparently described more experiences of the supernatural than today's followers.[57] But others see structure as their strength. They describe a kind of vitality in the subcultural sense of resistance produced by a church with especially stringent doctrine.[58] Charismatic subcultures do both—training and spontaneity, structure and experience, continuity and breakthrough—perhaps in sequence, perhaps simultaneously, but certainly well connected. A Bible read as infallible provides a seemingly immobile ethical structure, while the search for immediate, personal connection to God justifies relentless challenge to their own establishment. In this story, a training regime supported by an extensive bureaucracy provides a structure that nurtures institutional and individual moments of rebirth and renewal. Charismatic sociologist Margaret Poloma calls it "continuous charisma."[59] As with any musical instrument or dance, the structured practice of bodily technique is crucial to allowing experts to experience open improvisation. This tension has tremendous effects on the individuals immersed within it but also on the institutions: charismatics experience nonstop religious uprisings as new experience pushes against hardened church structures. It means they are breaking apart into new churches almost yearly. Yet, many groups appear to survive, and flourish, in the very Protestant storms they cultivate. At times, I wonder if the dynamic between cultivate, yield, and constrain might be simply another word for freedom.[60]

From Charles Finney through John Wesley and to the early Pentecostals, methodical effort—both on the part of organizers and participants—became increasingly central to their project. This is in keeping with what philosophers Charles Taylor's describes as central to the "Age of Mobilization," and Michel Foucault, a bit more skeptically, describes as increasing "discipline."[61] Both thinkers tell of a historical moment when the increasing rationalization of society meant that the modern self was more and more likely to be formed through an explicit method. This was the context for the emergence of the charismatic blend of method and release. It suggests to me that rather than imagine religiosity as a retreat from modernity,[62] religion can be very modern. Perhaps modern systems of methodical control shape the emotive and the sensual, when bodies and the spirits become the objects of technocratic manipulation, and when that gridding enables a broadly accessible and highly motivating experience of the spirit.

As Edith Blumhofer, a well-known AG academic, describes the first generations of Pentecostals, "they faced an insurmountable obstacle: they could formalize the message but they could not induce experience."[63] Yet, with all due credit to Blumhofer, it seems they could, to some degree, induce it. Not always, but sometimes. And yet, it is hard to blame her, for throughout the charismatic world, and throughout the United States, there are basically two positions on this question. Either a practice is spontaneous and therefore authentic and potentially spiritual. Or, on the other hand, it is an induced trance and therefore mechanical and worldly. As we have seen, it may be both.

Bibliographic Notes for Chapter 3: Attention, Arousal, and Release

Here is where the looping of this book turns local (see the looping conversation in the notes to the Prologue). This chapter outlines loops between three phenomenological-physiological experiences while thinking about how that loop is also shaped by practice given continuity through tradition and text.

Countless scholars have explored ritual processes, and some have noted relationships between attention and arousal, or arousal and release, though few examine all three together. We could look at Victor Turner's work, where transformative actions culminate in a cathartic release,[64] or Catherine Bell's illustration of how focused attention combined with a gradual increase in intensity can create meaningful and heightened ritual practices,[65] and even Clifford Geertz shows how events draw intense community attention and collective arousal. Thomas Csordas is unusual in addressing all three elements, describing how heightened attention to the body and emotional arousal in rituals lead to moments of catharsis or release, which are central to the healing process.[66]

In our work comparing the AAR spiral between Jhana meditations and speaking in tongues, we try and show how this process could make sense within a predictive processing framework. As attention and arousal coactivate, a spiraling interplay may unfold. For tongues practitioners, the focus is felt to be external on God, but the practical access to God is through internal sensations,[67] so they are looking inward. Stronger concentration narrows the scope of attention, boosting what computational neuroscientists call the "precision weighting" on the objects of focus.[68] The increased attention on an object of interest (e.g., God) means that the cognitive system is processing more detailed information about the object and thus perceives it more clearly, and has more confidence in its model of the object. Research shows that in general, uncertainty about perceptions leads to negative affect, while confidence typically causes positive affect.[69] As such, the more we pay attention to an object of experience, the more we may feel confident in our model of that object and therefore feel an influx of positive affect. Our cognitive system then comes to associate the influx of positive valence with that particular perceptual object. This is step one of the spiral: focused attention on an object of perception leads to more clarity and perceptual confidence, which in turn leads to positive valence that the brain associates with that object.

The second step of the spiral, after attention generates arousal, is that our attention is naturally drawn to perceptual objects that feel affectively valenced. In other words, affectively charged objects are more effortlessly salient, involuntarily drawing our attention toward them.[70] Thus, as the object of perception (God) becomes more positively valenced through either increased attention and clarity, compensation for sensory deprivation, and/or the release of free energy, then the practitioner's attention becomes more naturally and effortlessly drawn toward the object. This affect-driven increase in effortless attention then loops back to generate more perceptual clarity about the object, which further increases the positive affect associated with the object, resulting in a mutually reinforcing spiral. This dynamic seems to induce an experience of sustained, aroused attention that can be experienced by the practitioner as increasingly effortless.

We suspect that the practice of release plays a pivotal mediating role in the cyclic interplay of attention and arousal during speaking in tongues. Participants describe letting go—a release of physical, cognitive, and emotional holding and patterns. Release is especially difficult to define in this context, where physical, emotional, and cognitive forms of letting go seem to play back and forth with each other. But the simplest version is that in an atmosphere of increasing ease, words, bodies, and feelings can be released either with clear intention or by virtue of attending elsewhere. The spiral of attention and arousal can create an environment of effortlessness and ease, as we have described above. As the object of attention becomes more affectively valenced, maintaining focus becomes easier. Then, as our attentional and emotional systems relax, it becomes easier to let go even further. This sense of ease seems to build upon itself, leading to greater release.

One explanation for this is that sustained attention on a particular stimulus leads to repeated updates and confirmations of the brain's predictive model based on the focused input, reinforcing the brain's model for that stimulus. As a result, a perception of the object of focus may feel more fresh as it is refined and reinforced. Meanwhile, concentration utilizes attentional resources that would otherwise be focused on ruminative thoughts or ordinary sensory inputs. The predictive models for these unattended stimuli are then held less tightly which results in less consistency, and perhaps more freedom. As the thought patterns loosen, they may fade from consciousness altogether. The absence of those patterns may engender a feeling of joy or freedom, thus reinforcing the AAR spiral.[71]

Phenomenological data reveals that release is both facilitated by the interplay of attention and arousal that fosters an atmosphere of effortlessness, but also actively pursued by practitioners through repeated enactments. Practitioners seem comfortable with the paradox of actively surrendering. Following periods of intense focus and arousal, this deliberate yielding—whether to a divine presence or to an object of focus—seems to catalyze relaxation across somatic, emotional, and cognitive spheres.

Intriguingly, because this cycle recurs throughout each practice, practitioners report experiencing concurrent relaxation (parasympathetic activation) and arousal (sympathetic activation)—a state not typically emphasized in conventional relaxation research, which emphasizes how these systems are usually inversely related. While sympathetic and parasympathetic systems tend to coactivate only in passing, each rising as the other falls, they can indeed operate simultaneously, as suggested by Cacciopo and colleagues' autonomic space model, 1999.[72] This sustained arousal in high-intensity contemplative practices may stem in part from the unusual, prolonged coactivation of both systems, a phenomenon that warrants further exploration and could expand our understanding of autonomic responses in contemplative states.

Bibliographic Notes for Chapter 4: Feel and Say

Through a feel and a say and God's Hug, this chapter works the edges of mind-body dualism. The basic underlying thesis: if there are cultural differences in mind and body dualisms, then there must be a soft flexible space in culture where those differences can be cultivated—spiritual practice may be one of those.

Mind-body dualism often seems to have high stakes. Philosophers like Franz Fanon and Simone de Beauvoir argue that the separation between mind and body underpins the cultural foundations of sexism, classism, and racism.[73] Dominant ideas of "good" and "bad" often mirror these dualistic divides: the mind is seen as controlling the "vulgar" body, just as Europeans, whites, and men are seen as controlling the "others" in similar hierarchical constructs.

Anthropology, however, offers other possibilities. Many anthropologists outline non-dualistic perspectives in various cultures, showing that the separation of mind and body is not universal and that many societies integrate personhood, relationships, and the environment in ways that allow for different configurations of identity, equality, and social cohesion.[74] Yet others, like psychological anthropologist Rita Astuti, suggest that, in many ways, we are all dualists, a conclusion I initially found disappointing.[75]

At Stanford, our research team, in a paper led by Kara Weissman, examined this empirically. We studied how children from five different cultures categorize objects, bugs, and plants to see if they separate mind and body similarly to Europeans.[76] The findings are compelling: while all five groups classify entities into mind-like and body-like categories, the boundaries differ. Interestingly, the third element—emotions—sometimes aligns with the mind, sometimes with the body. This, to me, suggests that culture contains areas of ambiguity—liminal spaces where these divisions are worked out. I suspect spiritual experiences during which emotions and sensations intermingle are the kinds of things that play with these edges.

Anthropologists Catherine Lutz and Lila Abu-Lughod have observed that the meaning of a hug specifically varies by culture. In some societies, a hug symbolizes solidarity and unity, while in others, it is more personal, signifying intimacy and connection.[77] But the broader idea that cultural symbols and language shape emotions is classic.

Some scholars extend this exploration further. Marcel Mauss describes how cultural practices shape bodily comportment, which in turn shapes cultural perception.[78] Linguist George Lakoff highlights that metaphors deeply influence how we think, feel, and experience sensations.[79] Neuroscientist Antonio Damasio reinforces this, showing how thoughts trigger both emotional responses and physical sensations. Hugs, specifically, are what he would call a two-bodied experience.[80] Psychiatrist Daniel Stern notes that even imagining a hug can evoke an internal sense of emotional attunement, creating a physical sensation of being hugged.[81]

On a basic level, we know emotions are often interpretations of physical sensations: a racing heart and sweating can signal fear, excitement, anxiety, anger, or joy. Tears can indicate sadness, joy, frustration, relief, or empathy. An adrenaline rush can mean fear, euphoria, anger, motivation, or anticipation. Whether the sensation indicates excitement or anxiety, the physiological response is the same, understood as a basic affect that we interpret into a specific emotion. But in my view, the relationship is quite entwined. As Damasio notes, all thoughts carry an emotional component, and all emotions have a sensory aspect.

Charismatic experiences offer a way to understand the spaces where emotions and sensations intermingle. Instead of a straightforward mapping of affect to emotion through cognition, there exists a fluid continuum of sensation, feeling, and analysis, where these elements overlap and intertwine.

Bibliographic Notes for Chapter 5: The MRI

The question of "realness" within a culture has been a central preoccupation for anthropologists since the field's inception. From Franz Boas, Ruth Benedict, and Margaret Mead, who told us that reality is, to some degree, mediated by culture,[82] and Lévi-Strauss, who felt that there is something fundamentally real in the underlying patterns of human thought,[83] and later to thinkers who suggest we live amid multiple, simultaneous realities or ontologies[84]—this is the wheelhouse of anthropology. But this study doesn't settle on any one of these approaches.

I begin solidly in phenomenology—though not the sort that "brackets" anything—and then move across and through various approaches. I prefer to call it a series of loops, though at times it feels more like a wobbling journey. Ethnographic phenomenology examines lived experience, but then we cross into neurobiology to explore the anatomy of that experience, traveling between disciplines that offer vastly different conceptions of the real, and then back again.

In a sense, I am answering to two kinds of realness. First, my informant's question, much like a neuroscientist might—does this experience change the mind in tangible ways? Secondly, as an anthropologist, I'm drawn to what Daniel Dennett would call the "real patterns" and others might call "social facts"—the structures visible in the body, in subjective experience, and, intriguingly, in the spaces between.[85] It's here, between the neuroscientific and the phenomenological, that I hope to find some space for exploring what we call "the real."

Anthropology is full of methodological conversations about how we might treat things that are not clearly material as either real or unreal. This is especially obvious in conversations around things like race and culture where it seems the field has decided that social facts—things that are constructed by mutual engagement—are essentially facts.[86] Amy Hollywood, for instance, distinguished the real from the true and deemed all experience as real, but only true when third-person verifiable.[87] And I tend to follow that thread of thought but instead of two poles, I tend to imagine that all things are ephemeral and simply more or less sedimented, or sticky at a given moment of time. This would include cultural constructions as well as mountains. However, I am using the word "real" in this chapter in a different, more colloquial, manner. Real here means verifiable through some third-person test. With this approach, God's reality becomes impossible for me to determine and we are left exploring the effects of God, belief, or practice and the "real" there is the scientific real—the p value significance test that tells us this is likely replicable. Which is also a bit fuzzy if you think about it.

***

On MRIs: The reductionist science represented by tools like MRI has faced significant critique within science studies. Bruno Latour, for instance, argues that scientific knowledge is socially constructed through laboratory practices,[88] while Donna Haraway's concept of "situated knowledge" challenges the notion of a neutral, objective scientific gaze, requiring instead a situationally framed accountability.[89] Similarly, Evelyn Fox Keller demonstrates that scientific technologies, including brain imaging, tend to reinforce deterministic narratives about biology and behavior, often overlooking the complexity of individual and cultural experience.[90] As such, it is clear that scientific tools like MRIs and EEGs are not purely objective; they are shaped by the perspectives, values, and biases of those who design, interpret, and fund them (see also Martin, Good, and Dumit for further discussions on these critiques).[91]

Similarly, all of psychology is in the midst of a crisis in which well-established protocols and results have not been replicated. People are struggling to move forward with a science that is not meeting its own standards of replicability.[92]

Anthropology itself often appears to be in a state of perpetual crisis over the authority of its knowledge production, with frequent, intense debates over the value and ethics of ethnographic methodology. Many anthropologists question whether there is anything at all worthwhile in attempting to capture "objective" knowledge about cultures and whether efforts at positivist or universalist answers may risk imposing violent or reductive frameworks on diverse societies. Rather than objectivity, Clifford Geertz called for "thick description" as a means of understanding culture through interpretive nuance.[93] Ethnographic authority was critiqued by postcolonial scholars like Edward Said, who argued that ethnographic narratives often reinforce colonial hierarchies and perpetuate power imbalances.[94] This led to a wave of reflexive anthropology, emphasizing the need to acknowledge the ethnographer's positionality and the subjective nature of fieldwork.[95]

Anthropologists today often navigate these crises by promoting collaborative ethnography, which emphasizes partnerships between anthropologists and community members to co-construct knowledge. Collaborative approaches aim to overcome some ethical concerns by involving local perspectives and recognizing the co-dependency of knowledge production on both the ethnographer and the community.

Aiming to find a sweet spot between the dominance of "lone MRI cowboy" perspectives, the replication crisis, and ethnographic critiques of knowledge, I adopt a multimodal community-engaged approach. The interplay between biology and culture in this work aims to align with Margaret Lock's concept of "local biologies," illustrating how cultural context not only shapes biological understanding but also turns biological interpretations into cultural forces.[96] Additionally, Karen Barad's critique of traditional subject-object distinctions in scientific practice influences my approach. Barad argues that scientific measurements are active, relational processes affected by experimental setups, interpretive frameworks, and observer involvement, which complicates the idea that scientific tools can simply "reveal" reality. Instead, our work involves collaborative processes with our informants reading, critiquing, and helping to design the research—they actively construct it and we do too.[97]

The Psychology of Speaking in Tongues

I want to offer here a more thorough history of psychological and neuroscientific research into tongues prayer among charismatic evangelical Christians. Also, May[98] noted phenomena akin to tongues prayer among Quakers, Methodists, and Mormons, as well as indigenous shamans in Inuit traditions, in Borneo, Bali, and Haiti, and Hindus in India, to name but a few. He also drew connections to ancient sources, including the *Aeneid* and the Old Testament. In a different vein, psychologists have identified echoes of glossolalia in schizophrenia and manic-depressive psychosis,[99] and more recent studies have compared it to aphasia and hypnosis, though findings remain inconclusive.[100] Yet the degree to which these experiences overlap—neurologically, psychologically, or phenomenologically—remains unclear.

Two enduring debates have shaped the psychological understanding of speaking in tongues. The first concerns psychopathology: is this cascade of ecstatic, unintelligible speech a symptom of mental disorder—or, rather, a manifestation of a healthy, even transformative, spiritual state? The second addresses pretense: are practitioners knowingly performing for the sake of social status, or do they enter into something involuntary, maybe spontaneous, and deeply felt? These have given rise to three broad hypotheses concerning its origins and underlying mechanisms:

1 **Altered Mental States as Pathology**: The more critical view frames tongues prayer as a manifestation of disorganized thought and language—paralleling symptoms found in certain psychotic disorders.[101]

2 **Altered Mental States as Beneficial**: In contrast, this view emphasizes the psychological value of something that they also describe as relative disorganization, but they liken it to other altered states of consciousness—such as meditation or trance—that are known to foster emotional regulation and overall well-being.[102]

3 **Social Performance Hypothesis**: This third framework, which I explain pretty thoroughly in the main chapter of the book, downplays, and often fully dismisses, neurobiological accounts to interpret tongues prayer as a culturally learned behavior. Here, the apparent trance state is understood as a socially sanctioned performance—an expressive act shaped by ritual, expectation, and communal belief.[103]

These questions have not been fully resolved. Perhaps because the questions themselves are less gateways to understanding than conceptual impasses. Each offers a binary—sick or well, real or fake—often tied to an implicit ethical stance—good or bad, godly or heretical—when the practiced reality of tongues prayer might defy such divisions. It may be that versions of speech that sound like what we call tongues prayer can be performance, surrender, pathology, and transcendence—it can likely shift between them, and perhaps even be all at once. Which makes them interesting.

Speaking in tongues has frequently been associated with psychopathology, including schizophrenia, mood disorders, and dissociation.[104] Early clinical reports documented glossolalia in psychotic and neurotic patients (Maeder 1910; Finch 1959), reinforcing a view of it as symptomatic of mental disturbance.[105]

Later studies supported this link. Sargant (1957)[106] framed tongues as regressive behavior; Wood (1961)[107] found Pentecostals showed anxiety and disorganization; LaBarre (1962)[108] saw it as an expression of internal conflict, and Lapsley and Simpson (1964)[109] called it a dissociative defense. Klaus Thomas (1965)[110] linked tongues to pre-psychotic states in a suicide clinic. Pattison (1968)[111] noted pathology among low-income charismatics, though not in upper-class churches—highlighting potential class bias or contextual effects.

Kildahl (1972)[112] argued that psychological suggestibility primed individuals for glossolalia, a view echoed by Castelein (1984),[113] who tied it to dependence on authority. Morentz (1974),[114] however, identified more ambivalent traits: hostility, dependency, and a need for control, suggesting glossolalia could function as a coping mechanism. According to Qualben, as cited in Kildahl (1972),[115] 85 percent of practitioners of speaking in tongues experienced a distinct anxiety crisis prior to their speaking in tongues while Hine (1969)[116] reported that only 16 percent of practitioners experienced a crisis beforehand, while 84 percent described more gradual spiritual growth.

By the late 1960s, tongues prayer had spread beyond classical Pentecostalism into Catholic, Protestant, and nondenominational contexts. With this expansion came a shift in academic tone—from pathologizing to more balanced and even positive appraisals. Plog (1965)[117] found no abnormal personality traits among tongues speakers. Sherrill (1968)[118] described them as well-adjusted, and Gerlach and Hine (1968, 1970, 1974)[119] reported no signs of psychopathology, noting strong family cohesion and potential for social and economic empowerment.

Coulson and Johnson (1977)[120] found that Pentecostals had a more internal locus of control than Methodists, challenging Kildahl's earlier claims. Lovekin and Malony (1977)[121] noted only minor psychological differences, while Spanos and Hewitt (1979)[122] found no significant differences between them. Neanon and Hair (1983)[123] found that charismatic Christians were no more neurotic or imaginatively involved than noncharismatic Christians or the general population.

Later studies even suggested high emotional stability among tongues speakers. Francis and Kay (1995)[124] found them less neurotic; Grady and Loewenthal (1997),[125] Francis and Jones (1997),[126] Robbins et al. (1999),[127] and Francis and Robbins (2003)[128] confirmed these findings across clergy and lay populations, with tongues speakers showing greater emotional stability than their noncharismatic peers.

Oddly enough, even as study after study found little evidence of harm—and in many cases pointed to potential psychological and physiological benefits—the association between tongues prayer and psychopathology remains surprisingly persistent.

The Neurobiology of Spiritual Practice: Beyond the Obvious

Neurobiological research on speaking in tongues has grown steadily over the past several decades. Chris Lynn's studies (2010, 2011)[129] marked a significant starting point, showing that Pentecostal participants exhibited reduced stress biomarkers after glossolalia—comparable to the effects of mindfulness. Earlier, Pavelsky, Hart, and Malony (1975)[130] had divided tongues speakers into two groups: one resembling role-play with minimal neural change, and another—"process glossolalics"—exhibiting notable shifts in alpha wave activity, though these findings were never formally published. Persinger (1984)[131] added to this line of inquiry by observing spikes in temporal lobe and beta activity during glossolalia in one participant, suggesting possible microseizures, though the findings were not replicated in others of his subjects. Goodman (1988)[132] described a mix of arousal and release: decreased blood pressure, elevated heart rate, lower stress hormones, and increased theta brainwave activity—often linked to meditative or "flow" states. Burton (1993)[133] found alpha-to-beta EEG shifts in a serpent-handling preacher during glossolalia, supporting his trance interpretation. Schwartz (1999),[134] analyzing blood samples during worship, noted spikes in adrenaline, cortisol, and endorphins—proposing a "psychic reward system" that might explain the emotional reinforcement of the practice. Philipchalk and Mueller[135] examined hemispheric activity using carotid temperature as a proxy for blood flow and found greater right-hemisphere activation during glossolalia, contrasting with the left-dominant pattern of ordinary speech—though lacking rigorous controls. Newberg et al. (2006)[136] used SPECT imaging to show that glossolalia involves a reduction in dorsolateral prefrontal cortex activity, suggesting reduced volitional control. Walter et al. (2011)[137] found correlations between greater hours of tongues practice and increased gray matter in prefrontal regions. While valuable, earlier studies were often underpowered by today's standards. We aimed to update this work using a larger sample, current statistical thresholds, and stricter controls.

Agency Hubs

Our research suggests that the experience of agency may involve a dynamic relationship with two important hubs in the brain: the pre-supplementary motor area (pre-SMA) and temporoparietal junction (TPJ) both function as critical integration hubs in the neurocognitive architecture of the sense of agency, with converging evidence from structural, functional, and causal methodologies.[138] From early studies of the readiness potential[139] to more recent fMRI and TMS experiments, both regions have emerged as a linchpin in initiating internally generated action and mediating the subjective sense of agency—the feeling that "I am the one doing this."

Structurally, the pre-SMA serves as a transitional zone between the dorsolateral prefrontal cortex (DLPFC), anterior cingulate cortex (ACC), basal ganglia, SMA proper, and primary motor cortex (M1), allowing it to integrate volitional intention, motor preparation, and action selection.[140] Electrophysiologically, it shows early activation in internally generated movement, and task-based fMRI demonstrates increased pre-SMA activity during intentional binding and agency attribution.[141] The left TPJ, also facilitates connection between regional activity. It receives converging inputs from visual, somatosensory, auditory, and vestibular cortices and connects with the medial prefrontal cortex, posterior cingulate, and hippocampus, enabling the integration of multisensory input, and self–other distinctions.[142] Functional connectivity analyses show that both regions are embedded in large-scale brain networks— with pre-SMA situated in the frontoparietal control network and TPJ acting as a connector hub across the default mode, ventral attention, and sensorimotor networks.[143] Effective connectivity studies show the pre-SMA drives downstream motor regions during voluntary action,[144] while the TPJ compares predicted and actual sensory outcomes.[145] Causal evidence from TMS and tDCS demonstrates that disrupting either region alters agency judgments; disrupting the pre-SMA impairs not only the timing and selection of self-initiated actions but also the felt connection between action and outcome.[146] Lesions to the pre-SMA impair volitional action, and to the TPJ produce agency-related disturbances such as out-of-body experiences, and body ownership illusions.[147] Importantly for our study that joins agency release to language production, Walsh and colleagues associated the release of agency during hypnosis that involved writing with a reduction in activity of the left SMA, as well as altered functional connectivity between SMA and brain regions involved in language processing.[148] Collectively, these findings suggest that the pre-SMA and the TPJ serve as convergent computational nodes where motor intentions, predictive models, and sensory consequences are integrated, and the sense of agency is generated.[149]

However, because the right TPJ is implicated in both agency and social interaction it was unclear how it would respond in this context. One might expect activation during social interaction, particularly when a theory of another's mind is involved, as in relating to God (Schjoedt et al. 2009). Conversely, deactivation might be expected during the release of personal agency (Zito et al. 2020). In contrast, the left TPJ offered a clearer candidate for tracking the effects of agency release.

Bibliographic Notes for Chapter 6: Loosen the Mind?

This idea that creativity can emerge via altered states has deep roots. In the mid-1960s, Felicitas Goodman studied with anthropologist Erika Bourguignon, who mentored a crew of researchers excited by the exploration of trancelike experiences across the globe. Bourguignon held that altered states offer a path toward novel modes of thought and even innovative social relations.[150]

This led to a wonderful debate that suggests contrasting views about control, often associated with the frontal lobe, as a pathway to health and happiness. For example, Dr. Nora Volkow emphasized the brain's reward and inhibitory systems in understanding addiction, arguing that strengthening the prefrontal cortex, particularly its inhibitory control functions, is crucial for managing addictive behaviors by "overriding" impulses from more reactive areas like the limbic system.[151] Similarly, Dr. Russell Poldrack has researched the brain's inhibitory functions within the prefrontal cortex and pre-supplementary motor area (pre-SMA) as essential for managing conditions such as addiction and OCD.[152]

By contrast, scholars like Robin Carhart-Harris are more interested in the need for loosening, as he explores how psychedelic experiences can break up rigid mental patterns, potentially undoing ingrained cycles in conditions like addiction and depression.[153] Likewise, Judson Brewer suggests that mindfulness practices help "loosen" habitual patterns, reducing the brain's automatic responses and aiding in addiction recovery.[154] To be fair, they both see a need for balance, Carhart-Harris describes "criticality, where the brain is in the optimal tipping point between stasis and chaos, a site of high functioning, it is thought. FYI: we found something close to that in our study of Jhana meditation. We can also find arguments for balance from Bruce Wexler who explicitly argues that brain health requires a balance: the capacity to control impulses as well as the flexibility to adapt when established patterns become maladaptive.[155] Likewise, David Vago advocates for mindfulness-based interventions that not only enhance cognitive control but also allow the brain to relax habitual patterns through nonjudgmental awareness.[156]

***

Many anthropologists would challenge the straightforward equation of creativity with individual thought patterns that could be read in my chapter. I'm thinking of Tim Ingold and Howard Morphy who view creativity as embedded within daily practices and social interactions, which challenges the individualistic notion that resides in the testing of a person's creativity.[157] My response would be to look to the looping across chapters to see how this form of individual divergence is both cultivated through practice and then has tremendous effects on the sociopolitical trajectory of the charismatic movement. In other words, the looping in this book is meant as a direct response to these kinds of concerns. We can then at least ask if this somewhat reductionist moment has value in the broader context.

Others argue that rather than simply being about divergence, creativity requires structured spaces within which divergence can occur. Victor Turner's work on "liminality" and "communitas," for instance, explores how creativity and transformation often emerge from the tension between structure and anti-structure during rituals and social transitions.[158] This is my argument as well.

Bibliographic Notes for Chapter 7: Certainty

This chapter is the anthropological exploration of the ways the looping between bodies and culture shapes culture—it is the culture side. So, all the discussion of looping in the earlier notes is relevant and I won't bore you by repeating it.

I introduce the idea of ontological anxiety to join with a collection of anthropological understandings of the use of ontology: Holbraad's concept of ontological reflexivity that refers to how people emotionally defend their ontologies, especially when confronted with another framework;[159] and, Viveiros de Castro's theory of ontological perspectivism where Amazonian indigenous peoples see humans, animals, and spirits not as fundamentally different beings but as beings that share a similar essence, with differences emerging through their perspectives.[160] Similarly, Anna Tsing explores how global forces like capitalism, conservation, and modernization create "friction" when they encounter local ontologies, often provoking strong emotional responses.[161]

Bibliographic Notes for Chapter 8: Letting Go Brings Power

The key to this chapter is a philosophical divide noticed by historian of philosophy Paul Livingston whose book *The Politics of Logic: Badiou, Wittgenstein, and the Consequences of Formalism* helped me see the patterns in modern philosophical conversations about agency, especially the competing traditions that see agency in cognitive (Kant et al.) or affective (Rousseau et al.) terms.[162]

Cultivation, or a close kin, which is here taken to mean that we incrementally use cultural practices to change ourselves, has played a role in multiple theories of agency. Cultivation challenges the way many of us think about ritualized habits, and ritual more generally, both of which tend to be lumped together as unfree. As Catherine Bell puts it, ritual is usually seen as "particularly *thoughtless* action—routinized, habitual, or mimetic—and therefore the purely formal, secondary, and mere physical expression of logically prior ideas."[163] In response, she argues persuasively that when thoughts are deeply imprinted in the action, there is agency in extended cultivation, what she calls ritualization, as well as in moments of conscious deliberation.

Talal Asad describes the processes of secularization as cultivation, how in a secular society our sensory aptitudes are shaped by the repeated experiences of everyday life.[164] Marcel Mauss and Pierre Bourdieu tell us how our gait, our stance, and likely even our passions form slowly until they solidify in culturally and historically specific ways.[165] As with charismatic efforts to reconcile Godly and human agency, Philosopher William Connolly describes a "minority tradition"[166] of philosophy whose practice theories bring structure and agency together by joining the unconscious and the systematic, coherence to incoherence.[167] Connolly outlines what he calls a Spinozist-Deleuzian tradition with an ethic of "cultivation" that binds body, mind, and social life through its focus on "becoming." This is one philosophical side of the looping I have been talking about.

Cultivation is especially visible in the emerging anthropology of the senses where it is imagined that localities develop their own sensory capacities. According to Constance Classen, for instance, European cultures increasingly ignore and perhaps debase the sense of smell,[168] while sight has become more dominant.[169] More broadly, it seems that in some places, Protestants emphasize hearing, Catholics and Hindus seeing.[170] We know that in broad schemas, practices work with natural selection to change physiology. Dairy farming culture selects for high populations of lactose absorbers. Brain encephalization may have evolved through the increase of group size and the emergence of language.[171] These are long, slow processes.

But, cultivation is also relevant over a much tighter timeline. The contemporary Vietnamese have only recently—post-Communism—adopted a theory of mind that valorizes emotions and seems to intensify them as well, yet it seems somewhat established.[172] Likewise, anthropologist Sonya Pritzker describes how Americans learning Chinese medicine quickly come to feel emotions in their bodies.[173] Of course, as our study suggests, cultivation could work on the brain as well. Several recent studies have emphasized the role of religious practice in channeling neuroplasticity. Neuroscientist Andrew Newberg tells us that religious practice can, "permanently change the structure of those parts of the brain that control our moods, give rise to our conscious notions of self, and shape our sensory perceptions of the world."[174] Tanya Luhrmann describes a 6–9 month learning period by which evangelicals learn to hear God's voice in their prayer practices.[175] In other words, it may be that quite a bit can be modified if only subtly.[176] How deeply, and solidly, this change manifests is uncertain. Recent work on epigenetics suggests that even across one lifetime, very specific competences can crystalize and even be passed on to the next generation.[177]

***

Anthropologists also have often thought about how different cultures approach agency. This is juxtaposed to a dominant Western notion of the individual exerting their will, and the world following. Michael Scott,[178] for instance, talks about agency as microresistances, and one could follow that with Saba Mahmoud and R. Marie Griffith's argument that women use traditions as channels for their local forms of agency.[179] While these are both appropriate, I think charismatic code switching fits more closely with Bourdieu's[180] notion of the flexibility of practice where something akin to de Certeau's[181] "tactics" that enable switching in very much the way that Aiwha Ong describes as flexible citizenship.[182] Likewise, Sherry Ortner describes agency as multilayered, operating across various registers. She differentiates between small-scale actions, such as immediate, everyday decisions, and long-term strategies that unfold over extended periods.[183] Similarly, Akhil Gupta and James Ferguson discuss how agency functions across different spatial scales—local, national, and global—as well as temporal scales, showing that actions and influences are not confined to a single domain or time frame.[184] Alfred Gell's theory of extended agency and patiency posits that agency (the capacity to act or exert power) and patiency (the capacity to be affected or undergo experience) are distributed across broader systems that include tools, environments, and social structures.[185] He argues that agency and patiency are not opposites but deeply interrelated; the more an individual acts through extended means (such as tools or social systems), the more they are also subject to external influences shaping their experience. For instance, while a smartphone extends one's ability to communicate (agency), it also subjects the individual to notifications, messages, and data flows that influence their attention and responses (patiency).

William Mazzarella traces "patiency" back through theology, aesthetics, and therapeutic technique and within Peter Sloterdijk's history of "negative political theory" in which the monk, the nihilist, and those who reject the political all provide prototypes for actively releasing agency. As Mazzarella points out via Hannah Arendt, challenging agency-anxiety in this way is a response to a modern valuation of the active life. He points to Heidigger's discussions about the differences between "waiting," involving expectation, and "awaiting." Mazzarella finds surrender in even the most anxious of agency philosophies when he points out that even Kant believed that pausing was necessary for developing the higher processes that make us rational beings.

Then, as if he's been speaking about charismatics all along—which he was not—Mazzarella talks how Kant's image of letting go begins with spontaneous sensory experience, not with principles or rules. This letting go is triggered by the world around us, and also it's about our own capacity to resonate with that world. What could be a more fitting description of charismatic experience—the release, the embodied rupture, the cultivated attunement to something greater?

In psychology, agency is most often scaled tightly. There is a tremendous literature on the effects of agency on what is called intentional binding in which people change their subjective sense of timing depending upon their sense of control.[186] Others, however, describe extended scales: what Damasio calls dispositions, philosopher Giovanna Columbetti describes as "moods," others might call it habit.[187]

***

In scientific terms, scale and "scale effects" afford a space for emergent properties, top-down causality, and a collection of complexity effects that challenge reductive thinking.[188] Here I work with the notion of "consequential scale," a concept that allows anthropologists to recognize different scales as important in a given situation.[189]

Postmodernists also followed the impulse to rescale the question. As anthropologist Katie Stewart describes in *Ordinary Affects*, the emphasis on "something that throws itself together in a moment, an event and a sensation" is in direct reply to "the notion of a totalized system, of which everything is always already somehow a part." Breakthrough moments of immediate change, for Stewart, assuage the agency-anxiety produced by modern systematic thinking and experience.[190] And while leery of the idea that individual agency is a basic good, if we were to paint an evangelical history of agency from Calvinist predestination to Arminian individual choice—there has often been an impulse to reconcile preexisting direction (from God) with the capacity to affect the world around us.

Charismatic philosopher Paul Pomerville also explained that in noncharismatic theology, reason or rationality limits connection with God. This he termed the "noetic principle of theology (inflection, reason, epistemology, propositional statements on the confrontation of being)." Instead, he called for a charismatic return to immediacy, what he described as "the ontic principle (immediacy, presence, 'the earnest' of God, confrontation with reality)."[191] Put more simply, for Pomerville, modern approaches to spirituality that focus on reason are not effective at connecting people to God. By reversing this pattern and focusing on immediacy, he writes, charismatic evangelical practice enables modern rational people to know God. This is process philosophy and we could look to Whitehead and others for a fully fleshed out vision of the ways that change and capacity are entangled with time, but for our purposes, charismatics do somewhat similar work with the language of agriculture.

Bibliographic Notes for Chapter 9: Activism

The idea that powerful internal spiritual experience can generate an external attitude of resistance and even rebellion has been explored broadly by Marilyn Westerkamp, Laurie F. Maffly-Kipp, Betty Collier-Thomas, Phyllis Mack, Lawrence J. Friedman, Jean and John Comaroff, and more specifically for charismatics in the work of Walter Hollenweger, Ashon Crawley, Michael Wilkinson, and Mike Davis among others.[192]

Pentecostal theologian Amos Yong calls specifically for a revival of pentecostal benevolent service through a theological shift that he describes as a return to a focus on love which he sees as characteristic of early Pentecostalism as opposed to what he describes as a more recent emphasis on power (Yong, 2012a). You can follow the extended conversation on Godly Love that this intervention inspired through his edited books *The Science and Theology of Godly Love* (Yong 2012b) and *Godly Love: Impediments and Possibilities* (Yong 2012c).

The combination in *Tongues of Fire*, —however, in which the intimate inner details of the experience of fierce attention and letting go are probed for their concrete instantiations in the brain and body (and this experience becomes a prompt for certainty, agency, and action among charismatic evangelicals)— might take this conversation a step further.

Perhaps the central hypothesis underlying much of the research on mindfulness and now psychedelics as well is that internal states of peace and pleasure translate into external states of peace and kindness. If our minds are calm, our body, and our lives, are calm and peaceful. To apply this to charismatics would suggest that something about the ferocity of charismatic practice generates ferocious lives which can be demonstrated when we look at the history of splitting between sectarian charismatic church groups and is also a part of the present-day rightward intensity that the charismatic church is very much a part of. This book explores that hypothesis by simply looking closely. I look at charismatic practice and notice that it is not simply high arousal but also involves moments of intense focus as well as moments of quiet listening. I notice that this fierce mindfulness has a history in the Black prophetic tradition, that its politics may have generally been resistant and rebellious, but not always right wing.[193] And in the process, I hope to open the story of contemplation to include more than the quiet emptiness of mindfulness which was so strategically invited as the secular-seeming entry point for eastern traditions that could be compatible with western mind-body dualisms even while challenging them. Charismatic practice with its messy bodies and even messier experiences of voices and spiritual tactility has me joining Michael Lifshitz and Evan Thompson in expanding the story of contemplation to include the imaginative, chaotic, and spontaneous forms of the spiritual.[194]

Two major historiographic questions need some clarification. First, how important are charismatics to the politics of the Christian Right? Subjective statements abound. Joel Carpenter's is symptomatic of a clear trend: "We are now entering a new chapter of evangelical history, in which the pentecostal–charismatic movement is quickly supplanting the fundamentalist–conservative one is the most influential evangelical impulse at work today."[195] The "pentecostalization" of Catholicism and evangelicalism is another often discussed impression. The most visible evidence that charismatic practices have permeated evangelicalism is the strong leadership of charismatic churches in the National Association of Evangelicals.[196]

Second, there is also some significant debate about the class nature of charismatic evangelicalism which is also tied up in debates about its posture toward the secular modern world and capitalism in particular. I want to be clear that this is not a return to Anderson's argument that charismatics are poor and that this poverty is the reason for their dissociation. Instead, I am suggesting that resistance is cultivated by prayer practices as a charismatic sentiment, but not that it is specifically class-based. I am following Naomi Haynes[197] and others who seem to walk the line between those who see charismatics as middle class and those who see them as poverty-stricken, and instead point out that the demographics suggest lower socio-economic status, but the flavor of resistance is cross class and therefore may be somewhat rooted in prayer practice, not merely class experience.

There is certainly evidence that denominational affiliation often relates to social class.[198] And evidence that spiritual practice in general can generate resistance to dominant ways of being, especially class and racial hierarchies.[199] Sociologist Christian Lalive d'Epinay argues explicitly that charismatic evangelicalism is more than anything else a response to the specific forms of suffering generated by capitalist modernity. As he says, "[charismatic evangelicalism's] rise is parallel to that of the Marxist–socialist movements. They, like it, were born of the same one and the same need, both were nourished by the same rebelliousness and struggled by and large for the same clientele, but giving them very different orientation." For D'Epinay, charismatic practices were experientially born of life under capitalism, and their rebellious sensibilities meant that at the same time they repudiated it. As he writes, "[charismatic evangelicalism] is, on the one hand, the *expression* of real misery, and on the other a *protest* against real misery. It is the sigh of the creature who has been overwhelmed, the feeling of a heartless world, as well as the spirit of an age deprived of spirit." He explicitly compares charismatic organizing to a secular Marxism, "Is it not a paradox," he writes, "to find one protest just purely religious and spiritual and another purely social and political being born on the same terrain and developing in a parallel manner?"[200] Yet this story is difficult to reconcile with the image of the charismatic takeover of the capital in the service of Trump's right-wing agenda. Especially since the 1960s charismatic renewal among Catholics and the ensuing Third Wave of Pentecostalism, there has been a sense among some scholars that spirit-filled Christians have been found across all sorts of class positions and the previous generalizations about deprivation and, resistance, may no longer be applicable.[201]

My response: First, while there is certainly class variation in contemporary evangelicalism, the previous scholarship on the relationship between class and resistance and spiritual practice is still relevant. In my experience as an ethnographer, I think it is difficult to argue that the sense of resistance is not still very much present. The thought that the practice engenders a sense of certainty, agency, and possibility is something I hope to have shown in the last three chapters of this book. My point, however, is that this activation has been targeted differently in different eras. Second, while there has been some degree of charismatic practice among the middle class, according to Pew Foundation studies, charismatics are still relatively poor and undereducated compared to other denominations. This is especially true for a subset of charismatics, Pentecostals, of which the Assemblies of God is the largest group. According to Pew, Pentecostals are 20 percent more likely than the average US citizen to have only a high school degree, and 17 percent less likely to have completed college or more. They are about 10 percent more likely to be low income and 10 percent less likely to be high income than the average.[202]

My argument that we should expand our recognition of contemplative practice beyond a narrow form of mindfulness is an expansion of the arguments of Ronald Purser, Robert Sharf, Michael Lifshitz, and Evan Thompson.[203] The underlying thought that charismatic practice should be considered a mind-body training practice with significant internal consequence builds from the work of psychologist Michael McCullough on prayer in general with the specific focus on charismatic evangelicals derived from the work of anthropologists Tanya Luhrmann and Thomas Csordas, as well as psychologists Felicitas Goodman and Ralph Hood.[204]

Finally, it turns out that mindfulness, which was my initial subject for comparison, is really quite a narrow slice of meditative practice. The Richie Davidson, Ram Dass version of "be here now"[205] and also the more intensely experience-oriented versions that focus on the jhanas are both very small and recently revised threads of the Buddhist pantheon.[206] Robert Sharf argues that most versions of Buddhism are not at all interested in something akin to "experience" and that even those that claim it don't see it as part of the path toward Nirvana.[207] Ron Purser makes a related argument by calling mindfulness a new kind of Buddhism in which the practice has become part of a capitalist engine rather than an ethical structure for bettering the world.[208] In other words, when we say that mindfulness and charismatic worship are similar and yet different, this is true, but this comparison doesn't tell us much about Buddhism.

The bigger argument is simply that speaking in tongues, like mindfulness and other contemplative practices, is a real thing that changes our brains and our communities. Tongues prayer is similarly powerful, embodied, relaxing and transforming. While it may uniquely inspire a sense of resistance and enablement—which is worth celebrating and exploring further—it is apolitical, prone to both good use and to misuse, neither kind nor mean, and neither especially loving or hateful to people outside its innermost circle.

Notes

Prologue

1   D. W. Bebbington, *Evangelicalism in Modern Britain: A History from the 1730s to the 1980s* (Boston, MA: Unwin Hyman, 1989).

2   There are plenty of arguments about when tongues prayer first emerged; for non-evangelical versions, see "'The Tongue of Angels': Glossolalia among Mormonism's Founders"; "From the History of Glossolalia Studies. The Case of Hélène Smith on the Borderlines of Linguistics, Psychology, and Religion."

3   To think about the terms "evangelical," "Pentecostal," and "charismatic": Pentecostals were fundamentalist, and then as the 1950s brought out the new movement called neoevangelical, now called evangelical, the Pentecostals took that on to a significant degree. Many charismatics are evangelical, but not all (i.e., charismatic Catholics). Many evangelicals are charismatic or Pentecostal, but not all (i.e., Southern Baptists).

4   Anderson, *Studying Global Pentecostalism: Theories and Methods*.

5   Cutten, *Speaking with Tongues, Historically and Psychologically Considered*. See more in the bibliographic essay for chapter 5.

6   Lifshitz and Thompson, "What's Wrong with 'the Mindful Brain'?"; McNay, *Gender and Agency*.

7   Damasio, *Descartes' Error*.

8   Kuypers et al., "Ayahuasca Enhances Creative Divergent Thinking while Decreasing Conventional Convergent Thinking"; Schneider et al., "The Role of Mindfulness in Physical Activity."

9   Keltner and Haidt, "Social Functions of Emotions at Four Levels of Analysis"; Bai et al., "Awe, the Diminished Self, and Collective Engagement."

10   Carhart-Harris and Friston, "REBUS and the Anarchic Brain"; Yaden and Griffiths, "The Subjective Effects of Psychedelics Are Necessary for Their Enduring Therapeutic Effects."

11   Brahinsky, "Pentecostal Body Logics"; Brahinsky, *Pentecostal Missionary Training: Cultivating Body Logics, Converting Missionaries, Building A Movement, Dissertation*.

12   Hollenweger, *The Pentecostals*; Hollenweger, "Pentecostalism and Black Power."

13 Brahinsky, "Missionary Conversions."

14 Brahinsky, *Pentecostal Missionary Training: Cultivating Body Logics, Converting Missionaries, Building a Movement, Dissertation.*

15 Luhrmann and Morgain, "Prayer as Inner Sense Cultivation"; Luhrmann, Nusbaum, and Thisted, "'Lord, Teach Us to Pray.'"

16 Newberg et al., "The Measurement of Regional Cerebral Blood Flow during Glossolalia"; Persinger, "Striking EEG Profiles from Single Episodes of Glossolalia and Transcendental Meditation."

17 Hacking, "Looping Effects of Human Kinds."

18 The micro-phenomenological interviews were focused on AG-linked churches, two in the Bay Area and one that had recently left AG in the central valley. They included a broad mix of ages, genders, and races. The MRI data was from two churches in the Bay. The EEG and divergent thinking data included people from across northern California.

Chapter 1

1 He described his church as apostolic. I don't know which denomination it was, but they did speak in tongues.

2 Moore, *Shepherding Movement.*

3 Wink, Dillon, and Adrienne, "Religiousness, Spiritual Seeking, and Authoritarianism: Findings from a Longitudinal Study."

4 Anthropologist Julia Cassaniti has explained to me that "letting go" and "surrender" are not so obviously linked in Buddhist traditions.

5 Durkheim, *The Elementary Forms of the Religious Life.*

6 Strathern, *The Gender of the Gift*; Geertz, *Person, Time, and Conduct in Bali: An Essay in Cultural Analysis*; Taylor, *Sources of the Self.*

7 Several scholars have noted the planning and practice among charismatics that results in a sense of spontaneity (Luhrmann, *When God Talks Back*. Others suggest that a sense of spontaneity is an important element in the lasting effects of experience, especially around belief change (Lorini and Castelfranchi, "The Cognitive Structure of Surprise")).

8 Brahinsky, "Crossing the Buffer."

9 Luhrmann, *When God Talks Back.*

10 Carhart-Harris and Friston, "REBUS and the Anarchic Brain"; De Ruiter, Elzinga, and Phaf, "Dissociation."

11 Anderson, *Vision of the Disinherited.*

12 Davis, "Planet of Slums."

13 Pew Forum on Religion & Public Life, *Spirit and Power a 10-Country Survey of Pentecostals.*

14 Wendel, "Object-Based Epistemology at a Creationist Museum."

15 Rosenbaum, "Patient Teenagers?"

16 Marsden, *Fundamentalism and American Culture.*

17 Reich, *Selected Writings: An Introduction to Orgonomy.*

18 Thomas, *Revivalism and Cultural Change*; Connolly, "The Evangelical-Capitalist Resonance Machine."

Chapter 2

1 Wigger, *Taking Heaven by Storm Methodism and the Rise of Popular Christianity in America.*

2 Alland, "'Possession' in a Revivalistic Negro Church," 207.

3 Luhrmann, Nusbaum, and Thisted, "The Absorption Hypothesis."

4 Luhrmann, "A Hyperreal God and Modern Belief."

5 Samarin, *Tongues of Men and Angels*; Goodman, *Speaking in Tongues; a Cross-Cultural Study of Glossolalia [by] Felicitas D. Goodman.*

6 Asad, *Genealogies of Religion.*

7 Spanos et al., "Glossolalia as Learned Behavior: An Experimental Demonstration."

8 A note: white male control of Black women's spirituality is deeply problematic. At the same time, Dr. Stewart outspokenly advocates racial equality in a traditionally whites-only denomination.

9 I initially wondered if these training manuals might be a late twentieth century response to declension in Charismatic worship. However, in searching old AG book catalogs, I found a tradition of similar training texts running back to AG's first few decades, and their strategies are quite similar.

10 Huffman and Lindell, *Hungry? A Study in the Baptism in the Holy Spirit*, 13, 8.

11 Enloe, "The Nuts and Bolts of Ministering Spirit Baptism," 26–7; Griffin, "Communicating the Baptism of the Spirit to Students," 116.

12 Enloe, "Leading a Receiving Time," 85.

13 Enloe, "The Nuts and Bolts of Ministering Spirit Baptism," 27.

14 Cramer, "Preparing Yourself to Help Others," 47.

15 Crabtree, *Youth Ministry Institute Manual*, 134.

16 Cramer, "Preparing Yourself to Help Others," 42.er.

17 Gerhold, "Communicating the Character of the Holy Spirit to Kids," 110.

18 Enloe, "Ministering the Holy Spirit Baptism in Today's Culture," 53.

19 Crabtree, *Youth Ministry Institute Manual*, 135.

20 Huffman and Lindell, *Hungry? A Study in the Baptism in the Holy Spirit*, 8.

21 Crabtree, *Youth Ministry Institute Manual*, 134.

22 Huffman and Lindell, *Hungry? A Study in the Baptism in the Holy Spirit*, 12.

23 Crabtree, *Youth Ministry Institute Manual*, 134.

24 Erickson, "Fostering a Setting for People to Receive," 68.

25 Van Cappellen and Edwards, "Emotion Expression in Context."

26 Bullock, *When the Spirit Speaks: Making Sense of Tongues, Interpretation, and Prophecy*, 59.

27 Bullock, 8.

28 Bullock, 29.

29 Bullock, 53.

30 Bullock, 53.

31 Crabtree, *Youth Ministry Institute Manual*, 133–4.

32 Crabtree, 133.

33 Williams, *Spirit Cure*, 6.

34 Heyrman, *Southern Cross*.

35 Wigger, *Taking Heaven by Storm Methodism and the Rise of Popular Christianity in America*.

36 In her study of Brazilian Pentecostalism, Celia Loreto Mariz argues that Pentecostalism refigures hierarchies in a patently modern manner. "Many authors believe that Pentecostalism merely imitates a traditional relationship to authority and the supernatural and does not represent Pentecostalism, among other things, as a process of rationalization." Mariz, *Coping with Poverty*.

37 Poloma, *The Assemblies of God at the Crossroads*, 66.

38 Poloma, 41.

39 Taylor, *A Secular Age*.

40   Albrecht, *Rites in the Spirit.*

41   Bourdieu, *Pascalian Meditations.*

42   Brahinsky, "The Effects of Scale: What Pentecostalism and Neuroscience Teach Us about Habit, Affect and Agency."

Chapter 3

1   Hollenweger, *The Pentecostals.*

2   Brahinsky et al., "The Spiral of Attention, Arousal, and Release."

3   Posner, "Orienting of Attention."

4   Sharf, "Buddhist Modernism and the Rhetoric of Meditative Experience."

5   Todd et al., "Affect-Biased Attention as Emotion Regulation"; Ransom et al., "Affect-Biased Attention and Predictive Processing."

6   Angelina Lillard, "Ethnopsychologies: Cultural Variations in Theories of Mind," *Psychological Bulletin* 123, no. 1 (1998): 3–32; Julia L. Cassaniti and Tanya Marie Luhrmann, "The Cultural Kindling of Spiritual Experiences," *Current Anthropology* 55, no. S10 (December 2014): S333–43, https://doi.org/10.1086/677881; for an attention-based version of this question, see Richard E. Nisbett and Yuri Miyamoto, "The Influence of Culture: Holistic versus Analytic Perception," *Trends in Cognitive Sciences* 9, no. 10 (October 2005): 467–73, https://doi.org/10.1016/j.tics.2005.08.004.

7   Brahinsky et al., "The Spiral of Attention, Arousal, and Release."

Chapter 4

1   Damasio, *Self Comes to Mind.*

2   Luhrmann et al., "Sensing the Presence of Gods and Spirits across Cultures and Faiths."

3   Feld, *Sound and Sentiment: Birds, Weeping, Poetics, and Song in Kaluli Expression.*

4   Luhrmann and Morgain, "Prayer as Inner Sense Cultivation."

5   Yaden et al., "The Noetic Quality."

6   "Hearing Voices Website."

7   Luhrmann, *Of Two Minds.*

8   Gone, "Psychotherapy and Traditional Healing for American Indians."

9   Koenig, *The Healing Power of Faith.*

10 Longden, Corstens, and Dillon, "Recovery, Discovery and Revolution: The Work of Intervoice and the Hearing Voices Movement."

11 Beavan, Read, and Cartwright, "The Prevalence of Voice-Hearers in the General Population."

12 Read et al., "Childhood Trauma, Psychosis and Schizophrenia."

13 Romme and Escher, *Accepting Voices*.

14 Ohayon, "Prevalence of Hallucinations and Their Pathological Associations in the General Population."

Chapter 5

1   Josh Brahinsky, Michael Lifshitz, and Tanya Marie Luhrmann, "Steps toward a Neurophenomenology of Speaking in Tongues" (20 June 2024), in David Yaden and Michiel van Elk (eds), *The Oxford Handbook of Psychedelic, Religious, Spiritual, and Mystical Experiences* (online edn, Oxford Academic, 22 May 2024), https://doi.org/10.1093/oxfordhb/9780192844064.013.18.

2   Dennet, "Real Patterns."

3   McCrae and Elliott, "Spiritual Experiences in Temporal Lobe Epilepsy"; Mosini et al., "Neurophysiological, Cognitive-Behavioral and Neurochemical Effects in Practitioners of Transcendental Meditation—A Literature Review"; Persinger, "Religious and Mystical Experiences as Artifacts of Temporal Lobe Function."

4   Newberg et al., "The Measurement of Regional Cerebral Blood Flow during Glossolalia."

5   Limb and Braun, "Neural Substrates of Spontaneous Musical Performance"; Beaty et al., "A First Look at the Role of Domain-General Cognitive and Creative Abilities in Jazz Improvisation"; Beaty, "The Neuroscience of Musical Improvisation"; Liu et al., "Neural Correlates of Lyrical Improvisation."

6   Bahramzadeh Zoeram et al., "Hippocampal Orexin Receptor Blocking Prevented the Stress Induced Social Learning and Memory Deficits."

7   Walsh, Eisenlohr-Moul, and Baer, "Brief Mindfulness Training Reduces Salivary IL-6 and TNF-α in Young Women with Depressive Symptomatology."

8   Samarin, *Tongues of Men and Angels*; Goodman, *Speaking in Tongues; a Cross-Cultural Study of Glossolalia [by] Felicitas D. Goodman*.

9   Spanos et al., "Glossolalia as Learned Behavior: An Experimental Demonstration."

10 C. Farrer and C. D. Frith, "Experiencing Oneself vs Another Person as Being the Cause of an Action: The Neural Correlates of the Experience of Agency," *NeuroImage*

15, no. 3 (March 2002): 596–603, https://doi.org/10.1006/nimg.2001.1009; Philip Gerrans, "The Feeling of Thinking: Sense of Agency in Delusions of Thought Insertion," *Psychology of Consciousness: Theory, Research, and Practice* 2, no. 3 (2015): 291–300, https://doi.org/10.1037/cns0000060; Yukihito Yomogida et al., "The Neural Basis of Agency: An FMRI Study," *NeuroImage* 50, no. 1 (March 2010): 198–207, https://doi.org/10.1016/j.neuroimage.2009.12.054; Walsh et al., "The Functional Anatomy and Connectivity of Thought Insertion and Alien Control of Movement."

11 Jung, *History of Modern Psychology: Lectures Delivered at the ETH Zurich*; James, *The Varieties of Religious Experience*; James, *The Principles of Psychology Volume 1*.

12 Menzies, *Anointed to Serve*, 180.

13 John Kildahl, *The Psychology of Speaking in Tongues* (London: S.l., 1972).

14 Goodman, *Speaking in Tongues; a Cross-Cultural Study of Glossolalia [by] Felicitas D. Goodman.*

15 Samarin, *Tongues of Men and Angels*; Spanos et al., "Glossolalia as Learned Behavior: An Experimental Demonstration."

16 Samarin, "Reviewed Work(s): Speaking in Tongues: A Cross-Cultural Study of Glossolalia by Felicitas D. Goodman."

17 Goodman, "Altered Mental State vs. 'Style of Discourse.'"

18 Spanos et al., "Glossolalia as Learned Behavior: An Experimental Demonstration"; Spanos and Hewitt, "Glossolalia: A Test of the 'Trance' and Psychopathology Hypotheses."

19 McCrae and Elliott, "Spiritual Experiences in Temporal Lobe Epilepsy."

20 Persinger, "Experimental Simulation of the God Experience: Implications for Religious Beliefs and the Future of the Human Species"; Persinger et al., "The Electromagnetic Induction of Mystical and Altered States within the Laboratory"; Hu and Wu, "Michael Persinger & the GOD Experiments."

21 Newberg et al., "The Measurement of Regional Cerebral Blood Flow during Glossolalia."

22 Newberg et al.

23 Granqvist et al., "Sensed Presence and Mystical Experiences Are Predicted by Suggestibility, Not by the Application of Transcranial Weak Complex Magnetic Fields."

24 Azari et al., "Neural Correlates of Religious Experience"; Azari, Missimer, and Seitz, "Research."

25 Cristofori et al., "Neural Correlates of Mystical Experience."

26 Village, "Dimensions of Belief about Miraculous Healing"; Megevand et al., "Seeing Scenes."

27 Blackman, "Habit and Affect."

28 Arzy et al., "Neural Basis of Embodiment."

29 Blanke et al., "Hearing of a Presence"; Blanke et al., "Neurological and Robot-Controlled Induction of an Apparition."

30 Carlos Tinoco and Joao Ortiz, "Magnetic Stimulation of the Temporal Cortex: A Partial 'God Helmet' Replication Study," *Journal of Consciousness Exploration & Research* 5, no. 3 (April 201AD): 234–57; Michael A. Persinger, "Replication of God Helmet Experiment and Many Other of Our Results—a Blog by Dr. Michael A. Persinger," *Sacred Pathways—Blogs in Neurotheology* (blog), June 7, 2015, https://sacredneurology.com/2015/06/07/god-helmet-and-many-other-of-our-results-have-been-replicated-a-blog-by-dr-michael-a-persinger/.

31 Giuseppe A. Zito, Roland Wiest, and Selma Aybek, "Neural Correlates of Sense of Agency in Motor Control: A Neuroimaging Meta-Analysis," PLOS ONE 15, no. 6 (2020): e0234321, https://doi.org/10.1371/journal.pone.0234321. and Gethin Hughes, "The Role of the Temporoparietal Junction in Implicit and Explicit Sense of Agency," *Neuropsychologia* 113 (May 2018): 1–5, https://doi.org/10.1016/j.neuropsychologia.2018.03.020.

32 Veissière et al., "Thinking through Other Minds."

33 Daniel Goleman and Davidson Richard, *Altered Traits*, 2018.

34 Kornhuber and Deecke, "Brain Potential Changes in Voluntary and Passive Movements in Humans: Readiness Potential and Reafferent Potentials."

35 Seghezzi and Zapparoli, "Predicting the Sensory Consequences of Self-Generated Actions."

36 Walsh, Eisenlohr-Moul, and Baer, "Brief Mindfulness Training Reduces Salivary IL-6 and TNF-α in Young Women with Depressive Symptomatology."

37 Poldrack and Yarkoni, "From Brain Maps to Cognitive Ontologies."

38 Open Science Collaboration, "Estimating the Reproducibility of Psychological Science."

39 Albert Newen, Leon de Bruin, and Shaun Gallagher, *The Oxford Handbook of 4E Cognition*, 2018, https://doi.org/10.1093/oxfordhb/9780198735410.001.0001; Antoine Lutz and Evan Thompson, "Neurophenomenology: Integrating Subjective Experience and Brain Dynamics in the Neuroscience of Consciousness," *Journal of Consciousness Studies* 10, no. 9–10 (2003): 31–52; Francisco J. Varela and Cnrs Ura, "Neurophenomenology: A Methodological Remedy for the Hard Problem," *Journal of Consciousness Studies* 3, no. 4 (1996): 330–49.

40 We later received funding from the Bial Foundation and the Mind and Life Foundation, as well.

41 Damasio, *Descartes' Error*; Damasio, *Self Comes to Mind*.

42 Gallagher, *How the Body Shapes the Mind*.

43 Gethin Hughes, "The Role of the Temporoparietal Junction in Implicit and Explicit Sense of Agency," *Neuropsychologia* 113 (May 2018): 1–5. and Giuseppe A. Zito,

Roland Wiest, and Selma Aybek, "Neural Correlates of Sense of Agency in Motor Control: A Neuroimaging Meta-Analysis," *PLOS ONE* 15, no. 6 (2020): e0234321, https://doi.org/10.1371/journal.pone.0234321.

Chapter 6

1   Piff et al., "Higher Social Class Predicts Increased Unethical Behavior."

2   Anderson, Monroy, and Keltner, "Awe in Nature Heals."

3   Van Elk et al., "The Neural Correlates of the Awe Experience."

4   Takano and Nomura, "Neural Representations of Awe."

5   Guan et al., "Neural Basis of Dispositional Awe."

6   Piff et al., "Awe, the Small Self, and Prosocial Behavior."

7   Schneider et al., "The Role of Mindfulness in Physical Activity."

8   Preller and Vollenweider, "Modulation of Social Cognition via Hallucinogens and 'Entactogens.'"

9   Bahramzadeh Zoeram et al., "Hippocampal Orexin Receptor Blocking Prevented the Stress Induced Social Learning and Memory Deficits."

10   Matthew M. Nour et al., "Ego-Dissolution and Psychedelics: Validation of the Ego-Dissolution Inventory (EDI)," *Frontiers in Human Neuroscience* 10 (June 14, 2016): 201; Alexander V. Lebedev et al., "Finding the Self by Losing the Self: Neural Correlates of Ego-Dissolution under Psilocybin," *Human Brain Mapping* 36, no. 8 (August 2015): 3137–53, https://doi.org/10.1002/hbm.22833.

11   Schneider et al., "The Role of Mindfulness in Physical Activity"; Preller and Vollenweider, "Modulation of Social Cognition via Hallucinogens and 'Entactogens'"; Bahramzadeh Zoeram et al., "Hippocampal Orexin Receptor Blocking Prevented the Stress Induced Social Learning and Memory Deficits"; Nour et al., "Ego-Dissolution and Psychedelics"; Lebedev et al., "Finding the Self by Losing the Self"; Lebedev et al., "LSD-Induced Entropic Brain Activity Predicts Subsequent Personality Change."

12   Roland R. Griffiths et al., "Psilocybin Can Occasion Mystical-Type Experiences Having Substantial and Sustained Personal Meaning and Spiritual Significance," *Psychopharmacology* 187, no. 3 (August 2006): 268–83, https://doi.org/10.1007/s00213-006-0457-5; Roland R. Griffiths et al., "Mystical-Type Experiences Occasioned by Psilocybin Mediate the Attribution of Personal Meaning and Spiritual Significance 14 Months Later," *Journal of Psychopharmacology* 22, no. 6 (August 2008): 621–32, https://doi.org/10.1177/0269881108094300; Roland R. Griffiths et al., "Psilocybin-Occasioned Mystical-Type Experience in Combination with Meditation and Other Spiritual Practices Produces Enduring Positive Changes in Psychological Functioning and in Trait Measures of Prosocial Attitudes and Behaviors," *Journal of Psychopharmacology* 32, no. 1 (January 2018): 49–69, https://doi.

org/10.1177/0269881117731279; Frederick S. Barrett and Roland R. Griffiths, "Classic Hallucinogens and Mystical Experiences: Phenomenology and Neural Correlates," *Behavioral Neurobiology of Psychedelic Drugs*, Current Topics in Behavioral Neurosciences, 36 (2018): 393–430, https://doi.org/10.1007/7854_2017_474.

13   Nour et al., "Ego-Dissolution and Psychedelics."

14   Yang Bai et al., "Awe, the Diminished Self, and Collective Engagement: Universals and Cultural Variations in the Small Self," *Journal of Personality and Social Psychology* 113, no. 2 (August 2017): 185–209.

15   Bahramzadeh Zoeram et al., "Hippocampal Orexin Receptor Blocking Prevented the Stress Induced Social Learning and Memory Deficits." For Carhart-Harris, the richness of experience is measured by the free energy principle. The free energy principle works with predictive coding theories that recognize that our brains can't store endless information, so they function best by making good guesses (predictions) about the world and then modifying them when they turn out wrong. This leads to a strong internal impulse to resist disorder and minimize uncertainty to save us extra work (Friston, 2010). Carhart-Harris believes that free energy and entropy are the two linked elements of brain and mind, a "dual aspect monism" (Solms and Turnbull, 2003) that allows subjective experience to be mapped together with neuronal patterning.

16   Wolff et al., "Learning to Let Go."

17   Friston, "The Free-Energy Principle"; Friston, "A Theory of Cortical Responses"; Hinton and Sejnowski, "Optimal Perceptual Inference."

18   Barlow, "Possible Principles Underlying the Transformations of Sensory Messages."

19   Hubel and Wiesel, "Brain Mechanisms of Vision."

20   Sporns and Betzel, "Modular Brain Networks."

21   Rao and Ballard, "Predictive Coding in the Visual Cortex."

22   Friston, "The Free-Energy Principle."

23   Clark, *Surfing Uncertainty*.

24   Goodman, *Speaking in Tongues; a Cross-Cultural Study of Glossolalia [by] Felicitas D. Goodman*; Felicitas D. Goodman, "Body Posture and the Religious Altered State of Consciousness," accessed October 3, 2016, http://jhp.sagepub.com/content/26/3/81. full.pdf; Felicitas D. Goodman, "The Discomfiture of Religious Experience," *Religion* 21, no. 4 (October 1991): 339–43, https://doi.org/10.1016/0048-721X(91)90036-P; Felicitas D. Goodman, *Ecstasy, Ritual and Alternate Reality* (Bloomington, IN: Indiana University Press, 1988). Goodman followed others who had imagined tongues as a hopeful generator of moments of psychic or social reorientation— something akin to Maslow's peak experiences—that might lead to a breakdown and even reversal of previous behavioral and thought patterns Gerlach and Hine, "Five Factors Crucial to the Growth and Spread of a Modern Religious Movement." For some, the psychic reorientation became safe only within a church's social matrix

Lapsley and Simpson, "Speaking in Tongues"; Boisen, "Economic Distress and Religious Experience a Study of the Holy Rollers."

25   Grady and Loewenthal, "Features Associated with Speaking in Tongues (Glossolalia)."

26   Wacker, *Heaven Below: Early Pentecostals and American Culture.*

27   Newberg did wonder if tongues might evolve after extended practice. Brain scans of religious practice, however, have followed the established polarity by describing religion as a disinhibited trance or by contrast as a self-aware and concerted cognitive and or social practice (Azari, Missimer, and Seitz, "Research."). Azari et al. challenge others who argue that religious experience is marked by (dysfunctional) brain activity involving limbic structures—the "limbic marker hypothesis."

28   Guilford, *The Nature of Human Intelligence.*

29   Olson et al., "Naming Unrelated Words Predicts Creativity."

Chapter 7

1   Luhrmann, "Toward an Anthropological Theory of Mind."

2   Lillard, "Ethnopsychologies: Cultural Variations in Theories of Mind."

3   Pew Research Center, "When Americans Say They Believe in God, What Do They Mean."

4   Lord, "Spirit-Shaped Mission: A Holistic Charismatic Missiology."

5   Austin, *How to Do Things with Words.*

6   Wagner, *Confronting the Powers.*

7   Robbins, "Introduction."

8   Aulino, "From Karma to Sin."

9   Marsden, *Fundamentalism and American Culture*; Kazin, *The Populist Persuasion.*

10   Evans-Pritchard, *Witchcraft, Oracles and Magic among the Azande.*

11   Malinowski, *Argonauts of the Western Pacific.*

12   Mauss, *The Gift.*

Chapter 8

1   Lao-tzu., *Tao Tê Ching.*

2　Tolle, *The Power of Now: A Guide to Spiritual Enlightenment*.

3　Du Mez, *Jesus and John Wayne*.

4　Sapolsky, *Determined: A Science of Life without Free Will*.

5　Kant et al., *The Critique of Pure Reason.*

6　Freud and Freud, *The Interpretation of Dreams; and On Dreams*.

7　Gillespie, *Hegel, Heidegger, and the Ground of History*, 59.

8　Slingerland, *Trying Not to Try: The Art and Science of Spontaneity*.

9　Foucault, *Discipline and Punish*.

10　Morris and Spivak, *Can the Subaltern Speak?*, 11–12.

11　Here, "agency is the hiatus in iterability, the compulsion to install an identity through repetition, which requires the very contingency, the undetermined interval, that identity instantly seeks to foreclose." Butler, *Bodies That Matter*.

12　Likewise, philosopher Alain Badiou's concept of a void at the edge of formalism, Jacques Derrida's trace, Jacques Lacan's Real, even Carl Schmitt's exception, all offer a version of Gödel's theorem: there is no coherence if complete, and no completion if coherent. Badiou, *Being and Event*; Derrida, *Of Grammatology*; Laclau, *On Populist Reason*; Schmitt, *The Crisis of Parliamentary Democracy*; Livingston, *The Politics of Logic*. (Another group of theorists allowed the gaps to emerge between broader modes of existence instead of individual actions. Bourdieu, *La Noblesse d'Etat*; Deleuze et al., *What Is Philosophy?*; Latour, "Biography of an Inquiry." They imagined that the gap between coherent and incoherent, between complete and incomplete, might provide the space for affect, for the event, for hope, for resistance, and for agency.)

13　His later work does retract some of his early celebration of the isolated event.

14　Menzies, *Anointed to Serve: The Story of the Assemblies of God*, 325.

15　Pentecostal Evangel 1944_07_15, p 3.

16　Pentecostal Evangel 1936_10_10, p 5.

17　Badiou, *Saint Paul*.

18　Roberts, *The Baptism with the Holy Spirit*, 7, 9, 28–9.

19　McClung, *Azusa Street and Beyond*, 53.

20　Spittler, "Implicit Values in Pentecostal Missions," 409, 415.

21　Macgavran, *How Churches Grow*, 114–15.

22　Allen, *The Spontaneous Expansion of the Church*.

23　McClung, *Azusa Street and Beyond*, 5.

24 Paul Pomerville, *The Third Force in Missions: A Pentecostal Contribution to Contemporary Mission Theology* (Peabody, MA: Hendrickson Publishers, 1985), 73.

25 Badiou, *Saint Paul.*

26 "Fallow Ground," *PE* 1929_07_06, p 4.

27 W. E. Moody, "Have You Become Entangled?" PE 1940_5_4p2.

28 Moore and Obhi, "Intentional Binding and the Sense of Agency"; Christensen and Grünbaum, "Sense of Agency for Movements."

29 Damasio, *Self Comes to Mind.*

30 Kawakami et al., "Just Say No (to Stereotyping): Effects of Training in the Negation of Stereotypic Associations on Stereotype Activation."

31 Gollwitzer, Bayer, and McCulloch, "The Control of the Unwanted," 485, 487.

32 Damasio, *Self Comes to Mind.*

33 Donald, *A Mind so Rare*, 58.

34 Gazzaniga, *Who's in Charge?*, 131, 133, 135.

35 Gazzaniga, 125.

36 Sayre, "Ecological and Geographical Scale."

37 Choosing a scale performs what philosopher-physicist Karen Barad calls "a consequential cut" in the co-constitution of subject and object, and the onto-epistemological implications of such a fluid tool seem immense. Barad, *Meeting the Universe Halfway.*

38 Emerson and Smith, *Divided by Faith.*

Chapter 9

1 James, *The Varieties of Religious Experience.*

2 Williamson and Hood, "Spirit Baptism."

3 Davis, "Planet of Slums," 27.

4 Johns, *Pentecostal Formation*, 69.

5 Moreton, *To Serve God and Wal-Mart the Making of Christian Free Enterprise.*

6 Hollenweger, "Pentecostalism and Black Power"; Hollenweger, *The Pentecostals.*

7 Alexander, *Peace to War*; Pomerville, *The Third Force in Missions.*

8 Alexander, "An Analysis of the Emergence and Decline of Pacifism in the History of the Assemblies of God."

9   Davis, "Planet of Slums," 30–1.

10   Brown, *Love's Body,* 38.

11   Brown's call for poetry to replace politics prefigured Spivak's "poetics" by thirty years. His recognition of the polyphony and fertility of meanings set the stage for Deleuze's "excess." But then, what of the poeticity of symmetry (Jakobson) of a timetable (Pasternak), a wine list (Vjazemski), a clothes inventory (Gogol)? From Jakobson cited in Kirby, *Telling Flesh,* 36.

12   Haraway, *Simians, Cyborgs, and Women,* 181.

13   Moraga and Anzaldúa, *This Bridge Called My Back.* Anzaldua, *Speaking in Tongues,* 165.

14   Badiou, *Being and Event*; Agamben, *The Time That Remains*; Žižek, *The Puppet and the Dwarf.*

15   Cox, *Fire from Heaven*; Anderson, *Studying Global Pentecostalism: Theories and Methods*; Anderson and Hollenweger, *Pentecostals after a Century*; Meyer, *Translating the Devil.*

16   Lalive d'Epinay, *Haven of the Masses.*

17   van Klinken and Chitando, *Public Religion and the Politics of Homosexuality in Africa.*

18   Comaroff and Comaroff, "Occult Economies and the Violence of Abstraction"; Comaroff and Comaroff, *Millennial Capitalism and the Culture of Neoliberalism*; Coleman, *The Globalisation of Charismatic Christianity Spreading the Gospel of Prosperity.*

19   Young, *Bearing Witness against Sin.*

20   Friedman, *Gregarious Saints*; Mackie, *The Gift of Tongues*; Wesley, *Wesley's Standard Sermons Consisting of Fortyfour Discourses... to Which Are Added Nine Additional Sermons... Ed. and Annotated by Edward H. Sugden*; Mahmood, *Politics of Piety*; Collier-Thomas, *Jesus, Jobs, and Justice*; Comaroff, *Body of Power, Spirit of Resistance The Culture and History of a South African People.*

21   Anderson, *Vision of the Disinherited.*

22   Joutsa et al., "Brain Lesions Disrupting Addiction Map to a Common Human Brain Circuit."

23   Kuypers et al., "Ayahuasca Enhances Creative Divergent Thinking while Decreasing Conventional Convergent Thinking"; Schneider et al., "The Role of Mindfulness in Physical Activity"; Carhart-Harris and Friston, "REBUS and the Anarchic Brain."

24   Pollan, *How to Change Your Mind.*

25   Carhart-Harris et al., "Psychedelics and Connectedness"; Carhart-Harris and Goodwin, "The Therapeutic Potential of Psychedelic Drugs"; Yaden et al., "The Noetic Quality."

26 Griffiths et al., "Psilocybin Can Occasion Mystical-Type Experiences Having Substantial and Sustained Personal Meaning and Spiritual Significance."

27 Jungaberle et al., "Positive Psychology in the Investigation of Psychedelics and Entactogens"; Wolff et al., "Learning to Let Go."

28 Bahramzadeh Zoeram et al., "Hippocampal Orexin Receptor Blocking Prevented the Stress Induced Social Learning and Memory Deficits"; Ellison et al., "Prayer, Attachment to God, and Symptoms of Anxiety-Related Disorders among U.S. Adults"; Seeman, Dubin, and Seeman, "Religiosity/Spirituality and Health"; Tang, Hölzel, and Posner, "The Neuroscience of Mindfulness Meditation"; Gupta et al., "Prevalence and Determinants of Coronary Heart Disease in a Rural Population of India"; Koenig et al., "Commentary on 'Does Spirituality or Religion Positively Affect Mental Health?'"; Feinstein et al., "Burden of Cardiovascular Risk Factors, Subclinical Atherosclerosis, and Incident Cardiovascular Events across Dimensions of Religiosity"; Buck et al., "An Examination of the Relationship between Multiple Dimensions of Religiosity, Blood Pressure, and Hypertension"; Stausberg, "*Big Gods* in Review"; Ironson et al., "The Ironson-Woods Spirituality/Religiousness Index Is Associated with Long Survival, Health Behaviors, Less Distress, and Low Cortisol in People with HIV/AIDS"; Ferguson, Willemsen, and Castañeto, "Centering Prayer as a Healing Response to Everyday Stress."

29 Historian Karen Armstrong (2006) posits that empathy and compassion are central tenets across major world religions. Empirical studies also suggest that religious affiliation promotes ethical behaviors, fairness, and kindness Woods and Ironson, "Religion and Spirituality in the Face of Illness." Additionally, religiously invested individuals report heightened levels of "compassionate love" toward both acquaintances and strangers Sprecher and Fehr, "Compassionate Love for Close Others and Humanity"; Desiningrum, "Religiosity and Compassionate Love in Mother of Children with Autism Spectrum Disorder"; Asad et al., "Religious Orientation and Development of Pro- Social Behavior in Young Female Students," and score higher on personality traits like Agreeableness and Benevolence Saroglou, Delpierre, and Dernelle, "Values and Religiosity"; Ashton and Lee, "A Review of Personality/Religiousness Associations." Spiritual practices that specifically generate compassion are identified as direct drivers of prosocial behavior, with studies showing that even brief compassion practices have significant effects Berry et al., "Mindfulness Increases Prosocial Responses toward Ostracized Strangers through Empathic Concern"; Donald et al., "Does Your Mindfulness Benefit Others?"

30 Goleman and Richard, *Altered Traits*.

31 Beerel and Raffio, *Mindfulness*.

32 O. M. Klimecki, S. Leiberg, M. Ricard, and T. Singer, "Differential Pattern of Functional Brain Plasticity after Compassion and Empathy Training," *Social Cognitive and Affective Neuroscience* (2014), DOI:10.1093/scan/nsu014.

33 Goleman and Richard, *Altered Traits*, 106–7.

34 Wallmark et al., "Promoting Altruism through Meditation."

35 Garssen, Visser, and Pool, "Does Spirituality or Religion Positively Affect Mental Health?"

36 Frost, "Calming Meditation Increases Altruism, Decreases Parochialism."

37 Other researchers have divided mindfulness into components (describing, observing, nonjudging, aware acting, nonreacting) and showed that these influence empathy and active listening (SM Jones, "Mindfulness Training: Can It Create Superheroes?").

38 Arias et al., "Systematic Review of the Efficacy of Meditation Techniques as Treatments for Medical Illness"; Halifax, "A Heuristic Model of Enactive Compassion."

39 Kaplan and Berman, "Directed Attention as a Common Resource for Executive Functioning and Self-Regulation"; Wadlinger and Isaacowitz, "Fixing Our Focus."

40 Hafenbrack et al., "Helping People by Being in the Present"; Iwamoto et al., "Mindfulness Meditation Activates Altruism"; Berry et al., "Mindfulness Increases Prosocial Responses toward Ostracized Strangers through Empathic Concern."

41 Simonsson et al., "Effects of an 8-Week Mindfulness Course on Affective Polarization."

42 Berry et al., "Mindful Attention as a Skillful Means toward Intergroup Prosociality."

43 Di Bello et al., "The Compassionate Vagus"; Kogan et al., "Vagal Activity Is Quadratically Related to Prosocial Traits, Prosocial Emotions, and Observer Perceptions of Prosociality."

44 Batson, "Prosocial Motivation: Is It Ever Truly Altruistic?"; Eisenberg and Miller, "The Relation of Empathy to Prosocial and Related Behaviors"; Pang, Song, and Ma, "Effect of Different Types of Empathy on Prosocial Behavior"; Mazraeh et al., "The Role of Social Interest and Empathy on Helping Behaviors during Floods."

45 Batson et al., "Empathy, Attitudes, and Action"; McCauley, McAuliffe, and McCullough, "Does Empathy Promote Helping by Activating Altruistic Motivation or Concern about Social Evaluation?"

46 Durkheim, *The Elementary Forms of the Religious Life.*

47 Ahmed and Salas, "Implicit Influences of Christian Religious Representations on Dictator and Prisoner's Dilemma Game Decisions"; Ginges, Hansen, and Norenzayan, "Religion and Support for Suicide Attacks."

48 Argo, "Why Fight?"

49 Bruneau, Cikara, and Saxe, "Parochial Empathy Predicts Reduced Altruism and the Endorsement of Passive Harm"; Cikara et al., "Their Pain Gives Us Pleasure."

50 Richtel, "The Latest in Military Strategy"; Rothschild et al., "Mindfulness Meditation in the Israel Defense Forces."

51 Leary et al., *The Psychedelic Experience.*

52 Hartogsohn, "Constructing Drug Effects"; Hartogsohn, "Set and Setting, Psychedelics and the Placebo Response."

53 Brian Pace, Lucy In The Sky With Nazis: Psychedelics and the Right Wing, https://www.psymposia.com/magazine/, February 3, 2020.

54 Turner, *The Ritual Process.*

55 See Egalitarian Dynamics: Liminality, and Victor Turner's Contribution to the Understanding of Socio-historical Process.

56 Regnerus, *Forbidden Fruit.*

57 Reich and Wolfe, *The Mass Psychology of Fascism.*

Bibliographic Essays

1 Anderson and Hollenweger, *Pentecostals after a Century*, 1999; Anderson, "Revising Pentecostal History in a Global Perspective," 2005; Anderson, *Studying Global Pentecostalism: Theories and Methods*; Anderson, *Spreading Fires*; Anderson, "Revising Pentecostal History in a Global Perspective," 2005; Anderson, *Vision of the Disinherited*; Cox, *Fire from Heaven*; Anderson and Hollenweger, *Pentecostals after a Century*, 1999; Hollenweger, "Pentecostalism and Black Power"; Hollenweger, *The Pentecostals*; Pew Forum on Religion & Public Life, *Spirit and Power a 10-Country Survey of Pentecostals*; Mariz, *Coping with Poverty*; Albrecht, *Rites in the Spirit*; Yong, "The Word and the Spirit or the Spirit and the Word"; Wacker, *Heaven Below: Early Pentecostals and American Culture*; Coleman, *The Globalisation of Charismatic Christianity Spreading the Gospel of Prosperity*; Csordas, *The Sacred Self*; Bialecki, *A Diagram for Fire*; Luhrmann, *When God Talks Back*; McClung, *Azusa Street and Beyond*; Hayford and Moore, *The Charismatic Century*; Newman, *Race and the Assemblies of God Church the Journey from Azusa Street to the "Miracle of Memphis."*

2 Bialecki, Haynes, and Robbins, "The Anthropology of Christianity"; Bialecki, "The Bones Restored to Life: Dialogue and Dissemination in the Vineyard's Dialectic of Text and Presence"; Robbins, *Becoming Sinners*; Haynes, "Pentecostalism and the Morality of Money."

3 Poloma, *The Assemblies of God at the Crossroads*; Menzies, *Anointed to Serve*; Alexander, *Peace to War*; Alexander, "An Analysis of the Emergence and Decline of Pacifism in the History of the Assemblies of God"; Blumhofer, *The Assemblies of God*; Blumhofer, *Restoring the Faith*; Blumhofer, Spittler, "Corinthian Spirituality" in Wacker ed. *Pentecostal Currents in American Protestantism.*

4 Smith, *Thinking in Tongues.*

5   Ashon T. Crawley, *Blackpentecostal Breath*; Alexander, *Black Fire*; Gates, *The Black Church*; Kostarelos, *Feeling the Spirit: Faith and Hope in an Evangelical Black Storefront Church*.

6   Newberg et al., "The Measurement of Regional Cerebral Blood Flow during Glossolalia"; Persinger, "Striking EEG Profiles from Single Episodes of Glossolalia and Transcendental Meditation"; Goodman, *Speaking in Tongues; a Cross-Cultural Study of Glossolalia [by] Felicitas D. Goodman*; Spanos et al., "Glossolalia as Learned Behavior: An Experimental Demonstration"; Grady and Loewenthal, "Features Associated with Speaking in Tongues (Glossolalia)."

7   Seligman and Kirmayer, "Dissociative Experience and Cultural Neuroscience."

8   Csordas, "Somatic Modes of Attention"; Desjarlais and Jason Throop, "Phenomenological Approaches in Anthropology."

9   Wilkinson and Marmot, *Social Determinants of Health—The Solid Facts*.

10   Lifshitz, Sheiner, and Kirmayer, *Cultural Neurophenomenology of Psychedelic Thought*.

11   Noë, *Out of Our Heads*.

12   Clark, *Supersizing the Mind*.

13   Johnson, *Embodied Mind, Meaning, and Reason*.

14   Csordas, *The Sacred Self*; Jackson, "Where Thought Belongs"; Stoller, *The Power of the Between*.

15   Barsalou, "Grounded Cognition"; Ramstead, Veissière, and Kirmayer, "Cultural Affordances."

16   Roepstorff, Niewöhner, and Beck, "Enculturing Brains through Patterned Practices"; Roepstorff and Frith, "Neuroanthropology or Simply Anthropology?"; Domínguez Duque et al., "Neuroanthropology"; Lende and Downey, "Neuroanthropology And Its Applications."

17   Kleinman, *The Illness Narratives*; Good, *Medicine, Rationality, and Experience*; Hopper, *Reckoning with Homelessness*; Myers, *Recovery's Edge*; Jenkins, *Extraordinary Conditions*; Lester, *Famished*; Weisner, "Ecocultural Understanding of Children's Developmental Pathways."

18   Seligman, "The Unmaking and Making of Self."

19   Snodgrass, Most, and Upadhyay, "Religious Ritual Is Good Medicine for Indigenous Indian Conservation Refugees."

20   Astuti and Harris, "Understanding Mortality and the Life of the Ancestors in Rural Madagascar."

21   Lynn et al., "Salivary Alpha-Amylase and Cortisol among Pentecostals on a Worship and Nonworship Day"; Lynn et al., "Glossolalia Is Associated with Differences in Biomarkers of Stress and Arousal among Apostolic Pentecostals."

22 Davidson et al., "Alterations in Brain and Immune Function Produced by Mindfulness Meditation."

23 MacLean et al., "Intensive Meditation Training Improves Perceptual Discrimination and Sustained Attention"; Sahdra et al., "Enhanced Response Inhibition during Intensive Meditation Training Predicts Improvements in Self-Reported Adaptive Socioemotional Functioning."

24 Newberg, "The Neuroscientific Study of Spiritual Practices."

25 Chiao et al., "Theory and Methods in Cultural Neuroscience"; Han and Northoff, "Understanding the Self."

26 Buzsáki, *Rhythms of the Brain.*

27 Barad, *Meeting the Universe Halfway.*

28 Antoine Lutz and Evan Thompson, "Neurophenomenology: Integrating Subjective Experience and Brain Dynamics in the Neuroscience of Consciousness," *Journal of Consciousness Studies* 10, no. 9–10 (2003): 31–52; Francisco J. Varela and Cnrs Ura, "Neurophenomenology: A Methodological Remedy for the Hard Problem," *Journal of Consciousness Studies* 3, no. 4 (1996): 330–49; Greg Downey, "Neuroanthropology," in *The SAGE Handbook of Social Anthropology*, by Richard Fardon et al. (1 Oliver's Yard, 55 City Road, London EC1Y 1SP United Kingdom: SAGE Publications 2012), 243–60; Juan F. Domínguez D., "Neuroanthropology and the Dialectical Imperative," *Anthropological Theory* 12, no. 1 (March 2012): 5–27, https://doi.org/10.1177/1463499612436459; Joan Y. Chiao et al., "Cultural Neuroscience: Progress and Promise," *Psychological Inquiry* 24, no. 1 (January 2013): 1–19.

29 Brahinsky, "Pentecostal Body Logics"; Brahinsky, "Crossing the Buffer."

30 Spanos and Hewitt, "Glossolalia: A Test of the 'Trance' and Psychopathology Hypotheses"; Spanos et al., "Glossolalia as Learned Behavior: An Experimental Demonstration."

31 Classen, *Worlds of Sense*; Howes, *The Varieties of Sensory Experience.*

32 Gallagher, "On the Possibility of Naturalizing Phenomenology"; Newen, Bruin, and Gallagher, *The Oxford Handbook of 4E Cognition*; Lifshitz, Cusamano, and Raz, "Meditation and Hypnosis at the Intersection between Phenomenology and Cognitive Science"; Lutz and Thompson, "Neurophenomenology: Integrating Subjective Experience and Brain Dynamics in the Neuroscience of Consciousness"; Cardena, Lynn, and Krippner, *Varieties of Anomalous Experience.*

33 Varela, Thompson, and Rosch, *The Embodied Mind: Cognitive Science and Human Experience* (MIT Press, 1991).

34 Aulino, *Providing for Others: A Critical Phenomenology of Care in an Aging Thailand.*

35 Luhrmann, *When God Talks Back.*

36 James, *The Varieties of Religious Experience.*

37 Berger, *The Sacred Canopy; Elements of a Sociological Theory of Religion.*

38 Murphy and Throop, *Toward an Anthropology of the Will.*

39 Taves, *Religious Experience Reconsidered;* Hufford, "Beings without Bodies: An Experience-Centered Theory of the Belief in Spirits."

40 Joel Robbins, *Becoming Sinners* (Berkeley, CA: University of California Press, 2004); Jon Bialecki, Naomi Haynes, and Joel Robbins, "The Anthropology of Christianity," *Religion Compass* 2, no. 6 (November 2008): 1139–58; Naomi Haynes, "Pentecostalism and the Morality of Money: Prosperity, Inequality, and Religious Sociality on the Zambian Copperbelt: Pentecostalism and the Morality of Money," *Journal of the Royal Anthropological Institute* 18, no. 1 (March 2012): 123–39.

41 Bialecki, *A Diagram for Fire;* Luhrmann, *When God Talks Back;* Csordas, *The Sacred Self.*

42 Charles Hirschkind, "Is There a Secular Body?," *Cultural Anthropology* 26, no. 4 (November 2011): 633–47; Talal Asad, "Thinking about the Secular Body, Pain, and Liberal Politics," *Cultural Anthropology* 26, no. 4 (November 2011): 657–75; Felicity Aulino, "Perceiving the Social Body: A Phenomenological Perspective on Ethical Practice in Buddhist Thailand," *Journal of Religious Ethics* 42, no. 3 (September 2014): 415–41, https://doi.org/10.1111/jore.12064; Sarah Coakley, *Religion and the Body* (New York: Cambridge University Press, 1997); Marcel Mauss, "Techniques of the Body (1935)," in *Sociology and Psychology: Essays. Transl. by Ben Brewster.* (London: Routledge & Kegan Paul, 1979).

43 Chomsky and Foucault, *The Chomsky-Foucault Debate: On Human Nature.*

44 Gould, *Moving Politics: Emotion and ACT UP's Fight against AIDS.*

45 Connolly, "The Evangelical-Capitalist Resonance Machine."

46 Buchler, *Metaphysics of Natural Complexes.*

47 Marshall, *Political Spiritualities.*

48 Clifford, Marcus, and Fortun, *Writing Culture;* Donna Haraway, *Situated Knowledges.*

49 Kyle, *Evangelicalism.*

50 Gayatri, *In Other Worlds.*

51 McNay, *Gender and Agency.*

52 Albert Newen, Leon de Bruin, and Shaun Gallagher, *The Oxford Handbook of 4E Cognition,* 2018; "The_Evolution_of_Cognition_a_4E_Perspect."

53 Petitmengin et al., "Studying the Experience of Meditation through Micro-Phenomenology"; Bitbol and Petitmengin, "Neurophenomenology and the Micro-Phenomenological Interview"; Petitmengin and Bitbol, "The Validity of First-Person Descriptions as Authenticity and Coherence"; Petitmengin and Lachaux,

"Microcognitive Science"; Hurlburt and Schwitzgebel, *Describing Inner Experience?: Proponent Meets Skeptic.*

54 Csordas, "Ritualization of Life," 146.

55 Luhrmann, "The Absorption Hypothesis," 66. Mahmood, *Politics of Piety*; Hirschkind, *The Ethical Soundscape Cassette Sermons and Islamic Counterpublics.*

56 Bialecki, "The Bones Restored to Life: Dialogue and Dissemination in the Vineyard's Dialectic of Text and Presence"; Kirsch, *Spirits and Letters*; Elisha, *Moral Ambition Mobilization and Social Outreach in Evangelical Megachurches.* For the big picture, see Robbins, "Continuity Thinking and the Problem of Christian Culture"; Bell, *Ritual Theory, Ritual Practice.* Robbins provides a genealogy of continuity and moves toward rupture. Bell details ritual theory's approach to questions of continuity and rupture.

57 Poloma, *The Assemblies of God at the Crossroads.*

58 Kelley, *Why Conservative Churches Are Growing: A Study in Sociology of Religion.*

59 Poloma, *The Assemblies of God at the Crossroads.*

60 MacIntyre, *After Virtue.*

61 Charles Taylor, *A Secular Age* (Cambridge, MA: Belknap Press of Harvard University Press, 2007); Michel Foucault, *Discipline and Punish: The Birth of the Prison* (New York: Pantheon Books, 1977). For more direct versions of the above stories, one could compare Nathan O. Hatch, *The Democratization of American Christianity* (New Haven, CT: Yale University Press, 1989) to David Sehat, *The Myth of American Religious Freedom* (New York: Oxford University Press, 2011).

62 Talal Asad, *Genealogies of Religion: Discipline and Reasons of Power in Christianity and Islam* (Baltimore, MD: Johns Hopkins University Press, 1993). Margaret C. Jacob, *The Enlightenment: A Brief History with Documents* (Boston, MA: Bedford/St. Martin's, 2001), 18.

63 Blumhofer, *Restoring the Faith*, 152.

64 Turner, *The Ritual Process.*

65 Bell, *Ritual Theory, Ritual Practice.*

66 Csordas, *The Sacred Self.*

67 Brahinsky, "Pentecostal Body Logics."

68 Friston, Parr, and De Vries, "The Graphical Brain."

69 Joffily and Coricelli, "Emotional Valence and the Free-Energy Principle"; Hesp et al., "Deeply Felt Affect"; Seth and Friston, "Active Interoceptive Inference and the Emotional Brain."

70 Vuilleumier, "How Brains Beware"; Pessoa, "How Do Emotion and Motivation Direct Executive Control?"

71 Laukkonen and Slagter, "From Many to (n)One."

72 Berntson, Cacioppo, and Quigley, "Cardiac Psychophysiology and Autonomic Space in Humans: Empirical Perspectives and Conceptual Implications."

73 Fanon, *Black Skin, White Masks*; Beauvoir and Archer, *The Second Sex*.

74 De Castro, "Cosmological Deixis and Amerindian Perspectivism"; Scheper-Hughes and Lock, "The Mindful Body"; Moore, *A Passion for Difference*; Strathern, *The Gender of the Gift*.

75 Astuti, "Are We All Natural Dualists?"

76 Weisman et al., "Similarities and Differences in Concepts of Mental Life among Adults and Children in Five Cultures."

77 Lutz and Abu-Lughod, *Language and the Politics of Emotion*.

78 Mauss, "Techniques of the Body (1935)."

79 Lakoff and Johnson, *Metaphors We Live By*.

80 Damasio, *The Feeling of What Happens*.

81 Stern, *The Interpersonal World of the Infant*.

82 Boas, *The Mind of Primitive Man*; Benedict, *Patterns of Culture*; Mead, *Coming of Age in Samoa*.

83 Lévi-Strauss, *The Elementary Structures of Kinship*; Lévi-Strauss, *The Savage Mind*.

84 De Castro, "Cosmological Deixis and Amerindian Perspectivism"; Holbraad and Pedersen, *The Ontological Turn*; Mol, *The Body Multiple*; Cadena, *Earth Beings*; Descola, "Beyond Nature and Culture."

85 Dennet, "Real Patterns."

86 Durkheim, *The Rules of Sociological Method, and Selected Texts on Sociology and Its Method*.

87 Hollywood, *Acute Melancholia and Other Essays*.

88 Latour, *Laboratory Life*.

89 Donna Haraway, *Situated Knowledges*.

90 Keller, *Reflections on Gender and Science*.

91 Martin, *The Woman in the Body*; Good, *Medicine, Rationality, and Experience*; Dumit, *Picturing Personhood Brain Scans and Biomedical Identity*.

92 Shrout and Rodgers, "Psychology, Science, and Knowledge Construction."

93 Geertz, *The Interpretation of Cultures*.

94 Said, *Orientalism*.

95   Clifford, Marcus, and Fortun, *Writing Culture.*

96   Lock, "Recovering the Body."

97   Barad, *Meeting the Universe Halfway*; Lassiter, *The Chicago Guide to Collaborative Ethnography.*

98   May, "A Survey of Glossolalia and Related Phenomena in Non-Christian Religions."

99   Koic et al., "Glossolalia."

100 Chouiter and Annoni, "Glossolalia and Aphasia."

101 Cutten, *Speaking with Tongues, Historically and Psychologically Considered.*

102 Goodman, "Phonetic Analysis of Glossolalia in Four Cultural Settings"; Goodman, *Speaking in Tongues; a Cross-Cultural Study of Glossolalia [by] Felicitas D. Goodman.*

103 Samarin, *Tongues of Men and Angels*; Spanos et al., "Glossolalia as Learned Behavior: An Experimental Demonstration."

104 Cutten, *Speaking with Tongues, Historically and Psychologically Considered.*

105 Maeder, "La Langue d'un Aliene: Analyse d'un Cas de Glossolalie"; Finch, "God-Inspired or Self-Induced?"; both cited in Pattison, "Behavioral Science Research on the Nature of Glossolalia."

106 Sargant, "Some Cultural Group Abreactive Techniques and Their Relation to Modern Treatments."

107 Wood, "Culture and Personality Aspects of the Pentecostal Holiness Religion. Unpublished Doctoral Thesis."

108 La Barre, *They Shall Take up Serpents.*

109 Lapsley and Simpson, "Speaking in Tongues," September 1964; Lapsley and Simpson, "Speaking in Tongues," May 1964.

110 Cited in Pattison, "Behavioral Science Research on the Nature of Glossolalia."

111 Pattison.

112 Kildahl, *The Psychology of Speaking in Tongues.*

113 Castelein, "Glossolalia and the Psychology of the Self and Narcissism."

114 Cited in Pattison, "Behavioral Science Research on the Nature of Glossolalia."

115 Kildahl, *The Psychology of Speaking in Tongues.*

116 Hine, "Pentecostal Glossolalia toward a Functional Interpretation."

117 Cited in Richardson, "Psychological Interpretations of Glossolalia."

118 Sherrill, *They Speak with Other Tongues.*

119 Gerlach and Hine, "Five Factors Crucial to the Growth and Spread of a Modern Religious Movement"; Gerlach and Hine, *People, Power, Change; Movements of Social Transformation*; Gerlach, "Pentecostalism: Revolution or Counter-Revolution?"

120 Coulson and Johnson, "Glossollalia and Internal-External Locus of Control."

121 Lovekin and Malony, "Religious Glossolalia."

122 Spanos and Hewitt, "Glossolalia: A Test of the 'Trance' and Psychopathology Hypotheses."

123 Cited in Cartledge, "Interpreting Charismatic Experience: Hypnosis, Altered States of Consciousness and the Holy Spirit?"

124 Francis and Kay, "The Personality Characteristics of Pentecostal Ministry Candidates."

125 Grady and Loewenthal, "Features Associated with Speaking in Tongues (Glossolalia)."

126 Francis and Jones, "Personality and Charismatic Experience among Adult Christians."

127 Robbins, Hair, and Francis, "Personality and Attraction to the Charismatic Movement."

128 Francis and Robbins, "Personality and Glossolalia: A Study among Male Evangelical Clergy."

129 Lynn et al., "Salivary Alpha-Amylase and Cortisol among Pentecostals on a Worship and Nonworship Day"; Lynn et al., "Glossolalia Is Associated with Differences in Biomarkers of Stress and Arousal among Apostolic Pentecostals."

130 Cited in Malony and Lovekin, *Glossolalia*.

131 Persinger, "Striking EEG Profiles from Single Episodes of Glossolalia and Transcendental Meditation."

132 Goodman, *Ecstasy, Ritual and Alternate Reality*.

133 Burton, *Serpent-Handling Believers*.

134 Schwartz, *Faith, Serpents, and Fire*.

135 Philipchalk and Mueller, "Glossolalia and Temperature Change in the Right and Left Cerebral Hemispheres."

136 Newberg et al., "The Measurement of Regional Cerebral Blood Flow during Glossolalia."

137 Walter et al., "Brain Structural Evidence for a Frontal Pole Specialization in Glossolalia."

138 Sperduti et al., "Different Brain Structures Related to Self- and External-Agency Attribution"; Crivelli and Balconi, "The Agent Brain"; Haggard, "Sense of Agency in the Human Brain."

139 Libet et al., "Readiness-Potentials Preceding Unrestricted 'Spontaneous' vs. Pre-Planned Voluntary Acts."

140 Nachev et al., "The Role of the Pre-Supplementary Motor Area in the Control of Action."

141 Moore et al., "Disrupting the Experience of Control in the Human Brain"; Lau et al., *Attention to Intention*.

142 Carter and Huettel, "A Nexus Model of the Temporal–Parietal Junction"; Mars et al., "Connectivity-Based Subdivisions of the Human Right 'Temporoparietal Junction Area.'"

143 Cole et al., "Multi-Task Connectivity Reveals Flexible Hubs for Adaptive Task Control."

144 Cunnington et al., "Premovement Activity of the Pre-Supplementary Motor Area and the Readiness for Action."

145 Sperduti et al., "Different Brain Structures Related to Self- and External-Agency Attribution."

146 Moore et al., "Disrupting the Experience of Control in the Human Brain"; Seghezzi and Zapparoli, "Predicting the Sensory Consequences of Self-Generated Actions."

147 Farrer and Frith, "Experiencing Oneself vs Another Person as Being the Cause of an Action"; Blanke and Arzy, "The Out-of-Body Experience."

148 Walsh et al., "The Functional Anatomy and Connectivity of Thought Insertion and Alien Control of Movement."

149 Seghezzi and Zapparoli, "Predicting the Sensory Consequences of Self-Generated Actions"; Seghezzi et al., "The Brain in (Willed) Action"; Zito et al., "Neural Correlates of Sense of Agency in Motor Control."

150 Bourguignon, *Religion, Altered States of Consciousness and Social Change*.

151 Volkow, Koob, and McLellan, "Neurobiologic Advances from the Brain Disease Model of Addiction."

152 Poldrack, "Can Cognitive Processes Be Inferred from Neuroimaging Data?"

153 Carhart-Harris and Friston, "REBUS and the Anarchic Brain."

154 Brewer, *The Craving Mind*.

155 Wexler, *Brain and Culture*.

156 Vago and Silbersweig, "Self-Awareness, Self-Regulation, and Self-Transcendence (S-ART)."

157 Morphy, *Aboriginal Art*; Ingold, *The Perception of the Environment*.

158 Turner, *The Ritual Process*.

159 Holbraad and Pedersen, *The Ontological Turn*.

160 De Castro, "Cosmological Deixis and Amerindian Perspectivism."

161 Tsing, *Friction*.

162 Livingston, *The Politics of Logic*.

163 Bell, *Ritual Theory, Ritual Practice*, 19.

164 Asad, *Formations of the Secular*.

165 Mauss, "Techniques of the Body (1935)"; Bourdieu, *Outline of a Theory of Practice*.

166 Connolly, *Neuropolitics*, 91.

167 Bourdieu, *The Logic of Practice*, 10–13.

168 Classen, *Worlds of Sense*.

169 Majid and Levinson, "The Senses in Language and Culture."

170 Schmidt, *Hearing Things*; Dyrness, *Reformed Theology and Visual Culture*.

171 Li SC, "Biocultural Orchestration of Developmental Plasticity across Levels," 176.

172 Allen Tran cited in Luhrmann, "Toward an Anthropological Theory of Mind," 10.

173 Pritzker, "Thinking Hearts, Feeling Brains."

174 Newberg, *How God Changes Your Brain*, 7.

175 Luhrmann, *When God Talks Back*.

176 See also O'Hanlon, "Recovering the Subject Subaltern Studies and Histories of Resistance in Colonial South Asia"; Winkelman, *Shamanism a Biopsychosocial Paradigm of Consciousness and Healing*.

177 Carey, *The Epigenetics Revolution*.

178 *"Weapons of the Weak: Everyday Forms of Peasant Resistance"* (1985).

179 Mahmood, *Politics of Piety*; Griffith, *God's Daughters Evangelical Women and the Power of Submission*.

180 *"Outline of a Theory of Practice"* (1972).

181 *"The Practice of Everyday Life"* (1984).

182 *"Flexible Citizenship: The Cultural Logics of Transnationality"* (1999).

183 Ortner, *Anthropology and Social Theory*.

184 Gupta and Ferguson, *Anthropological Locations*.

185 Gell, *Art and Agency.*

186 Moore and Obhi, "Intentional Binding and the Sense of Agency." Shorter interval estimates usually indicate an increased sense of agency although Haggard, Martin, Taylor-Clarke, Jeannerod, and Franck (2003) found patients with schizophrenia reversed the norm.

187 Columbetti, *The Feeling Body: Affective Science Meets the Enactive Mind.*

188 Sayre, "Ecological and Geographical Scale."

189 It is equivalent to what ecologists call "operational scale."

190 Stewart, *Creolization*, 1, 7. Berlant, *Cruel Optimism*; Puar, *Terrorist Assemblages*; Ngai, *Ugly Feelings.*

191 Pomerville, *The Third Force in Missions*, 1985, 68.

192 Marilyn J. Westerkamp, *Women and Religion in Early America, 1600–1850: The Puritan and Evangelical Traditions*, 2020; Walter Hollenweger, *The Pentecostals* (Peabody, MA: Hendrickson, 1988); Walter J. Hollenweger, "Pentecostalism and Black Power," *Theology Today* 30, no. 3 (1973): 228–38; Ashon T. Crawley, *Blackpentecostal Breath: The Aesthetics of Possibility* (New York: Fordham University Press, 2016); Peter Marina and Michael Wilkinson, "Pentecostalism as Cultural Resistance: Music and Tongue-Speaking as Collective Response in a Brooklyn Church," *PentecoStudies: An Interdisciplinary Journal for Research on the Pentecostal and Charismatic Movements* 16, no. 2 (October 5, 2017): 216–42; Laurie F. Maffly-Kipp, *Setting Down the Sacred Past: African-American Race Histories* (Cambridge, MA: Belknap Press of Harvard University Press, 2010); Bettye Collier-Thomas, *Jesus, Jobs, and Justice: African American Women and Religion*, 1st ed (New York: Alfred A. Knopf, 2010); Phyllis Mack, "Religion, Feminism, and the Problem of Agency: Reflections on Eighteenth-Century Quakerism," *Signs Signs: Journal of Women in Culture and Society* 29, no. 1 (2003): 149–77; Phyllis Mack, *Heart Religion in the British Enlightenment: Gender and Emotion in Early Methodism* (Cambridge; New York: Cambridge University Press, 2008); Lawrence Jacob Friedman, *Gregarious Saints: Self and Community in American Abolitionism, 1830–1870* (Cambridge [Cambridgeshire]; New York: Cambridge University Press, 1982); Jean Comaroff, *Body of Power, Spirit of Resistance The Culture and History of a South African People* (Chicago, IL: University of Chicago Press, 2013).

193 Hollenweger, "Pentecostalism and Black Power"; Moreton, *To Serve God and Wal-Mart the Making of Christian Free Enterprise.*

194 Lifshitz et al., "What's Wrong with 'the Mindful Brain'? Moving Past a Neurocentric View of Meditation."

195 Carpenter, *Revive Us Again*, 237–8.

196 That is, Cloud, *The Pentecostal-Charismatic Movement: The History and Error.*

197 Haynes, "Pentecostalism and the Morality of Money"; Haynes, "Learning to Pray the Pentecostal Way."

198 McClung, *Azusa Street and Beyond.*

199 Wesley, *Wesley's Standard Sermons Consisting of Fortyfour Discourses ... to Which Are Added Nine Additional Sermons ... Ed. and Annotated by Edward H. Sugden*; Hollenweger, *The Pentecostals*; Hollenweger, "Pentecostalism and Black Power"; Ashon T. Crawley, *Blackpentecostal Breath*; Marina and Wilkinson, "Pentecostalism as Cultural Resistance"; Mahmood, *Politics of Piety*; Collier-Thomas, *Jesus, Jobs, and Justice*; Mack, "Religion, Feminism, and the Problem of Agency"; Mackie, *The Gift of Tongues*; Friedman, *Gregarious Saints*; Comaroff, *Body of Power, Spirit of Resistance The Culture and History of a South African People.*

200 Lalive d'Epinay, *Haven of the Masses*, 35.

201 Miller, *Reinventing American Protestantism*; Luhrmann, *When God Talks Back.*

202 Pew Forum on Religion & Public Life, *Spirit and Power a 10-Country Survey of Pentecostals.*

203 Ron Purser, *McMindfulness: How Mindfulness Became the New Capitalist Spirituality* (London: Repeater Books, 2019); Robert Sharf, "Buddhist Modernism and the Rhetoric of Meditative Experience," *Numen* 42, no. 3 (1995): 228–83; Michael Lifshitz and Evan Thompson, "What's Wrong with 'the Mindful Brain'? Moving Past a Neurocentric View of Meditation," in *Casting Light on the Dark Side of Brain Imaging*, edited by Amir Raz and Robert T. Thibault (London: Elsevier, 2019), 123–28.

204 Linda K. George et al., "Spirituality and Health: What We Know, What We Need to Know," *Journal of Social and Clinical Psychology* 19, no. 1 (March 2000): 102–16; T. M. Luhrmann, *When God Talks Back: Understanding the American Evangelical Relationship with God* (New York: Alfred A. Knopf, 2012); Thomas Csordas, *The Sacred Self: A Cultural Phenomenology of Charismatic Healing* (Berkeley, CA: University of California Press, 1994); Felicitas D. Goodman, *Speaking in Tongues; a Cross-Cultural Study of Glossolalia [by] Felicitas D. Goodman* (Chicago, IL: University of Chicago Press, 1972); W. Paul Williamson and Ralph W. Hood, "Spirit Baptism: A Phenomenological Study of Religious Experience," *Mental Health, Religion & Culture* 14, no. 6 (July 2011): 543–59.

205 Goleman and Richard, *Altered Traits.*

206 Cousins, "Buddhist Jhana: Its Nature and Attainment According to the Pali Sources."

207 Sharf, "Buddhist Modernism and the Rhetoric of Meditative Experience."

208 Puar, *Terrorist Assemblages.*

Bibliography

Agamben, Giorgio. *The Time That Remains: A Commentary on the Letter to the Romans.* Stanford, CA: Stanford University Press, 2005.

Ahmed, Ali M., and Osvaldo Salas. "Implicit Influences of Christian Religious Representations on Dictator and Prisoner's Dilemma Game Decisions." *The Journal of Socio-Economics* 40, no. 3 (May 2011): 242–6. https://doi.org/10.1016/j.socec.2010.12.013.

Alahmadi, Adnan. "Functional Connectivity Profiles of Ten Sub-Regions Within the Premotor and Supplementary Motor Areas: Insights into Neurophysiological Integration." *Diagnostics* 14, no. 17 (2024 [1990]). https://doi.org/10.3390/diagnostics14171990.

Albrecht, Daniel E. *Rites in the Spirit: A Ritual Approach to Pentecostal/Charismatic Spirituality.* Sheffield: Sheffield Academic Press, 1999.

Alexander, Estrelda. *Black Fire: One Hundred Years of African American Pentecostalism.* Downers Grove, IL: IVP Academic, 2011. http://www.h-net.org/reviews/showrev.php?id=41657.

Alexander, Paul. "An Analysis of the Emergence and Decline of Pacifism in the History of the Assemblies of God." *Peace Research Abstracts* 41, no. 4 (2004).

Alexander, Paul. *Peace to War: Shifting Allegiances in the Assemblies of God.* Scottdale, PA: Herald Press, 2009.

Alland, Alexander. "'Possession' in a Revivalistic Negro Church." *Journal for the Scientific Study of Religion* 1, no. 2 (1962): 204. https://doi.org/10.2307/1384699.

Allen, Roland. *The Spontaneous Expansion of the Church: And the Causes Which Hinder It.* London: World Dominion Press, 1927.

Anderson, Allan. "Revising Pentecostal History in a Global Perspective." In *Asian and Pentecostal: The Charismatic Face of Christianity in Asia,* edited by Allan Anderson and Edmond Tang. Oxford: Regnum Books International, 2005.

Anderson, Allan. *Spreading Fires: The Missionary Nature of Early Pentecostalism.* London: SCM Press, 2007.

Anderson, Allan. *Studying Global Pentecostalism: Theories and Methods.* Berkeley, CA: University of California Press, 2010.

Anderson, Allan, and Walter Jacob Hollenweger, eds. *Pentecostals After a Century: Global Perspectives on a Movement in Transition.* Sheffield: Sheffield Academic, 1999.

Anderson, Craig L., Maria Monroy, and Dacher Keltner. "Awe in Nature Heals: Evidence from Military Veterans, at-Risk Youth, and College Students." *Emotion* 18, no. 8 (2018): 1195. https://doi.org/10.1037/emo0000442.

Anderson, Robert Mapes. *Vision of the Disinherited: The Making of American Pentecostalism.* New York: Oxford University Press, 1979.

Argo, Nichole. "Why Fight?: Examining Self-Interested Versus Communally-Oriented Motivations in Palestinian Resistance and Rebellion." *Security Studies* 18, no. 4 (December 2, 2009): 651–80. https://doi.org/10.1080/09636410903368920.

Arias, Albert J., Karen Steinberg, Alok Banga, and Robert L. Trestman. "Systematic Review of the Efficacy of Meditation Techniques as Treatments for Medical Illness." *The Journal of Alternative and Complementary Medicine* 12, no. 8 (October 2006): 817–32. https://doi.org/10.1089/acm.2006.12.817.

Armstrong, Karen. *The Great Transformation: The Beginning of Our Religious Traditions.* 1st ed. New York: Knopf, 2006. http://site.ebrary.com/id/10115578.

Arzy, Shahar, Gregor Thut, Christine Mohr, Christoph M. Michel, and Olaf Blanke. "Neural Basis of Embodiment: Distinct Contributions of Temporoparietal Junction and Extrastriate Body Area." *Journal of Neuroscience* 26, no. 31 (August 2, 2006): 8074–81. https://doi.org/10.1523/JNEUROSCI.0745-06.2006.

Asad, Dr Shamaila, Samia Khalid, Sadaf Rehman, and Maham Abdullah. "Religious Orientation and Development of Pro-Social Behavior in Young Female Students." *Journal of Professional & Applied Psychology* 2, no. 2 (December 30, 2021): 189–98. https://doi.org/10.52053/jpap.v2i2.52.

Asad, Talal. *Formations of the Secular: Christianity, Islam, Modernity.* Stanford, CA: Stanford University Press, 2003.

Asad, Talal. *Genealogies of Religion: Discipline and Reasons of Power in Christianity and Islam.* Baltimore, MD: Johns Hopkins University Press, 1993.

Asad, Talal. "Thinking about the Secular Body, Pain, and Liberal Politics." *Cultural Anthropology* 26, no. 4 (November 2011): 657–75. https://doi.org/10.1111/j.1548-1360.2011.01118.x.

Ashton, Michael C., and Kibeom Lee. "A Review of Personality/Religiousness Associations." *Current Opinion in Psychology* 40 (August 2021): 51–5. https://doi.org/10.1016/j.copsyc.2020.08.023.

Astuti, Rita. "Are We All Natural Dualists? A Cognitive Developmental Approach*." *Journal of the Royal Anthropological Institute* 7, no. 3 (September 2001): 429–47. https://doi.org/10.1111/1467-9655.00071.

Astuti, Rita, and Paul Harris. "Understanding Mortality and the Life of the Ancestors in Rural Madagascar." *Cognitive Science: A Multidisciplinary Journal* 32, no. 4 (June 2008): 713–40.

Aulino, Felicity. "From Karma to Sin: A Kaleidoscopic Theory of Mind and Christian Experience in Northern Thailand." *Journal of the Royal Anthropological Institute* 26, no. S1 (April 2020): 28–44. https://doi.org/10.1111/1467-9655.13239.

Aulino, Felicity. "Perceiving the Social Body: A Phenomenological Perspective on Ethical Practice in Buddhist Thailand." *Journal of Religious Ethics* 42, no. 3 (September 2014): 415–41. https://doi.org/10.1111/jore.12064.

Aulino, Felicity. *Providing for Others: A Critical Phenomenology of Care in an Aging Thailand.* Ithaca, NY: Cornell University Press, 2019.

Austin, J. L. *How to Do Things with Words.* London: Oxford University Press, 1962.

Azari, Nina P., John Missimer, and Rudiger J. Seitz. "Religious Experience and Emotion: Evidence for Distinctive Cognitive Neural Patterns." *International Journal for the Psychology of Religion* 15, no. 4 (October 2005): 263–81. https://doi.org/10.1207/s15327582ijpr1504_1.

Azari, Nina P., Janpeter Nickel, Gilbert Wunderlich, Michael Niedeggen, Harald Hefter, Lutz Tellmann, Hans Herzog, Petra Stoerig, Dieter Birnbacher, and Rüdiger J. Seitz. "Neural Correlates of Religious Experience: Brain Activity and Religious Experience." *European Journal of Neuroscience* 13, no. 8 (April 2001): 1649–52. https://doi.org/10.1046/j.0953-816x.2001.01527.x.

Badiou, Alain. *Being and Event*. New York: Continuum, 2005.

Badiou, Alain. *Saint Paul: The Foundation of Universalism*. Stanford, CA: Stanford University Press, 2003.

Bahramzadeh Zoeram, Saeedeh, Mahmoud Elahdadi Salmani, Taghi Lashkarbolouki, and Iran Goudarzi. "Hippocampal Orexin Receptor Blocking Prevented the Stress Induced Social Learning and Memory Deficits." *Neurobiology of Learning and Memory* 157 (January 2019): 12–23. https://doi.org/10.1016/j.nlm.2018.11.009.

Bai, Yang, Laura A. Maruskin, Serena Chen, Amie M. Gordon, Jennifer E. Stellar, Galen D. McNeil, Kaiping Peng, and Dacher Keltner. "Awe, the Diminished Self, and Collective Engagement: Universals and Cultural Variations in the Small Self." *Journal of Personality and Social Psychology* 113, no. 2 (August 2017): 185–209.

Barad, Karen Michelle. *Meeting the Universe Halfway: Quantum Physics and the Entanglement of Matter and Meaning*. Druham, NC: Duke University Press, 2007.

Barlow, H. B. "Possible Principles Underlying the Transformations of Sensory Messages." In *Sensory Communication*, edited by Walter A. Rosenblith, 216–34. The MIT Press, 2012. https://doi.org/10.7551/mitpress/9780262518420.003.0013.

Barrett, Frederick S., and Roland R. Griffiths. "Classic Hallucinogens and Mystical Experiences: Phenomenology and Neural Correlates." *Behavioral Neurobiology of Psychedelic Drugs, Current Topics in Behavioral Neurosciences* 36 (2018): 393–430. https://doi.org/10.1007/7854_2017_474.

Barrett, Louise, "The Evolution of Cognition: A 4E Perspective." In *The Oxford Handbook of 4E Cognition*, edited by Albert Newen, Leon De Bruin, and Shaun Gallagher, Oxford Library of Psychology (online edn, Oxford Academic, 9 October 2018).

Barsalou, Lawrence W. "Grounded Cognition." *Annual Review of Psychology* 59, no. 1 (January 2008): 617–45. https://doi.org/10.1146/annurev.psych.59.103006.093639.

Batson, C. Daniel. "Prosocial Motivation: Is It Ever Truly Altruistic?" *Elsevier Advances in Experimental Social Psychology* 20 (1987): 65–122.

Batson, C. Daniel, Johee Chang, Ryan Orr, and Jennifer Rowland. "Empathy, Attitudes, and Action: Can Feeling for a Member of a Stigmatized Group Motivate One to Help the Group?" *Personality and Social Psychology Bulletin* 28, no. 12 (December 2002): 1656–66. https://doi.org/10.1177/014616702237647.

Beaty, Roger E. "The Neuroscience of Musical Improvisation." *Neuroscience & Biobehavioral Reviews* 51 (April 2015): 108–17.

Beaty, Roger E., Bridget A. Smeekens, Paul J. Silvia, Donald A. Hodges, and Michael J. Kane. "A First Look at the Role of Domain-General Cognitive and Creative Abilities in Jazz Improvisation." *Psychomusicology: Music, Mind, and Brain* 23, no. 4 (2013): 262–8. https://doi.org/10.1037/a0034968.

Beauvoir, Simone de, and Ellen Archer. *The Second Sex*. Translated by Constance Borde and Sheila Malovany-Chevallier. Complete and Unabridged. New York: Random House Audio, 2019. https://www.overdrive.com/search?q=74334BF2-EDD7-4402-8FB5-DFC54636CC23.

Beavan, Vanessa, John Read, and Claire Cartwright. "The Prevalence of Voice-Hearers in the General Population: A Literature Review." *Journal of Mental Health* 20, no. 3 (June 1, 2011): 281–92. https://doi.org/10.3109/09638237.2011.562262.

Bebbington, D. W. *Evangelicalism in Modern Britain: A History from the 1730s to the 1980s*. Boston, MA: Unwin Hyman, 1989.

Beerel, Annabel, and Tom Raffio. *Mindfulness: A Better Me; a Better You; a Better World*. Massachusetts: FLMI, 2018.

Bell, Catherine. *Ritual Theory, Ritual Practice*. New York: Oxford University Press, 1992.

Benedict, Ruth. *Patterns of Culture*. New York: Houghton Mifflen, 1934.

Berger, Peter L. *The Sacred Canopy; Elements of a Sociological Theory of Religion*. Garden City, NY: Doubleday, 1967.

Berlant, Lauren Gail. *Cruel Optimism*. Durham, NC: Duke University Press, 2011. http://public.eblib.com/choice/publicfullrecord.aspx?p=1172993.

Berntson, Gary G., John T. Cacioppo, and Karen S. Quigley. "Cardiac Psychophysiology and Autonomic Space in Humans: Empirical Perspectives and Conceptual Implications." *Psychological Bulletin* 114, no. 2 (1993): 296–322.

Berry, Daniel R., Athena H. Cairo, Robert J. Goodman, Jordan T. Quaglia, Jeffrey D. Green, and Kirk Warren Brown. "Mindfulness Increases Prosocial Responses Toward Ostracized Strangers Through Empathic Concern." *Journal of Experimental Psychology: General* 147, no. 1 (January 2018): 93–112. https://doi.org/10.1037/xge0000392.

Berry, Daniel R., Katie Rodriguez, Gin Tasulis, and Anna Maria C. Behler. "Mindful Attention as a Skillful Means Toward Intergroup Prosociality." *Mindfulness* 14, no. 10 (October 2023): 2471–84. https://doi.org/10.1007/s12671-022-01926-3.

Bialecki, Jon. *A Diagram for Fire: Miracles and Variation in an American Charismatic Movement*, 2017. https://doi.org/10.1525/california/9780520294202.001.0001.

Bialecki, Jon. "The Bones Restored to Life: Dialogue and Dissemination in the Vineyard's Dialectic of Text and Presence." In *The Social Life of Scriptures Cross-Cultural Perspectives on Biblicism*, edited by James S. Bielo, 136–56. New Brunswick, NJ: Rutgers University Press, 2009.

Bialecki, Jon, Naomi Haynes, and Joel Robbins. "The Anthropology of Christianity." *Religion Compass* 2, no. 6 (November 2008): 1139–58. https://doi.org/10.1111/j.1749-8171.2008.00116.x.

Bitbol, Michel, and Claire Petitmengin. "Neurophenomenology and the Micro-Phenomenological Interview." In *The Blackwell Companion to Consciousness*, edited by Susan Schneider and Max Velmans, 726–39. Chichester: John Wiley & Sons, Ltd, 2017. https://doi.org/10.1002/9781119132363.ch51.

Blackman, Lisa. "Habit and Affect: Revitalizing a Forgotten History." Edited by Tony Bennett, Francis Dodsworth, Greg Noble, Mary Poovey, and Megan Watkins. *Body & Society* 19, no. 2–3 (June 2013): 186–216. https://doi.org/10.1177/1357034X12472546.

Blanke, Olaf, and Shahar Arzy. "The Out-of-Body Experience: Disturbed Self-Processing at the Temporo-Parietal Junction." *The Neuroscientist* 11, no. 1 (2005): 16–24. https://doi.org/10.1177/1073858404270885.

Blanke, Olaf, Stéphanie Ortigue, Alessandra Coeytaux, Marie-Dominique Martory, and Theodor Landis. "Hearing of a Presence." *Neurocase* 9, no. 4 (August 2003): 329–39. https://doi.org/10.1076/neur.9.4.329.15552.

Blanke, Olaf, Polona Pozeg, Masayuki Hara, Lukas Heydrich, Andrea Serino, Akio Yamamoto, Toshiro Higuchi, et al. "Neurological and Robot-Controlled Induction of an Apparition." *Current Biology* 24, no. 22 (November 2014): 2681–6. https://doi.org/10.1016/j.cub.2014.09.049.

Blumhofer, Edith L., Russell Spittler, and Grant A. Wacker, eds. "Corinthian Spirituality." In *Currents in American Protestantism*, edited by Russel Spittler, 3–19. Urbana, IL: University of Illinois Press, 1999.

Blumhofer, Edith Waldvogel. *Restoring the Faith: The Assemblies of God, Pentecostalism, and American Culture.* Urbana, IL: University of Illinois Press, 1993.

Blumhofer, Edith Waldvogel. *The Assemblies of God: A Popular History.* Springfield, MO: Radiant Books, 1985.

Boas, Franz. *The Mind of Primitive Man.* Rev. ed/First Free Press paperback ed. New York: Free Press, 1965.

Boisen, Anton T. "Economic Distress and Religious Experience a Study of the Holy Rollers." *Psychiatry* 2, no. 2 (May 1939): 185–94. https://doi.org/10.1080/00332747.1939.11022237.

Bourdieu, Pierre. *La Noblesse d'Etat: Grandes écoles et Esprit de Corps.* Paris: Les Editions de minuit, 1989.

Bourdieu, Pierre. *Outline of a Theory of Practice.* New York: Cambridge University Press, 1977.

Bourdieu, Pierre. *Pascalian Meditations.* Cambridge: Polity Press, 2000.

Bourdieu, Pierre. *The Logic of Practice.* Stanford, CA: Stanford University Press, 1990.

Bourguignon, Erika. *Religion, Altered States of Consciousness and Social Change.* Columbus, OH: Ohio State University Press, 1973.

Brahinsky, Josh. "Crossing the Buffer: Ontological Anxiety Among US Evangelicals and an Anthropological Theory of Mind." *Journal of the Royal Anthropological Institute* 26, no. S1 (April 2020): 45–60. https://doi.org/10.1111/1467-9655.13240.

Brahinsky, Josh. "Missionary Conversions: How Missionary Encounters Pushed Fundamentalists Towards Evangelicalism." *HAU: Journal of Ethnographic Theory* 10, no. 3 (December 1, 2020): 828–43. https://doi.org/10.1086/711882.

Brahinsky, Josh. "Pentecostal Body Logics: Cultivating a Modern Sensorium." *Cultural Anthropology* 27, no. 2 (2012): 215–38.

Brahinsky, Josh. *Pentecostal Missionary Training: Cultivating Body Logics, Converting Missionaries, Building a Movement, Dissertation.* Santa Cruz, CA: University of California Press, 2014.

Brahinsky, Josh. "The Effects of Scale: What Pentecostalism and Neuroscience Teach Us About Habit, Affect and Agency." *Anthropological Theory* 18, no. 4 (2018): 478–501.

Brahinsky, Josh, Michael Lifshitz, and Tanya Marie Luhrmann. "Steps toward a Neurophenomenology of Speaking in Tongues" (20 June 2024). In *The Oxford Handbook of Psychedelic, Religious, Spiritual, and Mystical Experiences*, edited by David Yaden and Michiel van Elk (online edn, Oxford Academic, 22 May 2024). https://doi.org/10.1093/oxfordhb/9780192844064.013.18.

Brahinsky, Josh, Jonas Mago, Mark Miller, Shaila Catherine, and Michael Lifshitz. "The Spiral of Attention, Arousal, and Release: A Comparative Phenomenology of Jhāna Meditation and Speaking in Tongues." *American Journal of Human Biology* 36, no. 12 (December 2024): e24189. https://doi.org/10.1002/ajhb.24189.

Brewer, Judson. *The Craving Mind: From Cigarettes to Smartphones to Love—Why We Get Hooked and How We Can Break Bad Habits*. New Haven, CT: Yale University Press, 2018.

Brown, Norman Oliver. *Love's Body*. New York: Random House, 1966.

Bruneau, Emile G., Mina Cikara, and Rebecca Saxe. "Parochial Empathy Predicts Reduced Altruism and the Endorsement of Passive Harm." *Social Psychological and Personality Science* 8, no. 8 (November 2017): 934–42. https://doi.org/10.1177/1948550617693064.

Buchler, Justus. *Metaphysics of Natural Complexes*. New York: Columbia University Press, 1966.

Buck, Anna C., David R. Williams, Marc A. Musick, and Michelle J. Sternthal. "An Examination of the Relationship Between Multiple Dimensions of Religiosity, Blood Pressure, and Hypertension." *Social Science & Medicine* 68, no. 2 (January 2009): 314–22. https://doi.org/10.1016/j.socscimed.2008.10.010.

Bullock, Warren D. *When the Spirit Speaks: Making Sense of Tongues, Interpretation and Prophecy*. Springfield, MO: Gospel Publishing House, 2009.

Burton, Thomas G. *Serpent-Handling Believers*. 1st ed. Knoxville, TN: University of Tennessee Press, 1993.

Butler, Judith. *Bodies That Matter: On the Discursive Limits of "Sex."* New York: Routledge, 1993.

Buzsáki, G. *Rhythms of the Brain*. Oxford: Oxford University Press, 2006.

Cadena, Marisol de la. *Earth Beings: Ecologies of Practice Across Andean Worlds*. Lewis Henry Morgan Lectures. Durham, NC: Duke University Press, 2015. http://digitale-objekte.hbz-nrw.de/storage2/2017/03/27/file_5/7160488.pdf.

Cardena, Etzel, Steven Jay Lynn, and Stanley C. Krippner, eds. *Varieties of Anomalous Experience: Examining the Scientific Evidence*. Washington, DC: American Psychological Association, 2004.

Carey, Nessa. *The Epigenetics Revolution: How Modern Biology Is Rewriting Our Understanding of Genetics, Disease, and Inheritance*. New York: Columbia University Press, 2013.

Carhart-Harris, R. L., and K. J. Friston. "REBUS and the Anarchic Brain: Toward a Unified Model of the Brain Action of Psychedelics." Edited by Eric L. Barker. *Pharmacological Reviews* 71, no. 3 (July 2019): 316–44. https://doi.org/10.1124/pr.118.017160.

Carhart-Harris, Robin L., and Guy M. Goodwin. "The Therapeutic Potential of Psychedelic Drugs: Past, Present, and Future." *Neuropsychopharmacology* 42, no. 11 (October 2017): 2105–13. https://doi.org/10.1038/npp.2017.84.

Carhart-Harris, R. L., D. Erritzoe, E. Haijen, M. Kaelen, and R. Watts. "Psychedelics and Connectedness." *Psychopharmacology* 235, no. 2 (February 2018): 547–50. https://doi.org/10.1007/s00213-017-4701-y.

Carpenter, Joel. *Revive Us Again: The Reawakening of American Fundamentalism*. New York: Oxford University Press, 1997.

Carter, R. McKell, and Scott A. Huettel. "A Nexus Model of the Temporal–Parietal Junction." *Trends in Cognitive Sciences* 17, no. 7 (2013): 328–36. https://doi.org/10.1016/j.tics.2013.05.007.

Cartledge, Mark J. "Interpreting Charismatic Experience: Hypnosis, Altered States of Consciousness and the Holy Spirit?" *Journal of Pentecostal Theology* 13 (1999): 117–32.

Cassaniti, Julia L., and Tanya Marie Luhrmann. "The Cultural Kindling of Spiritual Experiences." *Current Anthropology* 55, no. S10 (December 2014): S333–43. https://doi. org/10.1086/677881.

Castelein, John Donald. "Glossolalia and the Psychology of the Self and Narcissism." *Journal of Religion & Health* 23, no. 1 (1984): 47–62. https://doi.org/10.1007/ BF00999899.

Cavanna, Federico, Martina G. Vilas, Matías Palmucci, and Enzo Tagliazucchi. "Dynamic Functional Connectivity and Brain Metastability During Altered States of Consciousness." *NeuroImage* 180 (October 2018): 383–95. https://doi.org/10.1016/j. neuroimage.2017.09.065.

Chiao, Joan Y., Ahmad R. Hariri, Tokiko Harada, Yoko Mano, Norihiro Sadato, Todd B. Parrish, and Tetsuya Iidaka. "Theory and Methods in Cultural Neuroscience." *Social Cognitive and Affective Neuroscience* 5, no. 2–3 (June 2010): 356–61. https://doi. org/10.1093/scan/nsq063.

Chiao, Joan Y., Bobby K. Cheon, Narun Pornpattananangkul, Alissa J. Mrazek, and Katherine D. Blizinsky. "Cultural Neuroscience: Progress and Promise." *Psychological Inquiry* 24, no. 1 (January 2013): 1–19. https://doi.org/10.1080/1047840X.2013.752715.

Chomsky, Noam, and Michel Foucault. *The Chomsky-Foucault Debate: On Human Nature.* New York: New Press, 2006.

Chouiter, Leila, and Jean-Marie Annoni. "Glossolalia and Aphasia: Related but Different Worlds." Edited by J. Bogousslavsky. *Frontiers of Neurology and Neuroscience* 42 (2018): 96–105. https://doi.org/10.1159/000475694.

Christensen, Mark Schram, and Thor Grünbaum. "Sense of Agency for Movements." *Consciousness and Cognition* 65 (October 2018): 27–47. https://doi.org/10.1016/j. concog.2018.07.002.

Cikara, M., E. Bruneau, J. J. Van Bavel, and R. Saxe. "Their Pain Gives Us Pleasure: How Intergroup Dynamics Shape Empathic Failures and Counter-Empathic Responses." *Journal of Experimental Social Psychology* 55 (November 2014): 110–25. https://doi. org/10.1016/j.jesp.2014.06.007.

Clark, Andy. *Supersizing the Mind: Embodiment, Action, and Cognitive Extension.* Oxford: Oxford University Press, 2008.

Clark, Andy. *Surfing Uncertainty: Prediction, Action, and the Embodied Mind.* Oxford: Oxford University Press, 2019.

Classen, Constance. *Worlds of Sense: Exploring the Senses in History and Across Cultures.* New York: Routledge, 1993.

Clifford, James, George E. Marcus, and Kim Fortun. *Writing Culture: The Poetics and Politics of Ethnography.* 25th anniversary ed. Berkeley, CA: University of California Press, 2010.

Cloud, David. *The Pentecostal-Charismatic Movement: The History and Error.* Port Huron, MI: Way of Life Literature, 2008.

Coakley, Sarah. *Religion and the Body.* New York: Cambridge University Press, 1997.

Cole, Michael W., Jeremy R. Reynolds, Jonathan D. Power, Grega Repovs, Alan Anticevic, and Todd S. Braver. "Multi-Task Connectivity Reveals Flexible Hubs for Adaptive Task Control." *Nature Neuroscience* 16, no. 9 (2013): 1348–55. https://doi.org/10.1038/ nn.3470.

Coleman, Simon. *The Globalisation of Charismatic Christianity Spreading the Gospel of Prosperity*. New York: Cambridge University Press, 2000.

Collier-Thomas, Bettye. *Jesus, Jobs, and Justice: African American Women and Religion*. 1st ed. New York: Alfred A. Knopf, 2010.

Columbetti, Giovanna. *The Feeling Body: Affective Science Meets the Enactive Mind*. Cambridge, MA: MIT Press, 2014.

Comaroff, Jean. *Body of Power, Spirit of Resistance the Culture and History of a South African People*. Chicago: University of Chicago Press, 2013.

Comaroff, Jean. "Occult Economies and the Violence of Abstraction: Notes from the South African Postcolony." *American Ethnologist* 26, no. 2 (1999): 279–303.

Comaroff, Jean, and John L. Comaroff. *Millenial Capitalism and the Culture of Neoliberalism*. Durham, NC: Duke University Press, 2005.

Connolly, William E. *Neuropolitics: Thinking, Culture, Speed*. Minneapolis, MN: University of Minnesota Press, 2002.

Connolly, William E. "The Evangelical-Capitalist Resonance Machine." *Political Theory* 33, no. 6 (2005): 869–86. https://doi.org/10.1177/0090591705280376.

Coulson, Jesse, and Ray Johnson. "Glossollalia and Internal-External Locus of Control." *Journal of Psychology and Theology* 5, no. 4 (September 1977): 312–17.

Cousins, L. S. "Buddhist Jhana: Its Nature and Attainment According to the Pali Sources." *Religion* 3, no. 2 (1973): 115–31.

Cox, Harvey. *Fire from Heaven: The Rise of Pentecostal Spirituality and the Reshaping of Religion in the Twenty-First Century*. Reading, MA: Addison-Wesley Publishing Company, 1995.

Crabtree, Loralie. *Youth Ministry Institute Manual: Bringing It All into Focus*. Springfield, MO: National Youth Dept., General Council of the Assemblies of God, 1998.

Cramer, Ken. "Preparing Yourself to Help Others." In *Helping Others Receive the Gift: Insights on Spirit Baptism from God's Word and Personal Experience*, edited by Tim Enloe and Randy Hurst. Springfield, MO: Gospel Publishing House, 2008.

Crawley, Ashon T. *Blackpentecostal Breath: The Aesthetics of Possibility*. New York: Fordham University Press, 2016.

Cristofori, Irene, Joseph Bulbulia, John H. Shaver, Marc Wilson, Frank Krueger, and Jordan Grafman. "Neural Correlates of Mystical Experience." *Neuropsychologia* 80 (January 2016): 212–20. https://doi.org/10.1016/j.neuropsychologia.2015.11.021.

Crivelli, Davide, and Michela Balconi. "The Agent Brain: A Review of Non-Invasive Brain Stimulation Studies on Sensing Agency." *Frontiers in Behavioral Neuroscience* 11 (November 2017): 229. https://doi.org/10.3389/fnbeh.2017.00229.

Csordas, Thomas. *The Sacred Self: A Cultural Phenomenology of Charismatic Healing*. Berkeley, CA: University of California Press, 1994.

Csordas, Thomas J. "Somatic Modes of Attention." *Cultural Anthropology: Journal of the Society for Cultural Anthropology* 8, no. 2 (1993): 135–56.

Cunnington, Ross, Christian Windischberger, and Ewald Moser. "Premovement Activity of the Pre-Supplementary Motor Area and the Readiness for Action: Studies of Time-Resolved Event-Related Functional MRI." *Human Movement Science* 24, no. 5–6 (2005): 644–56. https://doi.org/10.1016/j.humov.2005.10.001.

Cutten, George Barton. *Speaking with Tongues, Historically and Psychologically Considered.* New Haven, CT: Yale University Press, 1927.

Damasio, Antonio. *Descartes' Error: Emotion, Reason and the Human Brain.* London: Penguin, 2008.

Damasio, Antonio R. *Self Comes to Mind: Constructing the Conscious Brain.* New York: Pantheon Books, 2010.

Damasio, Antonio R. *The Feeling of What Happens: Body and Emotion in the Making of Consciousness.* 1st Harvest ed. San Diego, CA: Harcourt, 2000. http://media.obvsg.at/AC03054893-1001.

Davidson, Richard J., Jon Kabat-Zinn, Jessica Schumacher, Melissa Rosenkranz, Daniel Muller, Saki F. Santorelli, Ferris Urbanowski, Anne Harrington, Katherine Bonus, and John F. Sheridan. "Alterations in Brain and Immune Function Produced by Mindfulness Meditation." *Psychosomatic Medicine* 65, no. 4 (July 2003): 564–70. https://doi.org/10.1097/01.PSY.0000077505.67574.E3.

Davis, Mike. "Planet of Slums." *New Left Review*, no. 26 (2004): 5–35.

De Castro, Eduardo Viveiros. "Cosmological Deixis and Amerindian Perspectivism." *The Journal of the Royal Anthropological Institute* 4, no. 3 (September 1998): 469. https://doi.org/10.2307/3034157.

De Ruiter, Michiel B., Bernet M. Elzinga, and R. Hans Phaf. "Dissociation: Cognitive Capacity or Dysfunction?" *Journal of Trauma & Dissociation* 7, no. 4 (November 21, 2006): 115–34. https://doi.org/10.1300/J229v07n04_07.

Deleuze, Gilles, Félix Guattari, Hugh Tomlinson, and Graham Burchell. *What Is Philosophy?* New York: Columbia University Press, 1994.

Dennet, Daniel. "Real Patterns." *The Journal of Philosophy*, 88, no. 1 (1991): 27–51.

Derrida, Jacques. *Of Grammatology.* Baltimore, MD: Johns Hopkins University Press, 1976.

Descola, Philippe. "Beyond Nature and Culture: Forms of Attachment." *HAU: Journal of Ethnographic Theory* 2, no. 1 (March 2012): 447–71. https://doi.org/10.14318/hau2.1.020.

Desiningrum, Dinie Ratri. "Religiosity and Compassionate Love in Mother of Children with Autism Spectrum Disorder." *International Journal of Psychosocial Rehabilitation* 24, no. 1 (January 20, 2020): 1364–73. https://doi.org/10.37200/IJPR/V24I1/PR200235.

Desjarlais, Robert, and C. Jason Throop. "Phenomenological Approaches in Anthropology." *Annual Review of Anthropology* 40, no. 1 (October 21, 2011): 87–102. https://doi.org/10.1146/annurev-anthro-092010-153345.

Di Bello, Maria, Luca Carnevali, Nicola Petrocchi, Julian F. Thayer, Paul Gilbert, and Cristina Ottaviani. "The Compassionate Vagus: A Meta-Analysis on the Connection Between Compassion and Heart Rate Variability." *Neuroscience & Biobehavioral Reviews* 116 (September 2020): 21–30. https://doi.org/10.1016/j.neubiorev.2020.06.016.

Domínguez, D., and F. Juan "Neuroanthropology and the Dialectical Imperative." *Anthropological Theory* 12, no. 1 (March 2012): 5–27. https://doi.org/10.1177/1463499612436459.

Domínguez Duque, Juan F., Robert Turner, E. Douglas Lewis, and Gary Egan. "Neuroanthropology: A Humanistic Science for the Study of the Culture–Brain

Nexus." *Social Cognitive and Affective Neuroscience* 5, no. 2–3 (June 2010): 138–47. https://doi.org/10.1093/scan/nsp024.

Donald, James N., Baljinder K. Sahdra, Brooke Van Zanden, Jasper J. Duineveld, Paul W. B. Atkins, Sarah L. Marshall, and Joseph Ciarrochi. "Does Your Mindfulness Benefit Others? A Systematic Review and Meta-analysis of the Link Between Mindfulness and Prosocial Behaviour." *British Journal of Psychology* 110, no. 1 (February 2019): 101–25. https://doi.org/10.1111/bjop.12338.

Donald, Merlin. *A Mind so Rare: The Evolution of Human Consciousness*. New York: Norton, 2001.

Doricchi, Fabrizio. "The Functions of the Temporal–Parietal Junction." In *Handbook of Clinical Neurology*, vol. 187, 161–77. Elsevier, 2022. https://doi.org/10.1016/B978-0-12-823493-8.00020-1.

Downey, Greg. "Neuroanthropology." In *The SAGE Handbook of Social Anthropology*, edited by Richard Fardon, Olivia Harris, Trevor Marchand, Mark Nuttall, Cris Shore, Veronica Strang and Richard Wilson, 243–60. United Kingdom: SAGE Publications Ltd, 2012. https://doi.org/10.4135/9781446201077.n53.

Du Mez, Kristin Kobes. *Jesus And John Wayne: How White Evangelicals Corrupted a Faith and Fractured a Nation*. New York: Liveright Publishing Corp., 2021.

Dumit, Joseph. *Picturing Personhood Brain Scans and Biomedical Identity*. In-Formation Series. Baltimore, MD: Project Muse, 2021. https://muse.jhu.edu/book/85708/.

Durkheim, Émile. *The Elementary Forms of the Religious Life*. New York: Free Press, 1965.

Durkheim, Émile. *The Rules of Sociological Method, and Selected Texts on Sociology and Its Method*. London: Macmillan, 1982.

Dyrness, William A. *Reformed Theology and Visual Culture: The Protestant Imagination from Calvin to Edwards*. New York: Cambridge University Press, 2004.

Eisenberg, Nancy, and Paul A. Miller. "The Relation of Empathy to Prosocial and Related Behaviors." *Psychological Bulletin* 101, no. 1 (1987): 91–119. https://doi.org/10.1037/0033-2909.101.1.91.

Ellison, C. G., M. Bradshaw, K. J. Flannelly, and K. C. Galek. "Prayer, Attachment to God, and Symptoms of Anxiety-Related Disorders Among U.S. Adults." *Sociology of Religion* 75, no. 2 (June 1, 2014): 208–33. https://doi.org/10.1093/socrel/srt079.

Emerson, Michael O., and Christian Smith. *Divided by Faith: Evangelical Religion and the Problem of Race in America*. Oxford: Oxford University Press, 2000.

Enloe, Tim. "Leading a Receiving Time." In *Helping Others Receive the Gift: Insights on Spirit Baptism from God's Word and Personal Experience*, edited by Randy Hurst and Tim Enloe. Springfield, MO: Gospel Publishing House, 2008.

Enloe, Tim. "Ministering the Holy Spirit Baptism in Today's Culture." In *Helping Others Receive the Gift: Insights on Spirit Baptism from God's Word and Personal Experience*, edited by Randy Hurst and Gary Grogan. Springfield, MO: Gospel Publishing House, 2008.

Enloe, Tim. "The Nuts and Bolts of Ministering Spirit Baptism." In *Helping Others Receive the Gift: Insights on Spirit Baptism from God's Word and Personal Experience*, edited by Randy Hurst and Tim Enloe. Springfield, MO: Gospel Publishing House, 2008.

Erickson, Scott. "Fostering a Setting for People to Receive." In *Helping Others Receive the Gift: Insights on Spirit Baptism from God's Word and Personal Experience*, edited by Tim Enloe and Randy Hurst. Springfield, MO: Gospel Publishing House, 2008.

Evans-Pritchard, E. E. *Witchcraft, Oracles and Magic Among the Azande*. 1st ed. Oxford: Clarendon Press, 1963.

Fanon, Frantz. *Black Skin, White Masks*. Translated by Richard Philcox. 1st ed. New edition. Get Political. New York: Grove Press, 2008. http://catdir.loc.gov/catdir/ enhancements/fy0712/2006049607-d.html.

Farrer, C., and C. D. Frith. "Experiencing Oneself vs Another Person as Being the Cause of an Action: The Neural Correlates of the Experience of Agency." *NeuroImage* 15, no. 3 (March 2002): 596–603. https://doi.org/10.1006/nimg.2001.1009.

Feinstein, Matthew, Kiang Liu, Hongyan Ning, George Fitchett, and Donald M. Lloyd-Jones. "Burden of Cardiovascular Risk Factors, Subclinical Atherosclerosis, and Incident Cardiovascular Events Across Dimensions of Religiosity: The Multi-Ethnic Study of Atherosclerosis." *Circulation* 121, no. 5 (February 9, 2010): 659–66.

Feld, Steven. *Sound and Sentiment: Birds, Weeping, Poetics, and Song in Kaluli Expression*. Publications of the American Folklore Society. New Series; v. 5. Philadelphia, PA: University of Pennsylvania Press, 1982.

Ferguson, Jane K., Eleanor W. Willemsen, and MayLynn V. Castañeto. "Centering Prayer as a Healing Response to Everyday Stress: A Psychological and Spiritual Process." *Pastoral Psychology* 59, no. 3 (2010): 305–29. https://doi.org/10.1007/s11089-009-0225-7.

Feshchenko, V. V., and Lao Newman. "From the History of Glossolalia Studies. The Case of Hélène Smith on the Borderlines of Linguistics, Psychology, and Religion." *Cahiers Ferdinand de Saussure* 66 (2013): 67–79.

Finch, J. G. "God-Inspired or Self-Induced?" *Christian Herald*, no. 87 (1964): 12–19.

Foucault, Michel. *Discipline and Punish: The Birth of the Prison*. New York: Pantheon Books, 1977.

Francis, Leslie J., and Mandy Robbins. "Personality and Glossolalia: A Study Among Male Evangelical Clergy." *Pastoral Psychology* 51 (2003): 391–6.

Francis, Leslie J., and Susan H. Jones. "Personality and Charismatic Experience Among Adult Christians." *Pastoral Psychology* 45, no. 6 (January 1997): 421–8. https://doi. org/10.1007/BF02310642.

Francis, Leslie J., and William K. Kay. "The Personality Characteristics of Pentecostal Ministry Candidates." *Personality and Individual Differences* 18, no. 5 (May 1995): 581–94. https://doi.org/10.1016/0191-8869(94)00210-J.

Freud, Sigmund. *The Interpretation of Dreams; and on Dreams: (1900–1901)*. London: Hogarth Press, 1995.

Friedman, Lawrence Jacob. *Gregarious Saints: Self and Community in American Abolitionism, 1830–1870*. Cambridge and New York: Cambridge University Press, 1982.

Friston, Karl. "A Theory of Cortical Responses." *Philosophical Transactions of the Royal Society B: Biological Sciences* 360, no. 1456 (April 29, 2005): 815–36. https://doi. org/10.1098/rstb.2005.1622.

Friston, Karl. "The Free-Energy Principle: A Unified Brain Theory?" *Nature Reviews Neuroscience* 11, no. 2 (February 2010): 127–38. https://doi.org/10.1038/nrn2787.

Friston, Karl J., Thomas Parr, and Bert De Vries. "The Graphical Brain: Belief Propagation and Active Inference." *Network Neuroscience* 1, no. 4 (December 2017): 381–414. https://doi.org/10.1162/NETN_a_00018.

Frost, Karl. "Calming Meditation Increases Altruism, Decreases Parochialism." Preprint. Animal Behavior and Cognition, June 24, 2016. https://doi.org/10.1101/060616.

Gallagher, S. "On the Possibility of Naturalizing Phenomenology." In *The Oxford Handbook of Contemporary Phenomenology*, edited by D. Zahavi, 70–93. Oxford: Oxford University Press, 2012.

Gallagher, Shaun. *How the Body Shapes the Mind*. Oxford: Clarendon Press, 2013.

Garssen, Bert, Anja Visser, and Grieteke Pool. "Does Spirituality or Religion Positively Affect Mental Health? Meta-Analysis of Longitudinal Studies." *The International Journal for the Psychology of Religion* 31, no. 1 (February 27, 2020): 4–20. https://doi.org/10.1080/10508619.2020.1729570.

Gates, Henry Louis. *The Black Church: This Is Our Story, This Is Our Song*. New York: Penguin Press, 2021.

Gayatri, Spivak. *In Other Worlds: Essays on Cultural Politics*. London: Metheun, 1987.

Gazzaniga, Michael S. *Who's in Charge?: Free Will and the Science of the Brain*. New York: HarperCollins, 2011.

Geertz, Clifford. *Person, Time, and Conduct in Bali: An Essay in Cultural Analysis*. Cultural Report Series, No. 14. New Haven, CT: Yale University Press, 1966.

Geertz, Clifford. *The Interpretation of Cultures: Selected Essays*. Harper Colophon Books. New York: Basic Books, 1973. https://purl.fdlp.gov/GPO/gpo12195.

Gell, Alfred. *Art and Agency: An Anthropological Theory*. Oxford: Clarendon Press, 1998. http://catdir.loc.gov/catdir/enhancements/fy0604/97051845-t.html.

George, Linda K., David B. Larson, Harold G. Koenig, and Michael E. McCullough. "Spirituality and Health: What We Know, What We Need to Know." *Journal of Social and Clinical Psychology* 19, no. 1 (March 2000): 102–16. https://doi.org/10.1521/jscp.2000.19.1.102.

Gerhold, Jim. "Communicating the Character of the Holy Spirit to Kids." In *Helping Others Receive the Gift: Insights on Spirit Baptism from God's Word and Personal Experience*, edited by Tim Enloe and Randy Hurst. Springfield, MO: Gospel Publishing House, 2008.

Gerlach, Luther. "Pentecostalism: Revolution or Counter-Revolution?" In *Religious Movements in Contemporary America*, edited by Irving I. Zaretsky and Mark P. Leone. Princeton, NJ: Princeton University Press, 1974.

Gerlach, Luther P., and Virginia H. Hine. "Five Factors Crucial to the Growth and Spread of a Modern Religious Movement." *Journal for the Scientific Study of Religion* 7, no. 1 (1968): 23–40.

Gerlach, Luther P., and Virginia H. Hine. *People, Power, Change; Movements of Social Transformation*. Indianapolis, IN: Bobbs-Merrill, 1970.

Gerrans, Philip. "The Feeling of Thinking: Sense of Agency in Delusions of Thought Insertion." *Psychology of Consciousness: Theory, Research, and Practice* 2, no. 3 (2015): 291–300. https://doi.org/10.1037/cns0000060.

Gillespie, Michael Allen. *Hegel, Heidegger, and the Ground of History*. Chicago: University of Chicago Press, 1984.

Ginges, Jeremy, Ian Hansen, and Ara Norenzayan. "Religion and Support for Suicide Attacks." *Psychological Science* 20, no. 2 (February 2009): 224–30. https://doi.org/10.1111/j.1467-9280.2009.02270.x.

Goleman, Daniel, and Richard J. Davidson. *Altered Traits: Science Reveals How Meditation Changes Your Mind, Brain, and Body*. New York: Avery, 2017.

Gollwitzer, Peter, Ute Bayer, and Kathleen McCulloch. "The Control of the Unwanted." In *The New Unconscious*, edited by R. R. Hassin, J. S. Uleman, and J. A. Bargh, 485–515. Oxford and New York: Oxford University Press, 2005.

Gone, Joseph P. "Psychotherapy and Traditional Healing for American Indians: Exploring the Prospects for Therapeutic Integration." *The Counseling Psychologist* 38, no. 2 (February 2010): 166–235. https://doi.org/10.1177/0011000008330831.

Good, Byron. *Medicine, Rationality, and Experience: An Anthropological Perspective*. Lewis Henry Morgan Lectures. Cambridge: Cambridge University Press, 1994. http://catdir.loc.gov/catdir/toc/cam022/92045254.html.

Goodman, Felicitas D. "Altered Mental State vs. 'Style of Discourse:' Reply to Samarin." *Journal for the Scientific Study of Religion* 11, no. 3 (September 1972): 297. https://doi.org/10.2307/1384557.

Goodman, Felicitas D. "Body Posture and the Religious Altered State of Consciousness." Accessed October 3, 2016. http://jhp.sagepub.com/content/26/3/81.full.pdf.

Goodman, Felicitas D. *Ecstasy, Ritual and Alternate Reality*. Bloomington, IN: Indiana University Press, 1988.

Goodman, Felicitas D. "Phonetic Analysis of Glossolalia in Four Cultural Settings." *Journal for the Scientific Study of Religion* 8, no. 2 (1969): 227. https://doi.org/10.2307/1384336.

Goodman, Felicitas D. *Speaking in Tongues; a Cross-Cultural Study of Glossolalia [by] Felicitas D. Goodman*. Chicago: University of Chicago Press, 1972.

Goodman, Felicitas D. "The Discomfiture of Religious Experience." *Religion* 21, no. 4 (October 1991): 339–43. https://doi.org/10.1016/0048-721X(91)90036-P.

Gould, Deborah B. *Moving Politics: Emotion and ACT UP's Fight Against AIDS*. Chicago: University of Chicago Press, 2009.

Grady, Brian, and Kate Miriam Loewenthal. "Features Associated with Speaking in Tongues (Glossolalia)." *British Journal of Medical Psychology* 70, no. 2 (June 1997): 185–91. https://doi.org/10.1111/j.2044-8341.1997.tb01898.x.

Granqvist, Pehr, Mats Fredrikson, Patrik Unge, Andrea Hagenfeldt, Sven Valind, Dan Larhammar, and Marcus Larsson. "Sensed Presence and Mystical Experiences Are Predicted by Suggestibility, Not by the Application of Transcranial Weak Complex Magnetic Fields." *Neuroscience Letters* 379, no. 1 (April 2005): 1–6. https://doi.org/10.1016/j.neulet.2004.10.057.

Griffin, Allen. "Communicating the Baptism of the Spirit to Students." In *Helping Others Receive the Gift: Insights on Spirit Baptism from God's Word and Personal Experience*, edited by Tim Enloe and Randy Hurst. Springfield, MO: Gospel Publishing House, 2008.

Griffith, R. Marie. *God's Daughters Evangelical Women and the Power of Submission*. Berkeley, CA: University of California Press, 1997.

Griffiths, R. R., W. A. Richards, U. McCann, and R. Jesse. "Psilocybin Can Occasion Mystical-Type Experiences Having Substantial and Sustained Personal Meaning and Spiritual Significance." *Psychopharmacology* 187, no. 3 (August 2006): 268–83. https://doi.org/10.1007/s00213-006-0457-5.

Griffiths, Roland R., Matthew W. Johnson, William A. Richards, Brian D. Richards, Robert Jesse, Katherine A. MacLean, Frederick S. Barrett, Mary P. Cosimano, and Maggie A. Klinedinst. "Psilocybin-Occasioned Mystical-Type Experience in Combination with Meditation and Other Spiritual Practices Produces Enduring Positive Changes in Psychological Functioning and in Trait Measures of Prosocial Attitudes and Behaviors." *Journal of Psychopharmacology* 32, no. 1 (January 2018): 49–69. https://doi.org/10.1177/0269881117731279.

Griffiths, R. R., W. A. Richards, M. W. Johnson, U. D. McCann, and R. Jesse. "Mystical-Type Experiences Occasioned by Psilocybin Mediate the Attribution of Personal Meaning and Spiritual Significance 14 Months Later." *Journal of Psychopharmacology* 22, no. 6 (August 2008): 621–32. https://doi.org/10.1177/0269881108094300.

Guan, Fang, Yanhui Xiang, Outong Chen, Weixin Wang, and Jun Chen. "Neural Basis of Dispositional Awe." *Frontiers in Behavioral Neuroscience* 12 (September 11, 2018): 209. https://doi.org/10.3389/fnbeh.2018.00209.

Guilford, J. P. *The Nature of Human Intelligence.* New York: McGraw-Hill, 1967.

Gupta, Akhil, and James Ferguson. *Anthropological Locations: Boundaries and Grounds of a Field Science.* Berkeley, CA: University of California Press, 1997. http://bvbr.bib-bvb.de:8991/F?func=service&doc_library=BVB01&doc_number=007947958&line_number=0001&func_code=DB_RECORDS&service_type=MEDIA.

Gupta, Rajeev, H. Prakash, V. P. Gupta, and K. D. Gupta. "Prevalence and Determinants of Coronary Heart Disease in a Rural Population of India." *Journal of Clinical Epidemiology* 50, no. 2 (February 1997): 203–9. https://doi.org/10.1016/S0895-4356(96)00281-8.

Hacking, Ian. "Looping Effects of Human Kinds." In *Causal Cognition: A Multidisciplinary Debate: A Fyssen Foundation Symposium*, edited by Dan Sperber, Ann James Premack, David Premack, and Fondation Fyssen, 351–83. Oxford: Clarendon Press, 1995.

Hafenbrack, Andrew C., Lindsey D. Cameron, Gretchen M. Spreitzer, Chen Zhang, Laura J. Noval, and Samah Shaffakat. "Helping People by Being in the Present: Mindfulness Increases Prosocial Behavior." *Organizational Behavior and Human Decision Processes* 159 (July 2020): 21–38. https://doi.org/10.1016/j.obhdp.2019.08.005.

Haggard, Patrick. "Sense of Agency in the Human Brain." *Nature Reviews Neuroscience* 18, no. 4 (2017): 196–207. https://doi.org/10.1038/nrn.2017.14.

Halifax, Joan. "A Heuristic Model of Enactive Compassion." *Current Opinion in Supportive and Palliative Care* 6, no. 2 (June 2012): 228. https://doi.org/10.1097/SPC.0b013e3283530fbe.

Han, Shihui, and Georg Northoff. "Understanding the Self: A Cultural Neuroscience Approach." In *Progress in Brain Research*, 178: 203–12. Amsterdam: Elsevier, 2009. https://doi.org/10.1016/S0079-6123(09)17814-7.

Haraway, Donna. *Situated Knowledges: The Science Question in Feminism and the Privilege of Partial Perspective.* Ann Arbor, MI: Michigan Publishing, University of Michigan, 1988. http://hdl.handle.net/2027/spo.0499697.0014.310.

Haraway, Donna Jeanne. *Simians, Cyborgs, and Women: The Reinvention of Nature.* New York: Routledge, 1991.

Hartogsohn, Ido. "Constructing Drug Effects: A History of Set and Setting." *Drug Science, Policy and Law* 3 (January 2017): 205032451668332.

Hartogsohn, Ido. "Set and Setting, Psychedelics and the Placebo Response: An Extra-Pharmacological Perspective on Psychopharmacology." *Journal of Psychopharmacology* 30, no. 12 (December 2016): 1259–67. https://doi.org/10.1177/0269881116677852.

Hayford, Jack W., and S. David Moore. *The Charismatic Century: The Enduring Impact of the Azusa Street Revival*. New York: Warner Faith, 2006.

Haynes, Naomi. "Learning to Pray the Pentecostal Way: Language and Personhood on the Zambian Copperbelt." *Religion* 47, no. 1 (January 2, 2017): 35–50. https://doi.org/10.10 80/0048721X.2016.1225906.

Haynes, Naomi. "Pentecostalism and the Morality of Money: Prosperity, Inequality, and Religious Sociality on the Zambian Copperbelt: Pentecostalism and the Morality of Money." *Journal of the Royal Anthropological Institute* 18, no. 1 (March 2012): 123–39. https://doi.org/10.1111/j.1467-9655.2011.01734.x.

"Hearing Voices Website." n.d. https://www.hearing-voices.org/#content.

Hesp, Casper, Ryan Smith, Thomas Parr, Micah Allen, Karl J. Friston, and Maxwell J. D. Ramstead. "Deeply Felt Affect: The Emergence of Valence in Deep Active Inference." *Neural Computation* 33, no. 2 (February 1, 2021): 398–446. https://doi.org/10.1162/neco_a_01341.

Heyrman, Christine Leigh. *Southern Cross: The Beginnings of the Bible Belt*. Chapel Hill: University of North Carolina Press, 1997.

Hine, Virginia H. "Pentecostal Glossolalia Toward a Functional Interpretation." *Journal for the Scientific Study of Religion* 8, no. 2 (1969): 211. https://doi.org/10.2307/1384335.

Hinton, G. E., and T. J. Sejnowski. "Optimal Perceptual Inference." Proceedings of the IEEE conference on Compute Vision and Pattern Recognition, Washington, DC, 1983.

Hirschkind, Charles. "Is There a Secular Body?" *Cultural Anthropology* 26, no. 4 (November 2011): 633–47. https://doi.org/10.1111/j.1548-1360.2011.01116.x.

Hirschkind, Charles. *The Ethical Soundscape Cassette Sermons and Islamic Counterpublics*. New York: Columbia University Press, 2006.

Holbraad, Martin, and Morten Axel Pedersen. *The Ontological Turn: An Anthropological Exposition*. New Departures in Anthropology. Cambridge: Cambridge University Press, 2017.

Hollenweger, Walter. *The Pentecostals*. Peabody, MA: Hendrickson, 1988.

Hollenweger, Walter J. "Pentecostalism and Black Power." *Theology Today* 30, no. 3 (1973): 228–38.

Hollywood, Amy. *Acute Melancholia and Other Essays: Mysticism, History, and the Study of Religion*. New York: Columbia University Press, 2016.

Hopper, Kim. *Reckoning with Homelessness*. Ithaca, NY: Cornell University Press, 2003.

Howes, David. *The Varieties of Sensory Experience: A Sourcebook in the Anthropology of the Senses*. Buffalo, NY: University of Toronto Press, 1991.

Hu, Huping, and Maoxin Wu. "Michael Persinger & the GOD Experiments" *Scientific GOD Journal* 3, no. 10 (2012): 4.

Hubel, David H., and Torsten N. Wiesel. "Brain Mechanisms of Vision." *Scientific American* 241, no. 3 (September 1979): 150–62.

Huffman, Carey, and John Lindell. *Hungry? A Study in the Baptism in the Holy Spirit*. Springfield, MO: Gospel Pub. House, 2006.

Hufford, David. "Beings Without Bodies: An Experience-Centered Theory of the Belief in Spirits." In *Out of the Ordinary*. Logan, UT: Utah State University Press, 1995.

Hughes, Gethin. "The Role of the Temporoparietal Junction in Implicit and Explicit Sense of Agency." *Neuropsychologia* 113 (May 2018): 1–5.

Hurlburt, Russell T., and Eric Schwitzgebel. *Describing Inner Experience?: Proponent Meets Skeptic*. Cambridge, MA: MIT Press, 2011.

Ingold, Tim. *The Perception of the Environment: Essays on Livelihood, Dwelling and Skill.* London: Routledge, 2011.

Ironson, Gail, George F. Solomon, Elizabeth G. Balbin, Conall O'Cleirigh, Annie George, Mahendra Kumar, David Larson, and Teresa E. Woods. "The Ironson-Woods Spirituality/Religiousness Index Is Associated with Long Survival, Health Behaviors, Less Distress, and Low Cortisol in People with HIV/AIDS." *Annals of Behavioral Medicine* 24, no. 1 (February 2002): 34–48. https://doi.org/10.1207/S15324796ABM2401_05.

Iwamoto, Sage K., Marcus Alexander, Mark Torres, Michael R. Irwin, Nicholas A. Christakis, and Akihiro Nishi. "Mindfulness Meditation Activates Altruism." *Scientific Reports* 10, no. 1 (April 16, 2020): 6511. https://doi.org/10.1038/s41598-020-62652-1.

Jackson, Michael D. "Where Thought Belongs: An Anthropological Critique of the Project of Philosophy." *Anthropological Theory* 9, no. 3 (September 2009): 235–51. https://doi.org/10.1177/1463499609346984.

James, William. *The Principles of Psychology. Volume 1 Volume 1.* New York: Henry Holt and Company, 1918.

James, William. *The Varieties of Religious Experience: A Study in Human Nature.* New York: Barnes and Noble Classics, 2004 (1909).

Jenkins, Janis H. *Extraordinary Conditions: Culture and Experience in Mental Illness.* 1st ed. Oakland, CA: University of California Press, 2015. http://site.ebrary.com/id/11085798.

Joffily, Mateus, and Giorgio Coricelli. "Emotional Valence and the Free-Energy Principle." Edited by Tim Behrens. *PLoS Computational Biology* 9, no. 6 (June 13, 2013): e1003094. https://doi.org/10.1371/journal.pcbi.1003094.

Johns, Cheryl Bridges. *Pentecostal Formation: A Pedagogy Among the Oppressed.* Sheffield: Sheffield Academic Press, 1993.

Johnson, Mark. *Embodied Mind, Meaning, and Reason: How Our Bodies Give Rise to Understanding.* Chicago: University of Chicago Press, 2017.

Jones, Patrick. "Mindfulness Training: Can It Create Superheroes?" *Frontiers in Psychology* 10 (March 2019): 613.

Joutsa, Juho, Khaled Moussawi, Shan H. Siddiqi, Amir Abdolahi, William Drew, Alexander L. Cohen, Thomas J. Ross, Harshawardhan U. Deshpande, Henry Z. Wang, Joel Bruss, Elliot A. Stein, Nora D. Volkow, Jordan H. Grafman, Edwin van Wijngaarden, Aaron D. Boes, and Michael D. Fox "Brain Lesions Disrupting Addiction Map to a Common Human Brain Circuit." *Nature Medicine* 28, no. 6 (June 2022): 1249–55. https://doi.org/10.1038/s41591-022-01834-y.

Jung, C. G. *History of Modern Psychology: Lectures Delivered at the ETH Zurich.* Princeton, NJ: Princeton University Press, 2019.

Jungaberle, Henrik, Sascha Thal, Andrea Zeuch, Ansgar Rougemont-Bücking, Maximilian von Heyden, Helena Aicher, and Milan Scheidegger. "Positive Psychology in the Investigation of Psychedelics and Entactogens: A Critical Review." *Neuropharmacology* 142 (November 2018): 179–99. https://doi.org/10.1016/j.neuropharm.2018.06.034.

Kant, Immanuel, J. M. D. Meiklejohn, Thomas Kingsmill Abbott, James Creed Meredith, Immanuel Kant, Immanuel Kant, and Immanuel Kant. *The Critique of Pure Reason.* Chicago, IL: Encyclopædia Britannica, 1955.

Kaplan, Stephen, and Marc G. Berman. "Directed Attention as a Common Resource for Executive Functioning and Self-Regulation." *Perspectives on Psychological Science* 5, no. 1 (January 2010): 43–57. https://doi.org/10.1177/1745691609356784.

Kawakami, Kerry, Jasper Moll, Sander Hermsen, John F. Dovidio, and Abby Russin. "Just Say No (to Stereotyping): Effects of Training in the Negation of Stereotypic Associations on Stereotype Activation." *Journal of Personality and Social Psychology* 78 no. 5 (2000): 871–88.

Kazin, Michael. *The Populist Persuasion: An American History*. New York: Basic Books, 1995.

Keller, Evelyn Fox. *Reflections on Gender and Science*. 10th anniversary ed. New Haven, CT: Yale University Press, 1995.

Keltner, Dacher, and Jonathan Haidt. "Social Functions of Emotions at Four Levels of Analysis." *Cognition & Emotion* 13, no. 5 (September 1999): 505–21.

Kildahl, John. *The Psychology of Speaking in Tongues*. New York: Harper and Row, 1972.

Kirby, Vicky. *Telling Flesh: The Substance of the Corporeal*. New York: Routledge, 1997.

Kleinman, Arthur. *The Illness Narratives: Suffering, Healing, and the Human Condition*. New ed. New York: Basic Books, 2020.

Klinken, Adriaan van, and Ezra Chitando, eds. *Public Religion and the Politics of Homosexuality in Africa*. 1st ed. London: Routledge, 2016. https://doi.org/10.4324/9781315602974.

Koenig, Harold G. *The Healing Power of Faith: Science Explores Medicine's Last Great Frontier*. New York: Simon & Schuster, 1999. http://catdir.loc.gov/catdir/enhancements/fy0705/98032079-t.html.

Koenig, Harold G., Terrence D. Hill, Steven Pirutinsky, and David H. Rosmarin. "Commentary on 'Does Spirituality or Religion Positively Affect Mental Health?'" *The International Journal for the Psychology of Religion* (July 7, 2020): 1–18. https://doi.org/10.1080/10508619.2020.1766868.

Kogan, Aleksandr, Christopher Oveis, Evan W. Carr, June Gruber, Iris B. Mauss, Amanda Shallcross, Emily A. Impett, Ilmo van der Lowe, Bryant Hui, Cecilia Cheng, and Dacher Keltner "Vagal Activity Is Quadratically Related to Prosocial Traits, Prosocial Emotions, and Observer Perceptions of Prosociality." *Journal of Personality and Social Psychology* 107, no. 6 (December 2014): 1051–63. https://doi.org/10.1037/a0037509.

Koic, Elvira, Pavo Filakoviuc, Sanea Nad, and Ivan Celic. "Glossolalia." *Coll. Anthropology* 29, no. 1 (2005): 373–9.

Kornhuber, H. H., and L. Deecke. "Brain Potential Changes in Voluntary and Passive Movements in Humans: Readiness Potential and Reafferent Potentials." *Pflügers Archiv Für Die Gesamte Physiologie Des Menschen Und Der Tiere* 284, no. 1 (1965): 1–17.

Kostarelos, Frances. *Feeling the Spirit: Faith and Hope in an Evangelical Black Storefront Church*. South Carolina: University of Sotuh Carolina Press, 1995.

Kucyi, Aaron, Mojgan Hodaie, and Karen D. Davis. "Lateralization in Intrinsic Functional Connectivity of the Temporoparietal Junction with Salience- and Attention-Related Brain Networks." *Journal of Neurophysiology* 108, no. 12 (2012): 3382–92. https://doi.org/10.1152/jn.00674.2012.

Kuypers, K. P. C., J. Riba, M. de la Fuente Revenga, S. Barker, E. L. Theunissen, and J. G. Ramaekers. "Ayahuasca Enhances Creative Divergent Thinking While Decreasing Conventional Convergent Thinking." *Psychopharmacology* 233, no. 18 (September 2016): 3395–403.

Kyle, Richard G. *Evangelicalism: An Americanized Christianity*. New Brunswick, NJ: Transaction Publishers, 2006.

La Barre, Weston. *They Shall Take up Serpents: Psychology of the Southern Snake-Handling Cult.* Prospect Heights, IL: Waveland Press, 1962.

Laclau, Ernesto. *On Populist Reason.* London and New York: Verso, 2005.

Lakoff, George, and Mark Johnson. *Metaphors We Live By.* Chicago: The University of Chicago Press, 2003. http://www.gbv.de/dms/bowker/toc/9780226468013.pdf.

Lalive d'Epinay, Christian. *Haven of the Masses: A Study of the Pentecostal Movement in Chile.* London: Lutterworth Press, 1969.

Lao-tzu. *Tao Tê Ching.* 5th ed. London: Allen & Unwin, 1959.

Lapsley, James N. "Speaking in Tongues: Token of Group Acceptance and Divine Approval." *Pastoral Psychology* 15, no. 4 (May 1964): 48–55. https://doi.org/10.1007/BF01769602.

Lapsley, James N., and John H. Simpson. "Speaking in Tongues: Infantile Babble or Song of the Self?: Part II." *Pastoral Psychology* 15, no. 6 (September 1964): 16–24. https://doi.org/10.1007/BF01760225.

Lassiter, Luke E. *The Chicago Guide to Collaborative Ethnography.* Chicago Guides to Writing, Editing, and Publishing. Chicago: University of Chicago Press, 2005. http://catdir.loc.gov/catdir/enhancements/fy0621/2005006396-t.html.

Latour, Bruno. "Biography of an Inquiry: On a Book About Modes of Existence." *Social Studies of Science* 43, no. 2 (2013): 287–301.

Latour, Bruno. *Laboratory Life: The Construction of Scientific Facts.* Princeton: Princeton University Press, 2013. http://public.eblib.com/choice/publicfullrecord. aspx?p=1144731.

Lau, Hakwan C., Robert D. Rogers, Patrick Haggard, and Richard E. Passingham. "Attention to Intention." *Science* 303, no. 5661 (February 20, 2004): 1208–10

Laukkonen, Ruben E., and Heleen A. Slagter. "From Many to (n)One: Meditation and the Plasticity of the Predictive Mind." *Neuroscience & Biobehavioral Reviews* 128 (September 2021): 199–217. https://doi.org/10.1016/j.neubiorev.2021.06.021.

Leary, Timothy, Ralph Metzner, Ram Dass, and Karma-gliṅ-pa. *The Psychedelic Experience: A Manual Based on the Tibetan Book of the Dead.* New York: University Books, 1964.

Lebedev, A. V., M. Kaelen, M. Lövdén, J. Nilsson, A. Feilding, D. J. Nutt, and R. L. Carhart-Harris. "LSD-Induced Entropic Brain Activity Predicts Subsequent Personality Change." *Human Brain Mapping* 37, no. 9 (2016): 3203–13. https://doi.org/10.1002/hbm.23234.

Lebedev, Alexander V., Martin Lövdén, Gidon Rosenthal, Amanda Feilding, David J. Nutt, and Robin L. Carhart-Harris. "Finding the Self by Losing the Self: Neural Correlates of Ego-Dissolution Under Psilocybin: Finding the Self by Losing the Self." *Human Brain Mapping* 36, no. 8 (August 2015): 3137–53. https://doi.org/10.1002/hbm.22833.

Lende, Daniel H., and Greg Downey. "Neuoanthropology and Its Applications: An Introduction." *Annals of Anthropological Practice* 36, no. 1 (2012): 1–25. https://doi.org/10.1111/j.2153-9588.2012.01090.x.

Lester, Rebecca J. *Famished: Eating Disorders and Failed Care in America.* Oakland, CA: University of California Press, 2021.

Lévi-Strauss, Claude. *The Elementary Structures of Kinship.* Boston, MA: Beacon Press, 1969.

Lévi-Strauss, Claude. *The Savage Mind.* Nature of Human Society Series. Chicago and London: The University of Chicago Press; Weidenfeld and Nicolson Ltd., 1966.

Li SC. "Biocultural Orchestration of Developmental Plasticity Across Levels: The Interplay of Biology and Culture in Shaping the Mind and Behavior Across the Life Span." *Psychological Bulletin* 129, no. 2 (2003): 171–94.

Libet, Benjamin. "Do We Have Free Will?" In Libet, Freeman & Sutherland (eds), *The Volitional Brain, in Journal of Consciousness Studies* 6 (1999): 47–58.

Libet, B., E. W. Wright, and C. A. Gleason. "Readiness-Potentials Preceding Unrestricted 'Spontaneous' vs. Pre-Planned Voluntary Acts." *Electroencephalographv and Clinical Neurophysiology* 54 (1982): 322–35.

Lifshitz, Michael, E. P. Cusamano, and A. Raz. "Meditation and Hypnosis at the Intersection Between Phenomenology and Cognitive Science." In *Neuroscience, Consciousness, Spirituality, Vol. 2: The State of the Art of Meditation Research*, edited by S. Schmidt and H. Walach, 211–26. New York: Springer, 2014.

Lifshitz, Michael, Eli Sheiner, and Laurence J. Kirmayer. *Cultural Neurophenomenology of Psychedelic Thought*. Edited by Kalina Christoff and Kieran C. R. Fox. Vol. 1. Oxford: Oxford University Press, 2018.

Lifshitz, Michael, and Evan Thompson. "What's Wrong with 'the Mindful Brain'? Moving Past a Neurocentric View of Meditation." In *Casting Light on the Dark Side of Brain Imaging*, edited by Amir Raz and Robert Thibault, 123–8. London: Elsevier, 2019.

Lillard, Angelina. "Ethnopsychologies: Cultural Variations in Theories of Mind." *Psychological Bulletin* 123, no. 1 (1998): 3–32.

Limb, Charles J., and Allen R. Braun. "Neural Substrates of Spontaneous Musical Performance: An fMRI Study of Jazz Improvisation." Edited by Ernest Greene. *PLoS ONE* 3, no. 2 (February 27, 2008): e1679.

Liu, Siyuan, Ho Ming Chow, Yisheng Xu, Michael G. Erkkinen, Katherine E. Swett, Michael W. Eagle, Daniel A. Rizik-Baer, and Allen R. Braun. "Neural Correlates of Lyrical Improvisation: An fMRI Study of Freestyle Rap." *Scientific Reports* 2, no. 1 (December 2012): 1–8. https://doi.org/10.1038/srep00834.

Livingston, Paul M. *The Politics of Logic: Badiou, Wittgenstein, and the Consequences of Formalism*. New York: Routledge, 2012.

Lock, Margaret. "Recovering the Body." *Annual Review of Anthropology* 46, no. 1 (October 23, 2017): 1–14. https://doi.org/10.1146/annurev-anthro-102116-041253.

Longden, Eleanor, Dirk Corstens, and Jacqui Dillon. "Recovery, Discovery and Revolution: The Work of Intervoice and the Hearing Voices Movement." n.d.

Lord, Andrew. *Spirit-Shaped Mission: A Holistic Charismatic Missiology* (Studies in Pentecostal and Charismatic Issues). Milton Keynes, United Kingdom: Authentic Media, 2005.

Lorini, Emiliano, and Cristiano Castelfranchi. "The Cognitive Structure of Surprise: Looking for Basic Principles." *Topoi* 26, no. 1 (May 8, 2007): 133–49. https://doi.org/10.1007/s11245-006-9000-x.

Lovekin, Adams, and H. Newton Malony. "Religious Glossolalia: A Longitudinal Study of Personality Changes." *Journal for the Scientific Study of Religion* 16, no. 4 (December 1977): 383. https://doi.org/10.2307/1386224.

Luhrmann, T. M. "The Absorption Hypothesis: Learning to Hear God in Evangelical Christianity." *American Anthropologist* 112, no. 1 (February 23, 2010): 66–78. https://doi.org/10.1111/j.1548-1433.2009.01197.x.

Luhrmann, T. M. *Of Two Minds: An Anthropologist Looks at American Psychiatry*. 1st Vintage Books ed. New York: Vintage Books, 2001.

Luhrmann, T. M. *When God Talks Back: Understanding the American Evangelical Relationship with God*. New York: Alfred A. Knopf, 2012.

Luhrmann, T. M., and Rachel Morgain. "Prayer as Inner Sense Cultivation: An Attentional Learning Theory of Spiritual Experience." *Ethos* 40, no. 4 (December 2012): 359–89.

Luhrmann, T. M., Howard Nusbaum, and Ronald Thisted. "'Lord, Teach Us to Pray': Prayer Practice Affects Cognitive Processing." *Journal of Cognition and Culture* 13, no. 1–2 (January 1, 2013): 159–77.

Luhrmann, Tanya Marie, Kara Weisman, Felicity Aulino, Josh Brahinsky, John Dulin, Vivian Dzokoto, Cristine Legare, Michael Lifshitz, Emily Ng, Nicole Ross-Zehnder, and Rachel E. Smith. "Sensing the Presence of Gods and Spirits Across Cultures and Faiths." *PNAS* 118, no. 5 (2021): 1–8.

Luhrmann, Tanya. "A Hyperreal God and Modern Belief: Toward an Anthropological Theory of Mind." *Current Anthropology* 53, no. 4 (August 2012): 371–95. https://doi.org/10.1086/666529.

Luhrmann, Tanya. "Toward an Anthropological Theory of Mind." *Suomen: Journal of the Finnish Anthropological Society* 36, no. 4 (2011): 70.

Lutz, Antoine, and Evan Thompson. "Neurophenomenology: Integrating Subjective Experience and Brain Dynamics in the Neuroscience of Consciousness." *Journal of Consciousness Studies* 10, no. 9–10 (2003): 31–52.

Lutz, Catherine A., and Lila Abu-Lughod, eds. *Language and the Politics of Emotion.* Language and the Politics of Emotion. New York: Cambridge University Press, 1990.

Lynn, Christopher Dana, Jason J. Paris, Cheryl Anne Frye, and Lawrence M. Schell. "Glossolalia Is Associated with Differences in Biomarkers of Stress and Arousal Among Apostolic Pentecostals." *Religion, Brain & Behavior* 1, no. 3 (October 2011): 173–91. https://doi.org/10.1080/2153599X.2011.639659.

Lynn, Christopher Dana, Jason Paris, Cheryl Anne Frye, and Lawrence M. Schell. "Salivary Alpha-Amylase and Cortisol Among Pentecostals on a Worship and Nonworship Day." *American Journal of Human Biology* 22, no. 6 (November 2010): 819–22. https://doi.org/10.1002/ajhb.21088.

Macgavran, Donald. *How Churches Grow: The New Frontiers of Mission.* London: World Dominion Press, 1959.

Mack, Phyllis. "Religion, Feminism, and the Problem of Agency: Reflections on Eighteenth-Century Quakerism." *Signs Signs: Journal of Women in Culture and Society* 29, no. 1 (2003): 149–77.

Mackie, Alexander. *The Gift of Tongues.* New York: George H. Doran Company, 1921.

MacLean, Katherine A., Emilio Ferrer, Stephen R. Aichele, David A. Bridwell, Anthony P. Zanesco, Tonya L. Jacobs, Brandon G. King, Erika L. Rosenberg, Baljinder K. Sahdra, Phillip R. Shaver, B. Alan Wallace, George R. Mangun, and Clifford D. Saron. "Intensive Meditation Training Improves Perceptual Discrimination and Sustained Attention." *Psychological Science* 21, no. 6 (June 2010): 829–39. https://doi.org/10.1177/0956797610371339.

Maeder. "La Langue d'un Aliene: Analyse d'un Cas de Glossolalie." *Journal de psychologie normale et pathologique* 7 (1910): 563.

Mahmood, Saba. *Politics of Piety: The Islamic Revival and the Feminist Subject.* Princeton, NJ: Princeton University Press, 2005.

Majid, Asifa, and Stephen C. Levinson. "The Senses in Language and Culture." *Senses & Society* 6 (2011): 5–18.

Malinowski, Bronislaw. *Argonauts of the Western Pacific.* Routledge Classics. Hoboken, NJ: Taylor and Francis, 2014.

Malony, H. Newton, and A. Adams Lovekin. *Glossolalia: Behavioral Science Perspectives on Speaking in Tongues*. New York: Oxford University Press, 1985. http://catdir.loc.gov/catdir/enhancements/fy0639/84020606-d.html.

Marina, Peter, and Michael Wilkinson. "Pentecostalism as Cultural Resistance: Music and Tongue-Speaking as Collective Response in a Brooklyn Church." *PentecoStudies: An Interdisciplinary Journal for Research on the Pentecostal and Charismatic Movements* 16, no. 2 (October 5, 2017): 216–42. https://doi.org/10.1558/ptcs.32822.

Mariz, Cecília Loreto. *Coping with Poverty: Pentecostals and Christian Base Communities in Brazil*. Philadelphia, PA: Temple University Press, 1994.

Mars, R. B., J. Sallet, U. Schuffelgen, S. Jbabdi, I. Toni, and M. F. S. Rushworth. "Connectivity-Based Subdivisions of the Human Right 'Temporoparietal Junction Area': Evidence for Different Areas Participating in Different Cortical Networks." *Cerebral Cortex* 22, no. 8 (2012): 1894–903. https://doi.org/10.1093/cercor/bhr268.

Marsden, George. *Fundamentalism and American Culture: The Shaping of Twentieth Century Evangelicalism, 1870–1925*. New York: Oxford University Press, 2006.

Marshall, Ruth. *Political Spiritualities: The Pentecostal Revolution in Nigeria*. Chicago and London: The University of Chicago Press, 2009.

Martin, Emily. *The Woman in the Body: A Cultural Analysis of Reproduction*. Boston, MA: Beacon Press, 1992.

Mauss, Marcel. *The Gift: Forms and Functions of Exchange in Archaic Societies*. London: Cohen & West, 1969.

Mauss, Marcel. "Techniques of the Body." *Economy and Society* 2, no. 1 (1979): 70–88.

May, L. Carlyle. "A Survey of Glossolalia and Related Phenomena in Non-Christian Religions." *American Anthropologist* 58, no. 1 (February 1956): 75–96. https://doi.org/10.1525/aa.1956.58.1.02a00060.

Mazraeh, Nasrollah, Siamak Khodarahimi, Maeda Hesam, Ali Rasti, Sahar Mirghobad Khodarahmi, Najme Aganj, and Sonay Sheikhi. "The Role of Social Interest and Empathy on Helping Behaviors During Floods." *Anales de Psicología* 39, no. 1 (January 1, 2023): 119–26. https://doi.org/10.6018/analesps.515131.

McCauley, Thomas G., William H. B. McAuliffe, and Michael E. McCullough. "Does Empathy Promote Helping by Activating Altruistic Motivation or Concern About Social Evaluation? A Direct Replication of Fultz et al. (1986)." *Emotion (Washington, D.C.)*, July 8, 2024. https://doi.org/10.1037/emo0001339.

McClung, Grant. *Azusa Street and Beyond: Pentecostal Missions and Church Growth in the Twentieth Century*. South Plainfield, NJ: Bridge Publications, 1986.

McCrae, Niall, and Samantha Elliott. "Spiritual Experiences in Temporal Lobe Epilepsy: A Literature Review." *British Journal of Neuroscience Nursing* 8, no. 6 (December 2012): 346–51. https://doi.org/10.12968/bjnn.2012.8.6.346.

McNay, Lois. *Gender and Agency: Reconfiguring the Subject in Feminist and Social Theory*. Cambridge: Polity Press, 2000.

Mead, Margaret. *Coming of Age in Samoa*. Armed Services Editions (Series). New York: Editions for the Armed Services, 1945.

Megevand, P., D. M. Groppe, M. S. Goldfinger, S. T. Hwang, P. B. Kingsley, I. Davidesco, and A. D. Mehta. "Seeing Scenes: Topographic Visual Hallucinations Evoked by Direct Electrical Stimulation of the Parahippocampal Place Area." *Journal of Neuroscience* 34, no. 16 (April 16, 2014): 5399–405.

Menzies, William. *Anointed to Serve: The Story of the Assemblies of God*. Springfield, MO: Gospel Publishing House, 1971.

Meyer, Birgit. *Translating the Devil: Religion and Modernity Among the Ewe in Ghana*. Trenton, NJ: Africa World Press, 1999.

Miller, Donald E. *Reinventing American Protestantism: Christianity in the New Millennium*. Berkeley, CA: University of California Press, 1997.

Mol, Annemarie. *The Body Multiple: Ontology in Medical Practice*. Science and Cultural Theory. Durham, NC: Duke University Press, 2002.

Moore, Henrietta L. *A Passion for Difference: Essays in Anthropology and Gender*. Bloomington, IN: Indiana University Press, 1994.

Moore, James W., and Sukhvinder S. Obhi. "Intentional Binding and the Sense of Agency: A Review." *Consciousness and Cognition* 21, no. 1 (March 2012): 546–61. https://doi.org/10.1016/j.concog.2011.12.002.

Moore, James W., Diane Ruge, Dorit Wenke, John Rothwell, and Patrick Haggard. "Disrupting the Experience of Control in the Human Brain: Pre-Supplementary Motor Area Contributes to the Sense of Agency." *Proceedings of the Royal Society B: Biological Sciences* 277, no. 1693 (2010): 2503–9. https://doi.org/10.1098/rspb.2010.0404.

Moore, S. David. *Shepherding Movement*. London: T & T Clark International, 2004.

Moraga, Cherríe, and Gloria Anzaldúa. *This Bridge Called My Back: Writings by Radical Women of Color*. New York: Kitchen Table, Women of Color Press, 1983.

Moreton, Bethany. *To Serve God and Wal-Mart the Making of Christian Free Enterprise*. Cambridge, MA: Harvard University Press, 2009.

Morphy, Howard. *Aboriginal Art*. Art & Ideas. London: Phaidon, 1998. http://www.phaidon.com/store/art/aboriginal-art-9780714837529/.

Morris, Rosalind C., and Gayatri Chakravorty Spivak. *Can the Subaltern Speak?: Reflections on the History of an Idea*. New York: Columbia University Press, 2010.

Mosini, Amanda Cristina, Marcelo Saad, Camilla Casaletti Braghetta, Roberta de Medeiros, Mario Fernando Prieto Peres, and Frederico Camelo Leão. "Neurophysiological, Cognitive-Behavioral and Neurochemical Effects in Practitioners of Transcendental Meditation—A Literature Review." *Revista Da Associação Médica Brasileira* 65, no. 5 (May 2019): 706–13. https://doi.org/10.1590/1806-9282.65.5.706.

Murphy, Keith M, and C. Jason Throop. *Toward an Anthropology of the Will*. Stanford, CA: Stanford University Press, 2010.

Myers, Neely Laurenzo. *Recovery's Edge: An Ethnography of Mental Health Care and Moral Agency*. Nashville, TN: Vanderbilt University Press, 2015. https://search.ebscohost.com/login.aspx?direct=true&scope=site&db=nlebk&db=nlabk&AN=1128732.

Nachev, Parashkev, Henrietta Wydell, Kevin O'Neill, Masud Husain, and Christopher Kennard. "The Role of the Pre-Supplementary Motor Area in the Control of Action." *NeuroImage* 36 (2007): T155–63. https://doi.org/10.1016/j.neuroimage.2007.03.034.

Newberg, Andrew B. "The Neuroscientific Study of Spiritual Practices." *Frontiers in Psychology* 5 (March 18, 2014). https://doi.org/10.3389/fpsyg.2014.00215.

Newberg, Andrew B., and Mark Robert Waldman. *How God Changes Your Brain: Breakthrough Findings from a Leading Neuroscientist*. New York: Ballantine Books, 2009.

Newberg, Andrew B., Nancy A. Wintering, Donna Morgan, and Mark R. Waldman. "The Measurement of Regional Cerebral Blood Flow During Glossolalia: A Preliminary SPECT Study." *Psychiatry Research: Neuroimaging* 148, no. 1 (November 2006): 67–71.

Newen, Albert, Leon de Bruin, and Shaun Gallagher. *The Oxford Handbook of 4E Cognition*, 2018. https://doi.org/10.1093/oxfordhb/9780198735410.001.0001.

Newman, Joe. *Race and the Assemblies of God Church the Journey from Azusa Street to the "Miracle of Memphis."* Youngstown, NY: Cambria Press, 2007.

Ngai, Sianne. *Ugly Feelings.* Cambridge, MA: Harvard University Press, 2005. http://site.ebrary.com/id/10314241.

Nguyen, Vinh T., Michael Breakspear, and Ross Cunnington. "Reciprocal Interactions of the SMA and Cingulate Cortex Sustain Premovement Activity for Voluntary Actions." *The Journal of Neuroscience* 34, no. 49 (2014): 16397–407. https://doi.org/10.1523/JNEUROSCI.2571-14.2014.

Nisbett, Richard E., and Yuri Miyamoto. "The Influence of Culture: Holistic Versus Analytic Perception." *Trends in Cognitive Sciences* 9, no. 10 (October 2005): 467–73. https://doi.org/10.1016/j.tics.2005.08.004.

Noë, Alva. *Out of Our Heads: Why You Are Not Your Brain, and Other Lessons from the Biology of Consciousness.* 1st ed. New York: Hill and Wang, 2009.

Nour, Matthew M., Lisa Evans, David Nutt, and Robin L. Carhart-Harris. "Ego-Dissolution and Psychedelics: Validation of the Ego-Dissolution Inventory (EDI)." *Frontiers in Human Neuroscience* 10 (June 14, 2016): 269.

O'Hanlon, Rosalind. "Recovering the Subject Subaltern Studies and Histories of Resistance in Colonial South Asia." *Modern Asian Studies* 22, no. 1 (1988): 189–224.

Ohayon, Maurice M. "Prevalence of Hallucinations and Their Pathological Associations in the General Population." *Psychiatry Research* 97, no. 2 (December 27, 2000): 153–64. https://doi.org/10.1016/S0165-1781(00)00227-4.

Olson, Jay A., Johnny Nahas, Denis Chmoulevitch, Simon J. Cropper, and Margaret E. Webb. "Naming Unrelated Words Predicts Creativity." *Proceedings of the National Academy of Sciences* 118, no. 25 (June 22, 2021): e2022340118. https://doi.org/10.1073/pnas.2022340118.

Open Science Collaboration. "Estimating the Reproducibility of Psychological Science." *Science* 349, no. 6251 (August 28, 2015): aac4716–aac4716. https://doi.org/10.1126/science.aac4716.

Ortner, Sherry B. *Anthropology and Social Theory: Culture, Power, and the Acting Subject.* Durham, NC: Duke University Press, 2006. http://catdir.loc.gov/catdir/toc/ecip0612/2006012766.html.

Pang, YaLing, Chao Song, and Chao Ma. "Effect of Different Types of Empathy on Prosocial Behavior: Gratitude as Mediator." *Frontiers in Psychology* 13 (February 17, 2022): 768827. https://doi.org/10.3389/fpsyg.2022.768827.

Pattison, E. Mansell. "Behavioral Science Research on the Nature of Glossolalia." *JASA* 20, no. Sept (1968): 73–86.

Persinger, Michael A. "Experimental Simulation of the God Experience: Implications for Religious Beliefs and the Future of the Human Species." In *Neurotheology*, 267–84. CA: University Press, 2002.

Persinger, Michael A. "Religious and Mystical Experiences as Artifacts of Temporal Lobe Function: A General Hypothesis." *Perceptual and Motor Skills* 57, no. 3_suppl (December 1983): 1255–62. https://doi.org/10.2466/pms.1983.57.3f.1255.

Persinger, Michael A. "Replication of God Helmet Experiment and Many Other of Our Results—a Blog by Dr. Michael A. Persinger." *Sacred Pathways—Blogs in Neurotheology* (blog), June 7, 2015. https://sacredneurology.com/2015/06/07/god-helmet-and-many-other-of-our-results-have-been-replicated-a-blog-by-dr-michael-a-persinger/.

Persinger, Michael A. "Striking EEG Profiles from Single Episodes of Glossolalia and Transcendental Meditation." *Perceptual and Motor Skills* 58, no. 1 (February 1984): 127–33. https://doi.org/10.2466/pms.1984.58.1.127.

Persinger, Michael A., Kevin S. Saroka, Stanley A. Koren, and Linda S. St-Pierre. "The Electromagnetic Induction of Mystical and Altered States within the Laboratory." *Journal of Consciousness Exploration & Research* 1 (2010): 808–30.

Pessoa, Luiz. "How Do Emotion and Motivation Direct Executive Control?" *Trends in Cognitive Sciences* 13, no. 4 (April 2009): 160–6. https://doi.org/10.1016/j.tics.2009.01.006.

Petitmengin, Claire, and Jean-Philippe Lachaux. "Microcognitive Science: Bridging Experiential and Neuronal Microdynamics." *Frontiers in Human Neuroscience* 7 (2013): 1–6. https://doi.org/10.3389/fnhum.2013.00617.

Petitmengin, Claire, and Michel Bitbol. "The Validity of First-Person Descriptions as Authenticity and Coherence." *Journal of Consciousness Studies* 16, no. 10–12 (2009): 363–404.

Petitmengin, Claire, Martijn van Beek, Michel Bitbol, Jean-Michel Nissou, and Andreas Roepstorff. "Studying the Experience of Meditation through Micro-Phenomenology." *Current Opinion in Psychology* 28 (October 2018): 54–9.

Pew Forum on Religion & Public Life. *Spirit and Power a 10-Country Survey of Pentecostals.* Washington, DC: Pew Forum on Religion & Public Life, 2006.

Pew Research Center. "When Americans Say They Believe in God, What Do They Mean." April 25, 2018, 41.

PhD, Brian Pace. "Lucy In The Sky With Nazis: Psychedelics and the Right Wing." *Psymposia*, February 3, 2020. http://www.psymposia.com/magazine/lucy-in-the-sky-with-nazis-psychedelics-and-the-right-wing/.

Philipchalk, Ron, and Dieter Mueller. "Glossolalia and Temperature Change in the Right and Left Cerebral Hemispheres." *International Journal for the Psychology of Religion* 10, no. 3 (July 2000): 181–5. https://doi.org/10.1207/S15327582IJPR1003_04.

Piff, Paul K., Daniel M. Stancato, Stéphane Côté, Rodolfo Mendoza-Denton, and Dacher Keltner. "Higher Social Class Predicts Increased Unethical Behavior." *Proceedings of the National Academy of Sciences* 109, no. 11 (March 13, 2012): 4086–91. https://doi.org/10.1073/pnas.1118373109.

Piff, Paul K., Pia Dietze, Matthew Feinberg, Daniel M. Stancato, and Dacher Keltner. "Awe, the Small Self, and Prosocial Behavior." *Journal of Personality and Social Psychology* 108, no. 6 (2015): 883–99.

Poldrack, R. "Can Cognitive Processes Be Inferred from Neuroimaging Data?" *Trends in Cognitive Sciences* 10, no. 2 (February 2006): 59–63. https://doi.org/10.1016/j.tics.2005.12.004.

Poldrack, Russell A., and Tal Yarkoni. "From Brain Maps to Cognitive Ontologies: Informatics and the Search for Mental Structure." *Annual Review of Psychology* 67, no. 1 (January 4, 2016): 587–612. https://doi.org/10.1146/annurev-psych-122414-033729.

Pollan, Michael. *How to Change Your Mind: The New Science of Psychedelics.* New York: Penguin Publishing Group, 2019.

Poloma, Margaret M. *The Assemblies of God at the Crossroads: Charisma and Institutional Dilemmas.* 1st ed. Knoxville, TN: University of Tennessee Press, 1989.

Pomerville, Paul. *The Third Force in Missions: A Pentecostal Contribution To Contemporary Mission Theology.* Peabody, MA: Hendrickson Publishers, 1985.

Posner, Michael I. "Orienting of Attention." *Quarterly Journal of Experimental Psychology* 32, no. 1 (February 1980): 3–25. https://doi.org/10.1080/00335558008248231.

Preller, Katrin H., and Franz X. Vollenweider. "Modulation of Social Cognition via Hallucinogens and 'Entactogens'." *Frontiers in Psychiatry* 10 (December 3, 2019). https://doi.org/10.3389/fpsyt.2019.00881.

Pritzker, Sonya. "Thinking Hearts, Feeling Brains: Metaphor, Culture, and the Self in Chinese Narratives of Depression." *Metaphor and Symbol* 22, no. 3 (2007): 251–74.

Puar, Jasbir K. *Terrorist Assemblages: Homonationalism in Queer Times.* Durham, NC: Duke University Press, 2007.

Rae, Charlotte L., Laura E. Hughes, Michael C. Anderson, and James B. Rowe. "The Prefrontal Cortex Achieves Inhibitory Control by Facilitating Subcortical Motor Pathway Connectivity." *The Journal of Neuroscience* 35, no. 2 (2015): 786–94. https://doi.org/10.1523/JNEUROSCI.3093-13.2015.

Ramstead, Maxwell J. D., Samuel P. L. Veissière, and Laurence J. Kirmayer. "Cultural Affordances: Scaffolding Local Worlds through Shared Intentionality and Regimes of Attention." *Frontiers in Psychology* 7 (July 26, 2016). https://doi.org/10.3389/fpsyg.2016.01090.

Ransom, Madeleine, Sina Fazelpour, Jelena Markovic, James Kryklywy, Evan T. Thompson, and Rebecca M. Todd. "Affect-Biased Attention and Predictive Processing." *Cognition* 203 (October 2020): 104370. https://doi.org/10.1016/j.cognition.2020.104370.

Rao, Rajesh P. N., and Dana H. Ballard. "Predictive Coding in the Visual Cortex: A Functional Interpretation of Some Extra-Classical Receptive-Field Effects." *Nature Neuroscience* 2, no. 1 (January 1999): 79–87. https://doi.org/10.1038/4580.

Read, J., J. van Os, A. P. Morrison, and C. A. Ross. "Childhood Trauma, Psychosis and Schizophrenia: A Literature Review with Theoretical and Clinical Implications." *Acta Psychiatrica Scandinavica* 112, no. 5 (November 2005): 330–50. https://doi.org/10.1111/j.1600-0447.2005.00634.x.

Regnerus, Mark. *Forbidden Fruit: Sex & Religion in the Lives of American Teenagers.* New York: Oxford University Press, 2007.

Reich, Wilhelm. *Selected Writings: An Introduction to Orgonomy.* Toronto: Ambassador Books, 1961.

Reich, Wilhelm, and Theodore P. Wolfe. *The Mass Psychology of Fascism.* New York: Orgone Institute Press, 1946.

Richardson, James T. "Psychological Interpretations of Glossolalia: A Reexamination of Research." *Journal for the Scientific Study of Religion* 12, no. 2 (June 1973): 199. https://doi.org/10.2307/1384889.

Richtel, Matt. "The Latest in Military Strategy: Mindfulness." *The New York Times*, April 8, 2019, sec. Health. https://www.nytimes.com/2019/04/05/health/military-mindfulness-training.html.

Robbins, Joel. *Becoming Sinners*. Berkeley, CA: University of California Press, 2004.

Robbins, Joel. "Introduction: Global Religions, Pacific Island Transformations." *Journal of Ritual Studies* 15, no. 2 (2001): 7–12.

Robbins, Mandy, James Hair, and Leslie J. Francis. "Personality and Attraction to the Charismatic Movement: A Study Among Anglican Clergy." *Journal of Beliefs & Values* 20, no. 2 (October 1999): 239–46. https://doi.org/10.1080/1361767990200209.

Roberts, Oral. *The Baptism with the Holy Spirit: And the Value of Speaking in Tongues Today*. Tulsa, OK: The Author, 1971.

Roepstorff, Andreas, and Chris Frith. "Neuroanthropology or Simply Anthropology? Going Experimental as Method, as Object of Study, and as Research Aesthetic." *Anthropological Theory* 12, no. 1 (March 2012): 101–11. https://doi.org/10.1177/1463499612436467.

Roepstorff, Andreas, Jörg Niewöhner, and Stefan Beck. "Enculturing Brains Through Patterned Practices." *Neural Networks* 23, no. 8–9 (October 2010): 1051–9. https://doi.org/10.1016/j.neunet.2010.08.002.

Romme, M. A. J., and Sandra Escher. *Accepting Voices*. London: Mind Publications, 1993.

Rosenbaum, Janet Elise. "Patient Teenagers? A Comparison of the Sexual Behavior of Virginity Pledgers and Matched Nonpledgers." *Pediatrics* 123, no. 1 (January 2009): e110–20.

Rothschild, Sarit, Gilat Kaplan, Tomer Golan, and Yoram Barak. "Mindfulness Meditation in the Israel Defense Forces: Effect on Cognition and Satisfaction with Life—A Randomized Controlled Trial." *European Journal of Integrative Medicine* 10 (February 1, 2017): 71–4. https://doi.org/10.1016/j.eujim.2017.01.010.

Sahdra, Baljinder K., Katherine A. MacLean, Emilio Ferrer, Phillip R. Shaver, Erika L. Rosenberg, Tonya L. Jacobs, Anthony P. Zanesco, Brandon G. King, Stephen R. Aichele, David A. Bridwell, George R. Mangun, Shiri Lavy, B. Alan Wallace, and Clifford D. Saron. "Enhanced Response Inhibition During Intensive Meditation Training Predicts Improvements in Self-Reported Adaptive Socioemotional Functioning." *Emotion* 11, no. 2 (2011): 299–312. https://doi.org/10.1037/a0022764.

Said, Edward. *Orientalism*. London: Routledge & Kegan Paul, 1978.

Samarin, William J. "Reviewed Work(s): Speaking in Tongues: A Cross-Cultural Study of Glossolalia by Felicitas D. Goodman." *Language* 50, no. 1 (1974): 207–12.

Samarin, William J. *Tongues of Men and Angels: The Religious Language of Pentecostalism*. New York: Macmillan, 1972.

Sapolsky, Robert M. *Determined: A Science of Life Without Free Will*. New York: Penguin Press, 2023.

Sargant, William. "Some Cultural Group Abreactive Techniques and Their Relation to Modern Treatments." *Proceedings of the Royal Society of Medicine* 42, no. 5 (May 1949): 367–74. https://doi.org/10.1177/003591574904200520.

Saroglou, Vassilis, Vanessa Delpierre, and Rebecca Dernelle. "Values and Religiosity: A Meta-Analysis of Studies Using Schwartz's Model." *Personality and Individual Differences* 37, no. 4 (September 2004): 721–34. https://doi.org/10.1016/j.paid.2003.10.005.

Sayre, Nathan F. "Ecological and Geographical Scale: Parallels and Potential for
    Integration." *Progress in Human Geography* 29, no. 3 (2005): 276–90.
Scheper-Hughes, Nancy, and Margaret M. Lock. "The Mindful Body: A Prolegomenon
    to Future Work in Medical Anthropology." *Medical Anthropology Quarterly* 1, no. 1
    (March 1987): 6–41. https://doi.org/10.1525/maq.1987.1.1.02a00020.
Schjoedt, Uffe, Hans Stødkilde-Jørgensen, Armin W. Geertz, and Andreas Roepstorff.
    "Highly Religious Participants Recruit Areas of Social Cognition in Personal Prayer."
    Social Cognitive and Affective Neuroscience 4, no. 2 (June 1, 2009): 199–207. https://doi.
    org/10.1093/scan/nsn050.
Schmidt, Leigh Eric. *Hearing Things: Religion, Illusion, and the American Enlightenment.*
    Cambridge, MA: Harvard University Press, 2000.
Schmitt, Carl. *The Crisis of Parliamentary Democracy.* Cambridge, MA: MIT Press, 1985.
Schneider, J., P. Malinowski, P. M. Watson, and P. Lattimore. "The Role of Mindfulness
    in Physical Activity: A Systematic Review." *Obesity Reviews* 20, no. 3 (March 2019):
    448–63. https://doi.org/10.1111/obr.12795.
Schwartz, Scott W. *Faith, Serpents, and Fire: Images of Kentucky Holiness Believers.* Jackson,
    MS: University Press of Mississippi, 1999. https://search.ebscohost.com/login.aspx?dire
    ct=true&scope=site&db=nlebk&db=nlabk&AN=4676.
Seeman, Teresa E., Linda Fagan Dubin, and Melvin Seeman. "Religiosity/Spirituality
    and Health: A Critical Review of the Evidence for Biological Pathways." *American
    Psychologist* 58, no. 1 (2003): 53–63. https://doi.org/10.1037/0003-066X.58.1.53.
Seghezzi, Silvia, and Laura Zapparoli. "Predicting the Sensory Consequences of Self-
    Generated Actions: Pre-Supplementary Motor Area as Supra-Modal Hub in the Sense
    of Agency Experience." *Brain Sciences* 10, no. 11 (November 7, 2020): 825. https://doi.
    org/10.3390/brainsci10110825.
Seghezzi, Silvia, Eleonora Zirone, Eraldo Paulesu, and Laura Zapparoli. "The Brain
    in (Willed) Action: A Meta-Analytical Comparison of Imaging Studies on Motor
    Intentionality and Sense of Agency." *Frontiers in Psychology* 10 (April 2019): 804.
    https://doi.org/10.3389/fpsyg.2019.00804.
Seligman, Rebecca. "The Unmaking and Making of Self: Embodied Suffering and Mind-
    Body Healing in Brazilian Candomblé: Unmaking And Making the Self." *Ethos* 38, no.
    3 (September 2010): 297–320. https://doi.org/10.1111/j.1548-1352.2010.01146.x.
Seligman, Rebecca, and Laurence J. Kirmayer. "Dissociative Experience and Cultural
    Neuroscience: Narrative, Metaphor and Mechanism." *Culture, Medicine and Psychiatry*
    32, no. 1 (March 2008): 31–64. https://doi.org/10.1007/s11013-007-9077-8.
Seth, Anil K., and Karl J. Friston. "Active Interoceptive Inference and the Emotional
    Brain." *Philosophical Transactions of the Royal Society B: Biological Sciences* 371, no.
    1708 (November 19, 2016): 20160007. https://doi.org/10.1098/rstb.2016.0007.
Sharf, Robert. "Buddhist Modernism and the Rhetoric of Meditative Experience." *Numen*
    42, no. 3 (1995): 228–83. https://doi.org/10.1163/1568527952598549.
Sherrill, John L. *They Speak with Other Tongues.* Spire Books. Old Tappan, NJ: Revell,
    1968.
Shrout, Patrick E., and Joseph L. Rodgers. "Psychology, Science, and Knowledge
    Construction: Broadening Perspectives from the Replication Crisis." *Annual Review
    of Psychology* 69, no. 1 (January 4, 2018): 487–510. https://doi.org/10.1146/annurev-
    psych-122216-011845.

Simonsson, Otto, Olivier Bazin, Stephen D. Fisher, and Simon B. Goldberg. "Effects of an 8-Week Mindfulness Course on Affective Polarization." *Mindfulness* 13, no. 2 (February 2022): 474–83. https://doi.org/10.1007/s12671-021-01808-0.

Slingerland, Edward. *Trying Not to Try: The Art and Science of Spontaneity*. 2nd ed. New York: Crown Publishers, 2014.

Smith, James K. A. *Thinking in Tongues: Pentecostal Contributions to Christian Philosophy*. Grand Rapids, MI: William B. Eerdmans Pub. Co., 2010.

Snodgrass, Jeffrey G., David E. Most, and Chakrapani Upadhyay. "Religious Ritual Is Good Medicine for Indigenous Indian Conservation Refugees: Implications for Global Mental Health." *Current Anthropology* 58, no. 2 (April 2017): 257–84. https://doi.org/10.1086/691212.

Solms, M., and O. Turnbull. *The Brain and the Inner World: An Introduction to the Neuroscience of Subjective Experience*. London: Karnac, 2003.

Spanos, Nicholas P., and Erin C. Hewitt. "Glossolalia: A Test of the 'Trance' and Psychopathology Hypotheses." *Journal of Abnormal Psychology* 88, no. 4 (1979): 427–34.

Spanos, Nicholas P., Wendy P. Cross, Mark Lepage, and Marjorie Coristine. "Glossolalia as Learned Behavior: An Experimental Demonstration." *Journal of Abnormal Psychology* 95, no. 1 (1986): 21–3.

Sperduti, Marco, Pauline Delaveau, Philippe Fossati, and Jaqueline Nadel. "Different Brain Structures Related to Self- and External-Agency Attribution: A Brief Review and Meta-Analysis." *Brain Structure and Function* 216, no. 2 (2011): 151–7. https://doi.org/10.1007/s00429-010-0298-1.

Spittler, R. P. "Implicit Values in Pentecostal Missions." *Missiology: An International Review Missiology: An International Review* 16, no. 4 (1988): 409–24.

Sporns, Olaf, and Richard F. Betzel. "Modular Brain Networks." *Annual Review of Psychology* 67, no. 1 (January 4, 2016): 613–40. https://doi.org/10.1146/annurev-psych-122414-033634.

Sprecher, Susan, and Beverley Fehr. "Compassionate Love for Close Others and Humanity." *Journal of Social and Personal Relationships* 22, no. 5 (October 2005): 629–51. https://doi.org/10.1177/0265407505056439.

Spreng, R. Nathan, Jorge Sepulcre, Gary R. Turner, W. Dale Stevens, and Daniel L. Schacter. "Intrinsic Architecture Underlying the Relations Among the Default, Dorsal Attention, and Frontoparietal Control Networks of the Human Brain." *Journal of Cognitive Neuroscience* 25, no. 1 (2013): 74–86. https://doi.org/10.1162/jocn_a_00281.

Stausberg, Michael. "*Big Gods* in Review: Introducing Ara Norenzayan and His Critics." *Religion* 44, no. 4 (October 2, 2014): 592–608. https://doi.org/10.1080/0048721X.2014.954353.

Stern, Daniel N. *The Interpersonal World of the Infant: A View from Psychoanalysis and Developmental Psychology*. 1st pbk. ed. New York: Basic Books, 2000.

Stewart, Charles. *Creolization: History, Ethnography, Theory*. Walnut Creek, CA: Left Coast Press, 2007.

Stoller, Paul. *The Power of the Between*. Chicago: University of Chicago Press, 2008. https://www.press.uchicago.edu/ucp/books/book/chicago/P/bo5997326.html.

Strathern, Marilyn. *The Gender of the Gift: Problems with Women and Problems with Society in Melanesia*. Studies in Melanesian Anthropology. Berkeley, CA: University of California Press, 1988. https://doi.org/10.1525/california/9780520064232.001.0001.

Takano, Ryota, and Michio Nomura. "Neural Representations of Awe: Distinguishing Common and Distinct Neural Mechanisms." *Emotion* 22, no. 4 (June 2022): 669–77. https://doi.org/10.1037/emo0000771.

Tang, Yi-Yuan, Britta K. Hölzel, and Michael I. Posner. "The Neuroscience of Mindfulness Meditation." *Nature Reviews Neuroscience* 16, no. 4 (April 2015): 213–25. https://doi.org/10.1038/nrn3916.

Taves, Ann. *Religious Experience Reconsidered: A Building Block Approach to the Study of Religion and Other Special Things*. Princeton, NJ: Princeton University Press, 2009.

Taylor, Charles. *A Secular Age*. Cambridge, MA: Belknap Press of Harvard University Press, 2007.

Taylor, Charles. *Sources of the Self: The Making of the Modern Identity*. Cambridge, MA: Harvard University Press, 1989.

Thomas, George M. *Revivalism and Cultural Change: Christianity, Nation Building, and the Market in the Nineteenth-Century United States*. Chicago: University of Chicago Press, 1997.

Tinoco, carlos, and Joao Ortiz. "Magnetic Stimulation of the Temporal Cortex: A Partial 'God Helmet' Replication Study." *Journal of Consciousness Exploration & Research*, 5, no. 3 (April 2014): 234–57.

Todd, Rebecca M., William A. Cunningham, Adam K. Anderson, and Evan Thompson. "Affect-Biased Attention as Emotion Regulation." *Trends in Cognitive Sciences* 16, no. 7 (July 2012): 365–72. https://doi.org/10.1016/j.tics.2012.06.003.

Tolle, Eckhart. *The Power of Now: A Guide to Spiritual Enlightenment*. Novato, CA: New World Library, 1999.

Tsing, Anna Lowenhaupt. *Friction: An Ethnography of Global Connection*. Princeton, NJ: Princeton University Press, 2005.

Turner, Victor W. *The Ritual Process: Structure and Anti-Structure*. Chicago, IL: Aldine Publishing Company, 1969.

Vago, David R., and David A. Silbersweig. "Self-Awareness, Self-Regulation, and Self-Transcendence (S-ART): A Framework for Understanding the Neurobiological Mechanisms of Mindfulness." *Frontiers in Human Neuroscience* 6 (2012). https://doi.org/10.3389/fnhum.2012.00296.

Van Cappellen, Patty, and Megan Edwards. "Emotion Expression in Context: Full Body Postures of Christian Prayer Orientations Compared to Specific Emotions." *Journal of Nonverbal Behavior* 45, no. 4 (December 2021): 545–65. https://doi.org/10.1007/s10919-021-00370-6.

Van Elk, Michiel, M. Andrea Arciniegas Gomez, Wietske Van Der Zwaag, Hein T. Van Schie, and Disa Sauter. "The Neural Correlates of the Awe Experience: Reduced Default Mode Network Activity During Feelings of Awe." *Human Brain Mapping* 40, no. 12 (August 15, 2019): 3561–74. https://doi.org/10.1002/hbm.24616.

Veissière, Samuel P. L., Axel Constant, Maxwell J. D. Ramstead, Karl J. Friston, and Laurence J. Kirmayer. "Thinking Through Other Minds: A Variational Approach to Cognition and Culture." *Behavioral and Brain Sciences* 43 (2020). https://doi.org/10.1017/S0140525X19001213.

Village, Andrew. "Dimensions of Belief About Miraculous Healing." *Mental Health, Religion & Culture* 8, no. 2 (June 2005): 97–107. https://doi.org/10.1080/13674670420 00240374.

Vogel, Dan, and Scott C. Dunn. "'The Tongue of Angels': Glossolalia Among Mormonism's Founders." *Journal of Mormon History* 19, no. 2 (1993): 1–34.

Volkow, Nora D., George F. Koob, and A. Thomas McLellan. "Neurobiologic Advances from the Brain Disease Model of Addiction." Edited by Dan L. Longo. *New England Journal of Medicine* 374, no. 4 (January 28, 2016): 363–71. https://doi.org/10.1056/NEJMra1511480.

Vuilleumier, Patrik. "How Brains Beware: Neural Mechanisms of Emotional Attention." *Trends in Cognitive Sciences* 9, no. 12 (December 2005): 585–94. https://doi.org/10.1016/j.tics.2005.10.011.

Wacker, Grant. *Heaven Below: Early Pentecostals and American Culture.* Cambridge, MA: Harvard University Press, 2001.

Wadlinger, Heather A., and Derek M. Isaacowitz. "Fixing Our Focus: Training Attention to Regulate Emotion." *Personality and Social Psychology Review* 15, no. 1 (February 2011): 75–102. https://doi.org/10.1177/1088868310365565.

Wagner, C. Peter. *Confronting the Powers: How the New Testament Church Experienced the Power of Strategic-Level Spiritual Warfare.* Ventura, CA: Regal Books, 1996.

Wallmark, Erik, Kousha Safarzadeh, Daiva Daukantaitė, and Rachel E. Maddux. "Promoting Altruism Through Meditation: An 8-Week Randomized Controlled Pilot Study." *Mindfulness* 4, no. 3 (September 1, 2013): 223–34. https://doi.org/10.1007/s12671-012-0115-4.

Walsh, Eamonn, David A. Oakley, Peter W. Halligan, Mitul A. Mehta, and Quinton Deeley. "The Functional Anatomy and Connectivity of Thought Insertion and Alien Control of Movement." *Cortex* 64 (March 2015): 380–93. https://doi.org/10.1016/j.cortex.2014.09.012.

Walsh, Erin, Tory Eisenlohr-Moul, and Ruth Baer. "Brief Mindfulness Training Reduces Salivary IL-6 and TNF-α in Young Women with Depressive Symptomatology." *Journal of Consulting and Clinical Psychology* 84, no. 10 (October 2016): 887–97. https://doi.org/10.1037/ccp0000122.

Walter, Yoshija, Sebastian Dieguez, Michael Mouthon, and Lucas Spierer. "Brain Structural Evidence for a Frontal Pole Specialization in Glossolalia." *IBRO Reports* 9 (December 2020): 32–6. https://doi.org/10.1016/j.ibror.2020.06.002.

Weisman, Kara, Cristine H. Legare, Rachel E. Smith, Vivian A. Dzokoto, Felicity Aulino, Emily Ng, John C. Dulin, Nicole Ross-Zehnder, Joshua D. Brahinsky, and Tanya Marie Luhrmann. "Similarities and Differences in Concepts of Mental Life Among Adults and Children in Five Cultures." *Nature Human Behaviour* 5, no. 10 (October 2021): 1358–68. https://doi.org/10.1038/s41562-021-01184-8.

Weisner, Thomas S. "Ecocultural Understanding of Children's Developmental Pathways." *Human Development* 45, no. 4 (2002): 275–81. https://doi.org/10.1159/000064989.

Wendel, Paul J. "Object-Based Epistemology at a Creationist Museum." *Science & Education* 20, no. 1 (January 2011): 37–50. https://doi.org/10.1007/s11191-010-9287-2.

Wesley, John. *Wesley's Standard Sermons Consisting of Forty-four Discourses … to Which Are Added Nine Additional Sermons … Ed. and Annotated by Edward H. Sugden: Vol. 1–2.* London: Epworth, 1961.

Wexler, Bruce E. *Brain and Culture: Neurobiology, Ideology, and Social Change.* Cambridge, MA: MIT Press, 2006. http://site.ebrary.com/id/10173739.

Wigger, John H. *Taking Heaven by Storm Methodism and the Rise of Popular Christianity in America.* New York: Oxford University Press, 1998.

Wilkinson, R., and M. Marmot. *Social Determinants of Health—The Solid Facts.* 2nd ed. Geneva: WHO Regional Office for Europe, 2003.

Williams, Joseph W. *Spirit Cure: A History of Pentecostal Healing.* New York: Oxford University Press, 2013.

Williamson, W. Paul. "Spiritual Transformation: A Phenomenological Study Among Recovering Substance Abusers." *Pastoral Psychology* 62, no. 6 (December 2013): 889–906. https://doi.org/10.1007/s11089-012-0502-8.

Williamson, W. Paul, and Ralph W. Hood. "Spirit Baptism: A Phenomenological Study of Religious Experience." *Mental Health, Religion & Culture* 14, no. 6 (July 2011): 543–59. https://doi.org/10.1080/13674676.2010.493860.

Wink, Paul, Michele Dillon, and Prettyman Adrienne. "Religiousness, Spiritual Seeking, and Authoritarianism: Findings from a Longitudinal Study." *Journal for the Scientific Study of Religion* 46, no. 3 (September 2007): 321–35.

Winkelman, Michael. *Shamanism a Biopsychosocial Paradigm of Consciousness and Healing.* Santa Barbara, CA: Praeger, 2010.

Wolff, Max, Ricarda Evens, Lea J. Mertens, Michael Koslowski, Felix Betzler, Gerhard Gründer, and Henrik Jungaberle. "Learning to Let Go: A Cognitive-Behavioral Model of How Psychedelic Therapy Promotes Acceptance." *Frontiers in Psychiatry* 11 (February 21, 2020): 5.

Wood, W. W. "Culture and Personality Aspects of the Pentecostal Holiness Religion. Unpublished Doctoral Thesis." University of North Carolina, 1961.

Woods, Teresa E., and Gail H. Ironson. "Religion and Spirituality in the Face of Illness: How Cancer, Cardiac, and HIV Patients Describe Their Spirituality/ Religiosity." *Journal of Health Psychology* 4, no. 3 (May 1999): 393–412. https://doi.org/10.1177/135910539900400308.

Yaden, David B., and Roland R. Griffiths. "The Subjective Effects of Psychedelics Are Necessary for Their Enduring Therapeutic Effects." *ACS Pharmacology & Translational Science* 4, no. 2 (April 9, 2021): 568–72. https://doi.org/10.1021/acsptsci.0c00194.

Yaden, David B., Khoa D. Le Nguyen, Margaret L. Kern, Nancy A. Wintering, Johannes C. Eichstaedt, H. Andrew Schwartz, Anneke E. K. Buffone, Laura K. Smith, Mark R. Waldman, Ralph W. Hood Jr., Andrew B. Newberg. "The Noetic Quality: A Multimethod Exploratory Study." *Psychology of Consciousness: Theory, Research, and Practice* 4, no. 1 (2017): 54–62. https://doi.org/10.1037/cns0000098.

Yong, Amos. "The Word and the Spirit or the Spirit and the Word: Exploring the Boundaries of Evangelicalism in Relationship to Modern Pentecostalism." *Trinity Journal* 23, no. 2 (2002): 235–52.

Yong, Amos. 2012. "What's Love Got to Do with It? The Sociology of Godly Love and the Renewal of Modern Pentecostalism." *Journal of Pentecostal Theology* 21, no. 1 (2012a): 113–34. https://doi.org/10.1163/174552512X633321.

Yong, Amos, and Mathew Lee, eds. *The Science and Theology of Godly Love.* Northern Illinois University Press, 2012b.

Yong, Amos, and Mathew Lee, eds. *Godly Love: Impediments and Possibilities.* Lexington Books, 2012c.

Young, Michael P. *Bearing Witness Against Sin: The Evangelical Birth of the American Social Movement*. Chicago: University of Chicago Press, 2006.

Zito, Giuseppe A., Roland Wiest, and Selma Aybek. "Neural Correlates of Sense of Agency in Motor Control: A Neuroimaging Meta-Analysis." *PLOS ONE* 15, no. 6 (2020): e0234321. https://doi.org/10.1371/journal.pone.0234321.

Zito, Giuseppe A., Laura B. Anderegg, Kallia Apazoglou, René M. Müri, Roland Wiest, Martin grosse Holtforth, and Selma Aybek. "Transcranial Magnetic Stimulation over the Right Temporoparietal Junction Influences the Sense of Agency in Healthy Humans." *Journal of Psychiatry and Neuroscience* (July 1, 2020): 271–8. https://doi.org/10.1503/jpn.190099.

Zito, Giuseppe A., Roland Wiest, and Selma Aybek. "Neural Correlates of Sense of Agency in Motor Control: A Neuroimaging Meta-Analysis." *PLOS ONE* 15, no. 6 (2020): e0234321. https://doi.org/10.1371/journal.pone.0234321.

Žižek, Slavoj. *The Puppet and the Dwarf: The Perverse Core of Christianity*. Cambridge, MA: MIT Press, 2003.

Index

Page references in *italics* refer to figures & page numbers followed by "n" refers to end notes